T0331652

Developing Service-Oriented Applications Using the Windows Communication Foundation (WCF) Framework

Chirag Patel
Charotar University of Science and Technology, India

A volume in the Advances in Systems Analysis, Software Engineering, and High Performance Computing (ASASEHPC) Book Series

www.igi-global.com

Published in the United States of America by
    IGI Global
    Information Science Reference (an imprint of IGI Global)
    701 E. Chocolate Avenue
    Hershey PA 17033
    Tel: 717-533-8845
    Fax: 717-533-8661
    E-mail: cust@igi-global.com
    Web site: http://www.igi-global.com

Library of Congress Cataloging-in-Publication Data

Names: Patel, Chirag, 1981- author.
Title: Developing service-oriented applications using the Windows
   Communication Foundation (WCF) framework / by Chirag Patel.
Description: Hershey, PA : Information Science Reference, [2017]
Identifiers: LCCN 2016050990| ISBN 9781522519973 (hardcover) | ISBN
   9781522519980 (ebook)
Subjects: LCSH: Application software--Development. | Windows communication
   foundation (Software framework) | Internet programming. | Web services. |
   Service-oriented architecture (Computer science)
Classification: LCC QA76.76.A65 P388 2017 | DDC 006.7/6--dc23 LC record available at https://
lccn.loc.gov/2016050990

This book is published in the IGI Global book series Advances in Systems Analysis, Software Engineering, and High Performance Computing (ASASEHPC) (ISSN: 2327-3453; eISSN: 2327-3461)

British Cataloguing in Publication Data
A Cataloguing in Publication record for this book is available from the British Library.

All work contributed to this book is new, previously-unpublished material. The views expressed in this book are those of the authors, but not necessarily of the publisher.

Advances in Systems Analysis, Software Engineering, and High Performance Computing (ASASEHPC) Book Series

ISSN:2327-3453
EISSN:2327-3461

Editor-in-Chief: Vijayan Sugumaran, Oakland University, USA

MISSION

The theory and practice of computing applications and distributed systems has emerged as one of the key areas of research driving innovations in business, engineering, and science. The fields of software engineering, systems analysis, and high performance computing offer a wide range of applications and solutions in solving computational problems for any modern organization.

The **Advances in Systems Analysis, Software Engineering, and High Performance Computing (ASASEHPC) Book Series** brings together research in the areas of distributed computing, systems and software engineering, high performance computing, and service science. This collection of publications is useful for academics, researchers, and practitioners seeking the latest practices and knowledge in this field.

COVERAGE

- Engineering Environments
- Human-Computer Interaction
- Distributed Cloud Computing
- Metadata and Semantic Web
- Network Management
- Storage Systems
- Computer System Analysis
- Computer Networking
- Enterprise Information Systems
- Performance Modelling

IGI Global is currently accepting manuscripts for publication within this series. To submit a proposal for a volume in this series, please contact our Acquisition Editors at Acquisitions@igi-global.com or visit: http://www.igi-global.com/publish/.

Titles in this Series

For a list of additional titles in this series, please visit:
http://www.igi-global.com/book-series/advances-systems-analysis-software-engineering/73689

Resource Management and Efficiency in Cloud Computing Environments
Ashok Kumar Turuk (National Institute of Technology Rourkela, India) Bibhudatta Sahoo
(National Institute of Technology Rourkela, India) and Sourav Kanti Addya (National In-
stitute of Technology Rourkela,India)
Information Science Reference • ©2017 • 352pp • H/C (ISBN: 9781522517214) • US $205.00

Handbook of Research on End-to-End Cloud Computing Architecture Design
Jianwen "Wendy" Chen (IBM, Australia) Yan Zhang (Western Sydney University, Australia)
and Ron Gottschalk (IBM, Australia)
Information Science Reference • ©2017 • 507pp • H/C (ISBN: 9781522507598) • US $325.00

Innovative Research and Applications in Next-Generation High Performance...
Qusay F. Hassan (Mansoura University, Egypt)
Information Science Reference • ©2016 • 488pp • H/C (ISBN: 9781522502876) • US $205.00

Developing Interoperable and Federated Cloud Architecture
Gabor Kecskemeti (University of Miskolc, Hungary) Attila Kertesz (University of Szeged,
Hungary) and Zsolt Nemeth (MTA SZTAKI, Hungary)
Information Science Reference • ©2016 • 398pp • H/C (ISBN: 9781522501534) • US $210.00

Managing Big Data in Cloud Computing Environments
Zongmin Ma (Nanjing University of Aeronautics and Astronautics, China)
Information Science Reference • ©2016 • 314pp • H/C (ISBN: 9781466698345) • US $195.00

Emerging Innovations in Agile Software Development
Imran Ghani (Universiti Teknologi Malaysia, Malaysia) Dayang Norhayati Abang Jawawi
(Universiti Teknologi Malaysia, Malaysia) Siva Dorairaj (Software Education, New Zealand)
and Ahmed Sidky (ICAgile, USA)
Information Science Reference • ©2016 • 323pp • H/C (ISBN: 9781466698581) • US $205.00

Modern Software Engineering Methodologies for Mobile and Cloud Environments
António Miguel Rosado da Cruz (Instituto Politécnico de Viana do Castelo, Portugal) and
Sara Paiva (Instituto Politécnico de Viana do Castelo, Portugal)
Information Science Reference • ©2016 • 355pp • H/C (ISBN: 9781466699168) • US $210.00

For an enitre list of titles in this series, please visit:
http://www.igi-global.com/book-series/advances-systems-analysis-software-engineering/73689

www.igi-global.com

701 East Chocolate Avenue, Hershey, PA 17033, USA
Tel: 717-533-8845 x100 • Fax: 717-533-8661
E-Mail: cust@igi-global.com • www.igi-global.com

Table of Contents

Preface..vii

Acknowledgment xiv

Chapter 1
Introduction to Windows Communication Foundation Framework 1

Chapter 2
WCF Master Pieces.. 24

Chapter 3
WCF Programming Methodology 56

Chapter 4
Working with Address 102

Chapter 5
Working with Binding... 120

Chapter 6
Working with Contracts 167

Chapter 7
Client and Service.. 213

Chapter 8
Managing Transactions in WCF 283

Chapter 9
Reliable Communication in WCF.. 302

Chapter 10
Securing Message 335

Chapter 11
Hosting WCF Service 381

Chapter 12
Interoperability with Other Platforms 436

Appendix 469

About the Author 484

Index 485

Preface

I am wondering that why I am writing this book so late. But it is never too late. I have teaching graduate and post graduate students in computer applications since 2006. Since last four years I have been teaching the subject related to web service and WCF. I love to learn technology and explore it. I like the way WCF is designed and developed by Microsoft team thanks to them. I was attracted towards this technology as it shifted the entire paradigm from developing traditional web site to service oriented applications development. WCF is not just a web service, it is more than that. During teaching this subject I found that the subject is really useful for the developers as it unifies .NET Remoting, .Net web services (.ASMX) and Web Service Enhancements (WSE) in one technology called WCF.

I was motivated by many features of WCF which translated my thoughts into writing this book. Good thing about WCF is that it is tailor made for developing "Service Oriented Applications". It not only provides interoperability but also focuses on security of the message. WCF has powerful security infrastructure to build rich enterprise applications. Apart from this, you can provide reliable communication between service and client using reliable session and queuing support.

I think that many of the enterprise application developer are using WCF to build rich applications. There is no platform available in the market which provides everything available in WCF which includes transactions, security and reliable messaging support. The WCF services are rigid as you scale the services too. The biggest advantage is the declarative (attribute) way of programming in which a programmer is not required to write any algorithm to provide WCF feature. WCF takes care about providing those features one declared by the developer. This reduces the burden on developers and they can shift focus on developing their functional requirements. Earlier CORBA, RMI and other distributed technologies were available to develop distributed applications. The major issue with those earlier technologies was the interoperability with various platforms. WCF is also for distributed application development. A developer is not required to learn different technologies after learning WCF. Event they don't need to develop the communication protocols from scratch as it is taken care by binding in a program. Based on the selected binding related communication protocol is applied, a developer needs to just provide matching address with binding.

POTENTIAL READERS

I have written this book for the students who wish to dive deep into understanding of WCF and who are potential developer after completing their graduation. During teaching this subject I have created many videos of WCF programs. This book is also for the beginner –to-intermediate developers who are not familiar with the powerful capabilities of WCF. Initially the book covers pre-requisite concepts required to learn any web service. It includes serialization, loosely coupled, four tenant of SOA and many more. Sometimes the serialization concept is ignored by the student and developer community as they directly deal with it. But it is required to understand the concepts of serialization to know how message is translated from one form to another form.

I am demonstrated the concepts practically by providing inline examples and hands-on for implementing the concepts practically. WCF is applied in almost all the kinds of domains. In this book an effort is made to teach all the important concepts such as transaction, security and reliable messaging using theoretical concepts and hands-on examples. I have also explained the Microsoft Message Queuing (MSMQ) component available in Windows to integrate it with WCF program.

This book also covers all the hosting options such as Internet Information Services (IIS), Windows Service, Windows Activation Service (WAS) and self-hosting. This also differentiates WCF from other technologies as in the absence of dependent hosting options, a developer can write the program to host WCF service which is known as self-hosting. So WCF is like a generic vehicle with all the facilities such as riding on road, water or sky. It is up to the programmer to choose the way of riding. While choosing the riding option, you must know the pros and cons of it. This book covers major capabilities of WCF but it does not cover all the dimensions of web service communication. In general, the following topics are not fully covered in this book:

- Implementation of message contract using hands-on as most of the time the service contract and data contract is sufficient to develop any WCF service.
- In interoperability chapter the technical details about other programming languages such as JAVA, PHP and Android are not explained. As the purpose of that chapter is to write client code to consume WCF service in these platforms. It assumed that the reader of this chapter is expert in platforms such as JAVA, PHP or Android.

OUTLINE OF CHAPTERS

This book is organized in twelve chapters. All the chapters begin with fundamental concepts followed by hands-on examples. I recommend you to read Chapter 1, Chapter 2, and Chapter 3 in sequence and then you can reach other chapters in any order but it is advisable to read all the chapters in sequence to gain better understanding. Outline of each chapter is mentioned below:

Chapter 1: Introduction to Windows Communication Foundation Framework

This chapter provides in depth knowledge about important concepts related to pre-requisite concepts such as distributed computing, serialization, loosely coupled system, Service Oriented Architecture (SOA) etc. It also explains on four popular tenets of SOA. While developing any SOA, it is required to implement these tenets. After gaining understanding of basic concepts the chapter dives deep into the meaning and purpose of Windows Communication Foundation

(WCF) Framework. It explains the essential pieces required to develop any WCF service. The understanding of importance of WCF in developing rich enterprise applications is covered in depth with the advantages of using WCF. The chapter concludes with comparison between WCF and Web Service is explained to know why WCF is different than the web services.

Chapter 2: WCF Master Pieces

To develop any WCF service we must understand underlying concepts such as endpoint message and channel. In this chapter, fundamental concepts of end point, message and channel are explained. You will learn about core parts of endpoint which includes Address Binding and Contract. The major focus of this chapter is to understand message structure which is known as SOAP message. The theoretical concepts of message pattern are well explained in this chapter. You will also learn about various consumers of the SOAP. Towards the end of chapter you will understand about channel and elements of channel stack. The chapter concludes with demonstration of developing first WCF service with the test client. So after this chapter you will be able to develop at least a WCF service.

Chapter 3: WCF Programming Methodology

WCF has its unique way to write a program. A WCF program can be written via different ways. This chapter provides in depth knowledge of various programming methodologies. You will learn about syntax of writing a WCF program using each of the methodologies through hands-on examples. This chapter also covers steps required in developing WCF Service and hosting WCF service using one of the self-hosting options such as Console Project. It guides you steps by step to create configuration file using WCF Service Configuration editor. The chapter is concluded with demonstration of consuming the hosted WCF service in Android client.

Chapter 4: WCF Programming Methodology

The heart of endpoint is address. Without address a client cannot communicate with the service. In this chapter focus is on learning different address types and various formats of each type of addresses. The address is formatted according to the binding. You will also learn about programming address for service and client both using code and configuration method through hands-on examples. The in depth knowledge of absolute address and relative address is also provided in this chapter.

Chapter 5: Working with Binding

Just like address binding is also essential element of endpoint. Binding defines the communication protocol such as http, tcp, named pipe or MSMQ. This chapter explains about various bindings available in WCF. It provides in depth knowledge of practical implementation of each binding in WCF service. You will learn about capabilities and working of available built-in bindings. Creation of custom binding is also covered in this chapter. The chapter is concluded with demonstration of different bindings in one WCF service to know working of each binding practically.

Chapter 6: Working with Contracts

The third element of endpoint is contract. A contract tells client about what is available at the service. This chapter contains in depth understanding of various contracts available in WCF. The parameters of each contract well explained in this chapter. You will also learn the syntax through hands-on example of each parameter of each contract. The hands-on examples will help you in understanding the usage each contract in certain situation as all the contracts might not be needed in a program. The compulsory contract needed in any WCF service is a service contract.

Chapter 7: Client and Service

A client is a piece of code which initiates communication with service. This chapter provides in depth knowledge of client and different ways to create client code. It also explores details various service behaviors which can be helpful to implement advanced programming concepts in WCF. You will learn the practical implementation of all three message patterns using hands-on examples. The advanced concepts such as concurrency and session management are also well explained and demonstrated. The chapter is concluded with understating and implementation of exception handling mechanism in WCF.

Chapter 8: Managing Transactions in WCF

In any e-commerce application transaction management is inevitable. This chapter gets you familiar with general concepts of a transaction. You will learn about ACID properties of transaction. This chapter also explains the protocols used in transaction. You will also learn about different parameters of service contract and service behavior to implement transaction program in WCF. The chapter concludes with the practical demonstration of transaction program with the WCF service and .NET client.

Chapter 9: Reliable Communication in WCF

In Service-Oriented Applications, reliable delivery of message is expected. To provide reliable delivery of message WCF uses reliable messaging protocol. In this chapter fundamental concepts of reliable messaging are explained. The practical demonstration of sessional management using WCF is explained in depth. You will also learn about concepts of queue and implementation of queue through integrating MSMQ in WCF.

Chapter 10: Securing Message

In distributed and service-oriented applications, message security is essential. WCF provides robust security infrastructure to secure the message transferred between service and client. This chapter provides overview of basic security mechanisms. You will learn different level of security in this chapter. The chapter also covers various client credentials to be provided by client program using different bindings. The fundamental concepts of authentication and authorization are well explained in this chapter. These concepts are practically implemented using hands-on example towards the end of this chapter.

Chapter 11: Hosting WCF

A WCF service can be hosted using various hosting options available. A WCF service can be hosted using IIS, windows service, WAS or self-hosting options. This is the major advantage of WCF over the technology. This chapter explains each hosting options through hands-on example. The hosting and self-hosting options are compared at the end of this chapter.

Chapter 12: Interoperability with Other Platforms

The purpose of web service is to provide interoperability between various platforms. This chapter explains history of interoperability. It moves forward with practical demonstration of interoperating WCF with other platforms such as JAVA, PHP and Android. Therefore, this chapter is dedicated to the developer working on other platform who wants to consume WCF service in his/her native program.

Appendix: Service Chain Example

This appendix provides practical demonstration of service chain program. The theoretical concept of service chain is already discussed in chapter 7 but there is not room to place this program in any of the chapter. In several books, this concept is explained but not implemented practically. So in this appendix an effort is made to explain this concept practically.

ASSUMPTIONS AND SYSTEM REQUIREMENTS

I assume that the reads are familiar with basic .NET Framework and visual studio. The detailed steps are mentioned in all the practical demonstrations. It will guide you to develop WCF service, host it and create .NET client even you are not much familiar with .NET framework or visual studio. Following are the minimum requirements to execute the code samples discussed in this book:

- .NET Framework 4.0 or higher.
- Visual Studio 2010 or higher
- Windows 7 or higher
- Internet Information Service (IIS) 7.0 or higher
- Microsoft Message Queuing (MSMQ).

In this book, all the code sample are prepared in Visual Studio 2010 with .NET Framework 4.0 but this code samples can work in higher versions too as major focus of this book is too explain the concepts of WCF not the tool.

Some features are not installed by default in windows operating system. So you need to install it by turning that feature on in windows operating system. The components such as IIS and MSMQ are not installed by default so install these features by turning them on.

The Demonstrations.zip contains chapter wise visual studio solution. For each concept, different folders are created. The folder name resembles the concept being implemented.

You can use the programs or sample code discussed in this book; no separate permission is required for using any program of code sample in this book.

Acknowledgment

This is my first experience writing a book. I interacted with Kelsey Weitzel-Leishman for the review of a sample chapter. The sample chapter was reviewed and appreciated by the reviewers of Cyber Tech Publishing (Now IGI Global). So first and foremost I must thank Kelsey Weitzel-Leishman for having the trust in me to write my first book. She always encouraged me by reminding me at every deadline.

I always got the encouragement from Dr. Dharmendra Patel, HOD, CMPICA, CHARUSAT to continue writing during the painful time of structuring and arranging the book chapters.

Although I am the single author of this book, it is not possible to write without the support of several people. My family—my strength—motived me a lot to accomplish the mammoth task. My parents always showed their patience when I could not spend time with them. My lovely wife, Payal, took the burden of responsibilities on behalf me, who kept the house organized when I spent my time in writing this book. I thank my son, Vedant, and my niece, Aesha, for showing their patience when I said them, "I will spend my time soon after writing this book". I love you all. I swear that writing this book would have not been possible without your support.

Chapter 1
Introduction to Windows Communication Foundation Framework

After completing this chapter, you will be able to:

- Pre-requisite concepts required to learn Service Oriented Architecture (SOA).
- Understand the concepts related to SOA.
- Know the tenets of SOA and how these tenets are implemented in WCF.
- Understand Windows Communication Foundation (WCF) Framework.
- Understand the essential pieces of WCF.
- Differentiate between WCF and Web Service.
- Know the importance of WCF in developing professional applications.
- Understand the advantages of using WCF in building rich enterprise applications.

INTRODUCTION

The Windows Communication Foundation Framework is a unified program-ming model for building distributed and Service Oriented Applications (SOA) (Green, 2016). Before you build any WCF service, it is necessary to understand the concepts such as web service, distributed computing,

DOI: 10.4018/978-1-5225-1997-3.ch001

interoperability, and loosely coupled systems and SOA. These concepts are explained in the following section.

PRE-REQUISITE CONCEPTS

To learn any technology based on web service it is essential to learn the following topics in details to gain proper understanding.

Interoperability

Interoperability means the ability to communicate with other technology or language with ease. In object oriented programming we can design components which can be reused in the same technology or language. For instance Java Beans can be consumed in any Java application, but what about consuming these Java Beans in.Net? Interoperability solves this problem by providing loosely coupled architecture between diverse applications to communicate with one another. To have interoperability there must be some interface or common standards between the applications to communicate with each other. As shown in Figure 1, an application developed in JAVA is able to consume the functionality available in.NET application (regardless of the language such as C#, VB etc.) with ease. So it is possible because the systems are interoperable. Now how to provide interoperability? It is possible due to web service. So in the following section we will learn about web service and underlying concepts related to it.

Figure 1. Communication between.NET and Java

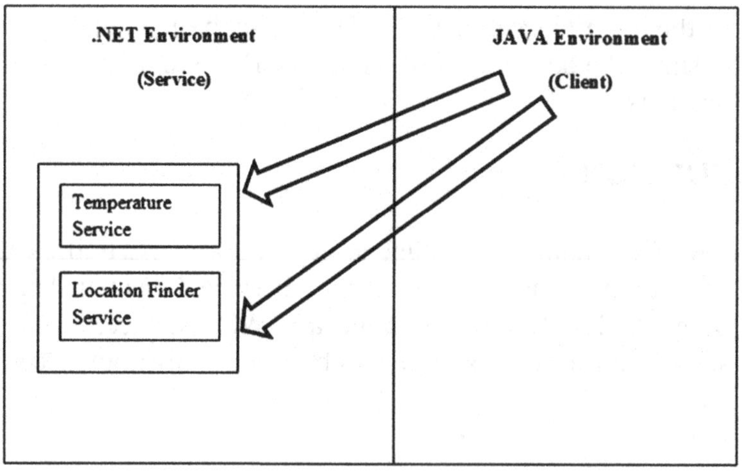

Web Service

A web service is a method of communication between two electronic devices over the World Wide Web. A web service is a software function provided at a network address over the web or the cloud, it is a service that is "always on" as in the concept of utility computing. The W3C (W3C Website) defines a "Web service" as:

A software system designed to support interoperable machine-to-machine interaction over a network. It has an interface described in a machine-processable format (specifically WSDL). Other systems interact with the Web service in a manner prescribed by its description using SOAP messages, typically conveyed using HTTP with an XML serialization in conjunction with other Web-related standards (Haas, 2004).

A Web Service can be developed in different languages such as C#. Net, JAVA or other programming languages. A.NET web service can be developed by using Microsoft Visual Studio 2010. Similarly a web service can be developed in JAVA using IDEs such as NetBeans or Eclipse. Once a web service is developed in any language it can be consumed in any other language without knowing more details about the web service. It is the pillar to provide interoperability between diverse systems. The client application needs to know the WSDL file only. Now questions arise that how diverse system communicate with each other as they are not having common data types. For instance, in C#.NET to store integer data, Int16, Int32, Int64 are available while in Java Integer wrapper class is available and in PHP no data types are available as it is a loosely typed language. So communication between these data types, concepts of serialization is used which is explained below.

Serialization

Serialization (Microsoft, 2015) is a process of translating data structures or object state into a format that can be stored (for example, in a file or memory buffer, or transmitted across a network connection link) and resurrected later in the same or another computer environment. This process of serializing an object is also called deflating or marshaling an object. The opposite operation, extracting a data structure from a series of bytes, is de=serialization (which is also called inflating or unmarshalling). So serialization process converts the data type of one language into common format understandable by both languages and then de-serialization is used to convert the data type

Figure 2. Serialization process

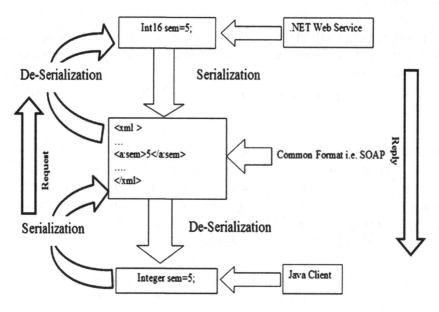

of common format in to language specific data type. For instance, a java client program consumes NET web service as illustrated in Figure 2. Now in JAVA, for storing integer values Integer data type is used. At the time of sending the request (shown by up arrow in vertical direction) to the.NET web service, serialization process converts it in to common format i.e. Simple Object Access Protocol(SOAP) as shown in Figure 2 in big rectangle in the middle. As SOAP is one of the formats used in the web service communication, it is shown in this example. Now as SOAP is understandable to both.NET and JAVA, after receiving request in SOAP form from JAVA, the.Net web service converts the SOAP format in to its original form i.e. Int16 as shown in the first rectangle in Figure 2. Same process happens in the reply process from.net web service to JAVA client shown in the down vertical arrow. So the serialization process plays a vital role in the web service communication for providing interoperability.

So we have seen that web service provides interoperability by using the concept of serialization and de-serialization. It also means by using web service we can design loosely coupled systems. In the following section, loosely coupled system is explained in brief.

Loosely Coupled

In software engineering subject, coupling has become the most popular topic of discussion for many authors. There are mainly two types of coupling: Tightly coupled systems and Loosely coupled systems. Tightly coupled system means the modules are closely dependent on each other and non-availability one module will not allow other dependent module to execute code independently. We will not focus on tight coupling any more as nowadays the systems are getting loosely coupled.

While in Loosely coupled system, the modules are not closely dependent on each other so system may work even in case of non-availability of one of the modules. As in web service communication the web service is developed in different language and client is developed in different language, both can exist separately, but for communication we require WSDL as discussed in the previous section of web service. In a loosely coupled system, individual components are designed separately with less dependency among each other. These components can be clubbed together to form the entire system so it is kind of plug and play system.

It is like the jigsaw puzzle for small kids in which the individual pieces can be used to form a particular shape. The typical exam is a personal computer in which mouse and keyboard are plug and play devices which can be attached and removed easily to and from the computer.

Distributed Computing

Distributed computing is a field of computer science that studies distributed systems. A distributed system is a software system in which components located networked computers communicate and coordinate their actions by passing messages. The components interact with each other in order to accomplish a common goal. So it is necessary to design different components to develop distributed system.

In recent days and upcoming years it will become necessary to develop such systems at large scale due to the increasing usage of mobile devices and easy availability of Internet.

Service-Oriented Architecture (SOA)

Service Oriented Architecture (SOA) is a loosely-coupled architecture which separates function in different independent units or services. It focuses on designing software in terms of services. It is a base for interoperability. As per W3C, SOA is defined as, "SOA is a set of components which can be invoked and whose interface descriptions can be discovered and published" (Haas, 2004).

It is a kind of distributed computing which works on the basis of the request/ reply design paradigm for synchronous and asynchronous communications. As it is mentioned earlier, various functions are divided into services and provided to the clients in the form of individual functions of that service. The main benefit SOA is that web services are loosely coupled in nature. For example, a web service can be implemented either in.NET, JAVA, PHP etc and the client, which consumes these services can be developed on same or other platforms such as Android, iOS etc.

In SOA, services have self-describing interfaces in the form of platform-independent XML documents. Web Services Description Language (WSDL) is the standard used to describe the services. This means that whether you develop the web service in.NET, JAVA or any other language you must generate WSDL for client program to consume it. Based on the specifications provided in the WSDL the request and reply are formed and serialization is done accordingly on client and service side. As we have discussed earlier in fig 2, during the serialization SOAP message is formed as a common format for both client and service. The schema of this message is defined by XML Schema (also called XML Schema Definition (XSD)). To discover new services available there is a registry called Universal Description, Discovery and Integration (UDDI) which maintained by the enterprise by a registry that acts as a directory listing. Applications can look up the services in that registry and invoke the service. So UDDI works like yellow pages where you would like to search new services available in your city. Data is passed through messages. In SOA data is passed through messages and available formats are SOAP, which is based on XML and JSON (JavaScript Object Notation). JSON is used in Representational State Transfer (REST) based services. SOA is widely used in cloud computing in recent days as organizations tend to provide services rather than developing products in the cloud environment. A programmer should design flexible system, while designing SOA and future changes should be accommodated in the system with ease. The services should be designed in loosely coupled, plug and play manner by providing interoperability with the other platforms. In the era of cloud computing focus should be to design Software as a Service (SaaS) while designing SOA.

As per Microsoft, while designing any SOA, the following four principles should be kept in mind (Microsoft, 2016):

- **Explicit Boundaries:** Services are responsible to expose the business functionalities which are to be provided to client through a well-defined contract. In.NET web service it can be done via [WebService] and [WebMethod] annotations while in WCF service contract is used to define all the operations which are to be provided to the client. The implementation details of the functions/methods are not available to the client and the client need not know it. As long as the client knows how to consume the service, location of service is not important for it. Services can be deployed anywhere without any specific platform needs and can be easily accessible by any client. Services should be easy to consume. The Service should user message instead of expensive Remote Procedure Calls (RPC). A service should not expose the implementation details to the client. The developers of service should provide an easy way for other developers to consume the service..NET Web services and WCF support this tenet as contracts are described in WSDL (Bustamante). All technologies also support location transparency as contract is independent of location of service.

- **Services Are Autonomous:** Services are built and deployed independently. Each service must be managed and versioned quickly. It must be replaceable. Redundancy should be used in the case of service failure or not available. Don't assume that your service will never fail. Provide the alternative in case of failure of the service. Proper exception handling and compensation logic must be associated with any service developed by the programmer. Services must be designed in the isolated manner to make it autonomous. Any exception in the service should not affect other service.

- **Services Share Schema and Contract, Not Class:** Service consumer should not be provided actual class or implementation details. The service contract must contain Message Exchange Patterns (MEP), message format defined by XML schema and other security policy related details. The main problem is the stability of the service, once it has been published, which cannot be altered without impacting the consumers. Internal policy regarding the data of service must not be disclosed to the client. The major challenge to the service is to apply the updates without affecting all the clients consuming the service. WCF supports this tenet as it does not share the logic at client side.

- **Service Compatibility Is Based on Policy:** Policy means explicit information about service. It is least understood tenet but it is very powerful in terms of implementation and security requirement of the service. It is not always possible to communicate certain requirements

Figure 3. Microsoft.NET framework folder in Windows OS

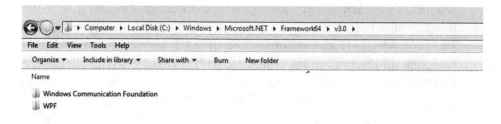

for service by using WSDL. Policy requirements can be used to have constraints such as to whom the access is provided and how it should be provided. For instance, as a security measure government may ask for various necessary documents while obtaining the SIM card for mobile device. People not following this policy (not providing necessary documents) are not allowed to buy the SIM card. In WCF the support for policy is completely hidden from the developers and policy details are incorporated in WSDL directly based on the configuration set by WCF for applying security and reliability (Bustamante).

WINDOWS COMMUNICATION FOUNDATION BASICS

What Is WCF?

WCF is a framework for building distributed systems and Service Oriented Architecture (SOA). It is the product of Microsoft. The WCF was introduced from .NET Framework 3.0 version which can be seen in the Fig1-3 which shows the .NET Framework under Microsoft Windows OS. It provides the programmer a flexible way to write a program in one machine to communicate with multiple machine across the network. It was originally known as Indigo or WinFX. It is installed with Windows Vista and it works on old windows version such as Windows XP and Windows 2003 Server. The WCF framework provides a uniform way to combine ASMX Web Services, .NET Remoting, Transactions and Message Queuing into a single programming unit. The core component which provides a way to write WCF program is System.ServiceModel.dll assembly which is available under the folder Windows Communication Foundation folder as shown in Figure 3. It contains plenty of namespaces, and classes to develop service oriented and distributed applications. You need to incorporate this assembly in your program to write

Figure 4. Overview of essential pieces of WCF

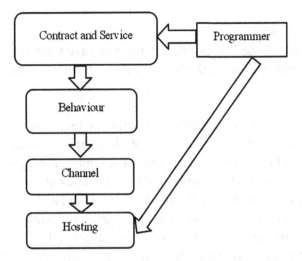

the code of WCF and without this assembly WCF program cannot be written. In this book we will discuss about developing WCF services using.NET Framework 4.0 using the Visual Studio 2010 IDE.

ESSENTIAL PIECES OF WCF: ELEMENTS OF WCF ARCHITECTURE

To write any WCF service a programmer needs to know certain important concepts of WCF as the writing WCF program is not as simple as writing any normal program. Therefore, it is necessary to under these concepts before developing any WCF service. In this section the essential pieces of WCF which are part of WCF architecture are explained in details. To develop the basic WCF service a programmer must know about essential pieces as shown in Figure 4. The following sections explain each piece in detail.

Contract

A contract is like a real life contract we sign. It provides a list of available functions to the client who want to consume the WCF service. A programmer must define alist of operations as part of the contract. There are different types of contracts available in WCF, such as:

1. Service Contract
2. Data Contract
3. Message Contract.
   a. Details about Data Contract and Message Contract are mentioned in Chapter 2 so in this section we will focus on Service Contract only.

A Service Contract is generally an Interface which provides list of operations which can be made available to the client to consume. A class can be a service contract too, but it is not good programming practice to designate class as a service contract as creates ambiguity. The example of class as service contract is discussed in Chapter 2. It is compulsory to provide at least one operation to a client otherwise the host program will return error at the time of hosting the service. In this section contract and service contracts are used interchangeably. An example of interface as service contract as per the C#.NET is shown below:

Example 1. A Service Contract Defined in WCF

```
[ServiceContract]
public interface ICalculator
{
    [OperationContract]
    int add(int no1, int no2);
}
```

Here, the interface ICalculator is an interface having the declaration of a method named as add. The interface looks similar as interface defined in other object oriented programming language such as JAVA. The only difference is the label [ServiceContract] above interface and [OperationContract] above the function. This indicates that a label is required to make the contract and functions available to the client program. Therefore, without these labels, the above code is useless and cannot be considered as part of the WCF service. There can be more than one service contract in a program. A programmer is directly communicating with the contract. After declaring the contract it must be implemented by a class which is also known as a service in WCF.

Service

A class which implements the [ServiceContract] is known as Service in WCF terminology. Here we used the word [ServiceContract] instead of interface because a class can be [ServiceContract] also. In this class implementation of [OperationContract] is written. The example of the service class is mentioned below:

Example 2. A Service Contract Defined in WCF

```
public class Calculator: ICalculator
{
            int add(int no1, int no2)
            {
              return no1+no2;
            }
      }
```

In this example, the class Calculator implements ICalculator interface which is defined as service contract in Example 1. So whenever the name of the service is asked, it must be a class which implements the service contract. There can be more than one service class in a program i.e. multiple classes can implement single service contract or single class can implement multiple contracts or multiple classes can implement multiple contracts. The programmer is directly associated with the service class.

So as per the Figure 4, programmer is responsible for writing the code of contract and service in a WCF program. Therefore, in some books, contracts are considered as layer1 of WCF framework architecture (Klein).

Behaviors

Behaviors are used to control the service runtime. As there are huge numbers of clients consuming the service when it is hosted in real environment, it is difficult to control the issues such as concurrency, flow control and other performance related issues of the service. A service should provide concurrency, quick availability without compromising the performance. So, behaviors play an important role to enable all these features when service is running. The behaviors can be set through the service and that is why programmers are not directly associated with it. A programmer can enable or disable behavior from the service program and WCF enables of disables the behavior as per the choice of the programmer. A programmer has to specify the type of behavior which is required in a program and no logic is required to enable to disable the behavior. Once the choice of providing particular behavior is made, WCF takes care about apply the particular behavior, a programmer need not to write any additional logic apart from just specifying the type of behavior and its allowed value. Therefore, a programmer is not directly related with wring the logic of applying the behavior. That is the reason of putting behavior as part of layer 2 in a WCF architecture (Klein). There are various behaviors such as Throttling behavior, Error behavior, Metadata behavior, instance behavior etc. The more details about these behaviors are covered in upcoming chapters.

Channel

A channel is the medium through with a client and service can communicate and exchange the messages. There are different types of channels created for various communication mechanisms. For instance, to communicate with http protocol http channel must be created. Likewise to communicate with the tcp protocol TCP channel must be created. Similar to behaviors the type of channel can be established by WCF based on the protocol specification done by a programmer. The detail of where to specify the protocol is provided in Chapter 2. A programmer just needs to provide the type of protocol to be applied and no logic is required by the programmer to create the channel. WCF takes care of creating a particular type of channel. Again, here a programmer is not directly associated with the logic on how to establish a particular type of channel. It is considered as part of layer 3 of the WCF architecture. There numerous types of channels such are HTTP channel, TCP channel, MSMQ channel etc. are available in WCF. The more details about these channels are available in the upcoming chapters.

Host

A service must be available to the client on anytime and anywhere basic. To make service available to clients it must be hosted first. A hosting is the process of making the service available to all the clients across the globe. After developing WCF service it is required to host the service. There are numerous hosting options available such as Internet Information Services (IIS), Self-hosting (Windows form or Console application) and Windows Service hosting. With all these options a programmer is directly associated to host the service. In self-hosting, a programmer needs to develop console application or windows form application to host the WCF service. It is also known as hosting under managed code as programming is done under the Common Language Runtime (CLR) of Microsoft.NET. In IIS hosting a programmer needs to publish the entire WCF service on IIS. In windows service hosting, a program based on window service in visual studio must be written by a programmer. In this hosting the service is hosted under the windows service environment which is a part of Windows Operating system. A programmer has a choice to start the service automatically when windows system starts. This is major benefit of this hosting option as once service is set as automatic human intervention is not required to start or stop the service.

These hosting options are part of the layer 4 of WCF architecture. A programmer is directly associated with hosting options which is also mentioned in Figure 4. The details about various hosting options are available throughout this book.

ESSENTIAL PIECES OF WCF: OTHER ELEMENTS

Apart from the important pieces of WCF architecture, it is required to learn other pieces which play major role in developing any WCF service. These elements are explained in the following section:

Endpoint

In WCF a communication between service and client is done through an endpoint. The endpoint contains address, binding and contract. Every endpoint must have at least these elements. The host program exposes a number of endpoints to the client program. A service must have at least one endpoint without which host program is not able to host the service and it throws the error. An endpoint can be defined via code or the configuration file. A programmer can prepare the configuration file by using a text editor such as notepad or other tool such as WCF service configuration editor which is discussed in Chapter 3.

Address

An address is a Uniform Resource Identifier (URI) which indicates the location of the service endpoint. It can be provided via code or configuration file. Every endpoint must have address.

Binding

A binding defines how a client can communicate with the service. Based on the binding the protocol of the address must be changed. Therefore, an address must match with binding or binding must have related address. Any mismatch results in an error. There is a list of predefined bindings available in WCF. Apart from these available bindings a programmer can design new custom bindings also.

Contract

Details about the contract is already explained in this section so it is not discussed further, but a contract means [ServiceContract] and not any other contracts whenever it is used as a part of endpoint in WCF.

Message

In WCF the communication between service and client is done through the message.

As a WCF service is based on the Simple Object Access Protocol (SOAP), the format of the message is as per SOAP specifications.

The in-depth details regarding endpoint and message are provided in Chapter 2. In the following Figure 5 the relationship between the essential pieces of WCF is explained to understand how WCF service works. It provides the clear understanding about role of each essential piece and interconnection between them. As shown in Figure 5, a WCF service is developed using contract and service which are discussed earlier. After the service is ready it must be hosted by some host program to make it available to the client. The WCF service can be hosted by any of the hosting options available. The steps are explained below:

1. A WCF service is developed and compiled.
2. The service is then hosted by using any of the hosting options available. It is waiting for client to communicate. In WCF communication is done through SOAP so a WSDL file is generated and provided to the client program.
3. A client communicates to the service by using WSDL file and channel is established between client and service. A channel is established at client side by the client program. Through channel client and service are able to send and receive messages by using endpoints at each side.

Figure 5. Interconnection between essential pieces of WCF service and client

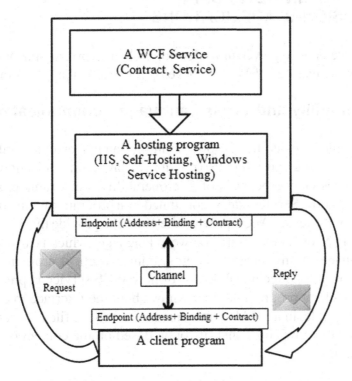

4. As the service exposes the functionality by using the contract it is necessary for the client to discover the contract and it is possible through endpoint as contract is a part of the endpoint.

5. Now client calls the function of service by sending the request by using message formatted SOAP which uses XML. The process of generating request message is known as serialization which is discussed in the preceding section. Upon receiving request from the client a service parses the message and converts data into its own native code. This process is known as de-serialization. Then the code of service is executed, reply is formed using SOAP message format and it is sent back to the client.

Here, client program can be developed in.NET, JAVA or any other language. In above communication usage of every essential piece is explained clearly. The important concepts such as endpoint channel and messages are discussed comprehensively in upcoming chapters.

USE OF WCF IN DEVELOPING PROFESSIONAL APPLICATIONS

WCF service is very powerful to develop rich enterprise applications. Following are the features of WCF to develop professional applications.

Interoperability and Cross Language Communication

Interoperability means diverse programming languages can communicate with each other with ease. It is also possible to have communication between different types device because of interoperability. For example, a service hosted in Window Service can be consumed by a program running on laptop, tablet or mobile device. WCF provides best ways to provide this kind of communication between devices and between languages which is also known as cross language communication. A programmer of client program does not need to know all the technical details of how WCF service is prepared and hosted. The client program needs to know about the interface to communicate. For example, in a SOAP communication a WSDL file is generated and client needs to know about this file only. Based on the content of WSDL a client program

Programming Flexibility

In the upcoming chapter we will discuss different way to writing and hosting a WCF programming. There is one single right way in WCF, but there can be multiple ways to do the same task and all the way might be right also (Klein). A programmer is given freedom to write the service code in different ways. For instance a programmer may create endpoint using code or configuration file and both ways might be right also.

Transactions

WCF supports development of transaction oriented applications. A transaction program can be integrated in WCF service by using the name space System. Transactions which is a part of System.Transactions assembly available under Microsoft.NET framework. This assembly is a part of the framework since framework version 2.0. In windows system a transaction can be processed by the component called Distributed Transaction Coordinator (DTC).

Security

By using WCF a programmer can develop distributed systems. The client and service send and receive message over the network. In a distributed network securing the message is essential. WCF provides robust security infrastructure to secure the message travelled between client and service. It provides the way to implement the security concepts such as integrity, confidentiality, authentication and authorization.

Reliability

WCF provides the flexible way of communication between client and service when either is not available. This is possible by integrating Microsoft Message Queuing (MSMQ) with WCF service. The major benefit of this communication is reliable delivery of message in case of non-availability of client or service. In reliable transfer the message is stored in the queue of windows system in case of the failure or crash of the system. Therefore, a programmer can integrate MSMQ with WCF to provide reliable communication which it is not possible with other technologies. WCF also provides functionality to create reliable sessions through reliable messaging channel which also helps to deliver the message in the case of failure.

Communication Protocols

In web service communication generally Http protocol is used. In WCF programmer has a choice to choose different protocols such as Http(s), Tcp, Named Pipe and MSMQ. This makes WCF flexible in terms of the protocols and a programmer can develop varies of services for browser (Http), for queue (MSMQ), for intranet (Tcp) and inter-process communication (Named Pipe).

Hosting

A host program is required to host the web service or web site. In the absence of this host program a service cannot be published and client cannot consume. A WCF service can be hosted on IIS or under the Windows Service. A programmer does not need to write a code to publish WCF service on these components of windows operating system. However a programmer can write his/her own program to host the WCF service. This is not possible in other technologies. Therefore, a programmer has alternative hosting options available in case of certain hosting options are not available.

ADVANTAGES OF WCF

Following are the advantages of using WCF:

Interoperability

WCF is interoperable with to other services and languages. This is not possible with.NET Remoting where only.NET client was able to consume the service.

Security and Reliability

WCF provides more security as compared to the.NET Web Services (.ASMX). To apply security in WCF extensive coding is not required. A programmer needs to configure attributes related to security and appropriate security is applied based on the attributes set by the programmer. Messages can be logged and traced by using Service Trace Viewer tool which is a major advantage of WCF as logging can be useful to investigate security issues. Moreover, reliable delivery of message can be guaranteed by using MSMQ with WCF program. A programmer can also create reliable sessions by using reliable message protocol and sessions are created automatically by WCF. A programmer needs to just change configuration of WCF service in order to have reliable session in it. This makes WCF really robust and powerful.

Error Handling

In WCF exceptions are handled in a different manner. The client program of WCF service can be another language. Therefore, WCF does not send the exception class to the client, but it converts exception to the SOAP faults just like request and reply and sends SOAP faults to the client. This is an efficient way of providing interoperability with the other technologies.

Serialization

In WCF it is possible to serialize almost all kinds of data types including hash tables which is not possible in web service. This provides better flexibility of working with different data types over web services.

Bindings

WCF supports various kinds of binding such as BasicHttpBinding, WSHttp-Binding, NetTcpBinding and other bindings including custom bindings. This feature is not available in the.NET Web Service. The.NET Web Services support only BasicHttpBinding. By using these bindings communication can be done using various protocols such as HTTP, TCP, Named Pipe and MSMQ.

Thread Support

A programmer can develop a multithreaded program by using WCF which is not available with the Web Services. Moreover, a programmer needs to only change certain configuration of WCF service to apply multithreading. No explicit coding required to manage the thread based program in WCF.

Duplex Communication

A two way communication in which, a WCF service can consume the functionality of client by calling it. This feature is not available in the traditional Web Service.

In duplex communication, both client and service can start communication at the same time. This provides flexibility to the developer to design two-way communication.

Development Support

To develop WCF service Microsoft Visual Studio with different versions is available. Microsoft Visual Studio is a complete package for developing any kind of.NET applications such as desktop applications, web based applications, mobile applications and other applications. To use this tool a programmer must obtain the license of it as it is not free and open source. A free express edition of Microsoft Visual Studio is available at the MSDN website for the initial learners like students and freelance developers (Green, 2016).

An open source project such as CodePlex provides tools for developing a WCF service program. It was launched by Microsoft in 2006 and now it has been widely used by a large number of programmers across the globe. It provides a number of tools as add-in or testing WCF service. Following are the tools available on it for various purposes:

- **WFCS.Blue:** It is the add-in for visual studio to develop WCF service using "contract first" development methodology. It is available at: http://wscfblue.codeplex.com.
- **WCFProxyGenerator:** It also an add-in for visual studio to offer the proxy of exception handling. It is available at: https://wcfproxygenerator.codeplex.com.
- **WCFMock:** It is a tool to perform unit testing on WCF services. It contains rich set of classes to do the black box testing. It reduces the burdon of writing lot of code to do the testing as it works like a wrapper to mock the unit testing of WCF service.

Another free light weight tool called as WCFStorm is also available to design WCF service with various configuration options.

WCF VS. WEB SERVICE

Table 1 contains difference between WCF and Web Service based on different parameters.

CONCLUSION

This chapter covers pre-requisite concepts required to learn WCF. It also explains the basic concepts of WCF. Following are the important points to summarize from this chapter:

- Diverse systems can communicate with each other because of interoperability.
- A web service designed in.NET can be consumed in JAVA with the ease and vice versa because of interoperability.
- A web service is always on and available.
- A web service is medium of communication between two electronic devices.
- Any client (Consumer) program can consume the web service by using Web Service Description Language (WSDL).
- A WSDL file must be generated for any web service.
- Serialization plays an important part in web service and interoperability

Table 1. Difference between WCF and web service

Sr. No	WCF	Web Service
1.	In WCF generally the operations are listed under the interface and implemented in the class.	In web service operations are directly implemented in the class no interface is defined for listing the operations of the service.
2.	The attribute [ServiceContract] is used to declare the interface as a service contract	The attribute [Web Service is used to declare the service class.
3.	The attribute [OperationContract] is used to expose the function as operation contract to the client program.	The attribute [WebMethod] is used to declare the function to be exposed to the client program.
4.	A WCF service can be hosted under IIS, Console Application, Windows Form Application and Windows Service	A web service can be hosted under IIS only.
5.	A WCF service can use non Http protocols	A web service uses Http protocol only. But Windows Activation Service under IIS allows to use net.tcp protocol.
6	In WCF one way, request-reply and duplex operations are supported	In Web service only one way and request-reply operations are supported
7	Default serializer is System.Runtime.Serialization	Default serializer is System.Xml.Serialization
8	Following message encoding options are available: XML 1.0, MTOM, Binary, Custom	Following message encoding options are available: XML 1.0, MTOM (Message Transmission Optimization Mechanism), DIME (Direct Internet Message Encapsulation), Custom
9	With WCF support, for security, reliable messaging and transaction is available	With Web Service, support for only security is available.

- Serialization converts one form of data to another form. De-Serialization does exactly same as serialization, but in reverse direction of serialization.
- Loosely coupled system is a kind of plug and play system.
- In a loosely coupled system, individual components are designed separately with less dependency among each other.
- In SOA, services have self-describing interfaces in the form of platform-independent XML documents. Web Services Description Language (WSDL) is the standard used to describe the services.
- UDDI is the registry for the services.
- In SOA service communicate through message and the message format can be SOAP or JSON.
- For designing SOA concepts such as a web service, loosely coupled system, interoperability and serialization can be very useful.
- Four tenets of SOA

- ○ Explicit boundaries
- ○ Services Are Autonomous
- ○ Services Share Schema and Contract, Not Class
- ○ Service Compatibility Is Based on Policy
- Windows Communication Foundation (WCF) Framework is a new platform to develop distributed and Service Oriented Applications (SOA).
- WCF combines various technologies such.NET Web Service,.NET Remoting into one unified programming model.
- Essential pieces of WCF
  - ○ Contract
  - ○ Service
  - ○ Behaviour
  - ○ Hosting
  - ○ Endpoint
    - ▪ Address
    - ▪ Binding
    - ▪ Contract
  - ○ Channel
  - ○ Message
- Major Features of WCF
  - ○ Security
  - ○ Reliability
  - ○ Transactions
  - ○ Interoperability
  - ○ Hosting
  - ○ Thread Support
- Advantages of WCF
  - ○ Interoperability.
  - ○ WCF provides robust security infrastructure with high reliability of data.
  - ○ A support for duplex communication is available in WCF.
  - ○ Multi-threading program support is available in WCF.
  - ○ Different communication protocols can be used by using different bindings such as BasicHttpBinding, WSHttpBinding, NetTcpBinding etc.
  - ○ A programmer can design the custom binding based on the requirement.
  - ○ Error handling is provided in good and efficient manner to provide interoperability with other technologies.

REFERENCES

Bustamante, M. L. (n.d.). *Leaning WCF*. O'Reilly.

Green, R. (2016). *Introduction to Windows Communication Foundation*. Microsoft. Retrieved from https://msdn.microsoft.com/en-us/library/dd936243.aspx

Haas, H., & Brown, A. (2004). *Web Services Glossary*. W3C. Retrieved from http://www.w3.org/

Klein, S. (n.d.). Professional WCF Programming. *WROX Publication.*

Microsoft. (2015). *Serialization (C# and Visual Basic)*. Retrieved from https://msdn.microsoft.com/en-us/library/ms233843.aspx

Microsoft. (2016). *Chapter 1: Service Oriented Architecture (SOA)*. Retrieved from http://msdn.microsoft.com/en-us/library/bb833022.aspx

Chapter 2
WCF Master Pieces

After completing this chapter, you will be able to:

- Learn basic concepts of Endpoint which includes Address Binding and Contract.
- Understand the underlying concepts of SOAP message.
- Understand the message communication patterns: One way, request reply and duplex.
- Gain knowledge about consumers of the message.
- Understand about channel and elements of channel stack.
- To develop first WCF service by using development server and WCF test client.

To develop any WCF service we must understand underlying concepts such as endpoint message and channel. In this chapter, fundamental concepts of end point, message and channel are explained. At the end of this chapter creating the first WCF service is explained.

DOI: 10.4018/978-1-5225-1997-3.ch002

Figure 1. Endpoint between service and client

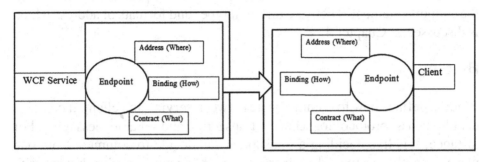

OVERVIEW OF ENDPOINT

The endpoint is the glue between service and client. Communication between client and service is done through the endpoint. Through endpoint a message is passed between client and service. A service must have at least one endpoint without which communication is not possible. It is like a USB port for communication between a computer and a pen drive or any other USB device. Furthermore, at least one USB port is required for communication otherwise data transfer is not possible. In Figure 1, a communication between a WCF service and .NET client through endpoint is presented. Once a client communicates with the service through particular endpoint it sends and receives message through that endpoint only. It is not possible that a client sends a message through one endpoint and receives message via another endpoint. An endpoint contains mainly three parts:

1. Address
2. Binding
3. Contract

Each part is introduced in Chapter 1. In this following section these parts are discussed in depth.

Address

Every endpoint must have unique address which is known as endpoint address. As WCF allows using different protocols such as Http, TCP, MSMQ etc. the format of address must be different for each protocol. An address specifies where the service is located without which it is not possible to communicate with the service. Therefore a service must provide the address in the endpoint element. There are different types and formats of address which is discussed in Chapter 4.

Binding

Binding defines how to communicate between service and client. It contains details such as protocol for security, transaction and reliable messaging. For instance, it is like deciding a transport when decide to commute from one place to another. A two wheeler vehicle might be easy to drive, but security is less as compared four wheeler vehicle. Furthermore, rule or protocols to drive a two wheeler are different than the rules or protocol to drive a four wheeler vehicle. Therefore, it is up to the user to choose the transport based on his/her choice and requirement. If security is not the essential requirement than a two wheeler vehicle might be the suitable option otherwise four wheeler vehicle can be chosen.

In WCF, there are some built-in bindings available. Some of the commonly used bindings are BasicHttpBinding, wsHTTPBinding, netTcpBinding and wsDualHttpBinding. Likewise, there are other built-in bindings available in WCF which are not listed here. A binding decides what kind of communication should be done between service and client. So bindings are more suitable for interoperability and there is less security or no security in these bindings. Moreover, the protocol of the address depends upon the type of binding selected. The binding must match with the protocol of address. For example, if a programmer chooses to use wsHTTPBinding, the protocol of address must be http or https. Using other protocols such as netTcpBinding results in the error while hosting the service. Apart from this built-in binding, a programmer can build custom binding also. The discussion on how to program the binding is included in Chapter 5.

Contract

A contract in endpoint is generally considered as [ServiceContract] annotation. Mainly it is an interface which contains a list of operations. It tells the client about the functions available in the service. It specifies a list of operations through [OperationContract] annotation. It also defines the communication patterns such as one way, request-reply or duplex. There must be at least one [OperationContract] otherwise it results in the error while hosting the service. Generally an interface is considered as [ServiceContract] on the other hand it is not necessary as a class can also be assigned as [ServiceContract]. But it creates ambiguity in the programmer's mind and it is not good programming practice to directly implementing the operations without declaring them into the interface.

There are other contracts such as [DataContract] and [MesageContract]. These contracts are discussed in details in Chapter 6.

Once the connection between client and service is established through endpoint, a communication between them is done through message which works on request-reply paradigm. In the following section details about a message is discussed.

OVERVIEW OF MESSAGE

A message is the basic unit of communication between client and service. A message is formatted according to the SOAP specifications and which uses XML as underlying language to prepare it. The basic structure of a message is shown in Figure 2.

A message contains three parts as shown in Figure 2. Each part is explained in detail below:

Envelope

It is the outermost part of the message. It contains other two parts: head and body. It contains information in the form of elements which include:

1. A namespace name.
2. An optional <header> element.
3. A compulsory <body> element.

Example 1. SOAP Envelope

```
<s:Envelope xmlns:a="http://www.w3.org/2005/08/addressing"
xmlns:s="http://www.w3.org/2003/05/soap-envelope">
…..
…..
</s:Envelope>
```

Here header and body parts are not shown in this example, but these parts are available in place where the dots (…) are shown.

Figure 2. Message structure

SOAP Envelope

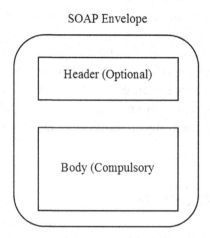

Header

A header element is optional. It may contain zero or more header block. It is used to include optional information such as sender details, security information and other user information. It must be the first element if it is included in the message. By default header element is included in the SOAP message. To remove it from the message, the concept of message contract can be applied.

Example 2. SOAP Header

```
…..
  <s:Header>
    <a:Action s:mustUnderstand="1">http://tempuri.org/ICal-
culator/add</a:Action>
    <a:MessageID>urn:uuid:f864e9b8-3aae-40a0-bcf9-
31d166c4f989</a:MessageID>
    <a:ReplyTo>
      <a:Address>http://www.w3.org/2005/08/addressing/
anonymous</a:Address>
    </a:ReplyTo>
  </s:Header>
…..
```

In above example the dots (…) can be replaced by envelope element and header element is part of envelope it cannot exist independently.

Body

A body is compulsory part of SOAP envelope. It is a child element of SOAP envelope node. It is the last element of SOAP envelope. It contains important information such as collection of data which is to be sent or received between service and client. Following is the example of typical body element:

Example 3. SOAP Body

```
…..
<s:Body>
    <add xmlns="http://tempuri.org/">
        <no1>5</no1>
        <no2>5</no2>
    </add>
  </s:Body>
</s:Envelope>
…..
```

In the above example the dots (…) can be replaced by envelope element and body element is part of the envelope it cannot exist independently.

The example of a SOAP message for the request from the client to service is shown in following example:

Example 4. SOAP Message (Request)

```
<s:Envelope xmlns:a="http://www.w3.org/2005/08/addressing"
xmlns:s="http://www.w3.org/2003/05/soap-envelope">
  <s:Header>
    <a:Action s:mustUnderstand="1">http://tempuri.org/ICal-
culator/add</a:Action>
    <a:MessageID>urn:uuid:f864e9b8-3aae-40a0-bcf9-
31d166c4f989</a:MessageID>
    <a:ReplyTo>
      <a:Address>http://www.w3.org/2005/08/addressing/
anonymous</a:Address>
    </a:ReplyTo>
  </s:Header>
  <s:Body>
    <add xmlns="http://tempuri.org/">
```

```
      <no1>5</no1>
      <no2>5</no2>
    </add>
  </s:Body>
</s:Envelope>
```

In above example, the entire message is shown with all three elements discussed in this section. As it is discussed earlier, the envelope is outermost element. The header and body elements are under the envelope and both are at the same level. In the body element the actual data which is to be transmitted to the service is shown. It contains the function name and parameter values. These values are passed by the client program at the time consuming the add function of the service. This indicates that no matter what kind of programming language a client uses, the functions and parameter are converted into message (XML) form due to the concept of serialization which is discussed in previous chapter.

In below example the SOAP message for the reply from service to client shown:

Example 5. SOAP Message (Reply)

```
<s:Envelope xmlns:s="http://www.w3.org/2003/05/soap-en-
velope" xmlns:a="http://www.w3.org/2005/08/addressing"
xmlns:u="http://docs.oasis-open.org/wss/2004/01/oasis-
200401-wss-wssecurity-utility-1.0.xsd">
  <s:Header>
    <a:Action s:mustUnderstand="1"    u:Id="_2">http://tem-
puri.org/ICalculator/addResponse</a:Action>
    <a:RelatesTo u:Id="_3">urn:uuid:c6e88fa9-2904-4bc8-b405-
556fa851dece</a:RelatesTo>
    <o:Security s:mustUnderstand="1" xmlns:o="http://docs.
oasis-open.org/wss/2004/01/oasis-200401-wss-wssecurity-se-
cext-1.0.xsd">
      <u:Timestamp u:Id="uuid-379f93d0-1462-4001-9c1c-
ab00e2873176-7">
        <u:Created>2016-04-10T11:38:29.625Z</u:Created>
        <u:Expires>2016-04-10T11:43:29.625Z</u:Expires>
      </u:Timestamp>
      <c:DerivedKeyToken u:Id="uuid-379f93d0-1462-4001-
9c1c-ab00e2873176-5" xmlns:c="http://schemas.xmlsoap.org/
```

```
ws/2005/02/sc">
        <o:SecurityTokenReference>
        <o:Reference URI="urn:uuid:6b7720c3-9358-4b3b-
9347-6f93d2974c9a" ValueType="http://schemas.xmlsoap.org/
ws/2005/02/sc/sct" />
        </o:SecurityTokenReference>
        <c:Offset>0</c:Offset>
        <c:Length>24</c:Length>
        <c:Nonce>yU2FsN/acp+YG6v+GIyA3A==</c:Nonce>
    </c:DerivedKeyToken>
    <c:DerivedKeyToken u:Id="uuid-379f93d0-1462-4001-
9c1c-ab00e2873176-6" xmlns:c="http://schemas.xmlsoap.org/
ws/2005/02/sc">
        <o:SecurityTokenReference>
        <o:Reference URI="urn:uuid:6b7720c3-9358-4b3b-
9347-6f93d2974c9a" ValueType="http://schemas.xmlsoap.org/
ws/2005/02/sc/sct" />
        </o:SecurityTokenReference>
        <c:Nonce>qkSNssISkULGluJpm2xwIQ==</c:Nonce>
    </c:DerivedKeyToken>
    <e:ReferenceList xmlns:e="http://www.w3.org/2001/04/
xmlenc#">
        <e:DataReference URI="#_1" />
        <e:DataReference URI="#_4" />
    </e:ReferenceList>
    <e:EncryptedData Id="_4" Type="http://www.
w3.org/2001/04/xmlenc#Element" xmlns:e="http://www.
w3.org/2001/04/xmlenc#">
        <e:EncryptionMethod Algorithm="http://www.
w3.org/2001/04/xmlenc#aes256-cbc" />
        <KeyInfo xmlns="http://www.w3.org/2000/09/xmldsig#">
          <o:SecurityTokenReference>
            <o:Reference ValueType="http://schemas.xmlsoap.
org/ws/2005/02/sc/dk" URI="#uuid-379f93d0-1462-4001-9c1c-
ab00e2873176-6" />
          </o:SecurityTokenReference>
        </KeyInfo>
        <e:CipherData>
        <e:CipherValue>wT71zFFI9ahxiYJ6TaiGEUWoPCT9nY7qTgP
Tn96IklpOHVG5mZA </e:CipherValue>
```

```
      </e:CipherData>
    </e:EncryptedData>
  </o:Security>
 </s:Header>
 <s:Body u:Id="_0">
   <addResponse xmlns="http://tempuri.org/">
    <addResult>10</addResult>
   </addResponse>
 </s:Body>
</s:Envelope>
```

In above example the format of message is similar as the request. In the body element the value which is returned from the service to client is shown. This indicates that no a code for WCF is written in C#.NET but it is converted in to message (XML) format. This has happen because of the concept of serialization.

In web service communication serialization plays important role as it convert the function, parameters and return value into SOAP message for request and reply. Furthermore, SOAP message is formatted using the XML which is understandable by almost all the programming languages and platform. A SOAP message plays important role in Service Oriented Architecture (SOA). In the following section, the consumers of the message are explained.

Message Consumers

In the previous section we have discussed about be message which travelled from client to service and vice versa. Apart from these two entities there can be another entity which can consume this message. In this section all these entities are explained.

Client

A client is program which consumes the service by calling the function of service. It always initiates communication to the service. Here the function call is converted in to request from as shown in Example 4. Now onwards throughout this book we will use the word request instead of function call. It sends the request to the client and waits for the reply. The communication from client to service is shown in Figure 3. It sends the message to service and waits for the reply if message pattern is not one way. Here the term client is considered as the code where the logic of consuming the service is written.

Figure 3. Client

Service

A service is also a program which receives a request from the client and sends the reply to particular client if the message pattern is not one way. The communication form service to client is shown in Figure 4. A service never initiates communication. After it is hosted it waits for the client to initiate communication. Upon receiving message from the client, it processes the message triggers some actions, executes the code and sends reply to the client. Here triggering means fetching the data from database or from another service. A service can serve more than one client at the same time. For this a service maintains a session for each client. For example, in a restaurant multiple clients come for the dinner. Now at a time multiple customers from different dinner table give order. In this case a waiter remembers the table number for each customer to deliver order to each client correctly. Two clients can consume the service by using the same endpoint at the same time. As service maintains session with each client it responds to each client and sends reply to each client correctly.

Here a service can call another service also i.e. a service becomes a client for another service. It is known as service chain. Service chain is shown in Figure 5. As shown in Figure 5, a client sends a request to the service 1 as per the step 1. Now service 1 is unable to provide the requested data to the

Figure 4. Service

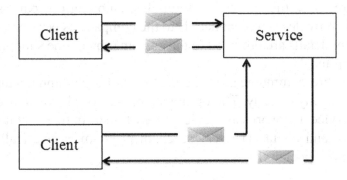

Figure 5. Service chain

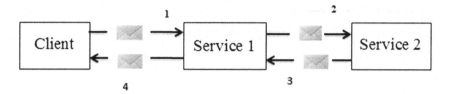

Figure 6. Service chain example

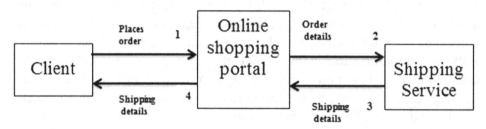

client so it communicates to the Service 2 as per step 2. Service 2 processes request of Service 1 and sends the reply back to Service 1 as shown in step 3. Upon getting the reply from Service 2, the first service i.e. Service 1 sends reply back to client. In the entire communication a client might not be aware about Service 2. It is also interesting to note that Service 1 behaves like a client for Service 2 and it behaves as Service for the client. Therefore, it is considered as client and service both in this communication. This fact is useful while doing actual implementation of service chain in WCF as in Service 1 additional configuration might be required.

Following is the example of service chain shown in Figure 6. A consumer buys a product online by placing an order as shown in step 1. The online shopping company confirms the order and contacts shipping company to ship the order placed by the customer as shown in step 2 and the customer is not aware about this communication. The shipping company ships the product and provides shipment details to the company as per step 3. Finally, the shipment details are provided to the customer by online shopping portal as shown in step 4.

In this entire communication a customer is not communicating to the shipping company directly. The online shopping portal works as client for shipping service and works as service for customer. In that way it becomes both service and client. The service chain program is practically implemented in the Appendix.

Figure 7. One way

Intermediaries

An intermediary can be considered as third party, client and service are not aware about it. It may sit between client and service. It works like a gateway between client and service. It may not consume the SOAP message. It might be useful to prevent unwanted message from the system. A programmer is not directly related to this component as it can be hardware too. As it does not consume message, it can be useful to route message or inspect message for security reasons.

A message can be sent to client and service based on the pattern of the message. In the following section message pattern is explained.

MESSAGE PATTERNS

There are mainly three message patterns available in WCF: (A) one way or simplex (B) Request-Reply (C) Duplex. Each method is described below:

(A) One way

It is known as single direction communication. It is also known as simplex communication. The popular example is a radio broadcasting system in which communication is done only in a single direction. After sending a request the client does not wait for the reply as a service does not send reply in this communication as shown in Figure 7. A service receives message processes it and does return anything to the client. If the service operation is one way it must have a void return type in the operation signature.

In WCF all the operations are request-reply by default so additional configuration is required to make the operation as one way even the operation is having return type as void. For example, in following code snippet an operation contract is declared as:

```
.....
[OperationContract]
void display ();
.....
```

Now above operation is declared as void but it is still considered as request-reply not one way. Therefore, some configuration from the WCF side is required to consider above operation as one way. Only void return type is allowed is this communication.

(B) Request-Reply

It is a two way communication but not at the same time. That is either entity can send the message at a time. The popular example is walky-talky in which at a time any one person can talk. In this communication a client sends the request to the service and waits for the reply. After receiving the request from a client, a service executes the code and return reply back to the client. The process is well presented in Figure 8. As discussed earlier in the service chain, a service may communicate with other service to provide the data to the client. As this is the default message pattern of communication in WCF, no additional configuration is required for this message pattern. An operation must have the return value for this communication otherwise it will result in error. Any return type is allowed in this communication.

Figure 8. Request-Reply

Figure 9. Duplex

(C) Duplex

It is a two way communication at the same time. Both client and service can send and receive message at the same time in this message pattern. The popular example is the telephone communication where both sender and receiver can talk with each other at the same time. In WCF duplex communication, a service can call the function of client so there must be another contract which must be implemented by a client to make this communication possible. The entire process is presented in Figure 9. As shown in Figure 9, the communication is done in both directions. When a communication is done in both directions at the same time there must be different channels for communication from client to service and service to client.

The implementation of all these patterns is explained in Chapter 7.

CHANNEL

A channel is a medium through the communication between service and client takes place. After message pattern is decided, endpoint is created but if channel is not established then communication cannot take place. As a client initiates communication, it also responsible to establish a channel. The entire process is presented in Figure 10. The steps shown in Figure 10 are explained below:

Step 1: A client uses address of the service through the endpoint to establish a channel. It sends the request to service.

Figure 10. Channel

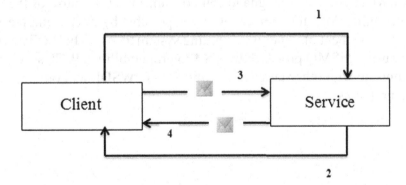

Step 2: If service receives the request to establish a channel from client, it accepts the request and channel is established otherwise error is generated and channel will not be established. In such cases steps 3 and 4 are not executed as the channel is not established message cannot be sent or received.

Step 3: Upon successful establishment of the channel, a client sends a message to service.

Step 4: A service receives the message from the client, processes it and sends reply to client if communication is not one way.

Channel Stack

A channel stack is the collection of various elements under a channel. These elements are explained below:

Security

There are two types of security available in WCF: Transport level security and Message level security. A transport level security is point to point security so entire message might not be secured. This security can be provided by several protocols such as HTTP or HTTPs. A message level security is end to end point security so entire message is secured. This security can be applied by using windows authentication and digital certificate. A programmer can apply custom credentials, authorization and tokens to provide the security.

Interoperability

In WCF various components over different platform and technology are combined together to build a channel. Several interoperability such as.NET interoperability, MSMQ interoperability and WS * Interoperability are possible in WCF. Any.NET language can consume WCF because of the.NET interoperability. MSMQ interoperability is possible by integrating message queuing component of windows operating system to WCF. In WCF it is possible by using MSMQ protocol. In WS * interoperability a WCF service can communicate with other languages using SOAP, WSDL and other security related protocols.

Message Patterns

It is very important to understand the message pattern to provide interoperability. The message pattern used by WCF service might not be supported in another client. Therefore, the message pattern must be chosen carefully by keeping the target environment in mind. For example

MSMQ does not support request-reply so it is not possible to apply request-reply message pattern for MSMQ interoperability.

Transports

In WCF there are different ways of communication based on the transport selected by a programmer. There are different transports such as HTTP, TCP, MSMQ and Name pipe are supported. Each of these transports is explained below:

HTTP

It is the fundamental protocol to interoperate with other system. Almost all the platform and languages support this protocol. As is connection less and stateless, the state is not maintained in this protocol. To use HTTPs protocol it is required to obtain certificate such as Transport Layer Security (TLS) or Secure Sockets Layer (SSL) from certified authorities.

TCP

It is a connection based protocol. Before sending the data a connection is established between service and client. It might not be supported by all platforms or languages. It is best suitable for the.NET interoperability. That is, it works well when a WCF service communicates with any.NET client.

MSMQ

For reliable messaging using queue this protocol is required. This protocol might not be supported by all platforms and languages.

Named Pipe

Named pipe is also known as inter-process communication. It can be used to communicate between two processes under same machine. It supports one

Figure 11. Visual studio IDE

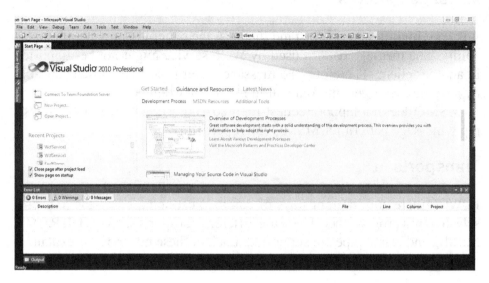

way and duplex communication. It is not suitable to develop distributed applications as it is designed for communication between two processes under the single machine. For example,

Creating first WCF Service

In this section we will learn step by step on how to create the first WCF service.

Step 1: Open Visual Studio 2010 from start-> Programs-> Microsoft Visual Studio 2010 folder or type devenv.exe in the run menu. The visual studio IDE will be opened as shown in Figure 11. This is the IDE in which all the.NET related program can be developed.

Step 2: Select File-> New Project option from the menu as shown in Figure 12. Specify programming language as Visual C#, WCF and select WCF Service library as the project type which is highlighted in Figure 12. Also select appropriate.NET Framework which is available at the top of this template window. In visual studio 2010 the highest framework is 4.0 and lowest framework is 2.0. Then after select appropriate path to save the project by clicking on the browse button. Finally provide the project name and click on the ok button to create the first WCF service.

Figure 12. Selecting WCF service

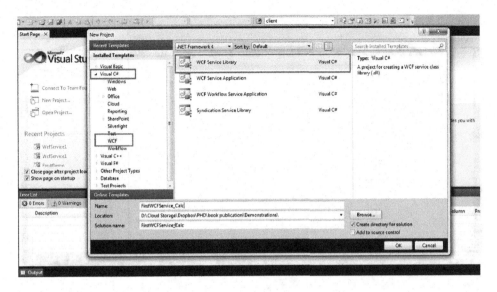

Step 3: A WCF service solution is opened with three main components IService1.cs, Service1.cs and App.config file in the solution explore. By default the code is IService1.cs file is opened which is shown in Figure 13. It this file an interface is defined under the name space. By default the name of interface is IService1 and it must be changed as per the requirement of the programmer. This interface is labeled as [ServiceContract] annotation which means that IService1 interface is the service contract and it must be referred as contract in the endpoint element. It comes from System.ServiceModel.ServiceContractAttribute. As discussed in chapter System.ServiceModel is the main building block to develop any WCF service and it is added under the references automatically in WCF Service library project. There are two operations available by default inside the interface definition. These operations are labeled as [OperationContract] annotation which means these operations are available to client. It comes from System.ServiceModel.OperationContractAttribute. If this annotation is missing, the operation is not made available to client. A programmer can add number of operations as per the requirement. At least one [OperationContract] is required otherwise it will result an error while hosting the service.

Figure 13. Solution explore with WCF service

Figure 14. Refactoring the interface

Here [DataContract] attribute is not explained as included in the upcoming chapters. In our example we intend to design simple calculator for basic four mathematics operations such as add, sub, mul and division which is mentioned in Step 4.

Figure 15. Renaming the interface using Re-factor

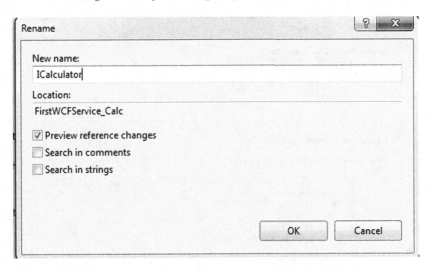

Step 4: Now rename the interface from IService1 to ICalculator by right clicking on interface as shown in Figure 14. Select the first option Rename to change the name of the interface and follow the sub sequent steps mentioned in Figure 15 and Figure 16. The interface name is changed now. The benefit of Refactor-Rename is that you don't need to change the name at other places where the objected referred. It automatically changes the name of the object everywhere it is referred in the code. Now write the declaration of all four operations with the heading [OperationContract] on each of them as shown in Figure 17.

Step 5: Now Open Service 1.cs file and change the name of the class Service 1 to Calculator as shown in Figure 18. Follow the similar steps shown in Figure 15 and Figure 16. Finally the name of the class is changed to "Calculator" as shown Figure 19. Here, this class implements interface and the interface is considered as [ServiceContract]. Therefore, the class which implements service contract is known as the service class. In this example service is "Calculator" as it implements the service contract "ICalculator". After changing the name of the service class remove the default functions of which were available by default when service was created. The class looks like as per Figure 19.

Step 6: Implement the interface by right clicking on the interface and selecting implement interface option as shown in Figure 20.

Figure 16. Applying rename operation through Re-factor

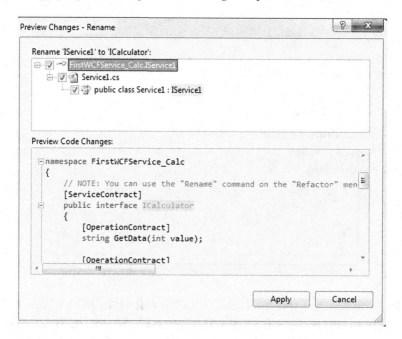

Figure 17. Adding the operations in [ServiceContract]

```
ISservice1.cs* ×
FirstWCFService_Calc.ICalculator                                        ▾  ♦ sub(int no1, in
    using System.Runtime.Serialization;
    using System.ServiceModel;
    using System.Text;
    namespace FirstWCFService_Calc
    {
        // NOTE: You can use the "Rename" command on the "Refactor" menu to change the interfac
        [ServiceContract]
        public interface ICalculator
        {
            [OperationContract]
            int add(int no1, int no2);
            [OperationContract]
            int sub(int no1, int no2);|
            [OperationContract]
            int mul(int no1, int no2);
            [OperationContract]
            int div(int no1, int no2);

            // TODO: Add your service operations here
        }

        // Use a data contract as illustrated in the sample below to add composite types to se
    }
```

Figure 18. Changing the name of the class using Refactor option

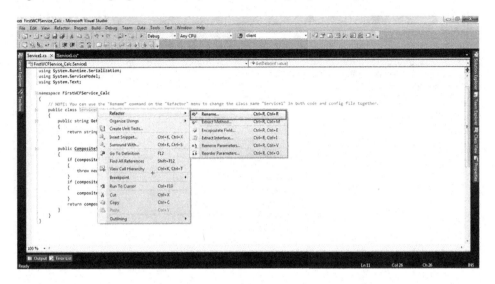

Figure 19. Service class after refactoring and removing the default operations

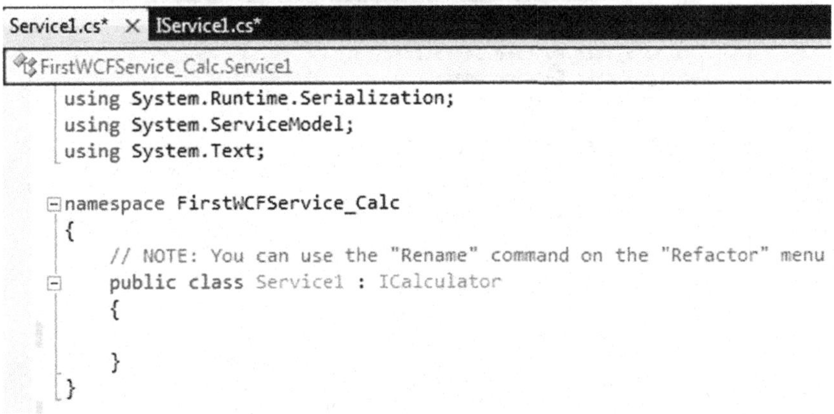

Step 7: In the empty body of each operation the default return value appears as shown in Figure 21. Remove the default values from the function body and write your logic with and return the value as shown in Figure 22 in which the updated logic is highlighted. Now the service is ready and the next step is to compile it.

Step 8: Right click on the project and select Build option from the context menu as shown in the Figure 23. The build option can also be selected from the Build menu of the menu bar. In case of no error the project is

Figure 20. Implementing service class

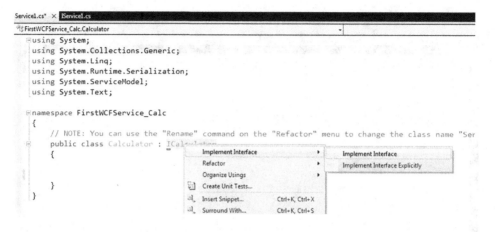

Figure 21. Service class with operations having default values

```
Service1.cs*  ×  IService1.cs*
FirstWCFService_Calc.Calculator
    using System.Runtime.Serialization;
    using System.ServiceModel;
    using System.Text;

  namespace FirstWCFService_Calc
  {
      // NOTE: You can use the "Rename" command on the "Refac
      public class Calculator : ICalculator
      {

          public int add(int no1, int no2)
          {
              throw new NotImplementedException();
          }

          public int sub(int no1, int no2)
          {
              throw new NotImplementedException();
          }

          public int mul(int no1, int no2)
          {
              throw new NotImplementedException();
          }

          public int div(int no1, int no2)
          {
              throw new NotImplementedException();
          }
      }
  }
```

Figure 22. Service class logic in each operation

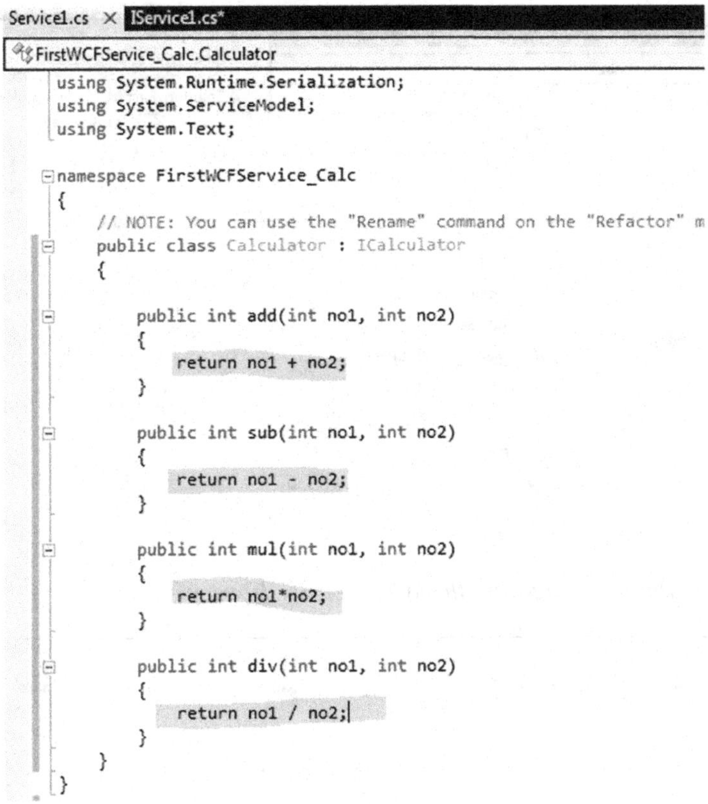

```
Service1.cs  ×  IService1.cs*
FirstWCFService_Calc.Calculator
    using System.Runtime.Serialization;
    using System.ServiceModel;
    using System.Text;

    namespace FirstWCFService_Calc
    {
        // NOTE: You can use the "Rename" command on the "Refactor" m
        public class Calculator : ICalculator
        {
            public int add(int no1, int no2)
            {
                return no1 + no2;
            }

            public int sub(int no1, int no2)
            {
                return no1 - no2;
            }

            public int mul(int no1, int no2)
            {
                return no1*no2;
            }

            public int div(int no1, int no2)
            {
                return no1 / no2;
            }
        }
    }
```

compiled an output is shown in the Figure 24. As the project is WCF service library the output is in the form of.dll (Dynamic Link Library). As we know it is not possible to execute the dll directly the service project must be hosted by a host program. In the host program this.dll file must be added as reference. This option will be discussed in the upcoming chapters. In this chapter we shall run this service by using the build-in development server of Visual Studio 2010. The test client program is provided by Visual Studio. Before running the service it is necessary to update the configuration file. It is mainly used to create endpoint and other configurations related to the service. It must have extension.config, and of file must be app.config. Changing the name or extension may lead to the error of not finding the configuration file. In the configuration file, contract and service name must be updated as per the program.

Figure 23. Compiling service project

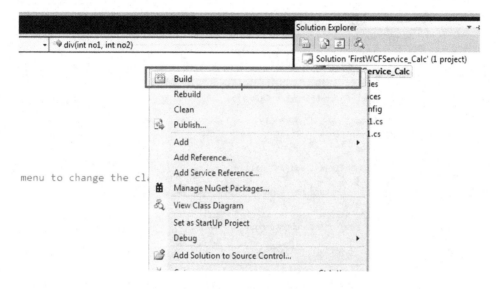

Figure 24. Output of compiling the WCF service library

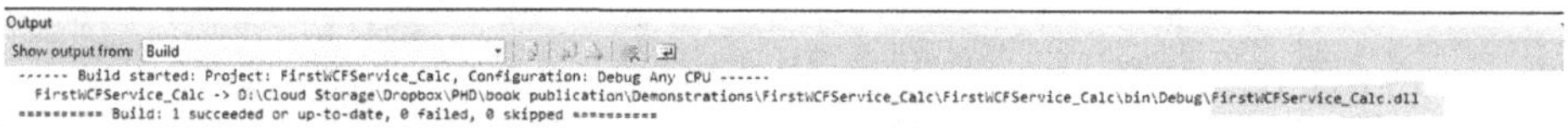

The configuration file is shown in Example 6. The service name is changed under the <service> element which is highlighted in this example. The contract name is changed under <endpoint> element which is also highlighted. As a service requires at least one endpoint, at least one <endpoint> is required in the configuration file.

```
Example 6. Configuration file:
<?xml version="1.0" encoding="utf-8" ?>
<configuration>
  <!-- When deploying the service library project, the
content of the config file must be added to the host's
 app.config file. System.Configuration does not support
config files for libraries. -->
  <system.serviceModel>
    <services>
      <service name="FirstWCFService_Calc.
```

```
Calculator"><endpoint address="" binding="wsHttpBinding"cont
ract="FirstWCFService_Calc.ICalculator">
          <identity>
            <dns value="localhost" />
          </identity>
        </endpoint>
        <endpoint address="mex" binding="mexHttpBinding"
contract="IMetadataExchange" />
        <host>
          <baseAddresses>
            <add baseAddress="http://localhost:8732/Design_
Time_Addresses/FirstWCFService_Calc/Service1/" />
          </baseAddresses>
        </host>
      </service>
    </services>
    <behaviors>
      <serviceBehaviors>
        <behavior>
          <!-- To avoid disclosing metadata information,
          set the value below to false and remove the meta-
data endpoint above before deployment
          -->
          <serviceMetadata httpGetEnabled="True"/>
          <!-- To receive exception details in faults for
debugging purposes,
          set the value below to true.  Set to false before
deployment
          to avoid disclosing exception information -->
          <serviceDebug includeExceptionDetailInFaults="Fal
se" />
        </behavior>
      </serviceBehaviors>
    </behaviors>
  </system.serviceModel>
</configuration>
```

Here both service name and contract name are written in a fully qualified manner. That is, the name must have a prefix of namespace in which that class or interface is defined. For example, the namespace in this program is

Figure 25. Run button

Figure 26. WCF Service host

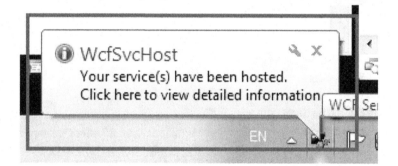

FirstWCFService_Calc. The service name is Calculator so the service name in the configuration file should be written as FirstWCFService_Calc.Calculator. The contract (interface) name is ICalculator so the contract name in the configuration file should be written as FirstWCFService_Calc.Calculator. Keep the other elements as it is for this program.

Step 9: Now click on the run button as shown in Figure 25, to launch WCF Service Host (WcfSvcHost) and WCF test client (wcftestclient). First the WCF Test Server is loaded and which can be opened from the taskbar as shown in Figure 26. After the host is loaded, the WCF test client is opened as shown in Figure 27. In this test client window all the operations are listed in the left panel. To test any operation you need to click on any of the function, and it will ask to you specify the parameter if any and then you can click on the invoke button to test the logic of the operation. In Figure 27, add operation is clicked so related parameters are shown. After clicking on invoke button, the response is returned under the response view below the request view which is also shown in Figure 27.

Figure 27. WCF test client (testing add operation)

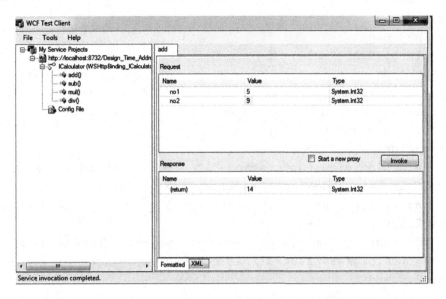

Apart from this view there is one XML view which shows actual form of request and response message in SOAP format. This format is discussed earlier in this chapter. The request is shown in Example 7. Likewise the response is shown in Example 8.

```
Example 7. SOAP request:
<s:Envelope xmlns:a="http://www.w3.org/2005/08/addressing"
xmlns:s="http://www.w3.org/2003/05/soap-envelope">
  <s:Header>
    <a:Action s:mustUnderstand="1">http://tempuri.org/
ICalculator/add</a:Action>
    <a:MessageID>urn:uuid:3905fdfe-2508-4ba3-a24e-
405ff98da15b</a:MessageID>
    <a:ReplyTo>
      <a:Address>http://www.w3.org/2005/08/addressing/
anonymous</a:Address>
    </a:ReplyTo>
  </s:Header>
  <s:Body>
    <add xmlns="http://tempuri.org/">
      <no1>5</no1>
      <no2>9</no2>
```

```
      </add>
    </s:Body>
</s:Envelope>
Example 8. SOAP Reply:
<s:Envelope xmlns:s="http://www.w3.org/2003/05/soap-enve-
lope" xmlns:a="http://www.w3.org/2005/08/addressing"
xmlns:u="http://docs.oasis-open.org/wss/2004/01/oasis-
200401-wss-wssecurity-utility-1.0.xsd">
  <s:Header>
    <a:Action s:mustUnderstand="1" u:Id="_2">http://tempuri.
org/ICalculator/addResponse</a:Action>
    <a:RelatesTo u:Id="_3">urn:uuid:c12bb099-6d9e-4412-af9a-
e82e8230c66c</a:RelatesTo>
    <o:Security s:mustUnderstand="1" xmlns:o="http://docs.
oasis-open.org/wss/2004/01/oasis-200401-wss-wssecurity-se-
cext-1.0.xsd">
      <u:Timestamp u:Id="uuid-5631774a-97bb-4ec3-9367-acf1b-
81b8add-7">
        <u:Created>2016-04-13T16:39:35.600Z</u:Created>
        <u:Expires>2016-04-13T16:44:35.600Z</u:Expires>
      </u:Timestamp>
      <c:DerivedKeyToken u:Id="uuid-5631774a-97bb-4ec3-9367-
acf1b81b8add-5" xmlns:c="http://schemas.xmlsoap.org/
ws/2005/02/sc">
        <o:SecurityTokenReference>
          <o:Reference URI="urn:uuid:c5ab626a-4280-4a71-
885c-5d4a075defb8" ValueType="http://schemas.xmlsoap.org/
ws/2005/02/sc/sct" />
        </o:SecurityTokenReference>
        <c:Offset>0</c:Offset>
        <c:Length>24</c:Length>
        <c:Nonce>eq87ZY1Ztop1EFAQeH0qRA==</c:Nonce>
      </c:DerivedKeyToken>
      <c:DerivedKeyToken u:Id="uuid-5631774a-97bb-4ec3-9367-
acf1b81b8add-6" xmlns:c="http://schemas.xmlsoap.org/
ws/2005/02/sc">
        <o:SecurityTokenReference>
          <o:Reference URI="urn:uuid:c5ab626a-4280-4a71-
885c-5d4a075defb8" ValueType="http://schemas.xmlsoap.org/
ws/2005/02/sc/sct" />
```

```
        </o:SecurityTokenReference>
        <c:Nonce>FXUuWuDu63PCdF2diEvRfQ==</c:Nonce>
      </c:DerivedKeyToken>
      <e:ReferenceList xmlns:e="http://www.w3.org/2001/04/
xmlenc#">
        <e:DataReference URI="#_1" />
        <e:DataReference URI="#_4" />
      </e:ReferenceList>
      <e:EncryptedData Id="_4" Type="http://www.w3.
org/2001/04/xmlenc#Element" xmlns:e="http://www.w3.
org/2001/04/xmlenc#">
        <e:EncryptionMethod Algorithm="http://www.w3.
org/2001/04/xmlenc#aes256-cbc" />
        <KeyInfo xmlns="http://www.w3.org/2000/09/xmldsig#">
         <o:SecurityTokenReference>
           <o:Reference ValueType="http://schemas.xmlsoap.
org/ws/2005/02/sc/dk" URI="#uuid-5631774a-97bb-4ec3-9367-
acf1b81b8add-6" />
         </o:SecurityTokenReference>
        </KeyInfo>
        <e:CipherData>
          <e:CipherValue>H24HPTS2vacW </e:CipherValue>
        </e:CipherData>
      </e:EncryptedData>
    </o:Security>
  </s:Header>
  <s:Body u:Id="_0">
    <addResponse xmlns="http://tempuri.org/">
      <addResult> 14 </addResult>
    </addResponse>
  </s:Body>
</s:Envelope>
```

Above request and reply are formed by using the concepts of serialization which is already discussed in Chapter 1. In this program the WCFsvcHost and WCF Test Client are provided by visual studio. In a real development of WCF service, these elements must be designed by the programmer. For IIS hosting it not required to write a host program otherwise a programmer must develop a program to host WCF service which is also known as self-hosting.

Likewise, in real development WCF Test Client should not be used. It should be used for debugging purpose only. A programmer must develop a client program in some programming language such as C#.NET, JAVA, PHP etc. Furthermore, in this program the configuration file is available by default, but in real development a programmer must create it manually or by using a tool. The configuration file must be created in the host program not in the service project.

Therefore, in real development generally three programs should be developed: a WCF Service, a Host program and a client. A host program is required for hosting WCF service on IIS, windows service, Windows Activation Service (WAS) or self-hosting. When IIS hosting is used only two projects are required. All the hosting options are explored with great details in Chapter 11.

In the forthcoming chapters, various hosting options are explained. The client program and other configurations are also explored in details.

CONCLUSION

In this chapter, basic concepts such as endpoint, message and channel are explained in depth. Without proper understanding of these concepts it is not possible to develop any WCF program. The following are important points to summarize from this chapter:

- Endpoint connects the client and service.
- Endpoint = Address+ Binding + Contract.
- Any WCF service must have at least one endpoint.
- An Address specifies where the service is and it is an URI.
- A Binding defines how to communicate between service and client.
- There are numbers of built-in bindings available in WCF and you can create your own customized binding also by using custom binding.
- A contract is generally [ServiceContract] when it is considered as a part of endpoint element. A class can work as [ServiceContract] too, but it is not good programming practice to do so.
- The communication between WCF service and client is done in the form of a SOAP message.
- The SOAP message is formatted using XML.
- There are different consumers of the message such as client, service and intermediaries.

- Three message patterns are available: one way, request-reply and duplex.
- By default the operations in WCF are request-reply.
- A channel must be established by client to send message to the service.
- Elements of the channel stack: security, interoperability, message pattern and transport.
- To develop WCF service a project type WCF service library must be selected in Visual Studio.
- There are three files in the WCF Service library project: an interface, a class and a configuration file. An interface is generally is labeled [ServiceContract] and it is referred as a contract in endpoint element. A class which implements [ServiceContract] is known as service class and it is referred as a service element in the configuration file. A configuration file must have extension.config.
- At least one <endpoint> element is required in the configuration file of service.
- A WCFsvcHost is a program provided by visual studio to host the WCF service for debugging and testing purpose only. It cannot be used in the real application development.
- A WCF Test Client is a program provided by visual studio to create test client for WCF service testing. It cannot be used in the real application development.
- The service name and contract name must have fully qualified name preceded by the namespace name in the configuration file.

Chapter 3
WCF Programming Methodology

After completing this chapter, you will be able to:

- Learn different programming methodologies available in WCF
- Learn steps required in developing WCF Service and Host WCF Service.
- Host WCF service using Console Project.
- Create Configuration file using WCF Service Configuration Editor.
- Consume WCF Service in.NET client.

In the previous chapter, I have discussed on master pieces of WCF. In this chapter different ways to develop a WCF service are discussed in detail. Some dependent components which are required to develop WCF are also well explained.

WCF AND OBJECT ORIENTED PROGRAMMING (OOP)

In the previous chapter, you learned about how to create first basic WCF service. In this entire book we will use C# language to develop the WCF service.

DOI: 10.4018/978-1-5225-1997-3.ch003

Table 1. Comparison between WCF service contract and normal OOP interface

A WCF Service Contract	Normal OOP Interface

[ServiceContract]
public interface ICalculator
{
[OperationContract]
int add(int no1, int no2);
[OperationContract]
int sub(int no1, int no2);
[OperationContract]
int mul(int no1, int no2);
[OperationContract]
int div(int no1, int no2);
}
	public interface ICalculator
	{
	
	int add(int no1, int no2);
	
	int sub(int no1, int no2);
	
	int mul(int no1, int no2);
	int div(int no1, int no2);
	}

The C# is object oriented programming language; therefore we can say that in WCF object oriented programming and Service Oriented Architecture (SOA) concepts are blended. To develop WCF service it is required to have strong fundamental knowledge of OOP concepts including interface and class. The comparison of a service contract and an OOP interface is shown in Table 1.

As shown in Table 1, the only difference between both methods that the attributes are applied in WCF program which are absent in the interface. Therefore, if the attributes are removed from WCF program, it is exactly same as the interface mentioned in the right side. Moreover, we can say that WCF is using OOP concepts to build Service Oriented Applications (SOA).

PROGRAMMING METHODS IN WCF

There are different programming methods available in WCF. Each method can have its own advantages and disadvantages. There are three programming methods in WCF: (A) Declarative (B) Explicit (B) Configuration. These methods are explained below:

(A) Declarative

In this method the annotations/ attributes are applied as label on the top of the particular part of the code. It is also useful to specify parameters to enable and customize certain features in the program as per the developer's choice. The example of the declarative method is shown in Example 1.

Example 1. Service contract with declarative methods:

```
[ServiceContract]
public interface ICalculator
{
        [OperationContract]
        int add(int no1, int no2);
        [OperationContract]
        int sub(int no1, int no2);
        [OperationContract]
        int mul(int no1, int no2);
        [OperationContract]
        int div(int no1, int no2);
      [OperationContract (IsOneWay=true)]
        void display(int no1, int no2);
}
```

Here in above example, [ServiceContract] and [OperationContract] are considered as attributes or labels. There no explicit coding is required to declare them. These labels are sufficient and the program will consider them as the label mentioned at the top of them. It is also possible to specify parameters to this attribute as it shown in fifth operation in Example 1. The parameter is "IsOneWay" and its value is given as true to indicate that the operation below this label is one way operation. Another example of declarative method in which attribute is mentioned over the service is shown in Example 2. As we can see in Example 2, an attribute is mentioned over the service class which is service behaviour and it helps to control the service runtime. In this example the parameter is not mentioned, but it is possible to provide the parameter using parenthesis just as the previous example.

Example 2. Service class with declarative method:

```
[ServiceBehavior]
public class Calculator: ICalculator
{
        ......

      ......

}
```

(B) Explicit

In this method of programming a programmer needs to write the code to work with interfaces and classes directly. As declarative method alone is not sufficient to write all the kinds of stuff explicit method is also required. For example, it is not possible to develop a program to find the factorial of the program using a declarative method. For that it is required to write code and declarative method is sufficient for it. The example of this method is shown in Example 3.

Example 3. Explicit method:

```
public class Calculator: ICalculator
{
        public int add(int no1, int no2)
        {
            return no1 + no2;
        }
        public int sub(int no1, int no2)
        {
            return no1 - no2;
        }
        public int mul(int no1, int no2)
        {
            return no1*no2;
        }
        public int div(int no1, int no2)
        {
            return no1 / no2;
        }
        public void display(int no1, int no2)
        {
          //do nothing as it is one way operation
        }
}
```

As shown in Example 3, it is required to write the code of operations mentioned in the class "Calculator". It is not possible to use declarative method to write the logic for each method. Therefore, it becomes compulsory to write the code using explicit method. Likewise, any code which is written to host the service is also known as the explicit method of programming.

(C) Configuration

In this method a configuration file is created which is used to apply certain configurations in a WCF program. A developer can specify endpoint, behaviour and other elements in this file. The main benefit of this method over explicit is that we don't need to compile the configuration in case of changes in it while it is required to compile the code in case of changes in the code. The example of the configuration file is presented in Example 4.

Example 4. Configuration file:

```xml
<?xml version="1.0" encoding="utf-8" ?>
<configuration>
   <system.serviceModel>
    <services>
      <service name="FirstWCFService_Calc.Calculator">
        <endpoint address="" binding="wsHttpBinding"
contract="FirstWCFService_Calc.ICalculator">

        </endpoint>
        <endpoint address="mex" binding="mexHttpBinding"
contract="IMetadataExchange" />
        <host>
          <baseAddresses>
            <add baseAddress="http://localhost:8732/Design_
Time_Addresses/
            FirstWCFService_Calc/Service1/" />
          </baseAddresses>
        </host>
      </service>
    </services>
    <behaviors>
      <serviceBehaviors>
        <behavior>

      <serviceMetadata httpGetEnabled="True"/>
        <serviceDebug includeExceptionDetailInFaults="False"
```

```
/>
        </behavior>
      </serviceBehaviors>
    </behaviors>
  </system.serviceModel>
</configuration>
```

As it is shown in Example 4, the configuration file is formatted using XML. If the endpoint is not defined through code, then it is compulsory to create a configuration file with endpoint element in it. In WCF the two types of configuration files can be possible: App.config and web.config. It is compulsory to have either of these names otherwise the host program is not able to find the configuration file. Furthermore, the configuration file must be there with the host program.

Priority of These Methods

When all these methods are used together at the same time in code, there can be conflict in applying certain settings. In WCF to tackle this problem priority is given among these methods. The order of execution is considered as follows:

1. First the attributes are applied.
2. Second Configuration is applied.
3. Lastly the Code (explicit) runs.

Therefore, the declarative method is given first, configuration method is given second and explicit method is given last priority in case of any conflict occurs. It is advisable to use all these methods together in any WCF project.

PUTTING ALL METHODS TOGETHER

In the section we will see the usage of all these methods practically. First, we will create the WCF service which was discussed in the Chapter 2 already. After that we will host the service using a host program which will contain two parts: code and configuration. The steps are shown below:

Step 1: Create the WCF Service

Open visual studio and select File->New->Project-> C#-> WCF Service library and follow the steps discussed in the Chapter 2 to create the WCF service. This solution contains two files. In one file the interface is declared which is also known as [ServiceContract] and in other file the class is created which implements the interface and it is also known as Service class. The example of a service contract file is shown in Example 5.

Example 5. Code of service contract:

```
using System;
using System.Collections.Generic;
using System.Linq;
using System.Runtime.Serialization;
using System.ServiceModel;
using System.Text;
namespace FirstWCFService_Calc
{
    [ServiceContract]
    public interface ICalculator
    {
        [OperationContract ]
        int add(int no1, int no2);
        [OperationContract]
        int sub(int no1, int no2);
        [OperationContract]
        int mul(int no1, int no2);
        [OperationContract]
        int div(int no1, int no2);
    }
}
```

The implementation class or service class code is mentioned in Example 6.

Example 6. Code of service class:

```
using System;
using System.Collections.Generic;
using System.Linq;
```

```
using System.Runtime.Serialization;
using System.ServiceModel;
using System.Text;
namespace FirstWCFService_Calc
{
    public class Calculator: ICalculator
    {
        public int add(int no1, int no2)
        {
            return no1 + no2;
        }
        public int sub(int no1, int no2)
        {
            return no1 - no2;
        }
        public int mul(int no1, int no2)
        {
            return no1*no2;
        }
        public int div(int no1, int no2)
        {
            return no1 / no2;
        }
    }
}
```

These steps are similar as steps done in Chapter 2. This project contains default App.config file which is required to host the service while using built-in host program of visual studio. But now we want to host this service by using the code so we need to create an executable project which will be considered as host program. In this program we will create the endpoint by using configuration file which is shown in step 2.

After the code is written in the WCF service project, right click on this project and select build option as shown in Figure 1 to compile it. The output of the compilation process is shown in Figure 2. As shown in Figure 2, the project is converted in Dynamic Link Library (Dll) which highlighted. Now the host program requires only Dll of this project to get service and contract details while preparing the configuration file.

Figure 1. Compiling the WCF service

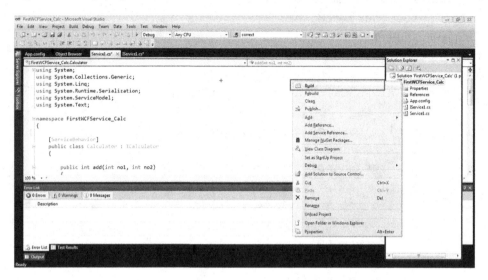

Figure 2. Output of compiling the WCF service

Step 2: Host the WCF Service Using Console Program

As discussed in Chapter 1, a WCF service can be hosted by various options. Self-hosting is one of the easiest option in which a developer can host WCF service using executable program such as console project or windows form

Figure 3. Adding new project

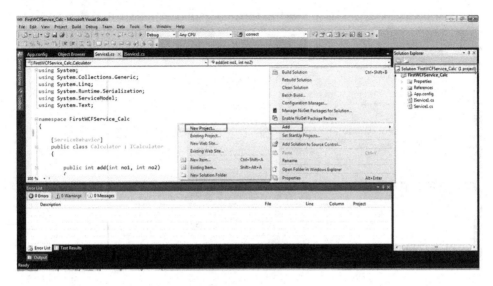

Figure 4. Wizard to select type of the project

project etc. In this section we will use console application project which is used to host the WCF service.

Now right click on the solution to and select new-> Project to add another project for hosting the service. It is shown in Figure 3. Same can be selected by using File menu also. After clicking on a new project option from

Figure 5. Layout of Console application project

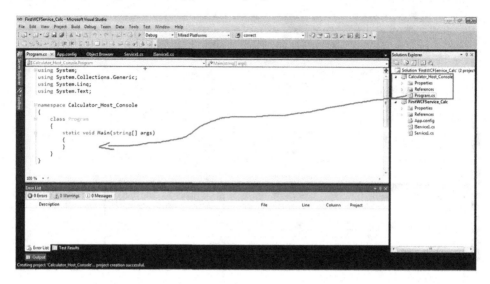

Figure 6. Adding service reference

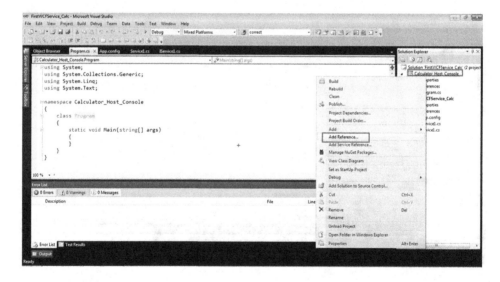

the context menu, it will show the options to select the type of project as shown in the Figure 4. Select C#->Windows and project type as a console application as highlighted in Figure 4. It will add another project in the same solution.

Figure 7. Adding service reference of System.ServiceModel

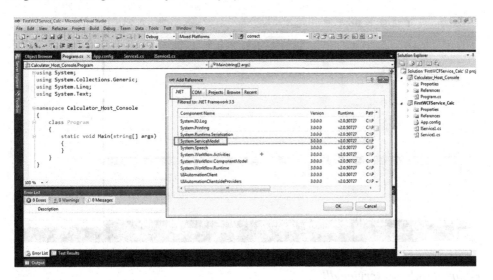

This newly added console application project has only one file called Program.cs as shown in Figure 5. It is file in which the main function is written which is the entry point of this program as output of this kind of project is.EXE. We will write the code for hosting in the main function of Program.cs file. To host the service ServiceHost class is used which is available in System.ServiceModel and to get the details about service and contract we require Dll of WCF service project which is already created when we compiled that project. Therefore, the console application project needs two references: one reference is of System.ServiceModel and another reference is of the Dll of WCF service which is available in the same solution in this example.

In the next step add the references of System.ServiceModel and service Dll one by one respectively. For adding references right click on the console application project and select add reference as shown in Figure 6. As System.ServiceModel is the part of.NET framework, click one the.NET tab, locate the System.ServiceModel Dll and click on ok button as shown in Figure 7. The System.ServiceModel reference is added and also import the reference in the code as shown in Figure 8. Now to add the reference of Dll of WCF service, again right click on the console application project and follow the steps mentioned Figure 6. As both project are under one solution, click on the project tab and Dll is by default is selected as shown in Figure 9.

Figure 8. Importing System.ServiceModel in code

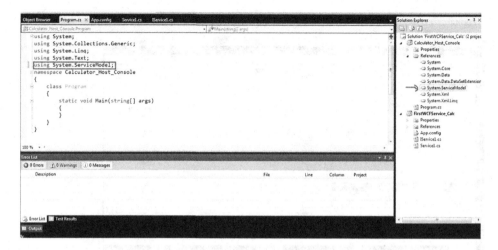

Figure 9. Adding service dll

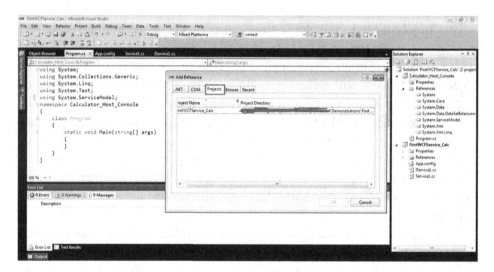

Then click on the ok button to add the reference. You can you browse tab also to add the reference when both projects are not the part of the same solution. The screen looks like the Figure 10 after adding the reference of WCF service Dll. Also import the reference in the Program.cs as shown in Figure 10. Now create the object of the ServiceHost class as shown in the Example 8. In the code the constructor of ServiceHost class requires type of service class. The service class in this example is Calculator so it is provided as a parameter of the constructor. The Open() method is used to host

Figure 10. After adding the reference of Dll of WCF service

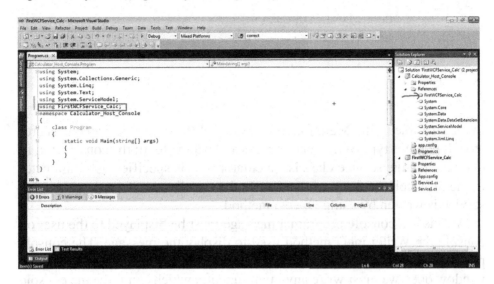

the service and make it available to the client if there is no error. Likewise the Close() method is used to stop the service and after executing this code service will not be available to any client. The code for hosting service in the main function is shown in Example 8.

Example 8. The code of main function to host WCF service:

```
using System;
using System.Collections.Generic;
using System.Linq;
using System.Text;
using FirstWCFService_Calc;
using System.ServiceModel;
namespace Calculator_Host_Console
{
    class Program
    {
        static void Main(string[] args)
        {
            ServiceHost host = new ServiceHost(typeof(Calcu
lator));
            host.Open();
            Console.WriteLine("Service is running press any
```

```
key to stop");
            Console.ReadKey();
            host.Close();
        }
    }
}
```

In the first line of the Main function, object of the class ServiceHost is created. It requires type of the service class as a parameter of the constructor. In our example the service class is Calculator so it is specified as a parameter of the ServiceHost class constructor. In the next line as the code to host the service is written by using Open() method.

As this is a console program a message must be displayed to the user on console the WriteLine() method used to display the message. The console program stops after execution and it closes the console window so to keep the window open we must write any input function which can force the console program to wait. In the example ReadKey() function is called, but any other methods which can take the input from the user can also be written for this purpose. Finally the host program is stopped and service is not available to the client if the user presses any key. This is done by using Close() method. Now right click on the console project and select build to compile it. Upon successful compilation of this project output window is displayed as shown in Figure 11. As shown in Figure 11, the output of the compilation process of the console application project is executable (.EXE) which is highlighted in Figure 11.

Now set the Console project as start up by right clicking and selecting set as a startup project option from the context menu as shown in Figure 12. Then click on the run button from the tool bar to run the project. The program is executed and error is displayed as shown in Figure 13. The meaning of this error is that endpoint is not defined in either code or configuration part of the program. Any WCF service must have at least one endpoint. An endpoint can be defined via code or configuration, but we will define the endpoint via a configuration file in this project as configuration method is more flexible as compared to other methods. So one configuration file is added in this project and then the XML tags related to WCF are added in this file using Service Configuration Editor.

To add the configuration file, right click on the console project and select Add->New Item option as shown in Figure 14.

The visual studio will open a dialog box to select the type of file to be added in the project as shown in Figure 15. Select General-> Configuration

Figure 11. Output of compiling console project

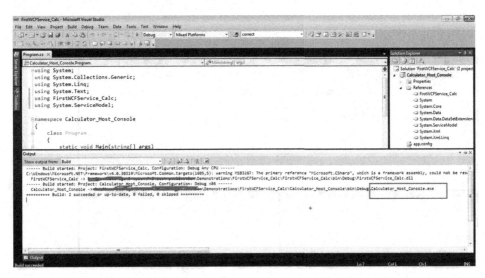

Figure 12. Setting console application project as startup project

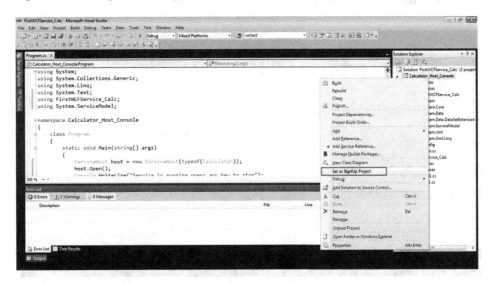

file as shown in Figure 15. The system provides default name of the configuration file as App.config which is highlighted at bottom in Figure 15. Please do not change the name of that file keep the name App.config only. The App.Config is added in the console project as shown in Figure 16. The default tags available in this file as shown on the left side of the Figure 16. To update this file WCF Service Configuration Editor can be used which helps to build configuration file easily.

Figure 13. End point error

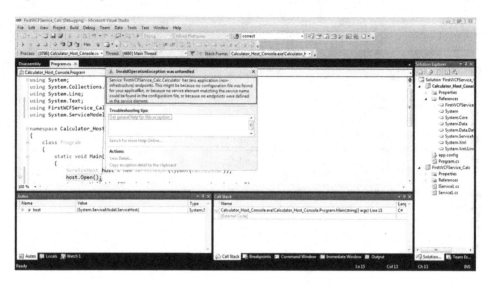

Figure 14. Adding configuration file

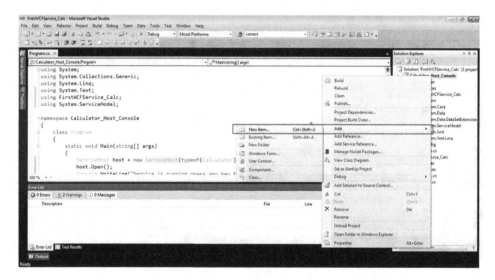

In the next step, the details to create configuration file using this tool is explained step-by-step.

Figure 15. Dialog box for selecting the item

Figure 16. Solution explorer after adding App.config file

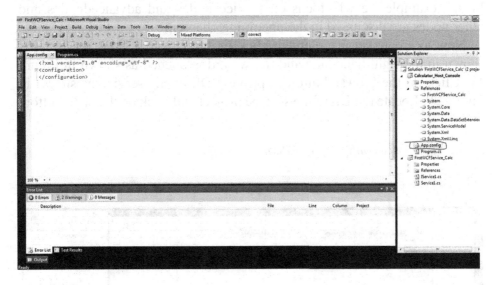

Step 2.1: Update App.Config File to Create an Endpoint Using Service Configuration Editor

Right click on the App.config file and select Edit WCF configuration option as shown in Figure 17. The WCF service configuration tool is opened as shown in Figure 18. As shown in Figure 18, the editor contains five nodes.

Figure 17. Selecting the option to edit App.config file

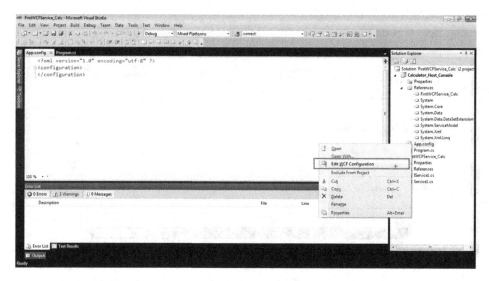

In this example we will focus on service nodes and advancednodes and other nodes are discussed in the upcoming chapters.

Now to create service element click on the Create a New Service link shown in the right hand side and the wizard is opened as shown in Figure 19. Click on the browse button to provide Dll of the service as shown in Figure 20. Locate the Dll of the service project and click on the open button.

Figure 18. Service configuration editor

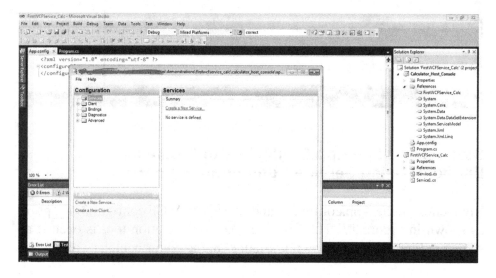

Figure 19. Wizard to select service type

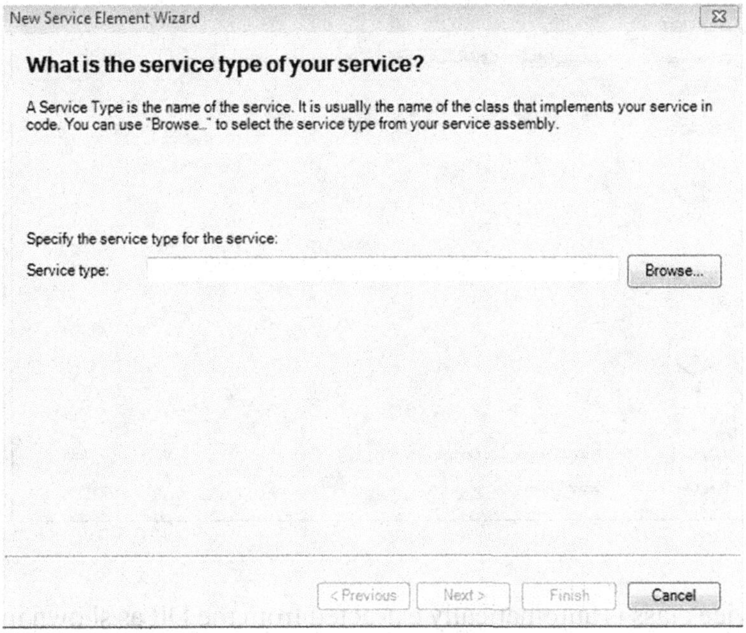

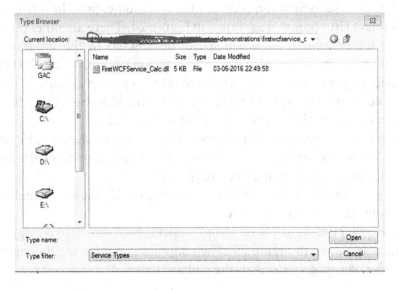

Figure 20. Locating service Dll

Figure 21. Selected service class

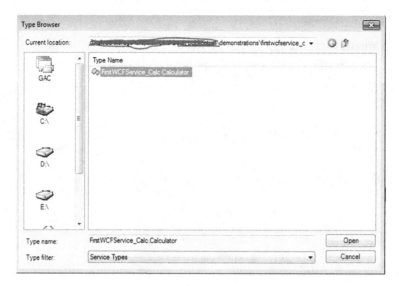

The Service class is automatically extracted from the Dll as shown in Figure 21 and then click on the open button to go to the next step in the wizard. The service name appears as shown in Figure 22.

Click on the next button to select the contract. As there is only on contract in the service project, service contract is selected by default as shown in Figure 23.

In the next step select the protocol for communication. In this example we will select Http protocol as shown in Figure 24. There are other protocols available for communication which can be applied in the program. The other protocols are discussed in upcoming chapters. Click on the Next button after selecting the protocol. The wizard to select type of web service interoperability appears as shown in Figure 25. Select Basic web service interoperability and click on Next button as shown in Figure 25.

The wizard asks you to enter the endpoint address as shown in Figure 26. Here it is not necessary to provide absolute endpoint address as we are going to provide base address in the upcoming steps.

Then go through the steps mentioned in Figure 26, Figure 27 and Figure 28 to create endpoint successfully.

Now expand the endpoint element by clicking on the + (plus) sign to see the details as shown in Figure 29. The endpoint is not having any name but a developer can specify name of the endpoint also.

Figure 22. Selected service in service element wizard

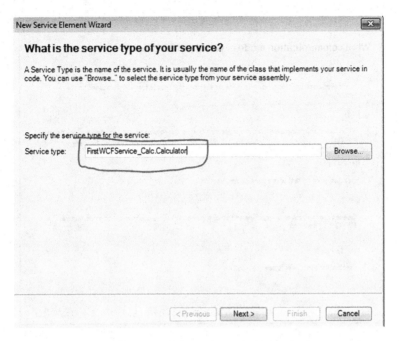

Figure 23. Selected contact in service element wizard

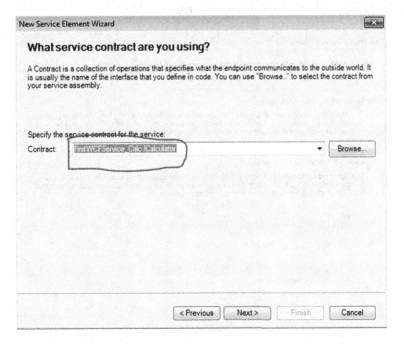

Figure 24. Selecting protocol

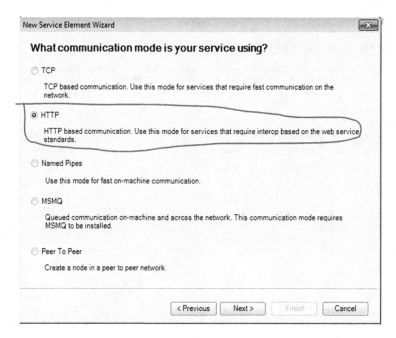

Figure 25. Selecting basic web service interoperability

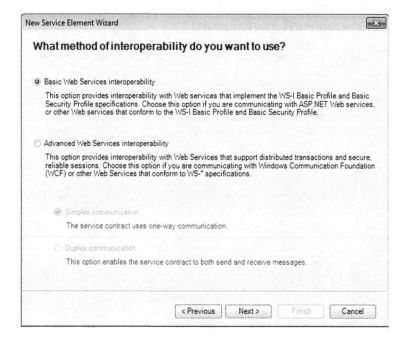

Figure 26. Specifying endpoint address

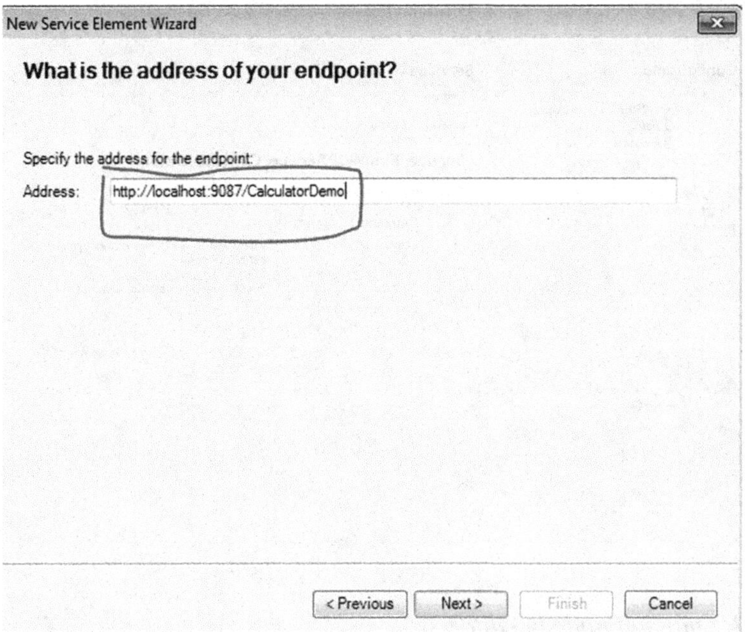

Figure 27. Endpoint is created

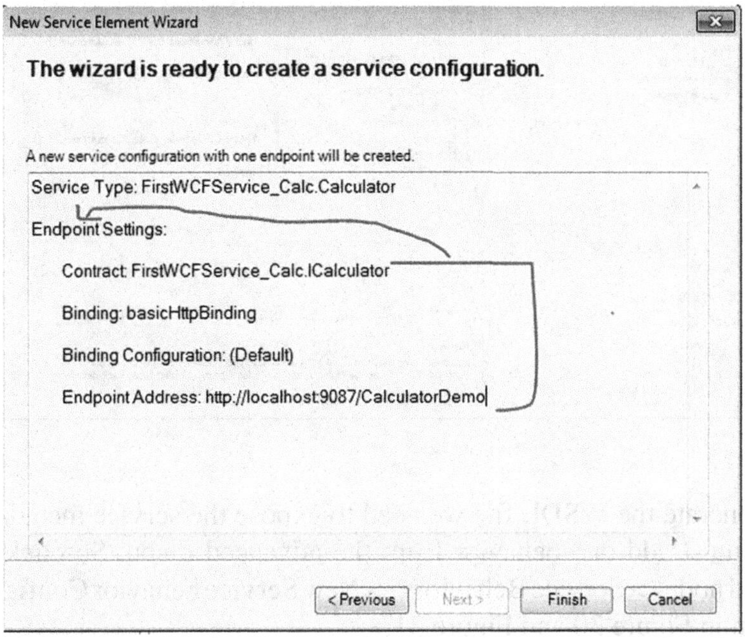

Figure 28. Endpoint

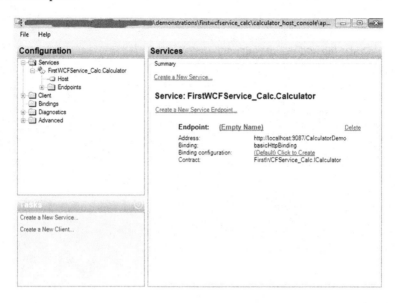

Figure 29. Endpoint node in editor

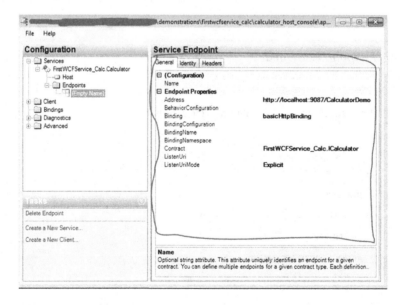

To generate the WSDL file we need to expose the service metadata. For that we must add one behavior from the advanced menu. So click on the advanced node -> Service Behaviors -> New Service behavior Configuration as shown in Figure 30 and Figure 31.

Figure 30. Advanced node

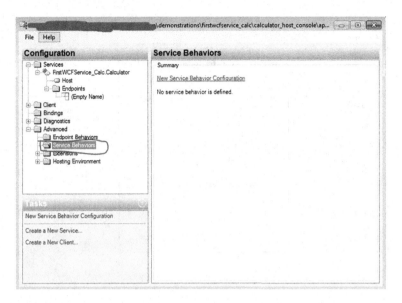

Figure 31. Selecting behavior from advanced menu

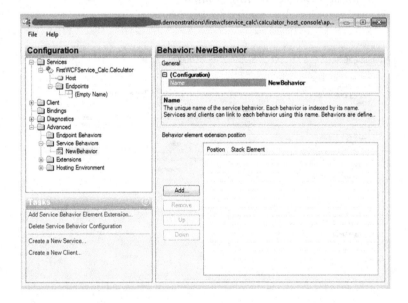

Now click on Add button to select the behavior as shown in Figure 32. Select serviceMetadata as shown in Figure 32 and click on Add button. The behavior is added as shown in Figure 33.

Figure 32. Selecting behavior

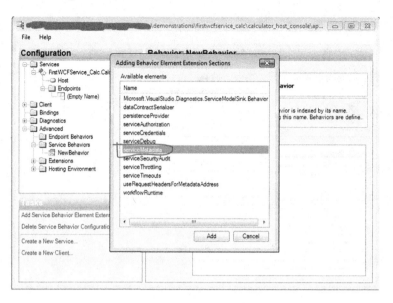

Figure 33. Editor screen after adding behavior

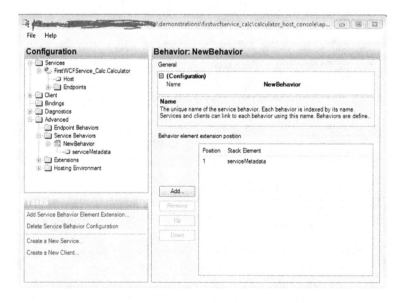

Now double click on the serviceMeatadata and set httpGetEnabled to true as shown in Figure 34.

Figure 34. Setting httpGetEnabled property of service behavior

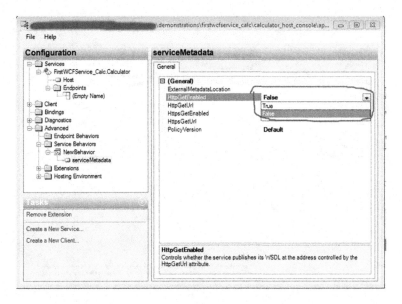

Then this behavior must be related with the service to enable it on service. So select service from the Services node and set behavior configuration property of that service with the behavior name as shown in Figure 35 and Figure 36.

Figure 35. Selecting behavior from the list

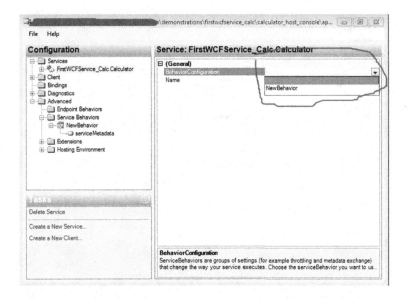

Figure 36. Relating behavior with service

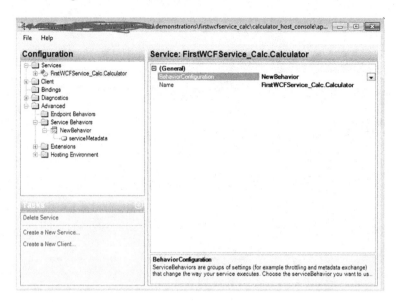

When we add service metadata behavior ->httpGetEnabled it is required to add base address of httpGetUrl. Here we will add based address. To add the base address expand service element and then click on host->base address and follow the steps mentioned from Figure 37 through Figure 39.

Figure 37. Expanding service element

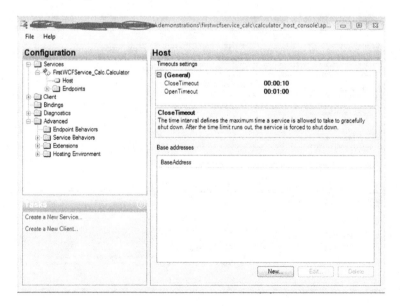

Figure 38. Providing the base address

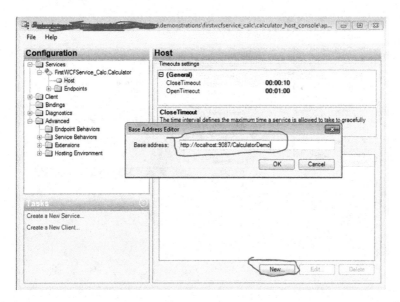

Figure 39. Added base address in editor

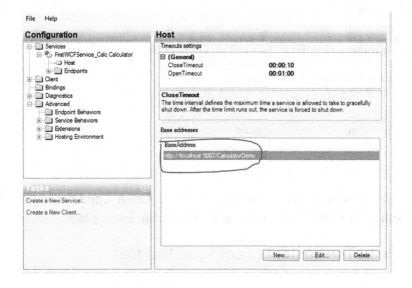

Then save the file using File-> Save menu as shown in Figure 40.

Then after close the editor using File->close menu or close button and the confirmation dialog box will appear as shown in Figure 41. Click on Yes or

Figure 40. Saving configuration file

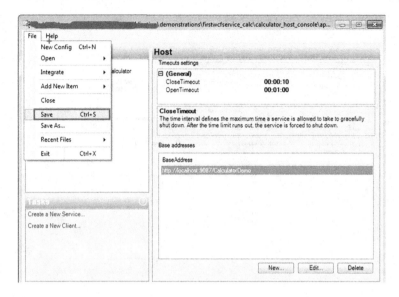

Figure 41. Dialog box to save the file

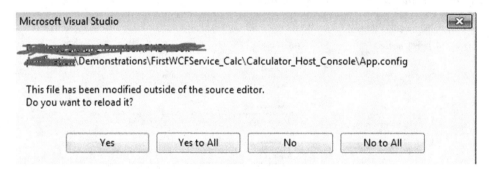

Yes to All button to save the configuration file. Open App.Config file in the visual studio to view the contents as illustrated in Example 9.

Example 9. The content of configuration file:

```
<?xml version="1.0" encoding="utf-8" ?>
<configuration>
    <system.serviceModel>
        <behaviors>
            <serviceBehaviors>
```

```
        <behavior name="NewBehavior">
            <serviceMetadata httpGetEnabled="true"
/>
        </behavior>
    </serviceBehaviors>
  </behaviors>
  <services>
    <service behaviorConfiguration="NewBehavior"
name="FirstWCFService_Calc.Calculator">
        <endpoint address="http://localhost:9087/
CalculatorDemo" binding="basicHttpBinding"
            bindingConfiguration=""
contract="FirstWCFService_Calc.ICalculator" />
        <host>
            <baseAddresses>
                <add baseAddress="http://local-
host:9087/CalculatorDemo" />
            </baseAddresses>
        </host>
    </service>
  </services>
  </system.serviceModel>
</configuration>
```

Step 2.2: Run the Host Program and Host the Service

This App. Config file is prepared by using the WCF service configuration editor. Now service is ready to be hosted as an endpoint is created in the configuration file as shown in Example 9.

Now compile the console application by using Right click on project -> Build option. As we discussed earlier the output of the console application project is executable (.EXE) as illustrated in Figure 42.

Now locate the EXE of the console application program and run it with the administrator credentials as shown in Figure 43. While using http address using self-hosting in windows operating system, it forces you to run the program with administrator privileges for security reason.

The program runs successfully and output window of console is shown in Figure 44.

Here service is hosted successfully as there is no error message. To test the service, type the base address of service in any browser. The output is

Figure 42. Output window after successful compilation of console application project

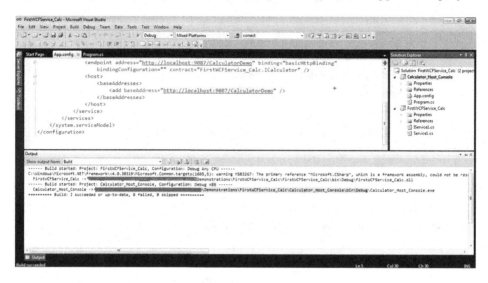

Figure 43. Running the EXE as Administrator

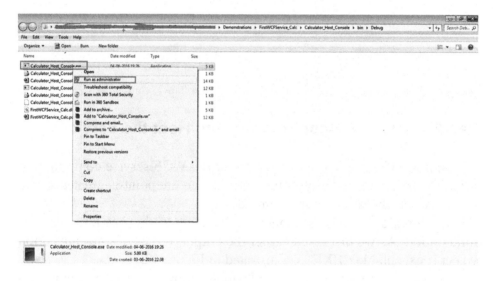

displayed in browser as shown in Figure 45. In this screen the sample code in c# and visual basic is shown to create object of class in client program. At client side, this class is known as proxy class. To consume the operation of the service object of proxy class must be created in client program. In

Figure 44. Output of running exe (Host program)

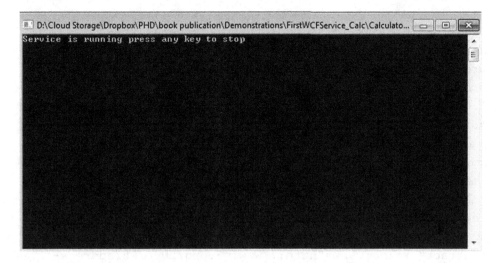

this example the proxy class is CalculatorClient as shown in Figure 45. So we will create object of this class in.NET client. Now Click on the WSDL file shown in Figure 45 and content of WSDL file are displayed as shown in Example 10.

Figure 45. Output in the browser

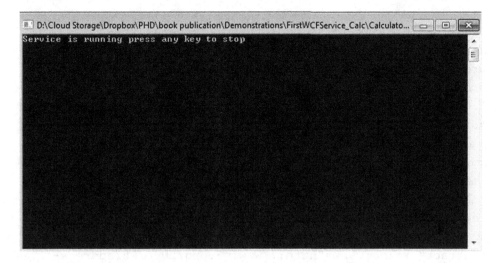

Example 10. WSDL File:

```
<wsdl:definitions xmlns:wsdl="http://schemas.xml-
soap.org/wsdl/" xmlns:soap="http://schemas.xmlsoap.
org/wsdl/soap/" xmlns:wsu="http://docs.oasis-open.
org/wss/2004/01/oasis-200401-wss-wssecurity-utility-
1.0.xsd" xmlns:soapenc="http://schemas.xmlsoap.org/
soap/encoding/" xmlns:wsam="http://www.w3.org/2007/05/
addressing/metadata" xmlns:tns="http://tempuri.org/"
xmlns:wsa="http://schemas.xmlsoap.org/ws/2004/08/addressing"
xmlns:wsp="http://schemas.xmlsoap.org/ws/2004/09/policy"
xmlns:wsap="http://schemas.xmlsoap.org/ws/2004/08/address-
ing/policy" xmlns:xsd="http://www.w3.org/2001/XMLSchema"
xmlns:msc="http://schemas.microsoft.com/ws/2005/12/wsdl/
contract" xmlns:wsaw="http://www.w3.org/2006/05/address-
ing/wsdl" xmlns:soap12="http://schemas.xmlsoap.org/wsdl/
soap12/" xmlns:wsa10="http://www.w3.org/2005/08/address-
ing" xmlns:wsx="http://schemas.xmlsoap.org/ws/2004/09/mex"
name="Calculator" targetNamespace="http://tempuri.org/">
<wsdl:types>
<xsd:schema targetNamespace="http://tempuri.org/Imports">
<xsd:import schemaLocation="http://localhost:9087/
CalculatorDemo?xsd=xsd0" namespace="http://tempuri.org/"/>
<xsd:import schemaLocation="http://localhost:9087/
CalculatorDemo?xsd=xsd1" namespace="http://schemas.micro-
soft.com/2003/10/Serialization/"/>
</xsd:schema>
</wsdl:types>
<wsdl:message name="ICalculator_add_InputMessage">
<wsdl:part name="parameters" element="tns:add"/>
</wsdl:message>
<wsdl:message name="ICalculator_add_OutputMessage">
<wsdl:part name="parameters" element="tns:addResponse"/>
</wsdl:message>
<wsdl:message name="ICalculator_sub_InputMessage">
<wsdl:part name="parameters" element="tns:sub"/>
</wsdl:message>
<wsdl:message name="ICalculator_sub_OutputMessage">
<wsdl:part name="parameters" element="tns:subResponse"/>
</wsdl:message>
```

```
<wsdl:message name="ICalculator_mul_InputMessage">
<wsdl:part name="parameters" element="tns:mul"/>
</wsdl:message>
<wsdl:message name="ICalculator_mul_OutputMessage">
<wsdl:part name="parameters" element="tns:mulResponse"/>
</wsdl:message>
<wsdl:message name="ICalculator_div_InputMessage">
<wsdl:part name="parameters" element="tns:div"/>
</wsdl:message>
<wsdl:message name="ICalculator_div_OutputMessage">
<wsdl:part name="parameters" element="tns:divResponse"/>
</wsdl:message>
<wsdl:portType name="ICalculator">
<wsdl:operation name="add">
<wsdl:input wsaw:Action="http://tempuri.org/ICalculator/add"
message="tns:ICalculator_add_InputMessage"/>
<wsdl:output wsaw:Action="http://tempuri.org/ICalculator/ad-
dResponse" message="tns:ICalculator_add_OutputMessage"/>
</wsdl:operation>
<wsdl:operation name="sub">
<wsdl:input wsaw:Action="http://tempuri.org/ICalculator/sub"
message="tns:ICalculator_sub_InputMessage"/>
<wsdl:output wsaw:Action="http://tempuri.org/ICalculator/
subResponse" message="tns:ICalculator_sub_OutputMessage"/>
</wsdl:operation>
<wsdl:operation name="mul">
<wsdl:input wsaw:Action="http://tempuri.org/ICalculator/mul"
message="tns:ICalculator_mul_InputMessage"/>
<wsdl:output wsaw:Action="http://tempuri.org/ICalculator/
mulResponse" message="tns:ICalculator_mul_OutputMessage"/>
</wsdl:operation>
<wsdl:operation name="div">
<wsdl:input wsaw:Action="http://tempuri.org/ICalculator/div"
message="tns:ICalculator_div_InputMessage"/>
<wsdl:output wsaw:Action="http://tempuri.org/ICalculator/di-
vResponse" message="tns:ICalculator_div_OutputMessage"/>
</wsdl:operation>
</wsdl:portType>
<wsdl:binding name="BasicHttpBinding_ICalculator"
type="tns:ICalculator">
```

```
<soap:binding transport="http://schemas.xmlsoap.org/soap/
http"/>
<wsdl:operation name="add">
<soap:operation soapAction="http://tempuri.org/ICalculator/
add" style="document"/>
<wsdl:input>
<soap:body use="literal"/>
</wsdl:input>
<wsdl:output>
<soap:body use="literal"/>
</wsdl:output>
</wsdl:operation>
<wsdl:operation name="sub">
<soap:operation soapAction="http://tempuri.org/ICalculator/
sub" style="document"/>
<wsdl:input>
<soap:body use="literal"/>
</wsdl:input>
<wsdl:output>
<soap:body use="literal"/>
</wsdl:output>
</wsdl:operation>
<wsdl:operation name="mul">
<soap:operation soapAction="http://tempuri.org/ICalculator/
mul" style="document"/>
<wsdl:input>
<soap:body use="literal"/>
</wsdl:input>
<wsdl:output>
<soap:body use="literal"/>
</wsdl:output>
</wsdl:operation>
<wsdl:operation name="div">
<soap:operation soapAction="http://tempuri.org/ICalculator/
div" style="document"/>
<wsdl:input>
<soap:body use="literal"/>
</wsdl:input>
<wsdl:output>
<soap:body use="literal"/>
```

```
</wsdl:output>
</wsdl:operation>
</wsdl:binding>
<wsdl:service name="Calculator">
<wsdl:port name="BasicHttpBinding_ICalculator"
binding="tns:BasicHttpBinding_ICalculator">
<soap:address location="http://localhost:9087/Calculator-
Demo"/>
</wsdl:port>
</wsdl:service>
</wsdl:definitions>
```

As WSDL file is ready it can be provided on any client program such as.NET, JAVA, PHP etc to consume the WCF service.

Step 3: Creating.NET Client to Consume the WCF Service

To consume the above hosted service in.NET client using a windows form project the steps are mentioned below:

1.   Open visual studio and select File-> New Project as shown in Figure 46.

Figure 46. Creating client project using the File menu

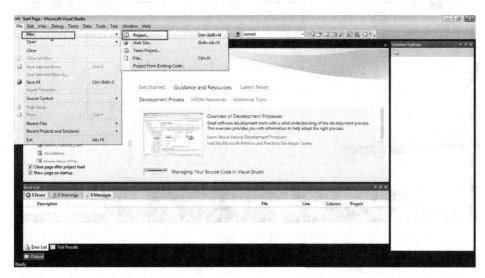

2. Select Visual C# -> Windows and Windows Forms Application as project type from the wizard as shown in Figure 47. Provide the path to save the project and give an appropriate name of the project

3. The Windows Form project appears in visual studio as shown in Figure 48. Change the name of Form using properties of the form. Design the form by taking appropriate controls from the tool box and the Form should look like as shown in Figure 48.

4. To consume to service using WSDL file right click on the project and click on add service reference as shown in Figure 49.

5. The window to provide a WSDL file appears as shown in in Figure 50. Provide the path of the WSDL of hosted service in the Address field and click on the go button. In the list of services the service is shown if it is hosted as shown in Figure 50, otherwise an error is displayed. Also change the default name of namespace shown at bottom in Figure 50. In this example, we have changed to name to Calc_Ref instead of the default name ServiceReference1. Click on the Ok button to return to the visual studio.

6. The service reference appears below the service references folder in the solution explorer as shown in Figure 51.

7. Import the service reference on the top of the code file (Form1.cs) as shown in Figure 52.

Figure 47. Selecting window forms application as project type

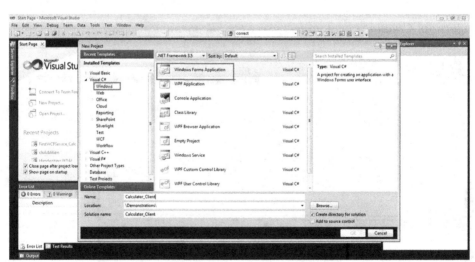

Figure 48. Windows Form project in visual studio

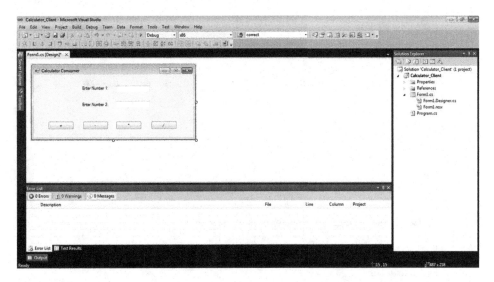

Figure 49. Adding service reference

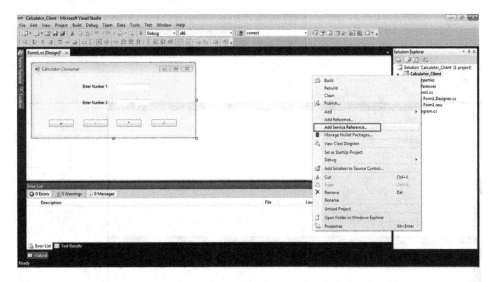

8. Write code in the click event of each button to consume the service using proxy class CalculatorClient as discussed earlier. The code is shown in Example 11.

Figure 50. Providing WSDL path

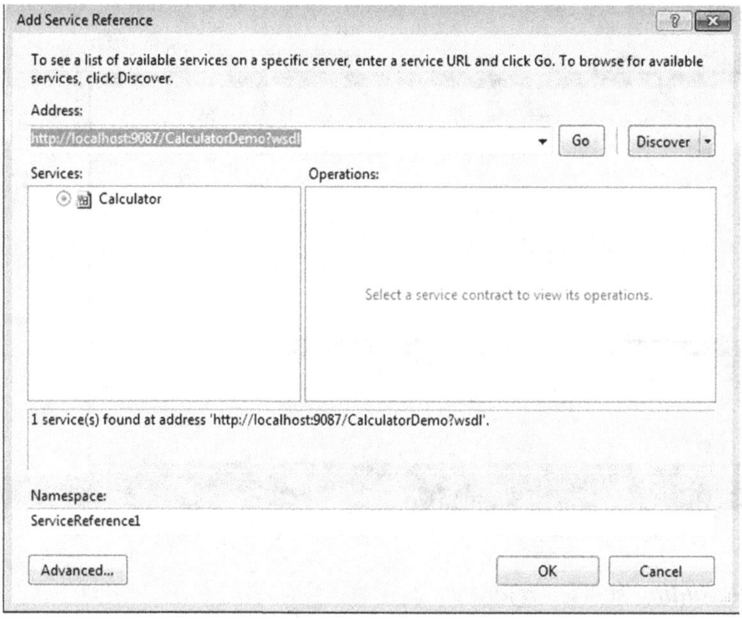

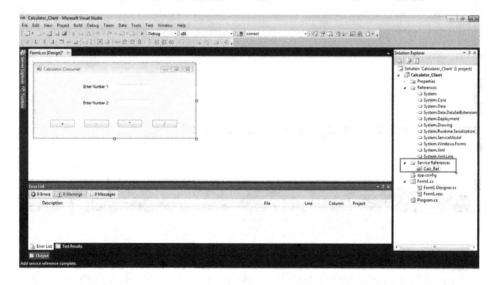

Figure 51. Service reference in visual studio

Figure 52. Importing service reference

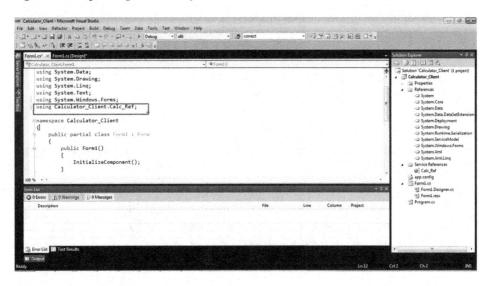

Example 11. Client Code:

```
 using System;
using System.Collections.Generic;
using System.ComponentModel;
using System.Data;
using System.Drawing;
using System.Linq;
using System.Text;
using System.Windows.Forms;
using Calculator_Client.Calc_Ref;
namespace Calculator_Client
{
    public partial class Form1: Form
    {
        int no1, no2;
        int ans;
        CalculatorClient proxy = new CalculatorClient();
        public Form1()
        {
            InitializeComponent();
        }
        private void btnPlus_Click(object sender, EventArgs
```

```
e)
        {
            no1 = Int16.Parse(tbNumber1.Text);
            no2 = Int16.Parse(tbNumber2.Text);
            ans = proxy.add(no1, no2);
            MessageBox.Show("Answer is "+ans);

        }
        private void btnMinus_Click(object sender, EventArgs
e)
        {
            no1 = Int16.Parse(tbNumber1.Text);
            no2 = Int16.Parse(tbNumber2.Text);
            ans = proxy.sub(no1, no2);
            MessageBox.Show("Answer is " + ans);
        }
        private void btnMult_Click(object sender, EventArgs
e)
        {

            no1 = Int16.Parse(tbNumber1.Text);
            no2 = Int16.Parse(tbNumber2.Text);
            ans = proxy.mul(no1, no2);
            MessageBox.Show("Answer is " + ans);
        }
        private void btnDiv_Click(object sender, EventArgs
e)
        {
            no1 = Int16.Parse(tbNumber1.Text);
            no2 = Int16.Parse(tbNumber2.Text);
            ans = proxy.div(no1, no2);
            MessageBox.Show("Answer is " + ans);
        }
    }
}
```

9. Now build the client project and execute it as shown in Figure 53 and Figure 54. In this output the testing done for addition operation. Likewise testing for other operations can be done as well which is left to the readers.

Figure 53. Providing input to test the output of the client program

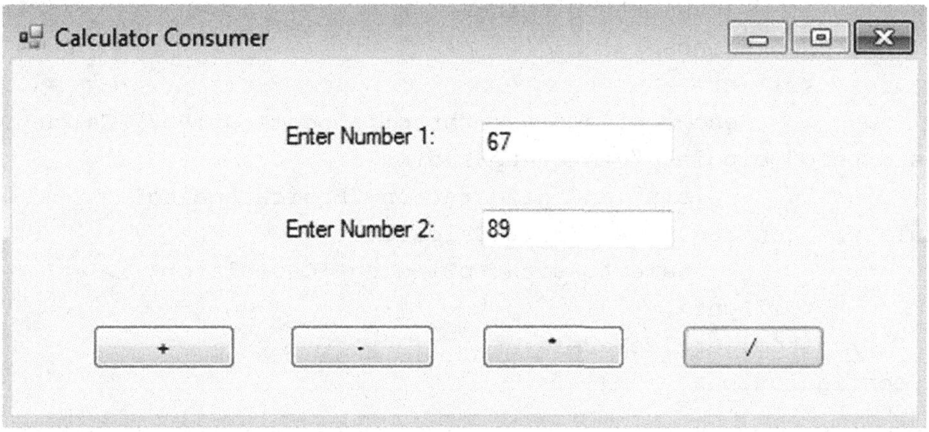

Figure 54. Output of addition (+) function

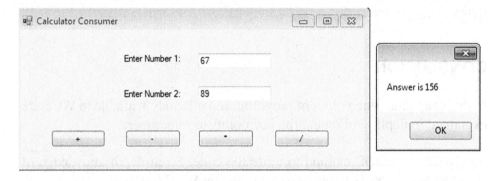

As we have discussed earlier an endpoint is also required at the.NET client side. When we add the service reference to the client project App.config is automatically created or updated with required elements in it. The code of App.config file is shown in Example 11.

Example 11. Client configuration file:

```
<?xml version="1.0" encoding="utf-8" ?>
<configuration>
    <system.serviceModel>
        <bindings>
            <basicHttpBinding>
                <binding name="BasicHttpBinding_ICalculator"
```

```
/>
        </basicHttpBinding>
      </bindings>
      <client>
        <endpoint address="http://localhost:9087/Calcu-
latorDemo" binding="basicHttpBinding"
          bindingConfiguration="BasicHttpBinding_ICal-
culator" contract="Calc_Ref.ICalculator"
          name="BasicHttpBinding_ICalculator" />
      </client>
    </system.serviceModel>
</configuration>
```

As shown in Example 11, the App.Config file of client program contains <client> tag in which the <endpoint> element is created which is directly taken from the service configuration file when we add the service reference to the client project.

CONCLUSION

In this chapter all three types of programming methods available in WCF are explained in depth. Following the key points to remember:

- WCF uses OOP method to write the code. So in-depth knowledge of OOP concepts is required to develop any WCF program.
- Generally an interface should be designated as service contract but class can also be considered as service contract.
- There are three methods of programming: declarative, explicit, configuration.
- In declarative method attributes are written using [] brackets. No additional coding is required after applying declarative method.
- In explicit method code is written.
- In configuration method configuration file is prepared. Configuration file name must be App.config or Web.config and other names are not allowed in order to host the service properly.
- The ServiceHost class is used to host the service while using console application project or windows forms application project.
- A service must have at least one endpoint.
- Endpoint must be available at the service and client side both.

- A client communicates with service using proxy class.
- To expose the service metadata and generate WSDL file, the service metadata behavior must be created and it must be related to the service. For BasicHttpBinding httpGetEnabled behavior must be set to true.
- To add service metadata behavior, it is required to add base address.
- Base address can be added under the host element which is the child element of service node.
- The configuration file can be created by using WCF Service Configuration Editor tool.
- It is not possible to use any single method to write any WCF service program. You can mix declarative, explicit and configuration methods to write any WCF service program.

Chapter 4
Working with Address

After completing this chapter, you will be able to:

- Learn in depth about the types address available in WCF
- Learn in depth about the formats of addresses in WCF
- Gain practical knowledge of programming the addresses.

The Address is very important part of any SOA application as without which client is unable to locate and consume the service. In this chapter focus is on learning different types of addresses and various formats of each type of addresses.

ADDRESS IN WCF

Each address type can have different formats as shown in Figure 1. As shown in Figure 1, the left hand side contains three type addresses and each address can be written by using different formats of address mentioned in right hand side of the Figure 1. This figure clears the ambiguity between the address

DOI: 10.4018/978-1-5225-1997-3.ch004

Figure 1. WCF Addresses

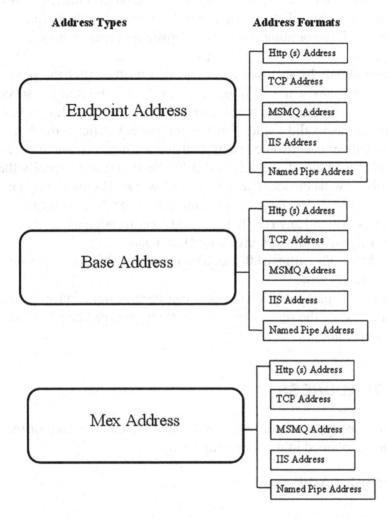

type and address format. An address contains several components which can be understood by following example.

The address in the below example is divided into three parts mentioned as numbers 1, 2 and 3.

1 3
http: //localhost:8080/CalculatorDemo
2

1. **Scheme/Protocol:** This is the first part which contains protocol for communication. In this example the protocol/scheme is http. It can be

written based on the binding selected by the programmer. For instance, if binding is BasicHttpBinding or wsHTTPBinding the protocol can be http. But if the binding is other netTcpBinding then protocol cannot be http.

2. **Name of Machine:** It is the second part written after the protocol. It can be machine name or domain name or IP address of the service on which it is hosted. The name localhost or loop back IP address 127.0.0.1 both are also valid values for this component. After a machine name port number can also be specified using a colon as separator. The port number is optional. Default port is 80. So if you don't specify the port number it will consider it as 80. In windows OS, IIS runs on port number so it is advisable to use the port number other than 80 for the service address to avoid any conflict. For instance the address

   a. **http: //localhost/CalculatorDemo** and

   b. **http: //localhost:80/CalculatorDemo**; both are considered as exactly same.

3. **Path:** This part is optional, but it can be the path of virtual directory while hosting the service on IIS. Multiple paths can be provided by using / operator.

TYPE OF ADDRESS

There are three types of addresses available in WCF and each of these addresses are explained in the following section.

(A) Endpoint Address

It is the address of endpoint through which client and service can communicate. Once the client is connected to the service through one endpoint all the other communications between them is done through the same endpoint. The example of the endpoint is shown as:

http: //localhost/CalculatorDemo

Every service must have at least one endpoint with absolute address as shown above.

(B) Base Address

It is also known as primary address which works as base address for one or more endpoints. In the presence of a base address endpoint address can be relative. If the base address is not available endpoint address must be absolute. For instance, following is the base address:

http://localhost/Service

Suppose there are three endpoints having a relative address as below:

- Endpoint 1: s1
- Endpoint 2: s2
- Endpoint 3: s3

Then the actual addresses of the endpoints are considered as:

- Endpoint 1: http://localhost/Service/s1
- Endpoint 2: http://localhost/Service/s2
- Endpoint 3: http://localhost/Service/s3

The base address cannot be relative. If the endpoint address and base address both are absolute then both are not considered as same and not related with each other.

(C) MEX Address

This address is used to expose the service metadata. Meaning of MEX is MetadataExchange which allows client to obtain the information about service in the absence of the service behavior service metadata httpGetEnabled. That means if service metadata behavior httpGetEnable is false and still if you want to expose the service meta data, a special endpoint called MEX endpoint should be created and it must have the address called MEX address.

FORMAT OF ADDRESS

As discussed earlier there are different formats of each type of addresses discussed in above section. The addresses are formatted according to binding is used in the endpoint. The binding must match with the related format of address otherwise an error is generated while hosting the service. For example the BasicHttpBinding or wsHTTPBinding must have either HTTP or HTTPs address formats and other formats are not allowed. Various formats are discussed below:

(A) HTTP Address

This is a familiar address which starts with http protocol. The format of address is given as:

http://<machine name/domain name/IP address>:[port number] / [Path]

Here the scheme http as second part is the machine name/domain name / IP address is already discussed in the previous section. Likewise port number and path are also discussed earlier in this chapter. The examples of HTTP address are shown below:

- **Address without Port Number (So default port will be 80):** http://localhost/CalcDemo
- **Address with Port Number:** http://localhost:9089/CalcDemo
- **Address without Path:** http://localhost:9089/
- **Address with Machine Name:** http://pc102:9089/CalcDemo
- **Address with Machine Name:** http://www.mycomputer.com/CalcDemo

(B) HTTPs Address

The format of this address is same as HTTP address the only difference the protocol. HTTPs is secured protocol which HTTP is not. To get HTTPs address we need to obtain the certificate from the certified authorities such as Verisign, Thwate etc. In local intranet IIS can be used create dummy certificate for testing purpose. The example of HTTPs address is given as:

https://www.mycomputer.com/CalcDemo

(C) TCP Address

The format for this address is also similar as HTTP or HTTPs only difference is the scheme. The scheme of this address starts with net.tcp. The syntax is given as:

net.tcp://<machine name/domain name/IP address>:[port number] / [Path]

The example is given as:

net.tcp://www.mycomputer.com/CalcDemo

The other examples are similar as examples shown in HTTP address so these examples are not repeated again here you just need to replace HTTP with net.tcp for TCP address format example. Please note that to use this address binding must be netTcpBinding.

(D) MSMQ Address

This format is used when integrating Microsoft Message Queue (MSMQ) in a WCF service. The format of this address different as shown below:

net.msmq://<host name>/[private] /queue_name

Here the scheme is net.msmq. The host name can be localhost, machine name, domain name or IP address. The keyword private is optional to indicate the queue is private under the message queuing component of windows OS. The private queue is available on the local machine and public queue is shared on a network.
The example is shown as:

net.msmq://pc102/private/myqueue

To use this address netMSMQBinding must be used and other bindings are not allowed.

(E) Named Pipe Address

This address is used to communicate between the two processes inside the same computer so port number is not required in this address. The example of process to process communication is the communication between Microsoft word and printer spooler service. The format is same as HTTP format, but port number is not allowed. An example of this address is shown below:

net.pipe://localhost/CalcService

Here the scheme is net.pipe and to use this address, binding must be net-MSMQBiding. Please note that endpoint having this address is not used to cross machine communication it for communication between two processes insider the same machine.

(F) IIS Address

This address is used when the WCF service is hosted on Internet Information Services (IIS). The format of address is:

<Scheme>://<domain namel machine name>[:port] /<virtual directory name>
/<.svc filename>

Here the scheme can be http or https and IIS 7.0 also supports net.tcp protocol. The domain name or machine name are already explained in the earlier section. Port number is optional and for IIS it is 80 by default. The virtual directory name is the name of the folder of the virtual directory which is created while hosting service on IIS. The file with.svc extension is required after the virtual directory. This file is also known as service file which is required to host any WCF service on IIS. The svc(service) file describes about contract and service available in WCF which helps IIS to obtain the information about the WCF service. The example of IIS address is shown below:

http://www.mycomputer.com/CalculatorDemo/CalcService.svc

PROGRAMMING ENDPOINT ADDRESS

An endpoint address can be defined via code or configuration file. As discussed in Chapter 3 configuration method is the better method. But there might be a need to create an endpoint through the code. In the following section we will learn about creating an endpoint at service side using code which is followed by the section to create an endpoint at client side using code.

Programming Endpoint Address at Service

In the previous chapter we have created endpoint using configuration file as shown in below example:

Example 1. Endpoint in Configuration File

```
<?xml version="1.0" encoding="utf-8" ?>
<configuration>
    <system.serviceModel>
        <behaviors>
            <serviceBehaviors>
                <behavior name="NewBehavior">
                    <serviceMetadata httpGetEnabled="true"
/>
                </behavior>
            </serviceBehaviors>
        </behaviors>
        <services>
            <service behaviorConfiguration="NewBehavior"
                name="FirstWCFService_Calc.Calculator">
                <endpoint address="http://localhost:9087/Cal
culatorDemo"binding="basicHttpBinding" bindingConfiguration=
""contract="FirstWCFService_Calc.ICalculator" />
                <host>
                    <baseAddresses>
                        <add baseAddress="http://local-
host:9087/CalculatorDemo" />
                    </baseAddresses>
                </host>
            </service>
        </services>
    </system.serviceModel>
</configuration>
```

The endpoint tag is highlighted with the bold letter. Now similar code can be written by using the function called AddServiceEndpoint which is overloaded method. The code written in Chapter 3 is re-written again after adding the function to create endpoint in Example 2

Example 2. Creating Endpoint using Code

```
using System;
using System.Collections.Generic;
using System.Linq;
```

```
using System.Text;
using FirstWCFService_Calc;
using System.ServiceModel;
namespace Calculator_Host_Console
{
    class Program
    {
        static void Main(string[] args)
        {
            ServiceHost host = new ServiceHost(typeof(Calcu
lator));
            host.AddServiceEndpoint(typeof(ICalculator), new
BasicHttpBinding(),"http://localhost:9087/CalculatorDemo");
            host.Open();
            Console.WriteLine("Service is running press any
key to stop");
            Console.ReadKey();
            host.Close();
        }
    }
}
```

Here the code of adding the service endpoint through AddServiceEndpoint method is highlighted. One of the version of this method is used in which the first argument is type of contract, second argument is the type of binding which is to be used so we created anonymous object of BasicHttpBinding class, third argument is the endpoint address which is http in this example as binding is BasicHttpBinding. In the presence of based address it can be left empty or you ca write String.Empty as third argument. To add the service metadata behavior following code is written as shown in Example 3.

Example 3. Adding Service Metadata Behavior

```
using System;
using System.Collections.Generic;
using System.Linq;
using System.Text;
using FirstWCFService_Calc;
using System.ServiceModel;
using System.ServiceModel. Description;
```

```
namespace Calculator_Host_Console
{
    class Program
    {
        static void Main(string[] args)
        {
            ServiceHost host = new ServiceHost(typeof(Calcu
lator));
            host.AddServiceEndpoint(typeof(ICalculator), new
BasicHttpBinding(),

"http://localhost:9087/CalculatorDemo");
            ServiceMetadataBehavior smb = new
ServiceMetadataBehavior();smb.HttpGetEnabled = true;host.De-
scription.Behaviors.Add(smb);
            host.Open();
            Console.WriteLine("Service is running press any
key to stop");
            Console.ReadKey();
            host.Close();
        }
    }
}
```

Here in this example to create the object of service metadata behavior, the object of ServiceMetadataBehavior class is created. This behavior is available under System.ServiceModel.Description so it must be imported in the code as highlighted in Example 3. After creating the object we need to set HttpGetEnabled to true which is a property of ServiceMetadataBehavior class so set is true as it is Boolean. The behavior must be added to the service by using Add method as shown in the third line of the highlighted code in Example 3. The code written in Example 3 is equivalent to the code of the configuration file as highlighted in in Example 4.

Example 4. Configuration File with Highlighted Code of Adding Behavior

```
<?xml version="1.0" encoding="utf-8" ?>
<configuration>
    <system.serviceModel>
```

```
        <behaviors><serviceBehaviors><behavior name="NewBeha
vior"><serviceMetadata httpGetEnabled="true" /></behavior></
serviceBehaviors></behaviors><services><service behaviorCon
figuration="NewBehavior"name="FirstWCFService_Calc.Calcula-
tor">
                <endpoint address="http://localhost:9087/
CalculatorDemo"
                    binding="basicHttpBinding"    bindingCon-
figuration=""
                    contract="FirstWCFService_Calc.ICalcula-
tor" />
                <host>
                    <baseAddresses>
                        <add baseAddress="http://local-
host:9087/CalculatorDemo" />
                    </baseAddresses>
                </host>
            </service>
        </services>
    </system.serviceModel>
</configuration>
```

Now to add the base address Uri class is used. It comes from System.Uri. To create the object of this class following code should be written as:

Uri baseaddress = new Uri ("http://localhost:9087/CalculatorDemo");
Multiple base addresses can be written by using the array as shown below:
Uri [] baseaddresses = new Uri []{new Uri("http://localhost:9087/Calcula-
    torDemo"),
new Uri("http://localhost:9092/CalculatorDemo")};

After creating the base address using the object of Uri class it must be passed as second argument of ServiceHost class as shown in below:

ServiceHost host = new ServiceHost (typeof (Calculator), baseaddress);

Now add the piece of code to add the base address to complete the code as shown in Example 5.

Example 5. Code to Create Endpoint

```
using System;
using System.Collections.Generic;
using System.Linq;
using System.Text;
using FirstWCFService_Calc;
using System.ServiceModel;
using System.ServiceModel.Description;
namespace Calculator_Host_Console
{
    class Program
    {
        static void Main(string[] args)
        {
            Uri baseaddress = new Uri("http://local-
host:9087/CalculatorDemo");ServiceHost host = new ServiceHos
t(typeof(Calculator),baseaddress);
            host.AddServiceEndpoint(typeof(ICalculator), new
BasicHttpBinding(),

"http://localhost:9087/CalculatorDemo");
            ServiceMetadataBehavior smb = new ServiceMetada-
taBehavior();
            smb.HttpGetEnabled = true;
            host.Description.Behaviors.Add(smb);
            host.Open();
            Console.WriteLine("Service is running press any
key to stop");
            Console.ReadKey();
            host.Close();
        }
    }
}
```

Here the highlighted code in Example 5 is equivalent to the highlighted code of configuration file as shown in Example 6.

Example 6. Configuration File with Highlighted Code of Adding Base Address

```xml
<?xml version="1.0" encoding="utf-8" ?>
<configuration>
    <system.serviceModel>
        <behaviors>
            <serviceBehaviors>
                <behavior name="NewBehavior">
                    <serviceMetadata httpGetEnabled="true"
/>
                </behavior>
            </serviceBehaviors>
        </behaviors>
        <services>
            <service behaviorConfiguration="NewBehavior"
             name="FirstWCFService_Calc.Calculator">
                <endpoint address="http://localhost:9087/
CalculatorDemo"
                  binding="basicHttpBinding"
                    bindingConfiguration=""
contract="FirstWCFService_Calc.ICalculator" />
                <host><baseAddresses><add
baseAddress="http://localhost:9087/CalculatorDemo" /></base-
Addresses></host>
            </service>
        </services>
    </system.serviceModel>
</configuration>
```

Therefore, if you write the code shown in Example 5 there is no need to create a configuration file as an endpoint is created using the code.

The endpoint address is divided into two types: Absolute address and Relative address. Both are discussed in the following sections.

Absolute Address

It is a fully qualified address which must start with the scheme discussed in the address format section. For example the address http://localhost:9890/CalcService is considered as absolute address. The endpoint having absolute an address might not need the base address. So in the presence of absolute address, snippet of explicit way of creating endpoint and configuration way of creating endpoint are shown in Example 7 and Example 8 respectively.

Example 7. The Snippet to Create Endpoint using Code

ServiceHost host = new ServiceHost(typeof(Calculator),baseaddress);
ServiceHost host = new ServiceHost(typeof(Calculator));

host.AddServiceEndpoint (typeof (ICalculator), new BasicHttpBinding (), "http://localhost:9087/CalculatorDemo");
  Therefore in above example it can be observed that Uri class is not required when endpoint is absolute. So if endpoint is absolute base address (Uri class) may be there or may not be there. Both cases are valid in the situation.

Example 8. The Snippet to Create Endpoint using Configuration File

```
<endpoint address="http://localhost:9087/Calculator-
Demo" binding="basicHttpBinding" bindingConfiguration=""
contract="FirstWCFService_Calc.ICalculator" />
            <host>
                <baseAddresses>
                    <add baseAddress="http://local-
host:9087/CalculatorDemo" />
                </baseAddresses>
            </host>
```

  The endpoint address is absolute the <host> tag is not required as shown in Example 8.

Relative Address

A relative endpoint address does not have fully qualified address. It does not start with any scheme such as http, net.tcp etc. The address such as service1 is considered as relative address. For relative endpoint address it is compulsory to have a base address. The blank address (not specifying it) is also considered as relative address. The example of a snippet of relative endpoint address in explicit method is given in Example 9.

Example 9. Relative Endpoint Address Code

ServiceHost host = new ServiceHost(typeof(Calculator),baseaddress);
host.AddServiceEndpoint(typeof(ICalculator), new BasicHttpBinding(),
    "CalculatorDemo");

OR

host.AddServiceEndpoint(typeof(ICalculator), new BasicHttpBinding(), "");

Here in the above example in the first function call of AddServiceEndpoint method, the relative address is given as "CalculatorDemo", and in the other call of AddServiceEndpoint method, the endpoint address is not written. In both situations it is compulsory to have a base address as shown in Example 10; otherwise it will result in an error.

Example 10. Relative Endpoint Address Code with Base Address

```
                    Uri baseaddress = new Uri ("http://loc-
alhost:9087/CalculatorDemo");
                    ServiceHost host = new ServiceHost (type
of(Calculator),baseaddress);
host.AddServiceEndpoint (typeof(ICalculator), new BasicHttp-
Binding(), "");
Likewise snippet for creating relative endpoint address us-
ing configuration file is shown in Example 11.
```

Example 11. The Relative Endpoint Address using Configuration Method

```
<service behaviorConfiguration="NewBehavior"
name="FirstWCFService_Calc.Calculator">
            <endpoint address=""
binding="basicHttpBinding"
            bindingConfiguration=""
contract="FirstWCFService_Calc.ICalculator" />
        <host>
            <baseAddresses>
```

Working with Address

Table 1. Types of addresses versus programming methods

Type of Address	Programming Methods	
	Explicit (Code)	Configuration
Endpoint Address	Class ServiceHost: Method: AddServiceEndpoint	<endpoint>
Base Address	Class Uri	<host> <baseAddresses> <add baseAddress= "" /> </baseAddresses> </host>

```
                    <add baseAddress="http://local-
host:9087/CalculatorDemo" />
                 </baseAddresses>
              </host>\
</service>
```

In the Table 1, the summary of endpoint address and base address with programming methods explicit and configuration is provided.

In the Table 2, the relation between endpoint address and base address is shown.

From the Table 2, it is observed that when base address is given, a relative endpoint address is given with some value, then the actual endpoint address is base address + relative endpoint address. Likewise when base address is given and relative endpoint address is given with no value both are same. When the base address actual and endpoint address is absolute both are not related at all. It is also interesting to note that base address cannot be relative. It is compulsory to have an absolute base address when it is included.

Table 2. Relation between endpoint address and base address

Sr. No	Values of Addresses		
	Base Address	Endpoint Address	Actual Endpoint Address
1.	http://localhost:9087	Service1	http://localhost:9087 /Service1
2.	http://localhost:9087		http://localhost:9087
3.	http://localhost:9087 /Service1	http://localhost:9090 /Service2	http://localhost:9090 /Service2

Programming Endpoint Address at Client

To work with the endpoint address at client side in C#.NET, EndpointAdress class is used. It contains several constructors to create the object. Following is the example of creating the object of EndpointAddress class:

EndpointAddress endpoint_address = new EndpointAddress ("http://local-host:9087/CalculatorDemo");

The code snippet of consuming the service in.NET client is shown in Example 12.

Example 12. Code of Consuming Service using EndpointAddress Class

```
…….. . .
…….. . .
…….. . .
CalculatorClient proxy = new CalculatorClient();
EndpointAddress endpoint_address = new
EndpointAddress("http://localhost:9087/CalculatorDemo");
        public Form1()
        {
            InitializeComponent();
        }
        private void btnPlus_Click(object sender, EventArgs
e)
        {
        proxy = newCalculatorClient("BasicHttpBinding_
ICalculator",endpoint_address);
            no1 = Int16.Parse(tbNumber1.Text);
            no2 = Int16.Parse(tbNumber2.Text);
            ans = proxy.add(no1, no2);
            MessageBox.Show("Answer is "+ans);


        }
……
……
……
```

Here in Example 12, in the constructor of CalculatorClient is the name of endpoint mentioned in the App.Config file of client program. The code in the click event of only plus button is shown in this example which is highlighted. Likewise code for other buttons can be written in the similar manner. As consuming WCF service using EndpointAddress class is not widely used, further detail regarding this class is not mentioned in this book. For more details regarding EndpointAddress class it is advisable to use object browser of visual studio.

CONCLUSION

Address is the heart of endpoint in WCF. Address also depends on the binding you choose. Depending upon the binding the format of address changes accordingly. Following are the important takeaways from this chapter:

- There are three types of address are available in WCF: Endpoint Address, Base Address, Mex Address. Each type of address has different formats.
- The format of address must match with the binding and vice versa.
- The AddServiceEndpoint method of ServiceHost class is used to create endpoint address through code.
- The Uri class is used to create base address through code.
- The Address can be absolute or relative.
- The relative endpoint address must have base address.
- The base address must be absolute.
- Port number is optional in any address.
- Default port is 80 and on windows OS IIS runs on this port by default.
- Named pipe address does not require port number.
- IIS Address requires service file (.Svc file).
- At service side if endpoint is created using code (explicit) method, configuration file is not required.
- It is advisable to use configuration method to create endpoint at service side. In unavoidable circumstances explicit (code) method should be used to create endpoint at service side.
- At client side to work with endpoint using code EndpointAddress class is used.

Chapter 5
Working with Binding

After completing this chapter, you will be able to:

- Gain understanding on different bindings available in WCF.
- Develop the WCF service using bindings.
- Gain practical exposure of using various binding WCF service in different scenarios.

This chapter explains about various bindings available in WCF. It provides in depth knowledge of practical implementation of binding in a WCF service. It also provides the difference between various built-in bindings. Creation of custom binding is also covered in this chapter.

INTRODUCTION TO BINDING

As address is an import part of endpoint, binding is also vital part of the endpoint as it decides how to communicate. It determines the protocol, message encoding and message pattern and vital features such as whether to provide

DOI: 10.4018/978-1-5225-1997-3.ch005

Table 1. Summary of each predefined binding with a scheme of address

Related Class	Configuration Name	Description	Scheme /Protocol
BasicHttpBinding	basicHttpBinding	A binding which is compatible with ASP.NET Web service (*.ASMX)	http /https
WSHTTPBinding	wsHttpBinding	A binding for reliable messaging, Transaction and security using latest web service standards using web service standards (WS*).	http/https
WSDualHttpBinding	wsDualHttpBinding	A binding for duplex communication	http/https
WSFederationBinding	wsFederationBinding	A binding to support federated security and WS* security standards	http/https
NetTcpBinding	netTcpBinding	A connection oriented binding which uses TCP binding	net.tcp
NetNamedPipeBinding	netNamedPipeBinding	A connection oriented binding to support inter-process communication.	net.pipe
NetMsmqBinding	netMsmqBinding	A binding to support reliable communication using Microsoft Message Queue (MSMQ)	net.msmq
NetPeerTcpBinding	netPeerTcpBinding	A binding to support peer to peer communication	net.tcp
MsmqIntegrationBinding	msmqIntegrationBinding	A binding to have the support of MSMQ components	net.msmq

security, transaction or reliable messaging. Based on the type of binding selected by a programmer related address format must be used which matches that binding. There several predefine bindings available in WCF. In the Table 1, the details of each predefined binding are summarized.

In the following section commonly used bindings are explained in details.

BasicHttpBinding

It is a binding which uses HTTP protocol as transport for WCF service to work similar as ASP.NET web service (*.ASMX). Therefore, the.NET web service clients can consume the WCF service easily using this binding. It uses the SOAP 1.1 of WS-I basic profile to interoperate with the old SOAP versions. The default setting of this binding using configuration file is shown in Example 1.

Example 1. BasicHttpBinding Default Settings

```
<basicHttpBinding>
                <binding name=" basicDefaults" closeTime-
out="00:01:00"
                openTimeout="00:01:00" receiveTime-
out="00:10:00" sendTimeout="00:01:00"
                allowCookies="false"
bypassProxyOnLocal="false" hostNameComparisonMode="StrongWi
ldcard"
                maxBufferSize="65536" maxBufferPool-
Size="524288"     maxReceivedMessageSize="65536"
                messageEncoding="Text"
textEncoding="utf-8" transferMode="Buffered"
                useDefaultWebProxy="true">
                <readerQuotas maxDepth="32" maxString-
ContentLength="8192" maxArrayLength="16384"
                    maxBytesPerRead="4096" maxNameTa-
bleCharCount="16384" />
                <security mode="None">
                    <transport
clientCredentialType="None" proxyCredentialType="None"
                        realm="" />
            <message clientCredentialType="UserName"
algorithmSuite="Default" />
                </security>
            </binding>
 </basicHttpBinding>
```

As shown in Example 1, this binding is not secured by default. But it can be changed by changing the security mode to message to transport. There is no support for transaction and reliable sessions in basic http binding. Therefore this binding cannot be used to develop the program of reliable sessions or transactions. It supports http and https protocols for communication. These setting can be changed in the code by using object of the class BasicHttp-Bindig as shown in the code snippet in Example 2.

Table 2. Features available in BasicHttpBinding

Features	Support	Default Value
Transaction	No	N/A
Reliable sessions	No	N/A
Security	Transport, Message)	None
Message Encoding	Text, MTOM (Message Transmission Optimization Mechanism)	Text
Protocols Supported	http, https	N/A
Duplex Communication	No	N/A

Example 2. Changing the Setting of Basic http Binding using Code

```
Uri baseaddress = new Uri("http://localhost:9087/Calculator-
Demo");
ServiceHost host = new ServiceHost(typeof(Calculator),basea
ddress);
 BasicHttpBinding basicbinding = new BasicHttpBinding();
 basicbinding.Security.Mode = BasicHttpSecurityMode.Message;
 basicbinding.MaxReceivedMessageSize = 10000;
 ServiceMetadataBehavior smb = new ServiceMetadataBehav-
ior();
 smb.HttpGetEnabled = true;
 host.Description.Behaviors.Add(smb);
 host.AddServiceEndpoint(typeof(ICalculator), basicbinding,
"");
 host.Open();
```

The summary of features supported in this binding is shown in Table 2.

WSHttpBinding

This binding support security, reliable session and transaction. It can be preferred over BasicHttpBinding to communicate with more recent web service communication. The default settings of WSHttpBinding are shown in Example 3.

Example 3. Default Security Settings for WSHttpBinding:

```
<wsHttpBinding>
                    <binding name=" wsHttpBindingDe-
faults" closeTimeout="00:01:00"
                    openTimeout="00:01:00" receiveTime-
out="00:10:00" sendTimeout="00:01:00"
                    bypassProxyOnLocal="false"
transactionFlow="false" hostNameComparisonMode="StrongWildc
ard"
                    maxBufferPoolSize="524288" maxReceived-
MessageSize="65536"
                    messageEncoding="Text"
textEncoding="utf-8" useDefaultWebProxy="true"
                    allowCookies="false">
                    <readerQuotas maxDepth="32" maxString-
ContentLength="8192" maxArrayLength="16384"
                       maxBytesPerRead="4096" maxNameTa-
bleCharCount="16384" />
                    <reliableSession ordered="true" inac-
tivityTimeout="00:10:00"
                       enabled="false" />
                    <security mode="Message">
                       <transport
clientCredentialType="Windows" proxyCredentialType="None"
realm="" />
                <message clientCredentialType="Windows"  nego
tiateServiceCredential="true"
                           algorithmSuite="Default"
establishSecurityContext="true" />
                    </security>
                 </binding>
              </wsHttpBinding>
```

This binding is secured by default and it provided message level security by default. It supports transaction and reliable messaging but by default both are disabled as shown in the configuration file as shown in Figure 3. The default settings can be changed in the code as per the snippet shown in Example 4. It supports http and https protocols for communication.

Example 4. Changing Default Setting of WSHttpBinding

```
Uri baseaddress = new Uri("http://localhost:9087/Calculator-
Demo");
ServiceHost host = new ServiceHost(typeof(Calculator),basea
ddress);
WSHttpBinding wsbinding = new WSHttpBinding();
wsbinding.Security.Mode = SecurityMode.None;
wsbinding.MaxReceivedMessageSize = 20000;
wsbinding.TransactionFlow = true;
OptionalReliableSession reliablesession=new OptionalReliab-
leSession();
 reliablesession.Enabled=true;
 wsbinding.ReliableSession = reliablesession;
 ServiceMetadataBehavior smb = new ServiceMetadataBehav-
ior();
 smb.HttpGetEnabled = true;
 host.Description.Behaviors.Add(smb);
 host.AddServiceEndpoint(typeof(ICalculator), wsbinding,
"");
 host.Open();
```

The summary of features supported in this binding is shown in Table 3.

NetTcpBinding

This binding is used for connection oriented communication. It is tailor made for interoperability between.NET to.NET communication. The default binding settings are shown in Example 5.

Table 3. Features available in WSHttpBinding

Features	Support	Default Value
Transaction	Yes	False
Reliable sessions	Yes	False
Security	Transport, Message	Message
Message Encoding	Text, MTOM	Text
Protocols Supported	http, https	N/A
Duplex Communication	No	N/A

Example 5. Default Settings of NetTcpBinding

```
<netTcpBinding>
                <binding name="netTcpDefaults" closeTime-
out="00:01:00"
                open Timeout="00:01:00" receiveTime-
out="00:10:00" sendTimeout="00:01:00"
                transactionFlow="false"
transferMode="Buffered" transactionProtocol="OleTransactio
ns"
                hostNameComparisonMode="StrongWildcard"
listenBacklog="10"
                maxBufferPoolSize="524288" maxBuffer-
Size="65536" maxConnections="10"
                maxReceivedMessageSize="65536">
                <readerQuotas maxDepth="32" maxString-
ContentLength="8192"  maxArrayLength="16384"
                    maxBytesPerRead="4096" maxNameTa-
bleCharCount="16384" />
                <reliableSession ordered="true" inac-
tivityTimeout="00:10:00"
                    enabled="false" />
                <security mode="Transport">
                <transport
clientCredentialType="Windows" protectionLevel="EncryptAndS
ign" />
                <message
clientCredentialType="Windows" />
                </security>
            </binding>
    </netTcpBinding>
```

This is binding is secured by default and it provides transport level security. Like WSHttpBinding it also supports reliable sessions and transactions. These features are disabled by default so we need to enable these features explicitly. This binding can be updated by using code as shown in the code snippet of Example 6.

Table 4. Features available in NetHttpBinding

Features	Support	Default Value
Transaction	Yes	False
Reliable sessions	Yes	False
Security	Transport, Message	Transport
Message Encoding	Binary	Binary
Protocols Supported	net.tcp	N/A
Duplex Communication	Yes	N/A

Example 6. Changing the Settings of NetTcpBinding using Code

```
Uri baseaddress = new Uri("net.tcp://localhost:9087/Calcula-
torDemo");          ServiceHost host = new ServiceHost(ty
peof(Calculator),baseaddress);NetTcpBinding nettcpbinding =
new NetTcpBinding();
nettcpbinding.Security.Mode = SecurityMode.None;
nettcpbinding.MaxReceivedMessageSize = 20000;
nettcpbinding.TransactionFlow = true;
OptionalReliableSession reliablesession = new OptionalReli-
ableSession();
reliablesession.Enabled = true;
nettcpbinding.ReliableSession = reliablesession;
host.AddServiceEndpoint(typeof(ICalculator), nettcpbinding,
"");
host.Open();
```

The summary of features supported in this binding is shown in Table 4.

WSDualHttpBinding

This binding is used for duplex communication. In duplex communication a client and service both can call each other at the same time. The default setting of this binding is shown in Example 7.

Example 7. Default Settings of WSDualHttpBinding

```
<wsDualHttpBinding>
        <binding name="wsDualDefaults"
        closeTimeout="00:01:00"
        openTimeout="00:01:00"
        receiveTimeout="00:010:00"
        sendTimeout="00:01:00"
        bypassProxyOnLocal="false"
        transactionFlow="false"
        maxBufferPoolSize="524288"
        maxReceivedMessageSize="65536"
        messageEncoding="Text"
        textEncoding="utf-8"
        useDefaultWebProxy="true">
        <reliableSession ordered="true"
          inactivityTimeout="00:10:00" />
        <security mode="Message">
     <message clientCredentialType="Windows "
      negotiateServiceCredential="true" algorithmSuite=" Ba-
sic256 " />
                </security>
        <readerQuotas            maxArrayLength="16384"
maxBytesPerRead="4096"       maxDepth="32"
maxNameTableCharCount="16384"        maxStringContent-
Length="8192 />     </binding>
</wsDualHttpBinding>
```

This bindings uses two way channel to communicate in both directions as communication in the both direction at the same time is possible in duplex communication. This binding is secured by default and message level security is provided by default by this binding. Reliable sessions are enabled by default and cannot be disabled as there is no option to disable reliable session in this binding. Transaction support is also available which is disabled by default but it can be enabled explicitly by the user. Please note that the service operations must be one way for this communication. The practical demonstration is explored in Chapter 7. The customization of this binding using code is depicted in Example 8.

Table 5. Features available in WSDualHttpBinding

Features	Support	Default Value
Transaction	Yes	False
Reliable sessions	Yes	True forever. Cannot be changed to False
Security	Transport, Message	Message
Message Encoding	Text, MTOM	Text
Protocols Supported	http, https	N/A
Duplex Communication	Yes	N/A

Example 8. Customizing WSDualHttpBinding using Code

```
WSDualHttpBinding WSDualHttpbinding = new WSDualHttpBind-
ing();
WSDualHttpbinding.Security.Mode = WSDualHttpSecurityMode.
None;
WSDualHttpbinding.MaxReceivedMessageSize = 15000;
WSDualHttpbinding.TransactionFlow = true;
ServiceMetadataBehavior smb = new ServiceMetadataBehavior();
smb.HttpGetEnabled = true;
host.Description.Behaviors.Add(smb);
host.AddServiceEndpoint(typeof(ICalculator), WSDualHttpbind-
ing, "");
host.Open();
```

The summary of features supported in this binding is shown in Table 5.

NetNamedPipeBinding

It connection oriented binding as NetTcpBinding. The purpose of using this binding is for communication between two processes inside the same machine i.e. inter-process communication. The default settings of this binding are depicted in Example 9.

Example 9. Default Settings of NetNamedPipeBinding

```
<netNamedPipeBinding>
  <binding name="netPipeDefaults" closeTimeout="00:01:00"
```

```
   hostNameComparisonMode="StrongWildcard" maxBufferPool-
Size="524288"
  maxBufferSize="65536" maxConnections="10"
  maxReceivedMessageSize="65536" openTimeout="00:01:00"
  receiveTimeout="00:10:00" sendTimeout="00:01:00"
transactionFlow="false"
  transactionProtocol="OleTransactions"
transferMode="Buffered">
   <readerQuotas maxArrayLength="16384" maxBytesPer-
Read="4096"
    maxDepth="32" maxNameTableCharCount="16384"
   maxStringContentLength="8192"/>
   <security mode="Transport">
   </security>
   </binding>
</netNamedPipeBinding>
```

This binding does not support reliable session. It provides transport level security and does not support message security. There is a support of transaction in this binding which is false by default but it can be updated explicitly by the programmer. The protocol used in this binding is net.pipe This binding can also be customized using code as depicted in Example 10.

Example 10. Customizing NetNamedPipeBinding using Code

```
Uri baseaddress = new Uri("net.pipe://localhost:9087/Calcu-
latorDemo");
ServiceHost host = new ServiceHost(typeof(Calculator),basea
ddress);
NetNamedPipeBinding NetNamedPipebinding = new NetNamedPipe-
Binding();
NetNamedPipebinding.Security.Mode = NetNamedPipeSecurity-
Mode.None;
NetNamedPipebinding.MaxReceivedMessageSize = 15000;
NetNamedPipebinding.TransactionFlow = true;
host.AddServiceEndpoint(typeof(ICalculator), NetNamedPipe-
binding, "");
host.Open();
```

The summary of features supported in this binding is shown in Table 6.

Table 6. Features available in NetNamedPipeBinding

Features	Support	Default Value
Transaction	Yes	False
Reliable sessions	No	N/A
Security	Transport	Transport
Message Encoding	Binary	Binary
Protocols Supported	net.pipe	N/A
Duplex Communication	Yes	N/A

NetMsmqBinding

This binding plays a vital role while using MSMQ for reliable communication. This binding is secured by default and has Transport level security by default. The default settings of this binding are depicted in Example 11.

Example 11. Default Setting of NetMsmqBinding

```
<netMsmqBinding>
                <binding name="NetMsmqBinding_IHello" clos-
eTimeout="00:01:00"
                openTimeout="00:01:00" receiveTime-
out="00:10:00" sendTimeout="00:01:00"
                deadLetterQueue="System" durable="true"
exactlyOnce="true"
                maxReceivedMessageSize="65536" maxRetry-
Cycles="2" receiveErrorHandling="Fault"
                receiveRetryCount="5" retryCycleDe-
lay="00:30:00" timeToLive="1.00:00:00"
                useSourceJournal="false"
useMsmqTracing="false" queueTransferProtocol="Native"
                maxBufferPoolSize="524288"
useActiveDirectory="false">
                <readerQuotas maxDepth="32" maxString-
ContentLength="8192" maxArrayLength="16384"
                    maxBytesPerRead="4096" maxNameTa-
bleCharCount="16384" />
                <security mode="Transport">
                <transport msmqAuthenticationMode="W
```

```
indowsDomain" msmqEncryptionAlgorithm="RC4Stream"
                              msmqProtectionLevel="Sign"
msmqSecureHashAlgorithm="Sha1" />
                         <message
clientCredentialType="Windows" />
                    </security>
                 </binding>
              </netMsmqBinding>
```

There is not support of transaction in this binding. The reliable sessions are enabled by default and there is no way to disable it in this binding just as WSDualHttpBinding. The binding can be customized using code as depicted in Example 12.

Example 12. Customizing NetMsMqBinding

```
Uri baseaddress = new Uri("http://localhost:9087/Calculator-
Demo");
ServiceHost host = new ServiceHost(typeof(Calculator),basea
ddress);
NetMsmqBinding NetMsmqbinding = new NetMsmqBinding();
NetMsmqbinding.Security.Mode = NetMsmqSecurityMode.None;
NetMsmqbinding.MaxReceivedMessageSize = 300000;
host.AddServiceEndpoint(typeof(ICalculator), NetMsmqbinding,
" net.msmq://localhost/private/wcfqueue");
host.Open();
```

In this binding the service operations must be one way as duplex communication. The practical implementation of queue is explained in Chapter 9.
The summary of features supported in this binding is shown in Table 7.

Customized Binding

Apart from the built-in bindings available a programmer has a choice to create the custom binding. The custom binding using service configuration can be created as per the following steps.

Step 1: Open service configuration editor by right clicking on the configuration file as discussed in Chapter 3.In the editor screen right click on

Table 7. Features available in NetMsmqBinding

Features	Support	Default Value
Transaction	Yes	False
Reliable sessions	Yes	True forever. Cannot be changed to False
Security	Transport, Message	Transport
Protocols Supported	net.msmq	N/A
Duplex Communication	Yes	N/A

Figure 1. Adding new binding

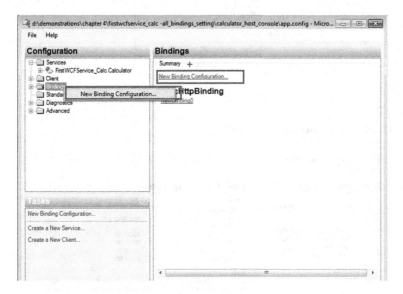

bindings and click on the New Binding Configuration or click that option directly on right hand side as shown in Figure 1.

Step 2: Choose the customBinding from the list of available bindings as shown in Figure 2

Step 3: The custom binding is created as shown in Figure 3. By default it contains two elements as shown in Figure 3. These elements can be added or removed as per the requirement. The steps to add the elements are well explained in upcoming steps.

Step 4: The new element extension sections can be added by clicking on Add button. After clicking on the Add button, the list of available extensions are displayed as shown in Figure 4. To add the security element, select it and click on Add button.

Figure 2. Adding new binding

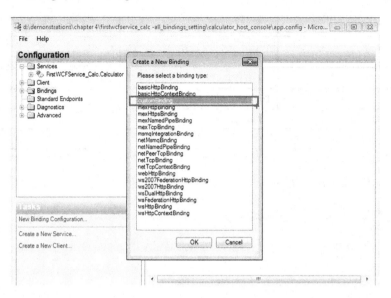

Figure 3. After selecting custom binding

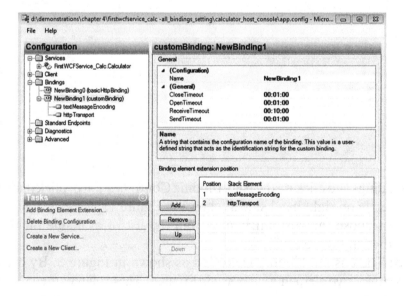

Step 5: After clicking on Add button the extension is added as shown in Figure 5.

Step 6: The details of security element can be viewed by selecting element from the security node which is available under the newly added binding as shown in Figure 6.

Figure 4. Adding new Binding Element Extension sections

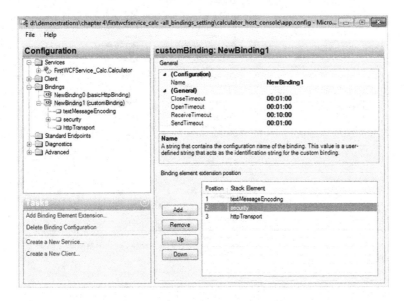

Figure 5. Editor screen after adding security element

Figure 6. The details of security element

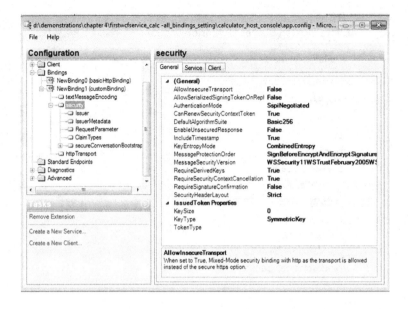

Figure 7. Removing the element

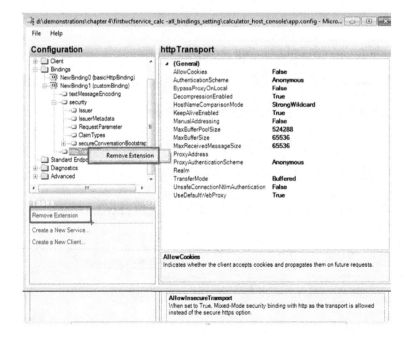

Figure 8. Adding the element

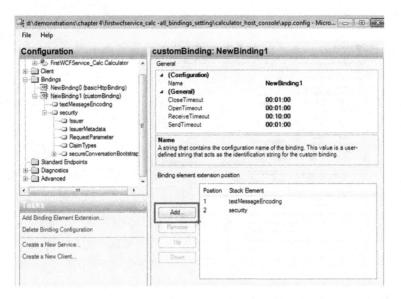

Step 7: An element can be removed from the binding configuration too. To remove the element select it->right click on it and click on Remove Extension option from the context menu or from the link shown below in Figure 7. In this figure we have selected httpTransport element which must be removed from the customBinding.

Step 8: As per the previous step the element httpTransport is removed from the list as shown in Figure 8. Likewise an element can be added in the binding configuration also. To add the element click on the Add button as illustrated in Figure 8.

Step 9: The list of available elements are displayed as shown in Figure 9. In this example, we will add tcpTransport for connection oriented communication. Select the tcpTransport as shown in Figure 9 and click on the Add button.

Step 10: The tcpTranport element is added in the new binding configuration as shown in Figure 10.

Step 11: The added tcpTransport has similar characteristics as the NetTcp-Binding. The default settings of NetTcpBinding is shown in Figure 11. To view these setting just locate the tcpTransport element under the custom binding node and click on it the default settings as displayed as shown in Figure 11. After finishing updating custom binding save the configuration file using File->Save menu and return to the visual studio by closing the service configuration editor The code snippet of newly added custom binding in the configuration file is shown in Example 13.

Figure 9. Selecting the element to be added

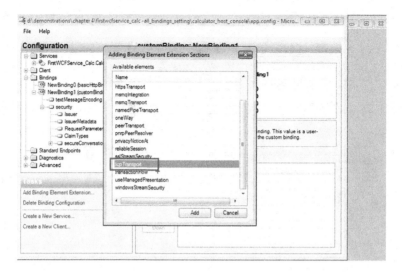

Figure 10. Editor screen after adding the element

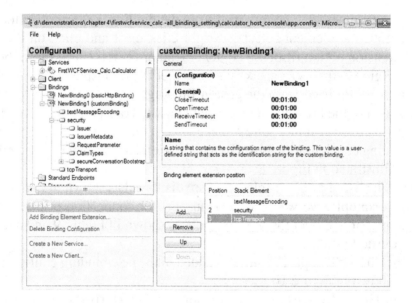

Figure 11. The details of tcpTranport

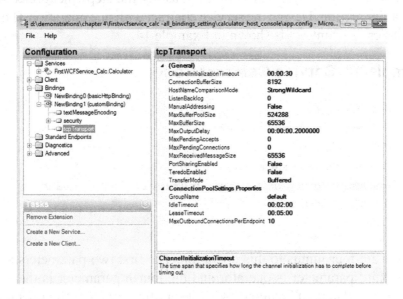

Example 13. Custom Binding in Configuration File

```
<customBinding>
            <binding name="NewBinding1">
                <textMessageEncoding />
                <security />
                <tcpTransport  />
            </binding>
</customBinding>
```

PUTTING BINDINGS TOGETHER

In this section working of multiple binding with practical demonstration is explained. We used BasicHttpBinding, WSHttpBinding and NetTcpBinding in one WCF service. The.NET client having a GUI interface is provided to choose any one binding from the list of bindings and consume the service accordingly. The WCF service is developed which works as basic mathematical subject tutor for a child. In the host program three endpoints will be created as there are three bindings used in this program. The steps are mentioned below.

Step 1: Create the WCF service library, as per the steps mentioned in the earlier section. Design the service contract with one operation The code of Service contract is shown in Example 14.

Example 14. Service Contract Code

```
[ServiceContract]
public interface IMathTutor
{
    [OperationContract]
    Boolean Check_Answer(int operand1, int operand2, String
op, int user_answer);
}
```

There are four inputs to this operation. The first two parameters are operands, third parameter is operator and the fourth parameter is the answer which is calculated and entered by the user after applying the operator i.e. +,-,* or / on the operand 1 and operand2. If the answer is correct the operation returns true, otherwise it returns false.

Step 2: Implement the service class by writing the logic of the operation contract as shown in Example 15.

Example 15. The Code of Service Class

```
public class MathTutor: IMathTutor
    {
        public bool Check_Answer(int operand1, int operand2,
String op, int user_answer)
        {
            int correct_ans = 0;
            if (op == "+")
                correct_ans = operand1 + operand2;
            else if (op == "-")
                correct_ans = operand1 - operand2;
            else if (op == "*")
                correct_ans = operand1 * operand2;
            else //operation is division
                correct_ans = operand1 / operand2;
            //matching the actual answer i.e.correct_ans
```

```
variable
          //and answer entered by user i.e. user_answer
variable
          if (correct_ans == user_answer)
              return true;
          else
              return false;
      }
    }
```

Step 3: Compile the WCF service project and generate the Dll of the service to host it. The location of Dll file is at \bin\debug or \bin\release

Step 4: Create the console application project as discussed in Chapter 3 to host the service. Add the required Dll files in this project i.e. Dll of service file and reference of System.ServiceModel. The code of Program. cs file is shown in Example 15.

Example 15. The Code of Program.cs File of Console Application Project

```
using System;
using System.Collections.Generic;
using System.Linq;
using System.Text;
using System.ServiceModel;//reference of System.ServiceModel
using System.ServiceModel.Description; //reference for cre-
ating object of

// ServiceEndpoint Class
using Math_Tutor;  //reference of service
namespace Math_Tutor_Console_Host
{
    class Program
    {
        static void Main(string[] args)
        {
            ServiceHost host = new
ServiceHost(typeof(MathTutor));
            host.Open();
            foreach (ServiceEndpoint endpoint in host.De-
```

```
scription.Endpoints)
            {
                Console.WriteLine("Service is running at " +
endpoint.Address + "\n Binding =" + endpoint.Binding);
            }
            Console.WriteLine("Press any key to stop");
            Console.ReadKey();
            host.Close();
        }
    }
}
```

Step 5: In the console application project add the configuration file by right clicking on the project and select the new item as shown in Figure 12. Then go through the steps mentioned in Figure 13 and Figure 14 to add the configuration file in the console project. As discussed earlier keep the configuration file name as App.config.

Step 6: To edit the configuration file, right click on it and click on Edit WCF Configuration from the context menu as shown in Figure 15. The WCF Service configuration is opened, which is shown in Figure 16. The WCF configuration editor can be opened the Tools menu of visual studio also.

Step 7: To add the new service element, select the Services node which is first node and then click on create a new service link on the right side as shown in Figure 16. The wizard to select the service class is displayed as shown in Figure 17.

Figure 12. Adding the configuration file

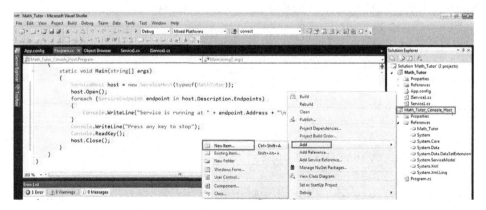

Figure 13. Selecting the file type as configuration file

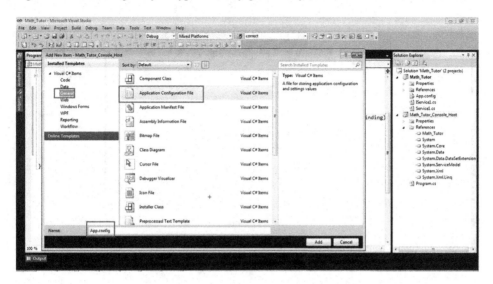

Figure 14. App.Config file added in console application project

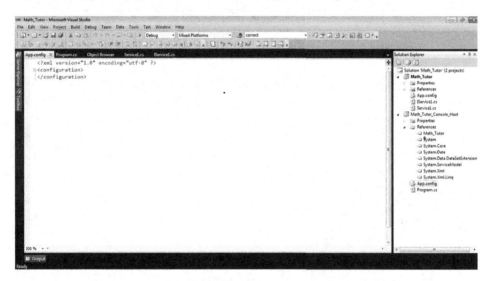

Step 8: Locate the Dll of service project using browse button as shown in Figure 18. Then click on the next button to select the service file which is automatically extracted from the Dll as shown in Figure 19. Select the service file and click on the open button. The service file is selected as shown in Figure 20. Then click on the next button to select the contract type.

Figure 15. Right clicking on App.Config file

Figure 16. WCF service configuration editor

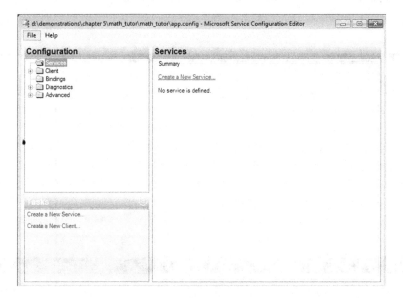

Step 9: As shown in Figure 21, in the wizard the contract is selected by default as there is only one service contract in this project. Click on the next button. The wizard to select protocol appears as shown in Figure 22. Select HTTP radio button.

Figure 17. Selecting service type

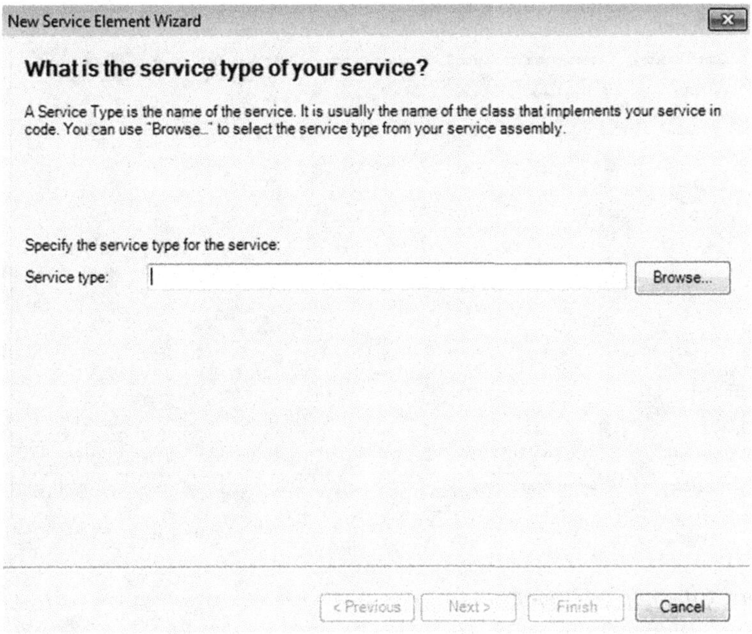

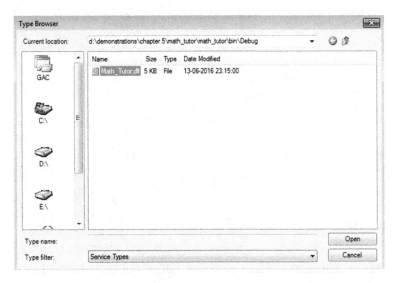

Figure 18. Locating Dll of service project

Figure 19. Selecting the service file

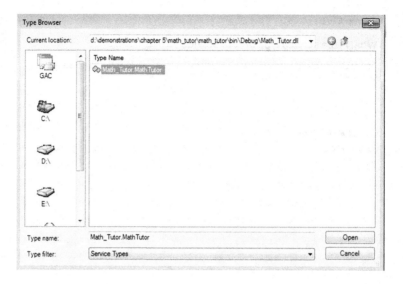

Figure 20. Selected Service file in the wizard

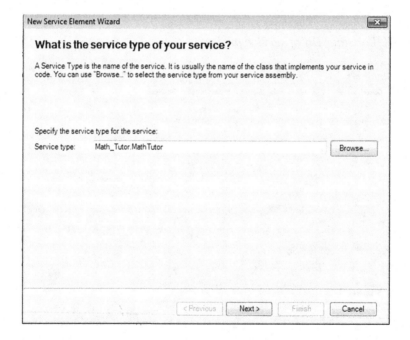

Figure 21. Selected contract file in the wizard

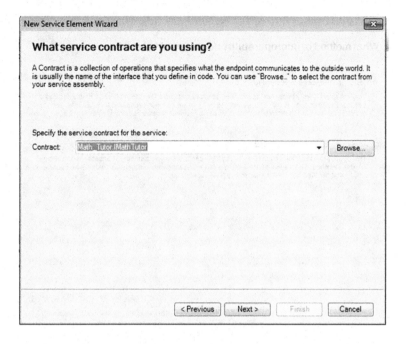

Figure 22. Selecting the protocol for communication

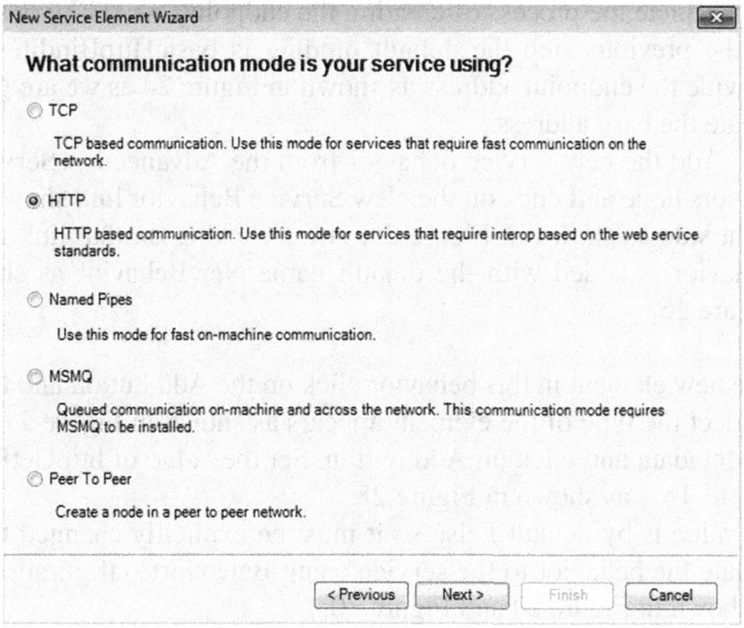

Figure 23. Selecting basic web service interoperability

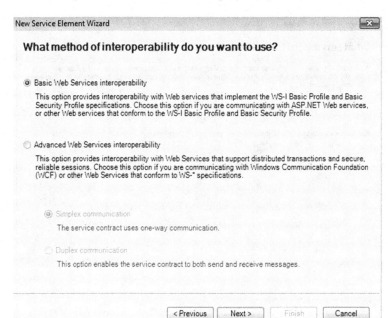

Step 10: Then go through the steps mentioned in Figure 23 and Figure 24 to complete the process of creating the endpoint. As HTTP is selected in the previous step the default binding is basicHttpBinding. Don't provide the endpoint address as shown in Figure 24 as we are going to create the base address.

Step 11: Add the new service behavior from the Advanced ->Service Behaviors node and click on the New Service Behavior link shown in the right side as shown in Figure 25. After clicking on that link the new behavior is added with the default name NewBehavior as shown in Figure 26.

In the new element in this behavior click on the Add button and the wizard to select the type of the element appears as shown in Figure 27. Select serviceMetadata and click on Add button. Set the value of httpGetEnabled property to True as shown in Figure 28.

This value is by default False so it must be explicitly changed to True. Then relate the behavior to the service using BehaviorConfiguration property as shown in Figure 29 and Figure 30.

Figure 24. Specifying endpoint address

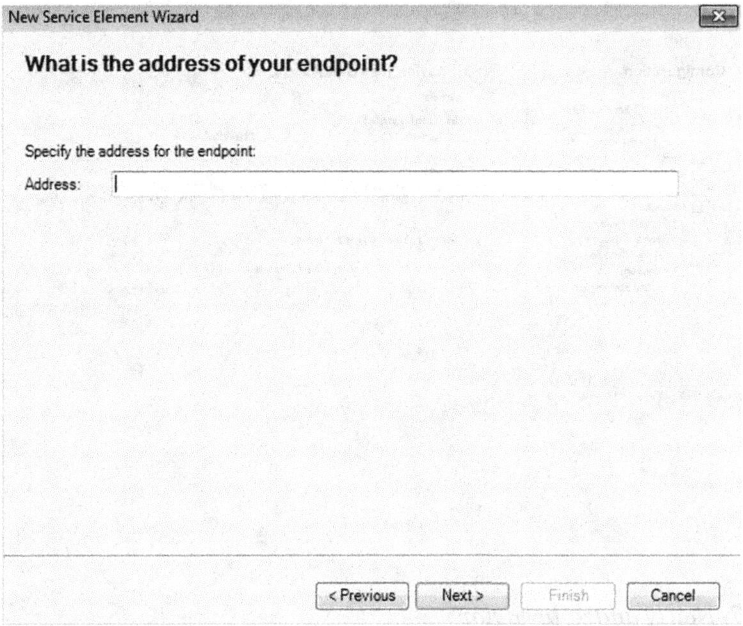

Figure 25. Creating new service behavior

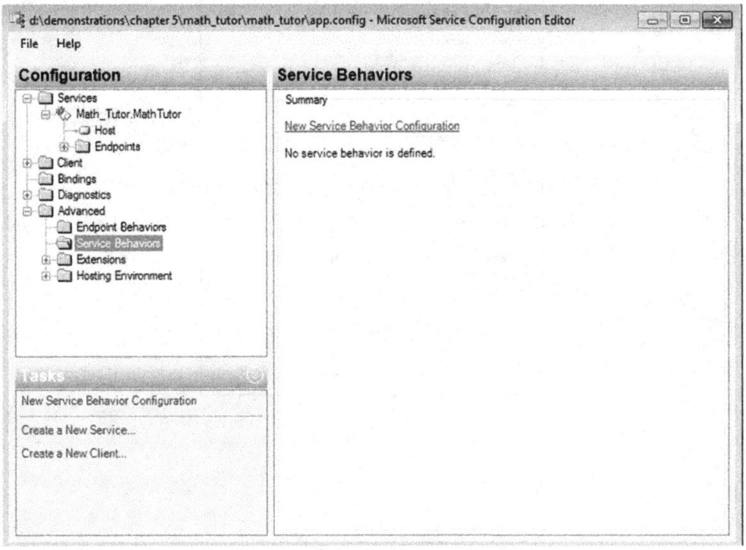

Figure 26. Adding new service behavior

Figure 27. Newly added behavior

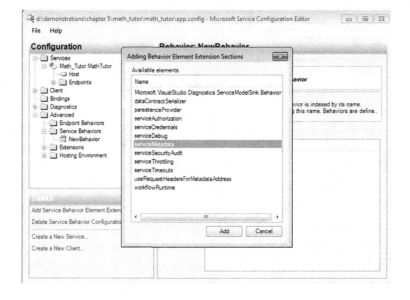

Step 12: As discussed in Chapter 3, adding the service metadata behavior requires to have base address, so add the base address using host element under the Services-> service (i.e.Math_tutor.MathTutor) as shown in Figure 31.

Figure 28. Setting httpGetEnabled to True

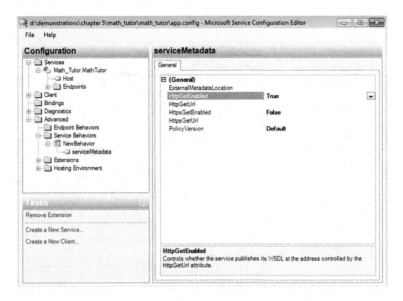

Figure 29. Setting behaviorConfiguration for the Service

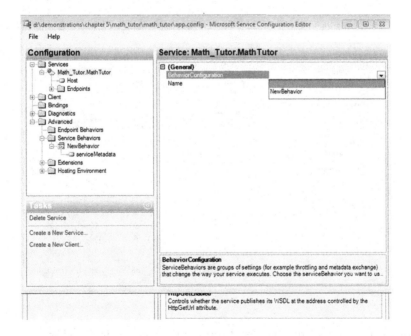

Figure 30. Setting behaviorConfiguration for the Service

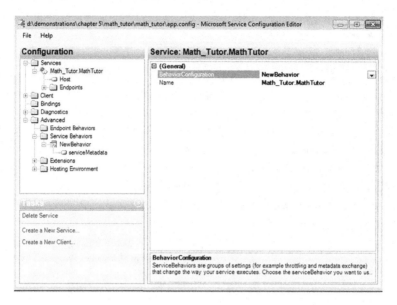

Figure 31. Selecting the host element

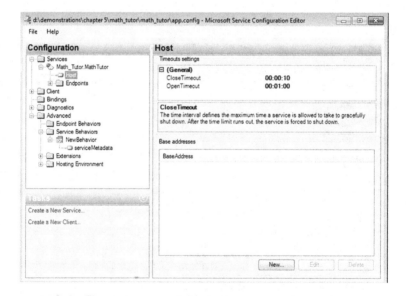

Click on the new button to add the new base address as shown in figure 32. Provide the value of base address as shown in Figure 32 and click on OK button. Then click on the endpoint form the Endpoints node the first endpoint with the basicHttpBinding is shown in Figure 33.

Figure 32. Adding base address

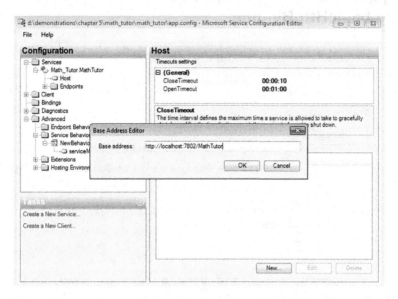

Figure 33. Endpoint with basicHttpBinding

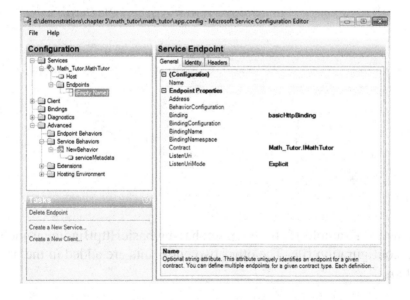

After adding this endpoint the App.Config file looks like as shown in Example 16.

Example 16. App. Config File After Adding basicHttpBinding

```xml
<?xml version="1.0" encoding="utf-8" ?>
<configuration>
    <system.serviceModel>
        <behaviors>
            <serviceBehaviors>
                <behavior name="NewBehavior">
                    <serviceMetadata httpGetEnabled="true"
/>
                </behavior>
            </serviceBehaviors>
        </behaviors>
        <services>
            <service behaviorConfiguration="NewBehavior"
name="Math_Tutor.MathTutor">
                <endpoint address=""
binding="basicHttpBinding" bindingConfiguration=""
                    contract="Math_Tutor.IMathTutor" />
                <host>
                    <baseAddresses>
                        <add baseAddress="http://local-
host:7802/MathTutor" />
                    </baseAddresses>
                </host>
            </service>
        </services>
    </system.serviceModel>
</configuration>
```

As shown in Example 16, the endpoint having basicHttpBinding is included in the configuration file. The other two endpoints are added in the upcoming steps.

Step 13: Add another endpoint having netTcpBinding. To do so, right click on the endpoints and click on New Service Endpoint from the context menu of from the link provided at the bottom as shown in Figure 34. It will create another endpoint with default binding as basicHttpBinding as shown in Figure 35.

Figure 34. Adding new endpoint

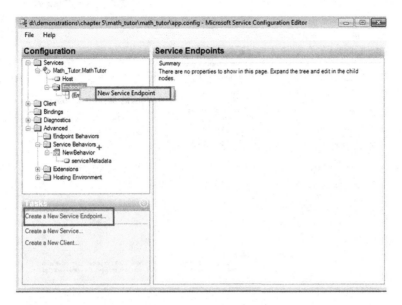

Figure 35. Newly added endpoint

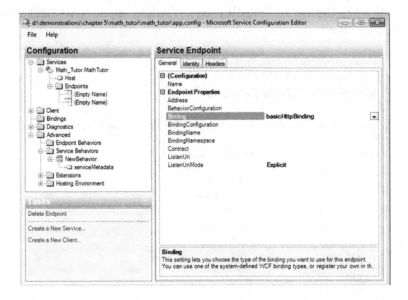

Now provide the address of this endpoint as net.tcp address and changed the binding to netTcpBinding as shown in Figure 36.

Figure 36. Setting address and binding

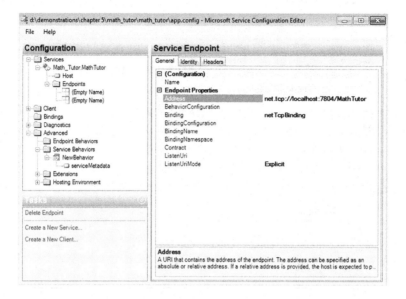

Step 14: Now provide the contract details by selecting the Contract element as shown in Figure 37. The ellipse (…) button appears to select contract. Click on that button.

Figure 37. Selecting the contract element

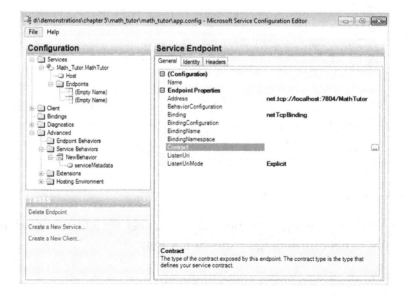

Step 15: Locate the Dll of the service and click on Open button as shown in Figure 38. The wizard automatically selects the contract as there is only one service contract as shown in Figure 39. Select the contract and click on the Open button. Another endpoint having netTcpBinding appears on the screen as shown in Figure 40.

After adding this endpoint the configuration file looks like as shown in Example 17.

Example 17. App.Config file after adding netTcpBinding:

```
<?xml version="1.0" encoding="utf-8" ?>
<configuration>
    <system.serviceModel>
        <behaviors>
            <serviceBehaviors>
                <behavior name="NewBehavior">
                    <serviceMetadata httpGetEnabled="true"
/>
                </behavior>
            </serviceBehaviors>
```

Figure 38. Locating service Dll

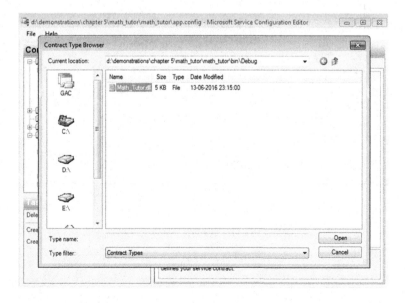

Figure 39. Extracted contract from Dll

Figure 40. Another endpoint having netTcpBinding in editor screen

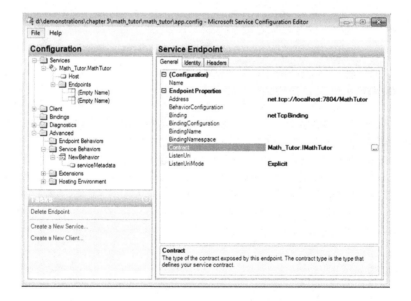

```
            </behaviors>
            <services>
                <service behaviorConfiguration="NewBehavior"
name="Math_Tutor.MathTutor">
                    <endpoint address=""
binding="basicHttpBinding" bindingConfiguration=""
                        contract="Math_Tutor.IMathTutor" />
                    <endpoint address="net.tcp://localhost:7804/
MathTutor" binding="netTcpBinding"bindingConfiguration=""
contract="Math_Tutor.IMathTutor" />
                    <host>
                        <baseAddresses>
                            <add baseAddress="http://local-
host:7802/MathTutor" />
                        </baseAddresses>
                    </host>
                </service>
            </services>
        </system.serviceModel>
</configuration>
```

Step 16: Add the third endpoint having wsHttpBinding by using similar steps which were used to add endpoint having netTcpBinding. These steps are exactly same except the binding name which must be changed as wsHttpBinding from default basicHttpBinding and therefore not explained again here. Provide endpoint address as http address. Click on File->Save menu of Service Configuration editor and close it to return to the visual studio scree. After adding all three endpoints the configuration file looks like as shown in Example 18.

Example 18. Configurations file after adding all three endpoints:

```
<?xml version="1.0" encoding="utf-8" ?>
<configuration>
  <system.serviceModel>
    <behaviors>
      <serviceBehaviors>
        <behavior name="NewBehavior">
          <serviceMetadata httpGetEnabled="true" />
```

159

```
        </behavior>
      </serviceBehaviors>
    </behaviors>
    <services>
      <service behaviorConfiguration="NewBehavi
or" name="Math_Tutor.IMathTutor"><endpoint address=""
binding="basicHttpBinding" bindingConfiguration=""contra
ct= "Math_Tutor.IMathTutor" /><endpoint address="net.tcp://
localhost:7804/MathTutor" binding="netTcpBinding"bindingCon
figuration="" contract="Math_Tutor.IMathTutor" /><endpoint
address= "http://localhost:7803/MathTutor" binding= "wsHttp-
Binding" bindingConfiguration="" contract="Math_Tutor.IMath-
Tutor" />
        <host>
          <baseAddresses>
            <add baseAddress="http://localhost:7802/MathTu-
tor" />
          </baseAddresses>
        </host>
      </service>
    </services>
  </system.serviceModel>
</configuration>
```

Step 17: Now host project (console application) is ready compile it to generate the.EXE of this project. Locate the.EXE file and run it as Administrator privilege because of windows security feature as shown in Figure 41.

The output is shown in Figure 42. As shown in Figure 42 the host program is running. Now create the.NET client to consume this service.

Step 18: Create the window forms project by using the steps mentioned in Chapter 3. Design the layout of the client program as shown in Figure 43.

Step 19: Add the reference of service WSDL by using Add Service reference option as discussed in Chapter 3. So these steps are not repeated here. On the client side the configuration file including client tag is generated after completing the steps. This file is very important when service has more than one endpoint. The content of App. Config of the client program is shown in Example 19.

Figure 41. Running console application project using Administrator privilege

Computer ▸ Local Disk (D:) ▸ Demonstrations ▸ Chapter 5 ▸ Ma
File Edit View Tools Help
Organize ▾ Open Burn New folder
Name
Type
Size
Math_Tutor.dll
Application extens...
5 KB
Math_Tutor.pdb
Program Debug D...
12 KB
Math_Tutor_Conso
Math_Tutor_Conso
Math_Tutor_Conso
Math_Tutor_Conso
Open
Run as administrator
Troubleshoot compatibility
Scan with 360 Total Security
Run in 360 Sandbox
Add to archive...
Add to "Math_Tutor_Console_Host.rar"
Compress and email...
Compress to "Math_Tutor_Console_Host.rar" and email
Pin to Taskbar
Pin to Start Menu
Restore previous versions
Send to
Cut
Copy
Create shortcut
Delete
Rename
Properties

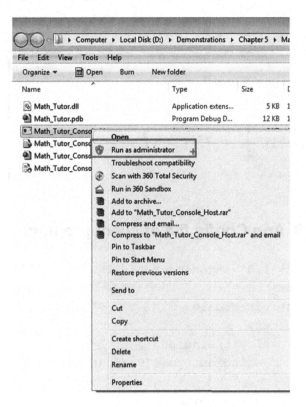

Figure 42. Output of host program

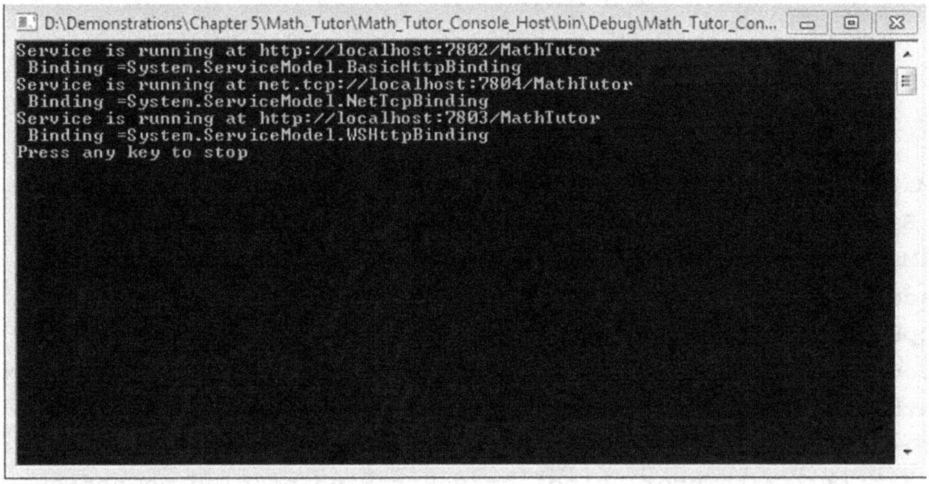

D:\Demonstrations\Chapter 5\Math_Tutor\Math_Tutor_Console_Host\bin\Debug\Math_Tutor_Con...
Service is running at http://localhost:7802/MathTutor
Binding =System.ServiceModel.BasicHttpBinding
Service is running at net.tcp://localhost:7804/MathTutor
Binding =System.ServiceModel.NetTcpBinding
Service is running at http://localhost:7803/MathTutor
Binding =System.ServiceModel.WSHttpBinding
Press any key to stop

Figure 43. Designing controls at client project

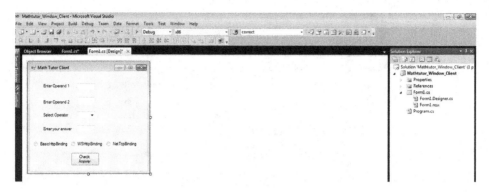

Example 19. App.Config file of client program:

```
<?xml version="1.0" encoding="utf-8" ?>
<configuration>
    <system.serviceModel>
        <bindings>
            <basicHttpBinding>
                <binding name="BasicHttpBinding_IMathTutor"
/>
            </basicHttpBinding>
            <netTcpBinding>
                <binding name="NetTcpBinding_IMathTutor" />
            </netTcpBinding>
            <wsHttpBinding>
                <binding name="WSHttpBinding_IMathTutor" />
            </wsHttpBinding>
        </bindings>
            <client><endpoint address="http://localhost:7802/
MathTutor" binding="basicHttpBinding"bindingConfiguration=
"BasicHttpBinding_IMathTutor" contract="Mathtutor_Client.
IMathTutor"name="BasicHttpBinding_IMathTutor" /><endpoint
address="net.tcp://localhost:7804/MathTutor" binding="netT
cpBinding"bindingConfiguration="NetTcpBinding_IMathTutor"
contract="Mathtutor_Client.IMathTutor"name="NetTcpBinding_IM
athTutor"><identity><userPrincipalName value="india1\india"
/></identity></endpoint><endpoint address="http://local-
host:7803/MathTutor" binding="wsHttpBinding"bindingConfigura
```

```
tion="WSHttpBinding_IMathTutor" contract="Mathtutor_Client.
IMathTutor"name="WSHttpBinding_IMathTutor"><identity><userPr
incipalName value="india1\india" /></identity></endpoint></
client>
    </system.serviceModel>
</configuration>
```

As shown in Example 19, there are three <endpoint> tags under <client> node. Every endpoint has name element. This name is useful in code while consuming the service using that particular name. Therefore, in the constructor of the proxy class the name of endpoint can be specified to communicate through that endpoint. For instance, the endpoint name WSHttpBinding_IMathTutor can be provided as parameter to the proxy class to communicate with the enpoint having wsHttpBinding.

The code of the client program is mentioned in Example 20.

Example 20. Code of Client Program

```
using System;
using System.Collections.Generic;
using System.ComponentModel;
using System.Data;
using System.Drawing;
using System.Linq;
using System.Text;
using System.Windows.Forms;
using Mathtutor_Window_Client.Mathtutor_Client;
namespace Mathtutor_Window_Client
{
    public partial class frmMathTutor: Form
    {
        public frmMathTutor()
        {
            InitializeComponent();
        }
        private void btnCheckAnswer_Click(object sender,
EventArgs e)
        {
            int operand1, operand2;
            //fetching the values of operand1 and operand 2
```

```
            operand1 = Int16.Parse(tbOperand1.Text);
            operand2 = Int16.Parse(tbOperand2.Text);
            //Selecting value of operator from combo box
            String math_operator = cbOperator.SelectedItem.
ToString();
            //Fetching value of user answer
            int user_answer = Int16.Parse(tbUser_Ans.Text);
            String endpoint_name = null;
           // Checking which binding is selected
            if (rbBasicHttpBinding.Checked == true)  //if
basic http binding is selected
                endpoint_name = "BasicHttpBinding_IMathTu-
tor";
            else if (rbWSHttpBinding.Checked == true) // if
ws http binding is selected
                endpoint_name = "WSHttpBinding_IMathTutor";
            else                                        // if
net tcp binding is selected
                endpoint_name = "NetTcpBinding_IMathTutor";
            Boolean ans;
            MathTutorClient proxy = new
MathTutorClient(endpoint_name);
            ans = proxy.Check_Answer(operand1, operand2,
math_operator, user_answer);
            String msg = "Your answer is";
            if (ans == true)
                msg = msg + " Correct";
            else
                msg = msg + " Incorrect";
            MessageBox.Show(msg);
        }
    }
}
```

Here in this code the radio button of related endpoint. Based on the selected binding the name of related endpoint is set from the App.Config file which shown in Example 19. Then the endpoint name is passed to the proxy class constructor which is highlighted. The client will communicate through that endpoint only.

Step 20: Now run the client program to view the output as shown in Figure 44 and Figure 45. As shown in Figure 44 the values of operands are provided, the operator is selected from the combo box and user answer is entered which is correct in this example. Then the NetTcpBinding is selected and Check Answer button is clicked. On the click event the name of endpoint having NetTcpBinding is passed in the proxy class constructor and output is shown in Figure 45. The program can be further tested by providing incorrect answer and selecting other binding it will provide similar output.

CONCLUSION

In this chapter, all the important bindings are explained in depth. The important points are mentioned below:

- Binding determines how to communicate. It decides protocol, message encoding and message communication patterns.
- A binding must match with the address format discussed in Chapter 4.
- BasicHttpBinding is not secured by default, but can be customized to provide security.

Figure 44. Output of client project – providing input values

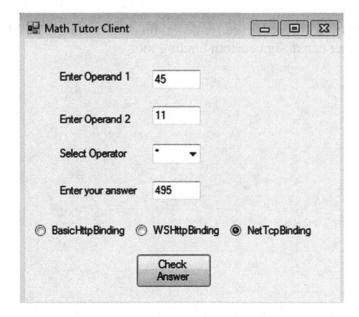

Figure 45. Output of client project – output with message box

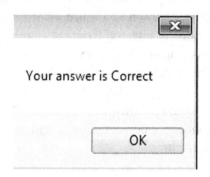

- All the bindings can be customized either using configuration file or code file.
- To customize the binding using configuration file XML tags are used.
- To customize the binding using code file, related class is available and we need to create the object of that class to customize that binding.
- Reliable session is enabled in WSDualHttpBinding and NetMsmqBinding and it cannot the disabled in these binding.
- For WSDualHttpBinding and NetMsmqBinding the service operations must be one way.
- NetTcpBinding is ideal for.NET to.NET communication i.e. WCF service and.NET client.
- NetTcpBinding and NetMsmqBinding are connection oriented bindings.
- Apart from the predefined (build-in) bindings available in WCF, a programmer can design custom binding too.

Chapter 6
Working with Contracts

This chapter dives you deep into the last element of endpoint which is contract. It contains in depth understanding of various contracts available in WCF.

After completing this chapter, you will be able to:

- Gain understanding about contracts available in WCF.
- Understand the importance of using contracts
- Learn practical implementation of each contract.

INTRODUCTION TO CONTRACTS

A contract is similar to the real life contract we sign. In WCF it is an agreement between client and service to restrict the boundary of the service operations. It is also important to know about contract as it is related serialization too. A service and client must agree on contract for communication to happen. There are mainly three types of contracts available in WCF: Service Contract,

DOI: 10.4018/978-1-5225-1997-3.ch006

Data Contract and Message Contract. Each of these contracts is explained in details in the following sections.

Service Contract

A service contract contains a list of operations made available to the client. It also defines:

- Message pattern (Oneway, request-reply, duplex)
- Protocol and serialization format
- Datatype of the operations
- Grouping of the operations

A service contract is represented by [ServiceContract] annotation. The operations are labelled as [OperationContract] annotation. The example of service contract is shown in Example 1.

Example 1. Example of Service Contract

```
[ServiceContract]
public interface ICalculator
{
    [OperationContract]
    int add(int no1, int no2);
    [OperationContract]
    int sub(int no1, int no2);
    [OperationContract]
    int mul(int no1, int no2);
    [OperationContract]
    int div(int no1, int no2);
}
```

It is required to have at least [OperationContract]. The operations having a label [OperationContract] are available to the client. The code in Example 1 is re-written again after removing [OperationContract] from several operations as shown in Example 2.

Example 2. Service Contract After Removing [OperationContract] From Some

```
                    Operations:
[ServiceContract]
 public interface ICalculator
 {
      int add(int no1, int no2);
      [OperationContract]
      int sub(int no1, int no2);
      int mul(int no1, int no2);
      [OperationContract]
      int div(int no1, int no2);
 }
```

As shown in Example 2, the operations add and mul are not having a label [OperationContract] so a client program cannot consume these methods The [ServiceContract] is generally an interface and it must be implemented by a service class as it is interface. The implementation of service contract of Example 1 is shown in Example 3.

Example 3. Implementation of Service Contract using Service Class

```
public class Calculator: ICalculator
{
        public int add(int no1, int no2)
        {
            return no1 + no2;
        }
        public int sub(int no1, int no2)
        {
            return no1 - no2;
        }
        public int mul(int no1, int no2)
        {
            return no1*no2;
        }
        public int div(int no1, int no2)
        {
```

```
        return no1 / no2;
    }
}
```

A class can work as [ServiceContract] too. In this situation interface is not required and a class must be labelled [ServiceContract]. The example of a class being a [ServiceContract] is depicted in Example 4.

Example 4. Class as Service Contract

```
[ServiceContract]
public class Calculator
{
        [OperationContract]
    public int add(int no1, int no2)
      {
            return no1 + no2;
      }
      [OperationContract]
    public int sub(int no1, int no2)
      {
            return no1 - no2;
      }


        [OperationContract]
    public int mul(int no1, int no2)
      {
            return no1*no2;
      }
      [OperationContract]
    public int div(int no1, int no2)
      {
            return no1 / no2;
      }
}
```

In this example no interface is required and class behaves like a service contract and service class both. Therefore while creating a configuration file you need to provide contract as class name and service name as class name too. The way provided in Example 4 leads to ambiguity and it is not a better programming practice to directly write the code without interface, this method of programming should be avoided. So we will not use the method presented in Example 4. A service contract has several parameters which is discussed in section below.

PARAMETERS OF [SERVICE CONTRACT]

The attribute [ServiceContract] comes from the class System.ServiceModel. ServiceContractAttribute. The [ServiceContract] attribute contains several parameters which can be written like a method parameters. More than parameters can be applied to this attribute in any order. Following are different parameters available for this attribute:

- CallbackContract
- ConfigurationName
- Name
- Namespace
- ProtectionLevel
- SessionMode

Each parameter is explained in details in following sections.

CallbackContract

This parameter is used for duplex communication. It is the value of the call back contract interface which must be implemented as client side. It requires type of the interface so typeof operator is required while specifying its value. Default value of this parameter is null. The example of this parameter is shown in Example 5.

Example 5. CallbackContract Parameter Example

```
[ServiceContract (CallbackContract=
typeof(IClientCallback))]
public interface ICalculator
{
    . . . .
    . . . .
```

```
}
[ServiceContract]
public interface IClientCallback
{
        . . . .
        . . . .
}
```

As shown in Example 5, the type of operator is applied which takes an interface name as value of CallbackContract. This interface must be defined in the code as shown below the first [ServiceContract]. The call back interface IClientCallback is defined in the service program, but it must be implemented by a client. The practical implementation is of duplex communication is explained in Chapter 7.

ConfigurationName

This parameter is used to change the reference of the name of the contract in the configuration file. The data type of this parameter is a string. If it is not specified, then the default value is fully qualified name of the [ServiceContract] i.e. namespace.servicecontract name. The code snippet of changing the configuration name is shown in Example 6.

Example 6. Changing the Configuration Name of Service Contract

```
[ServiceContract (ConfigurationName="Calc")]
 public interface ICalculator
{
        ….. .
        ….. .
}
```

Now the code snippet of configuration file (App.Config) of host program is shown in Example 7 in which the contract name is not changed.

Example 7. Code Snippet of App.Config of the Host Program

```
<service behaviorConfiguration="NewBehavior"
name="FirstWCFService_Calc.Calculator">
```

```
                <endpoint address=""
binding="basicHttpBinding" bindingConfiguration=""
contract="FirstWCFService_Calc.ICalculator"/>
                <host>
                    <baseAddresses>
                        <add baseAddress="http://local-
host:9087/CalculatorDemo"/>
                    </baseAddresses>
                </host>
</service>
```

Now keeping the same name which is highlighted in above example, results an error such as:

The contract name 'FirstWCFService_Calc.ICalculator' could not be found in the list of contracts implemented by the service 'Calculator

This error occurred because because we provided the value of parameter ConfigurationName to Calc so in the configuration file now contract name should be referred as on Calc without namespace name as shown in the updated code snippet of App.Config file of the host program in Example 8.

Example 8. Code Snippet of the Updated App.Config File of Host Program

```
<service behaviorConfiguration="NewBehavior"
name="FirstWCFService_Calc.Calculator">
            <endpoint address="" binding="basicHttpBinding"
bindingConfiguration="" contract="Calc"/>
                <host>
                    <baseAddresses>
                        <add baseAddress="http://local-
host:9087/CalculatorDemo"/>
                    </baseAddresses>
                </host>
 </service>
```

Name

This parameter is used to change the name of <portType> element in the WSDL file while service is hosted. The default value is the name of the interface. The data type is a String which can be any user defined value. The code snippet of specifying this parameter is shown in Example 9.

Example 9. Code Snippet to Specifying Name Parameter

```
[ServiceContract (Name="NewCalc_Name")]
public interface ICalculator
{
        ….

        ….

}
```

After applying this parameter the value in the <portType> element in WSDL file is changed to the new name NewCalc_Name which is depicted in the code snippet of WSDL file in Example 10.

Example 10. The Code Snippet of WSDL Showing <portType> Element

```
<wsdl:portType name="NewCalc_Name">
- <wsdl:operation name="add">
  <wsdl:input wsaw:Action="http://tempuri.org/NewCalc_Name/
add" message="tns:NewCalc_Name_add_InputMessage" />
  <wsdl:output wsaw:Action="http://tempuri.org/NewCalc_Name/
addResponse" message="tns:NewCalc_Name_add_OutputMessage" />
  </wsdl:operation>
- <wsdl:operation name="sub">
  <wsdl:input wsaw:Action="http://tempuri.org/NewCalc_Name/
sub" message="tns:NewCalc_Name_sub_InputMessage" />
  <wsdl:output wsaw:Action="http://tempuri.org/NewCalc_Name/
subResponse" message="tns:NewCalc_Name_sub_OutputMessage" />
  </wsdl:operation>
- <wsdl:operation name="mul">
  <wsdl:input wsaw:Action="http://tempuri.org/NewCalc_Name/
mul" message="tns:NewCalc_Name_mul_InputMessage" />
  <wsdl:output wsaw:Action="http://tempuri.org/NewCalc_Name/
mulResponse" message="tns:NewCalc_Name_mul_OutputMessage" />
  </wsdl:operation>
- <wsdl:operation name="div">
  <wsdl:input wsaw:Action="http://tempuri.org/NewCalc_Name/
```

```
div" message="tns:NewCalc_Name_div_InputMessage" />
  <wsdl:output wsaw:Action="http://tempuri.org/NewCalc_Name/
divResponse" message="tns:NewCalc_Name_div_OutputMessage" />
  </wsdl:operation>
  </wsdl:portType>
```

Namespace

This parameter is used to change the namespace name in the WSDL file. The datatype of this parameter is string. The default value of this parameter is http://temuri.org. The code snippet of applying this parameter is illustrated in Example 11.

Example 11. Code snippet to change the Namespace:

```
[ServiceContract(Namespace = "http://www.techzusiastic.
com")]
public interface ICalculator
{
        ….
        ….
}
```

ProtectionLevel

This parameter specifies the protection level of the service contract. It secures the message based of the value of these parameters. The value of this parameter comes from System.Net.Security.ProtectionLevel enum. It has three values as discussed below:

- None: It does authentication only. No other security mechanisms are applied.
- Encrypt and Sign: It provides integrity and confidentiality of the data transmitted over the wire. So the data is encrypted.
- Sign: It ensures integrity of the data sent over the wire but does not provide encryption.

The value of this parameter is applied in the hierarchical manner as [OperationContract] also has this parameter. The value specified at the level is considered as the default value of the [OperationContract] if there is no value provided at [OperationContract] level.

The default value of this parameter depends on the binding. If the value of this parameter is not given and binding supports security, then the default value is EncryptAndSign. If the value of this parameter is not given and binding does not support security, then the default value is set as None. The code snippet of setting this parameter is shown in Example 12.

Example 12. Code Snippet to Apply ProtectionLevel Parameter

```
[ServiceContract(ProtectionLevel=System.Net.Security.Protec-
tionLevel.Sign)]
public interface ICalculator
{
        ….
        ….
}
```

In above example the value of the parameter is set as System.Net.Security. ProtectionLevel.Sign so it provides integrity only.

SessionMode

This parameter is used to ensure whether the contract supports reliable session or not. The value of this parameter comes from SessionMode enum. It contains three values as discussed below:

- **Allowed:** Allows reliable sessions if the binding supports reliable session and there is explicit request to establish the session.
- **Required:** It forces a contract to establish a reliable session at all time. An error is generated if the binding does not support reliable session. For example, setting value Require and in basicHttpBinding results in an error as basicHttpBinding does not support reliable session.
- **NotAllowed:** It never supports reliable session even the binding supports reliable session and there is a request to establish a session.

The code snippet of specifying this parameter is shown in Example 13.

Example 13. Code snippet to specify SessionMode parameter:

```
[ServiceContract(SessionMode = SessionMode.Required)]
public interface ICalculator
{
...
...
}
```

In above example the parameter value is set as SessionMode.Required which forces contract to establish reliable session at all time.

PARAMETERS OF [OPERATION CONTRACT]

The [OperationContract] attribute comes from System.ServiceModel.Operation ContractAttribute class. This attribute is a part of [ServiceContract] and it specifies the method that is to be exposed to the client. As discussed earlier the method not having the label [OperationContract] is not available to the client. Following are the parameters of [OperationContract] attribute:

- Name
- IsOneWay
- Action
- ReplyAction
- AsyncPattern
- IsInitiating
- IsTerminating
- ProtectionLevel

These parameters can be used in any order and more than parameters can be provided. Each parameter is explained in details in the following section.

Name

This parameter changes the name of the <operation name> element in the WSDL file. When overloaded operations are used, WCF does not support to have same name in WSDL. It generates an error while hosting the service. So it is required to use a Name parameter on the operations having the same name. The data type of this parameter is a string and the default value is the name of the operation. The code snippet of this specifying this parameter is shown in Example 14.

Example 14. Specifying the Name Parameter of [OperationContract]

```
[ServiceContract]
public interface ICalculator
{
        [OperationContract (Name="Addition")]
        int add(int no1, int no2);
        [OperationContract]
        int add(int no1, int no2, int no3);
        [OperationContract]
        int sub(int no1, int no2);
        [OperationContract]
        int mul(int no1, int no2);
        [OperationContract]
        int div(int no1, int no2);
}
```

As depicted in the above example, there are two operations having same name add. In the first add operation two parameters are passed and in another operation three parameters are passed. If we don't apply Name parameter on any of these operations, then error will be generated while hosting the service. Therefore the Name parameter is provided in the first [OperationContract] which takes two parameters. Now the service is hosted successfully and part of the WSDL file having <operation name> element is shown in Example 15.

Example 15. WSDL File Having <operation name> Element

```
...
- <wsdl:operation name="Addition">
  <wsdl:input wsaw:Action="http://tempuri.org/ICalculator/
Addition" message="tns:ICalculator_Addition_InputMessage" />
  <wsdl:output wsaw:Action="http://tempuri.org/ICalculator/
AdditionResponse" message="tns:ICalculator_Addition_Output-
Message" />
  </wsdl:operation>
- <wsdl:operation name="add">
```

```
<wsdl:input wsaw:Action="http://tempuri.org/ICalculator/
add" message="tns:ICalculator_add_InputMessage" />
  <wsdl:output wsaw:Action
```

As shown in above example the name of first operation is changed to Addition in the <wsdl:operation name> and the second operation name is as it which is highlighted in Example 15.

IsOneWay

This parameter determines whether the operation is one way or request reply. The date type of this parameter is boolean which take either true or false value. The default value of this parameter is false.So by default all the operations in WCF are request reply. The code snippet example is shown in Example 16.

Example 16. Example of One Way Operations

```
[ServiceContract]
public interface IJobPlacement
{

        [OperationContract (IsOneWay=false)]
        Boolean Login(String username);
        [OperationContract (IsOneWay=true)]
        void display_jobs();
        [OperationContract]
        void apply_for_job(String username);
}
```

In the above example, there are three operations. In the first operation IsOneWay is set to false which means that the operation is request-reply. In the second operation IsOneWay is set to true which indicates that the operation is one way. In the third operation no parameter is specified, so this operation is considered as a request-reply by default even the return type of the operation is void. So in above example first and third operations are similar as both are request reply.

It is important to note that the one way operations must have a void return type but operations having void return type are not one way if IsOneway is not set to true on them. Therefore, to declare any operation as one way it is compulsory to set IsOneWay=true as parameter of [OperationContract]. The code snippet in the Example 17 results in an error while hosting the service.

Example 17. Oneway Operation with Return Type

```
{

        [OperationContract (IsOneWay=true)]
        Boolean Login(String username);
}
```

In the above code the operation is set as one way, but the return type of the operation is a Boolean which is invalid as operation returns nothing so it must be void.

The major problem with one way operation is that client does not have to wait for the reply so there is no acknowledgement on whether the service has completed the operation or not.

Action

It is used to change the value of action element of the action property of <input> tag of operation in the WSDL file. The data type of this parameter is a string. Default value is formed by namespace name and operation name. The code snippet to apply this parameter is illustrated in Example 18.

Example 18. Code Snippet to Apply Action Parameter

```
[ServiceContract]
public interface ICalculator
{
        [OperationContract (Name="Addition",Action="http://
www.google.com")]
        int add(int no1, int no2);
}
```

After setting the value of this parameter the value of action element the <input> tag is changed to http://www.google.com as depicted in part of WSDL file in Example 19.

Example 19. Part of WSDL file having input tag and action element:

```
<wsdl:operation name="Addition">
<wsdl:input wsaw:Action="http://www.google.com"
message="tns:ICalculator_Addition_InputMessage" />
<wsdl:output wsaw:Action="http://tempuri.org/ICalculator/Ad-
ditionResponse" message="tns:ICalculator_Addition_OutputMes-
sage" />
</wsdl:operation>
```

ReplyAction

It is used to change the value of action element of the <output> tag of operation in the WSDL file. The data type of this parameter is a string. Default
value is formed by name space name and operation name. The code snippet
to apply this parameter is illustrated in Example 20

Example 20. Code Snippet to Apply ReplyAction Parameter

```
[ServiceContract]
public interface ICalculator
{
        [OperationContract (Name="Addition",ReplyAction="ht
tp://www.google.com")]
        int add(int no1, int no2);
}
```

After setting the value of this parameter the value of action element the
<output> tag is changed to http://www.google.com as depicted in part of
WSDL file in Example 21.

Example 21. Part of WSDL file having output tag and action element

```
<wsdl:portType name="ICalculator">
<wsdl:operation name="Addition">
<wsdl:input wsaw:Action="http://tempuri.org/ICalculator/Ad-
dition" message="tns:ICalculator_Addition_InputMessage" />
  <wsdl:output wsaw:Action="http://www.google.com"
```

```
message="tns:ICalculator_Addition_OutputMessage" />
   </wsdl:operation>
```

AsyncPattern

This parameter is used for asynchronous operations. The data type of this parameter is Boolean. The default value of this parameter is false. The asynchronous operations have pair of Begin and End methods. The begin method must have related end method. The WCF forwards incoming message to Begin method first, then the results of End method are forwarded to outbound message. For asynchronous communication to work AsyncPattern value must be set to true as illustrated in the code snippet in Example 22.

Example 22. Code Snippet to Specify ASyncPattern

```
[ServiceContract]
public interface IJobPlacement
{
        [OperationContract]
        IAsyncResult BeginRegister(String username, String
password, String email,
        AsyncCallback cb, object state);
        void Endregister(IAsyncResult iar);
}
```

As shown in the above example the Begin method has two additional parameters. The result of Begin method is stored in IAsyncResult object which is passed to the End method to return the result.

IsInitiating

This parameter is useful while implementing the reliable sessions. It determines that whether the operation is the first operation to be called while initiating the session. The data type of this parameter is Boolean. The default value of this parameter is False. To use this parameter it is required to use the binding which supports the reliable session. It is important to note that SessionMode parameter of [ServiceContract] is also required. The code snippet of applying this parameter is illustrated in Example 23.

Example 23. Code Snippet of Applying IsInitiating Parameter

```
[ServiceContract (SessionMode=SessionMode.Required)]
public interface IJobPlacement
{
        [OperationContract (IsInitiating=true)]String
register(String username, String password, String email);
        [OperationContract (IsTerminating=false)]
        void Login(String username);
        [OperationContract (IsTerminating=false)]
        void display_jobs();
        [OperationContract (IsTerminating=true)]
        void apply_for_job(String username);
}
```

In above example the operation register must be called first by the client program as it is initiating operation.

IsTerminating

This parameter is useful while implementing the reliable sessions. It determines that whether the operation is the last operation to be called during the session termination. The data type of this parameter is Boolean. The default value of this parameter is False. To use this parameter, it is required to use the binding which supports the reliable session. It is important to note that SessionMode parameter of [ServiceContract] is also required. The code snippet of applying this parameter is illustrated in Example 24.

Example 24. Code Snippet of Applying IsTerminating Parameter

```
[ServiceContract (SessionMode=SessionMode.Required)]
public interface IJobPlacement
{
        [OperationContract (IsInitiating=true)]
        String register(String username, String password,
String email);
        [OperationContract (IsTerminating=false)]
        void Login(String username);
        [OperationContract (IsTerminating=false)]
```

```
        void display_jobs();
        [OperationContract (IsTerminating=true)]void apply_
for_job(String username);
}
```

In above example the operation apply_for_job must be called by the client program during session termination as is it terminating operation. No other operation should be called after calling the apply_for_job operation.

ProtectionLevel

This parameter specifies the protection level of the operation contract. The value comes from System.Net.Security.ProtectionLevel enum. It has three values as discussed below:

- **None:** It does authentication only. No other security mechanisms are applied.
- **Encrypt and Sign:** It provides integrity and confidentiality of the data transmitted over the wire. So data is encrypted.
- **Sign:** It ensures integrity of the data sent over the wire but does not provide encryption.

The value is this parameter is applied in the hierarchical manner as [ServiceContract] also has this parameter. If the service contract provides the value of ProtectionLevel and operation contract does provide value the value of service contract is considered as default value of that operation. The code snippet of applying this parameter is illustrated in Example 25.

Example 25. Applying ProtectionLevel Parameters

```
[ServiceContract (ProtectionLevel=System.Net.Security.Pro-
tectionLevel.Sign)]
public interface IJobPlacement
{
    [OperationContract(ProtectionLevel = System.Net.Secu-
rity.ProtectionLevel.EncryptAndSign)]
    String register(String username, String password,
String email);
        [OperationContract (ProtectionLevel=System.Net.Secu-
rity.ProtectionLevel.EncryptAndSign)]
```

```
        void Login(String username);
        [OperationContract]
        void display_jobs();
}
```

As shown in the above example ProtectionLevel parameter is provided in first two operations as EncryptAndSign so for this function the value of ProtectionLevel parameter is considered as EncryptAndSign. In the third operation this parameter is not applied so the default value is taken from the value of ProtectionLevel parameter of [ServiceContract] which is Sign in this example. Therefore the default value of the third operation is considered as ProtectionLevel.Sign.

DATA CONTRACT

A data contract is used to serialize the data type which is not available in.NET. It comes from System.Runtime.Serialization.DataContractAttribute class. The default serializer engine in WCF is DataContractSerializer engine while in web service the XmlSerializerFormat engine is used. It is written as [DataContract] on the top of the type which is to be declared as data contract. The concept of serialization and deserialization is well explained in Chapter 1. So when a user defined/complex data type such as class or enum is used, it must be declared as data contract. It is also important to note that when the complex type is specified as parameter or return type of the operation, then only data contract is required otherwise it is not required to declare the complex type as data contract. The code snippet in Example 26 illustrates the syntax of specifying data contract in the code.

Example 26. Specifying Data Contract

```
[ServiceContract]
public interface IStudRecord
{
        [OperationContract]
        void insert_stud(Student stud);
        [OperationContract]
        Student find_stud(String stud_id);

}
```

```
[DataContract]
public class Student
{
        [DataMember]
        String stud_id;
        [DataMember]
        String stud_name;
        [DataMember]
        int semester;
        [DataMember]
        String Branch;
}
```

In the above example, there are two operations. In the first operation Student class is passed as parameter and in second operation Student class is the return type. Here Student class in the.NET data so it must be created first and labelled as [DataContract]. Please note that the elements inside the [DataContract] class must be labelled as [DataMember] otherwise the elements not having a label [DataMember] are not serialized and will be included in the request (SOAP) and response (SOAP).

PARAMETERS OF [DATA CONTRACT] ATTRIBUTE

[DataContract] has few parameters available. The important parameters are listed below:

• Name
• NameSpace

These parameters are well explained in below sections.

Name

This parameter is used to represent the name of data contract in the request and response. The data type of this parameter is a string. Default value is the name of the class. The snippet to apply is parameter is depicted in Example 27.

Example 27. Apply Name Parameter to [DataContract]

```
[DataContract (Name="StudentData")]
public class Student
{
        [DataMember]
        public  String stud_id;
        [DataMember]
        public String stud_name;
        [DataMember]
        public int semester;
        [DataMember]
      public  String Branch;
}
```

NameSpace

It is used to change the URI of the namespace of the data contract. The data type of this parameter is string. Default value is the CLR namespace i.e. http://schemas.datacontract.org/2004/07. The snippet to use this parameter is shown in Example 28.

Example 28. Applying NameSpace Parameter:

```
[DataContract(Name = "StudentData", Namespace = "www.techzu-
siastic.com")]
public class Student
{
        [DataMember]
        public  String stud_id;
        [DataMember]
        public String stud_name;
        [DataMember]
        public int semester;
        [DataMember]
       public  String Branch;
}
```

PARAMETERS OF [DATA MEMBER] ATTRIBUTE

The [DataMember] attribute is used to specify whether to serialize the element of [DataContract] or not. Just like [DataContract] it also has several parameters to customize it. The important parameters are listed below:

- Name
- Order
- EmitDefaultValue
- IsRequired

In the following section each parameters are explained in details.

Name

It is used to change the name of the data member. The data type of this parameter is string. Default value of this parameter is name of the data member. The code snippet to change the name of a data member using this parameter is shown in Example 29.

Example 29. Changing the Name of Data Member

```
[DataContract]
public class Student
{
        [DataMember (Name="Student ID")]
        public  String stud_id;
        [DataMember (Name="Student Name")]
        public String stud_name;
        [DataMember]
        public int semester;
        [DataMember]
        public  String Branch;
}
```

As shown in the above example, the Name parameter is applied in first two data members. So the name of the first data member is represented as Student ID and name of the second data member is represented as Student Name in the request and response. The names of other data member are not changed as Name parameter is not applied to them.

Order

This parameter is used to change the order of appearance of the data member in XML request and response. The data type of this parameter is an integer. If this parameter value is not specified, then the order is decided based on the ascending order of alphabets. The code snippet of XML request without changing the order property is shown in Example 30.

Example 30. XML Request without Changing the Order

```
<s:Body>
  <insert_stud xmlns="http://tempuri.org/">
    <stud xmlns:d4p1="http://schemas.datacontract.
org/2004/07/DataContractDemo" xmlns:i="http://www.
w3.org/2001/XMLSchema-instance">
      <d4p1:Branch i:nil="true" />
      <d4p1:semester>0</d4p1:semester>
      <d4p1:stud_id i:nil="true" />
      <d4p1:stud_name i:nil="true" />
    </stud>
  </insert_stud>
</s:Body>
```

As shown in above example the default order is ascending sequence of alphabet when Order parameter of [DataMember] is not specified. Now let us provide the Order parameter as shown in the Example 31.

Example 31. Specifying Order Parameter of [DataMember]

```
[DataContract]
public class Student
{
        [DataMember (Order=4)]
        public String stud_id;
        [DataMember (Order=6)]
        public String stud_name;
        [DataMember (Order=11)]
        public int semester;
        [DataMember (Order=25)]
        public String Branch;
```

```
}
```

In the above code the [DataMember] having lowest value will appear first in the XML request and response. It is not necessary to maintain the sequence or but it can be in ascending order. The lowest value of this parameter is the highest priority of putting that element first in the XML. The part of XML request after applying changes as per Example 10 is Shown in Example 32.

Example 32. Part of XML Request

```
<s:Body>
    <insert_stud xmlns="http://tempuri.org/">
        <stud xmlns:d4p1="http://schemas.datacontract.
org/2004/07/DataContractDemo" xmlns:i="http://www.
w3.org/2001/XMLSchema-instance">
            <d4p1:stud_id i:nil="true" />
            <d4p1:stud_name i:nil="true" />
            <d4p1:semester>0</d4p1:semester>
            <d4p1:Branch i:nil="true" />
        </stud>
    </insert_stud>
</s:Body>
```

As shown in Example 21 the stud_id element appears first as it was having the lowest value of the Order parameter and other elements appear in the similar manner. Following are the rules to remember while using this parameter:

- The value of the Order parameter must be non-negative.
- If more than one data members have same order, then order is decided based on the ascending order of the alphabets.

EmitDefaultValue

This parameter is used to determine whether the data member should be serialized or not when the default value of the member provide. This means if no value for that data member is provided by consuming the operation of the service this parameter can decide whether to serialize that member or not. The data type of this parameter is True. The default value of this parameter is True. So by default it will serialize all the members. Setting the value False will not serialize the members which are having default value i.e. no value is provided for that member. The code snippet for this parameter is illustrated in Example 33.

Example 33. Specifying the EmitDefaultValue

```
[DataContract]
    public class Student
    {
        [DataMember (EmitDefaultValue=false)]
        public String stud_id;
        [DataMember (EmitDefaultValue=false)]
        public String stud_name;
        [DataMember]
        public int semester;
        [DataMember]
        public String Branch;
    }
```

As shown in the above code the first two members will not be serialized if the client program keeps the default values of these members and other two members will be serialized even if client program keeps the default value of these members. So,this this client program we supplied the default value of all the parameters and XML request is generated based on these values which is illustrated in Example 34.

Example 34. XML Request after Applying EmitDefaultValue

```
<s:Body>
    <insert_stud xmlns="http://tempuri.org/">
        <stud xmlns:d4p1="http://schemas.datacontract.
org/2004/07/DataContractDemo" xmlns:i="http://www.
w3.org/2001/XMLSchema-instance">
            <d4p1:Branch i:nil="true" />
            <d4p1:semester>0</d4p1:semester>
        </stud>
    </insert_stud>
</s:Body>
```

The data members having a false value of EmitDefaultValue are not serialized and not included in the XML request in Example 33. The main purpose of this parameter is to reduce the size of XML file of request and reply. It is important to note that when no default value is provided there is no meaning of using this parameter. That means if non default value is provided, setting EmitDefaultValue to true or false does not matter.

IsRequired

This parameter is used to serialize the data member compulsorily. The data type of this parameter is a Boolean. The default value of this parameter is false. The code snippet to apply this parameter is shown in Example 35.

Example 35. Applying IsRequired Parameter:

```
[DataContract]
public class Student
{
        [DataMember (IsRequired=true)]
        public String stud_id;
}
```

In above example stud_id will be serialized and will be included in XML request and response file. A care should be take while using this parameter with EmitDefaultValue parameter. Setting EmitDefaultValue=false, IsRequired=true and providing default value of that data member generates following error:

Member stud_id in type DataContractDemo.Student cannot be serialized. This exception is usually caused by trying to use a null value where a null value is not allowed. The 'stud_id' member is set to its default value (usually null or zero). The member's EmitDefault setting is 'false', indicating that the member should not be serialized. However, the member's IsRequired setting is 'true', indicating that it must be serialized. This conflict cannot be resolved. Consider setting 'stud_id' to a non-default value. Alternatively, you can change the EmitDefaultValue property on the DataMemberAttribute attribute to true, or changing the IsRequired property to false.

PROGRAMMING [DATA CONTRACT]

In this section you will learn about how to create a WCF service which includes data contract. Then this service is hosted using console application project discussed earlier. A Windows Form application is created to consume the service. The steps are mentioned in following section.

Step 1: Create a WCF service library project and write the code of service contract as shown in Example 36.

Example 36. Code of service contract:

```
using System;
using System.Collections.Generic;
using System.Linq;
using System.Runtime.Serialization;
using System.ServiceModel;
using System.Text;
namespace DataContractDemo
{
    [ServiceContract]
    public interface IStudRecord
    {
        [OperationContract]
        void insert_stud(Student stud);
        [OperationContract]
        Student find_stud(String stud_id);
    }
    [DataContract]
    public class Student
    {
        [DataMember]
        public String stud_id;
        [DataMember]
        public String stud_name;
        [DataMember]
        public int semester;
        [DataMember]
        public String Branch;
```

```
    }
}
```

Step 2: Write the code of service class as depicted in Example 37.

Example 37. Code of service class as:

```
using System;
using System.Collections.Generic;
using System.Linq;
using System.Runtime.Serialization;
using System.ServiceModel;
using System.Text;
namespace DataContractDemo
{
    public class StudRecord: IStudRecord
    {
        List<Student> all_students = new List<Student>();
        public void insert_stud(Student stud)
        {
            all_students.Add(stud);
        }
        public Student find_stud(string stud_id)
        {
            Student found_stud = null;
            foreach (Student stud in all_students)
            {
                if (stud_id == stud.stud_id)
                {
                    found_stud = stud;
                    break;
                }
            }
            return found_stud;
        }
    }
}
```

In the insert_stud operation the new stud object is inserted in the generic list while in find_stud operation the student information is returned whose student id is provides as parameter.

Step 3: Design the console application by adding references of service and System.ServiceModel as discussed earlier. Write the code in Program. cs file as illustrated in Example 38. Also prepare the configuration file as illustrated in Example 39.

Example 38. Code of Program.cs

```
using System;
using System.Collections.Generic;
using System.Linq;
using System.Text;
using System.ServiceModel;
using DataContractDemo;
using System.ServiceModel.Description;
namespace DataContract_Host
{
    class Program
    {
        static void Main(string[] args)
        {
            ServiceHost host=new ServiceHost(typeof(StudReco
rd));
            host.Open();
            ServiceEndpoint endpoint=host.Description.End-
points[0];
            Console.WriteLine("Service is running at " + end-
point.Address);
            Console.WriteLine("Press any key to stop");
            Console.ReadKey();
            host.Close();
        }
    }
}
```

Example 39. Content of App.Config file:

```xml
<?xml version="1.0" encoding="utf-8" ?>
<configuration>
    <system.serviceModel>
        <behaviors>
            <serviceBehaviors>
                <behavior name="NewBehavior">
                    <serviceMetadata httpGetEnabled="true"
/>
                </behavior>
            </serviceBehaviors>
        </behaviors>
        <services>
            <service behaviorConfiguration="NewBehavior"
name="DataContractDemo.StudRecord">
                <endpoint address=""
binding="basicHttpBinding" bindingConfiguration=""
                    contract="DataContractDemo.IStudRecord"
/>
                <host>
                    <baseAddresses>
                        <add baseAddress="http://local-
host:8056/StudentService" />
                    </baseAddresses>
                </host>
            </service>
        </services>
    </system.serviceModel>
</configuration>
```

Step 4: Now host the service by locating the.EXE of the host project and providing administrator credentials. The output of hosting the service is shown in Figure 1. The WSDL file can be viewed in the browser by providing the URI of the base address. The WSDL file is shown in Example 40.

Figure 1. Output of host program

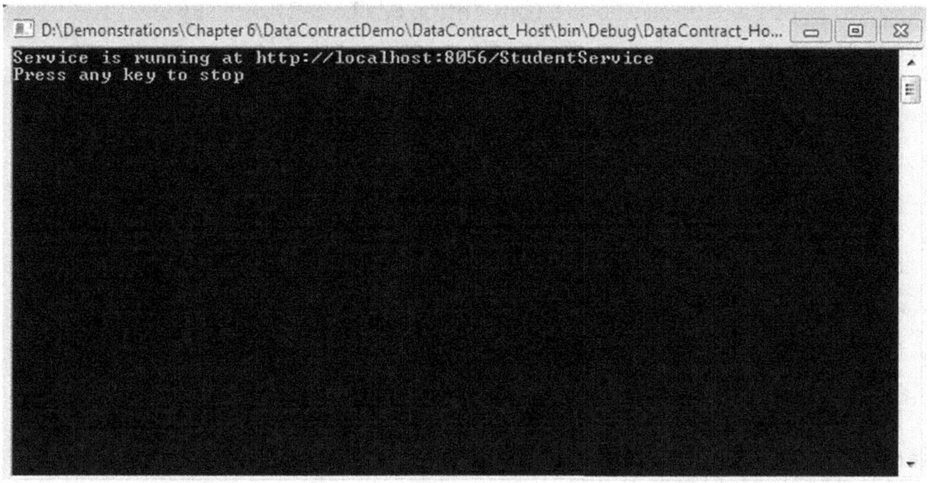

Example 40. Content of WSDL File:

```
<?xml version="1.0" encoding="utf-8" ?>
- <wsdl:definitions name="StudRecord"
targetNamespace="http://tempuri.org/" xmlns:wsdl="http://
schemas.xmlsoap.org/wsdl/" xmlns:soap="http://schemas.
xmlsoap.org/wsdl/soap/" xmlns:wsu="http://docs.oasis-
open.org/wss/2004/01/oasis-200401-wss-wssecurity-utili-
ty-1.0.xsd" xmlns:soapenc="http://schemas.xmlsoap.org/
soap/encoding/" xmlns:wsam="http://www.w3.org/2007/05/
addressing/metadata" xmlns:tns="http://tempuri.org/"
xmlns:wsa="http://schemas.xmlsoap.org/ws/2004/08/addressing"
xmlns:wsp="http://schemas.xmlsoap.org/ws/2004/09/policy"
xmlns:wsap="http://schemas.xmlsoap.org/ws/2004/08/address-
ing/policy" xmlns:xsd="http://www.w3.org/2001/XMLSchema"
xmlns:msc="http://schemas.microsoft.com/ws/2005/12/wsdl/
contract" xmlns:wsaw="http://www.w3.org/2006/05/address-
ing/wsdl" xmlns:soap12="http://schemas.xmlsoap.org/wsdl/
soap12/" xmlns:wsa10="http://www.w3.org/2005/08/addressing"
xmlns:wsx="http://schemas.xmlsoap.org/ws/2004/09/mex">
- <wsdl:types>
- <xsd:schema targetNamespace="http://tempuri.org/Imports">
  <xsd:import schemaLocation="http://localhost:8056/
```

```
StudentService?xsd=xsd0" namespace="http://tempuri.org/" />
  <xsd:import schemaLocation="http://localhost:8056/
StudentService?xsd=xsd1" namespace="http://schemas.micro-
soft.com/2003/10/Serialization/" />
  <xsd:import schemaLocation="http://localhost:8056/
StudentService?xsd=xsd2" namespace="http://schemas.datacon-
tract.org/2004/07/DataContractDemo" />
  </xsd:schema>
  </wsdl:types>
- <wsdl:message name="IStudRecord_insert_stud_InputMessage">
  <wsdl:part name="parameters" element="tns:insert_stud" />
  </wsdl:message>
- <wsdl:message name="IStudRecord_insert_stud_OutputMes-
sage">
  <wsdl:part name="parameters" element="tns:insert_studRe-
sponse" />
  </wsdl:message>
- <wsdl:message name="IStudRecord_find_stud_InputMessage">
  <wsdl:part name="parameters" element="tns:find_stud" />
  </wsdl:message>
- <wsdl:message name="IStudRecord_find_stud_OutputMessage">
  <wsdl:part name="parameters" element="tns:find_studRe-
sponse" />
  </wsdl:message>
- <wsdl:portType name="IStudRecord">
- <wsdl:operation name="insert_stud">
  <wsdl:input wsaw:Action="http://tempuri.org/IStudRecord/
insert_stud" message="tns:IStudRecord_insert_stud_InputMes-
sage" />
  <wsdl:output wsaw:Action="http://tempuri.org/IStudRecord/
insert_studResponse" message="tns:IStudRecord_insert_stud_
OutputMessage" />
  </wsdl:operation>
- <wsdl:operation name="find_stud">
  <wsdl:input wsaw:Action="http://tempuri.org/IStudRecord/
find_stud" message="tns:IStudRecord_find_stud_InputMessage"
/>
  <wsdl:output wsaw:Action="http://tempuri.org/IStudRecord/
find_studResponse" message="tns:IStudRecord_find_stud_Out-
putMessage" />
```

```
    </wsdl:operation>
    </wsdl:portType>
 -  <wsdl:binding name="BasicHttpBinding_IStudRecord"
 type="tns:IStudRecord">
    <soap:binding transport="http://schemas.xmlsoap.org/soap/
 http" />
 -  <wsdl:operation name="insert_stud">
    <soap:operation soapAction="http://tempuri.org/IStudRe-
 cord/insert_stud" style="document" />
 -  <wsdl:input>
    <soap:body use="literal" />
    </wsdl:input>
 -  <wsdl:output>
    <soap:body use="literal" />
    </wsdl:output>
    </wsdl:operation>
 -  <wsdl:operation name="find_stud">
    <soap:operation soapAction="http://tempuri.org/IStudRe-
 cord/find_stud" style="document" />
 -  <wsdl:input>
    <soap:body use="literal" />
    </wsdl:input>
 -  <wsdl:output>
    <soap:body use="literal" />
    </wsdl:output>
    </wsdl:operation>
    </wsdl:binding>
 -  <wsdl:service name="StudRecord">
 -  <wsdl:port name="BasicHttpBinding_IStudRecord"
 binding="tns:BasicHttpBinding_IStudRecord">
    <soap:address location="http://localhost:8056/StudentSer-
 vice" />
    </wsdl:port>
    </wsdl:service>
    </wsdl:definitions>
```

Step 5: Develop windows forms application project as client application and design the screen as shown in Figure 2. In this screen the form is designed for insert_student only. Similarly you can design the screen for another operation which left to the readers as self-study assignment.

Figure 2. Form design of client project

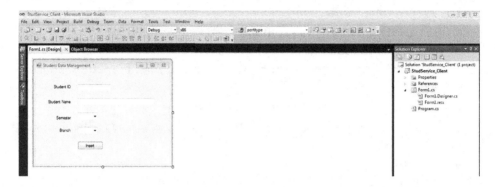

Step 6: Add the reference of service using Add Service option menu to generate the proxy class from the WSDL file. Write the code of client program as depicted in Example 41. The generated App.Config file at client program is shown in Example 42.

Example 41. Code of Client Program

```
using System;
using System.Collections.Generic;
using System.ComponentModel;
using System.Data;
using System.Drawing;
using System.Linq;
using System.Text;
using System.Windows.Forms;
using StudService_Client.Stud_ClientRef;
namespace StudService_Client
{
    public partial class frmStudManagement: Form
    {
        public frmStudManagement()
        {
            InitializeComponent();
        }
        private void btnInsert_Click(object sender, Even-
tArgs e)
        {
```

```
        Student stud = new Student();
        String stud_id = tbStudID.Text;
        String stud_name = tbStudName.Text;
        int sem = Convert.ToInt16(cbSemester.Select-
edItem.ToString());
        String branch = cbBranch.SelectedItem.To-
String();
        StudRecordClient proxy = new StudRecordClient("B
asicHttpBinding_IStudRecord");
        stud.stud_id = stud_id;
        stud.stud_name = stud_name;
        stud.semester = sem;
        stud.Branch = branch;
        proxy.insert_stud(stud);
    }
  }
}
```

Example 42. App.Config file of Client Program

```
<?xml version="1.0" encoding="utf-8" ?>
<configuration>
    <system.serviceModel>
        <bindings>
            <basicHttpBinding>
                <binding name="BasicHttpBinding_IStudRecord"
/>
            </basicHttpBinding>
        </bindings>
        <client>
            <endpoint address="http://localhost:8056/Stu-
dentService" binding="basicHttpBinding"
                bindingConfiguration="BasicHttpBinding_IStu-
dRecord" contract="Stud_ClientRef.IStudRecord"
                name="BasicHttpBinding_IStudRecord" />
        </client>
    </system.serviceModel>
</configuraion>
```

Step 7: Now compile the client program and run it after successful compilation. The output is depicted in Figure 3. Provide all the input value and click on the insert button. The system will not provide any reply and operation is void, but if no error is generated the record is inserted into local data structure of service program.

MESSAGE CONTRACT

A message contract is used to modify the header and body parts of the SOAP message. Use this attribute, if you need to have additional control over the SOAP otherwise data contract is sufficient in most of the applications. It comes from System.ServiceModel.MessageContractAttribute. To use the message contract return type and parameter of the operation must be message contract otherwise an error is generated while hosting the service. Just like data contract the attribute [MessageContract] is written on a user defined type. The element inside [MessageContract] class are labeled either [MessageHeader] or [MessageBodyMember]. The elements having [MessageHeader] label are placed as in the header part of SOAP request and reply while the elements having [MessageBodyMember] label are placed in the body part of the SOAP request and reply. The snippet of applying this attribute is illustrated in Example 43.

Figure 3. Output of client project

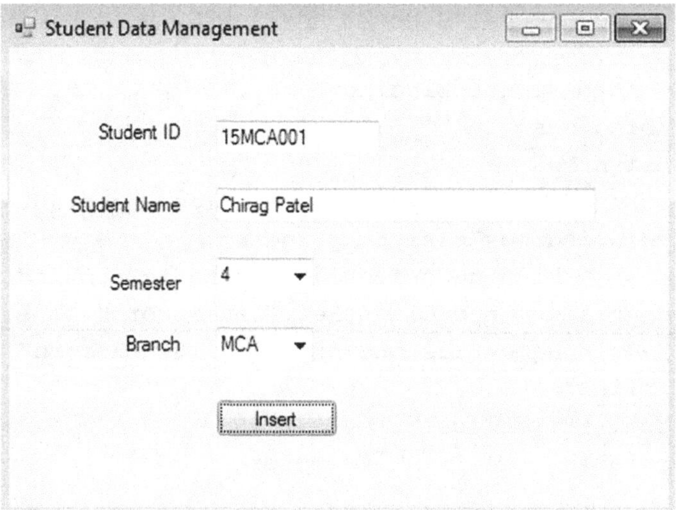

Example 43. Applying [MessageContract]

```
[ServiceContract]
public interface IStudRecord
{
        [OperationContract]
        Student insert_stud(Student stud);
}
[MessageContract ]
public class Student
{
        [MessageHeader ]
        public String stud_id;
        [MessageHeader]
        public String stud_name;
        [MessageBodyMember]
        public int semester;
        [MessageBodyMember]
        public String Branch;
}
```

As shown in above example the Student class is considered as [Message-Contract]. The return type and the parameter both are message contract as highlighted in Example 42. In this example first two elements stud_id and stud_name are labeled as [MesseageHeader] so the elements must be placed in the header part of the SOAP request and reply. Likewise the other two elements semester and Branch are labelled as [MessageBodyMember] so these elements must be placed in the body part of SOAP request and reply. The SOAP request, including [MessageContract] is shown in Example 44.

Example 44. SOAP Request

```
<s:Envelope xmlns:a="http://www.w3.org/2005/08/addressing"
xmlns:s="http://www.w3.org/2003/05/soap-envelope">
  <s:Header>
    <a:Action s:mustUnderstand="1">http://tempuri.org/IStu-
dRecord/insert_stud</a:Action>
    <h:stud_id xmlns:h="http://tempuri.org/">3</h:stud_
id><h:stud_name xmlns:h="http://tempuri.org/">adsfasd</
h:stud_name>
```

```
    <a:MessageID>urn:uuid:fd66158c-6281-487f-90af-
ee2a7f796f97</a:MessageID>
    <a:ReplyTo>
     <a:Address>http://www.w3.org/2005/08/addressing/
anonymous</a:Address>
    </a:ReplyTo>
  </s:Header>
  <s:Body>
    <Student xmlns="http://tempuri.org/">
      <Branch>mca</Branch><semester>5</semester>
    </Student>
  </s:Body>
</s:Envelope>
```

As expected the first two elements are placed in header and last two elements are placed in body part which is highlighted in Example 45.

PARAMETERS OF [MESSAGE CONTRACT]

[MessageContract] has few parameters and we have listed important parameter below:

- ProtectionLevel

  This parameter is explained in details in following section.

ProtectionLevel

This parameter specifies the protection level of the message contract. The value comes from System.Net.Security.ProtectionLevel enum. It has three values as discussed below:

- **None:** It does authentication only. No other security mechanisms are applied.
- **Encrypt and Sign:** It provides integrity and confidentiality of the data transmitted over the wire. So data is encrypted.
- **Sign:** It ensures the integrity of the data sent over the wire but does not provide encryption.

The value of this parameter is applied in the hierarchical manner as [MessageHeader] and [MessageBodyMember] also have this parameter. The value specified at the level is considered as the default value of these two elements there is no value provided at [MessageHeader] or [MessageBodyMember] level.

The default value of this parameter depends upon the binding. If the value of this parameter is not given and binding supports security, then the default value is EncryptAndSign. If the value of this parameter is not given and binding does not support security, then the default value is set as None. An error is generated if protection level is higher the security configured in binding. For example, setting the protection level EncryptAndSign in basicHttpBinding generates error as basicHttpBinding is not secured by default. The code snippet of setting this parameter is shown in Example 45.

Example 45. Specifying the ProtectionLevel Parameter

```
[MessageContract (ProtectionLevel=System.Net.Security.Pro-
tectionLevel.EncryptAndSign)]
public class Student
{
        [MessageHeader]
        public String stud_id;
        [MessageHeader]
        public String stud_name;
        [MessageBodyMember]
        public int semester;
        [MessageBodyMember]
        public String Branch;
}
```

PARAMETERS OF [MESSAGE HEADER]

The attribute [MessageHeader] is used to place the element in the header part of the request or response. It comes from System.ServiceModel.MessageHeaderAttribute. It has several parameters and these parameters can be applied in any order. Multiple parameters can be provided at the same time by using comma separator. The important parameters are listed below:

● Name

- NameSpace
- ProtectionLevel

Each of these parameters are presented in the following section with great details.

Name

This parameter is used to override the name of the element in the header part of the request or reply. The data type of this parameter is a string. The default value the name of the element. The code snippet to apply this parameter is depicted in Example 46.

Example 46. Applying Name Parameter

```
[MessageContract]
public class Student
{
        [MessageHeader (Name="Student_ID")]
        public String stud_id;
}
```

Now in the header element of SOAP request or reply Student_ID will appear instead of stud_id.

NameSpace

It is used to update the namespace in the header of SOAP request or reply. The data type of this parameter is a string. The default value of this parameter is the address provided by the CLR. The code snippet to apply this parameter is depicted in Example 47.

Example 47. Applying NameSpace Parameter

```
[MessageContract]
 public class Student
 {
        [MessageHeader (Namespace="http://www.techzusiastic.
com")]
```

```
        public String stud_id;
}
```

ProtectionLevel

This parameter specifies the protection level of the message header. The value comes from System.Net.Security.ProtectionLevel enum. It has three values as discussed below:

- **None:** It does authentication only. No other security mechanisms are applied.
- **Encrypt and Sign:** It provides integrity and confidentiality of the data transmitted over the wire. So the data is encrypted.
- **Sign:** It ensures the integrity of the data sent over the wire but does not provide encryption.

The code snippet of setting this parameter is depicted in Example 48. Default value is System.Net.Security.ProtectionLevel.EncryptAndSign if the binding support security otherwise default value is System.Net.Security. ProtectionLevel.None.

Example 48. Specify the ProtectionLevel

```
[MessageContract]
 public class Student
 {
        [MessageHeader (ProtectionLevel=System.Net.Security.
ProtectionLevel.None)]
        public String stud_id;
}
.
```

PARAMETERS OF [MESSAGE BODY MEMBER]

The attribute [MessageBodyMember] is used to place the element in the body part of the SOAP request or reply. It comes from System.ServiceModel.MessageBodyMemberAttribute. It has several parameters which are listed below:

- Name

- NameSpace
- Order
- ProtectionLevel

These parameters are explained below.

Name

This parameter is used to override the name of the element in the body part of the request or reply. The data type of this parameter is a string. Default value the name of the element. The code snippet to apply this parameter is depicted in Example 49.

Example 49. Applying Name Parameter

```
[MessageContract]
public class Student
{
        [MessageHeader]
        public String stud_id;
        [MessageHeader]
        public String stud_name;[MessageBodyMember
(Name="Current_Semester")]
        public int semester;
        [MessageBodyMember]
        public String Branch;
}
```

Now in SOAP body part Current_Semester will appear instead of semester.

Namespace

It is used to update the namespace in the body of SOAP request or reply. The data type of this parameter is a string. Default value of this parameter is address provided by the CLR. The code snippet to apply this parameter is depicted in Example 50.

Example 50. Applying Namespace Parameter

```
[MessageContract]
public class Student
        [MessageHeader]
        public String stud_id;
        [MessageHeader]
        public String stud_name;
        [MessageBodyMember (Namespace="http://www.techzusi-
astic.com")]public int semester;
        [MessageBodyMember]
        public String Branch;
}
```

Order

This parameter is used to change the order of appearance of the message body member in XML request and response. The data type of this parameter is an integer. If this parameter value is not specified, then the order is decided based on the ascending order of alphabets. The code snippet to apply this parameter is illustrated in Example 51.

Example 51. Applying Order Parameter

```
[MessageContract]
public class Student
{
        [MessageHeader]
        public String stud_id;
        [MessageHeader]
        public String stud_name;
        [MessageBodyMember (Order=1)]
        public int semester;
        [MessageBodyMember(Order=5)]
        public String Branch;
}
```

In above code the [MessageBodyMember] having lowest value will appear first in the XML request and response. It is not necessary to maintain the sequence or but it can be in ascending order. The lowest value of this parameter is the highest priority of putting that element first in the XML. The part of XML request after applying changes as per Example 50 is shown in Example 52

Example 52. Request After Applying Order Parameter

```
<s:Envelope xmlns:s="http://schemas.xmlsoap.org/soap/enve-
lope/">
  <s:Header>
    <Action s:mustUnderstand="1" xmlns="http://schemas.mi-
crosoft.com/ws/2005/05/addressing/none">http://tempuri.org/
IStudRecord/insert_stud</Action>
      <h:stud_id i:nil="true" xmlns:i="http://www.w3.org/2001/
XMLSchema-instance" xmlns:h="http://tempuri.org/" />
      <h:stud_name i:nil="true" xmlns:i="http://www.
w3.org/2001/XMLSchema-instance" xmlns:h="http://tempuri.
org/" />
  </s:Header>
  <s:Body>
    <Student xmlns="http://tempuri.org/">
      <semester>0</semester><Branch i:nil="true"
xmlns:i="http://www.w3.org/2001/XMLSchema-instance" />
    </Student>
  </s:Body>
</s:Envelope>
```

As illustrated in the above example, the semester element appears before the Branch element in the <body> element. This has happened because the order of semester element is lower than the order of Branch element which is set in Example 50. Following are the rules to remember while using this parameter:

- The value of the Order parameter must be non-negative.
- If more than one message body members have same order, then order is decided based on the ascending order of the alphabets.

ProtectionLevel

This parameter specifies the protection level of the message body member. The value comes from System.Net.Security.ProtectionLevel enum. It has three values as discussed below:

- **None:** It does authentication only. No other security mechanisms are applied.
- **Encrypt and Sign:** It provides integrity and confidentiality of the data transmitted over the wire. So data is encrypted.
- **Sign:** It ensures integrity of the data sent over the wire but does not provide encryption.

The code snippet of setting this parameter is depicted in Example 47. The default value is System.Net.Security.ProtectionLevel.EncryptAndSign if the binding support security otherwise default value is System.Net.Security. ProtectionLevel.None.

The demonstration of message contract is not shown and it is left to the readers as self-learning exercise because the program is similar as the data contract demonstration. You need to change the data type of insert_stud operation to Student from void in the service program. The rest of the elements such as host and client are same as the data contract demonstration.

CONCLUSION

In this chapter, all three contracts are explained in depth. A contract is the third element of the endpoint. As WCF follows contract first development strategy, through understanding of each contract is required. You have also learned about syntax of each parameter of a contract in depth. Following are the important points to ponder from this chapter:

- A client and service must agree on the contract to communicate.
- There are three contracts available in WCF: Service Contract, Data Contract and Message Contract.
- Service Contract is generally an interface, but the class can behave like a service contract.
- It is better programming practice to create an interface as [ServiceContract].

- All the one way operations must have a void return type but the operations having void return type are not one way.
- All the contracts have several parameters to override the default settings.
- The CallbackContract parameter of [ServiceContract] is used to duplex communication.
- Data Contract is useful for serializing the complex data type.
- Message Contract is useful for having additional control over the SOAP message.
- To use message contract with the program, the return type and parameter both must be [MessageContract].
- To change the default order of [DataMember] and [MessageBodyMember] Order parameter is used
- The ProtectionLevel parameter can be applied on [ServiceContract] and [OperationContract]. It is applied based on the hierarchy. If this parameter is not provided at [OperationContract] its default value is taken from the ProtectionLevel of [ServiceContract].
- The ProtectionLevel parameter can also be applied on [MessageContract], [MessageContract], [MessageHeader] and [MessageBodyMember]. It is applied based on the hierarchy. If this parameter is not provided for [MessageHeader] and [MessageBodyMember], the default value is taken from the ProtectionLevel of [MessageContract].

Chapter 7
Client and Service

Generally, a client initiates communication to the service that is why it is included first in the title of this chapter. This chapter provides in depth knowledge of client and different ways to create client code. It also explores details various service behaviors which can be helpful to implement advanced programming concepts in WCF.

After completing this chapter, you will be able to:

- Gain understanding about above client.
- Learn various element available which are generated in client code
- Gain understanding about service.
- Practical implementation of message patterns.
- Gain understanding about service behaviors.
- Implement concurrency and session management.
- Handle the exception in WCF service and client.

DOI: 10.4018/978-1-5225-1997-3.ch007

CLIENT

A client is a piece of code which initiates communication with the service. It communicates with the service through the endpoint. There are certain underlying objects which are generated while consuming the service using the proxy class object. A programmer must know about these objects. The communication between client and service id illustrated in Figure 1. As illustrated in Figure 1, a proxy object is available at client side which communicates with the service using endpoints generated on both sides. Proxy generation is done in two ways.

- One way is to use Add Service Reference option of visual studio which calls the svcutil.exe program in the background. This option is already discussed in the preceding chapters, but readers are not aware about that the proxy class generation is done by the utility called svcutil.exe
- Another way is to create object of ChannelFactory class which is available in System.ServiceModel. This option is tailor made for the.NET client, but it will not work for interoperability with other languages.

These two methods are explained in great details in the following sections.

Generating proxy using svcutil.exe

To apply this option, modify the code of service discussed for data contract and let us follow the steps mentioned below:

Step 1: Create the WCF service library in visual studio and write the code of service contract as illustrated in Example 1.

Figure 1. Client and service communication

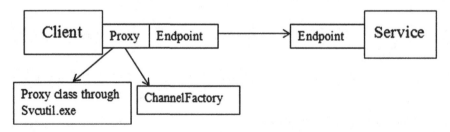

Example 1. Service Contract Code

```
using System;
using System.Collections.Generic;
using System.Linq;
using System.Runtime.Serialization;
using System.ServiceModel;
using System.Text;
namespace DataContractDemo
{
```

// NOTE: You can use the "Rename" command on the "Refactor" menu to change the interface name "IService1" in both code and config file together.

```
    [ServiceContract]
    public interface IStudRecord
    {
        [OperationContract]
        Boolean insert_stud(Student stud);

    }
    [DataContract]
    public class Student
    {
        [DataMember]
        public String stud_id;
        [DataMember]
        public String stud_name;
        [DataMember]
        public int semester;
        [DataMember]
        public String Branch;
    }
}
```

As shown in Example 1, the operation returns Boolean if the record is successfully inserted in the list of students.

Step 2: Write code of the service class as shown in Example 2. Then compile the service project and generate dll.

Example 2. Code of Service Class

```
using System;
using System.Collections.Generic;
using System.Linq;
using System.Runtime.Serialization;
using System.ServiceModel;
using System.Text;
namespace DataContractDemo
{
    public class StudRecord: IStudRecord
    {
        List<Student> all_students = new List<Student>();
        public Boolean insert_stud(Student stud)
        {
            if (stud != null)
            {
                all_students.Add(stud);
                return true;
            }
            else
                return false;
        }
    }
}
```

Step 3: Create the console application project with the two endpoints as shown
in the App.Config file in Example 3. Then write the code in Program.
cs file as depicted in Example 4.

Example 3. App.Config File of Host Program

```
<?xml version="1.0" encoding="utf-8" ?>
<configuration>
    <system.serviceModel>
        <behaviors>
            <serviceBehaviors>
                <behavior name="NewBehavior">
                    <serviceMetadata httpGetEnabled="true"
/>
```

```
                </behavior>
            </serviceBehaviors>
        </behaviors>
        <services>
            <service behaviorConfiguration="NewBehavior"
name="DataContractDemo.StudRecord">
                <endpoint address="" binding="wsHttpBinding"
bindingConfiguration=""
                    contract="DataContractDemo.IStudRecord"
/>
                <endpoint address="net.tcp://localhost:9091/
StudService2" binding="netTcpBinding"
                    bindingConfiguration=""
contract="DataContractDemo.IStudRecord" />
                <host>
                    <baseAddresses>
                        <add baseAddress="http://local-
host:8090/StudentService" />
                    </baseAddresses>
                </host>
            </service>
        </services>
    </system.serviceModel>
</configuration>
```

Example 4. Code of Program.cs File

```
using System;
using System.Collections.Generic;
using System.Linq;
using System.Text;
using System.ServiceModel;
using DataContractDemo;
using System.ServiceModel.Description;
namespace DataContract_Host
{
    class Program
    {
        static void Main(string[] args)
        {
```

```
        ServiceHost host=new ServiceHost(typeof(StudReco
rd));
        host.Open();
        foreach (ServiceEndpoint endpoint in host.De-
scription.Endpoints)
        {
            Console.WriteLine("Service is running at " +
endpoint.Address);
        }
        Console.WriteLine("Press any key to stop");
        Console.ReadKey();
        host.Close();
    }
  }
}
```

Step 4: Compile console application project, generate exe and execute it under the administrator privileges. The output is shown in Figure 2. Now type the base address in the any browser. The base address is available in the App.Config you can copy it also. The output after typing the base address in the browser is shown as in Figure 3.

Figure 2. Client and service communication

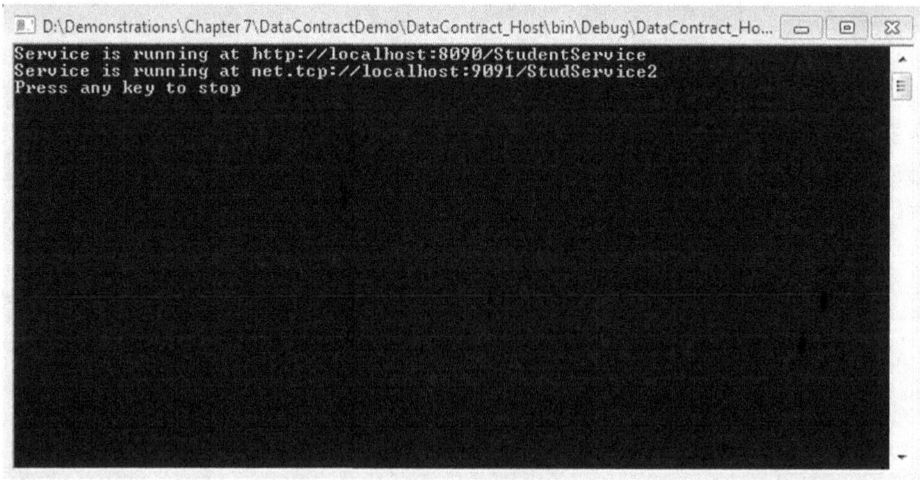

Figure 3. Viewing base address in browser

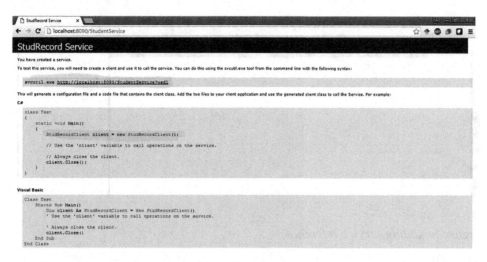

As shown in Figure 3, the output in browser is displayed. Two important things should be understood here. First, there is command called svcutil.exe shown on top and the instruction is also mentioned below it. The instruction tells that svcutil.exe is used to generate the proxy class and Configuration file for the client. The second thing is the code sample shown in the C# and Visual Basic. As we are writing the code in C#, we will discuss about C# only. The code illustrates the name of proxy class which writing the code in the client project to consume the service. That means in this example we need to create object of StudRecordClient class in client program. This class is also known as a proxy class as it behaves like a service class but it is not a service class and works a proxy for the service class. This fulfills the one of the tenets of SOA which tells service shares schemas and contract not actual class.

Step 5: Create a windows forms application project and design the form layout as shown in Figure 4.

Step 6: Now to add the reference of service right click on the project and click on the Add Service Reference as illustrated in Figure 5. Also observe that there is no configuration file in the solution explorer of client project as of now.

Step 7: The Add service reference wizard appears as shown in Figure 6. Copy or type the URI of WSDL path and click on the Go button, the service is listed. Provide the name of the Namespace at bottom the text box and click on OK button.

Figure 4. Screen design of form of client project

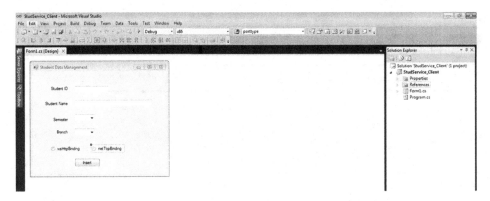

Figure 5. Adding service reference

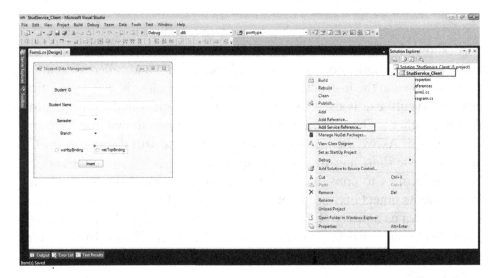

Step 8: This is the time at which the svcutil.exe comes into the focus. On the click event of Ok button visual studio internally calls svcutil.exe file to generate proxy class and App.Config (or Web.Config). This process is not visible to the programmer, but the proxy is created and App.Config file is added in this client project as illustrated in Figure 7. The content of App.Config is shown in Example 5.

Client and Service

Figure 6. Adding service reference

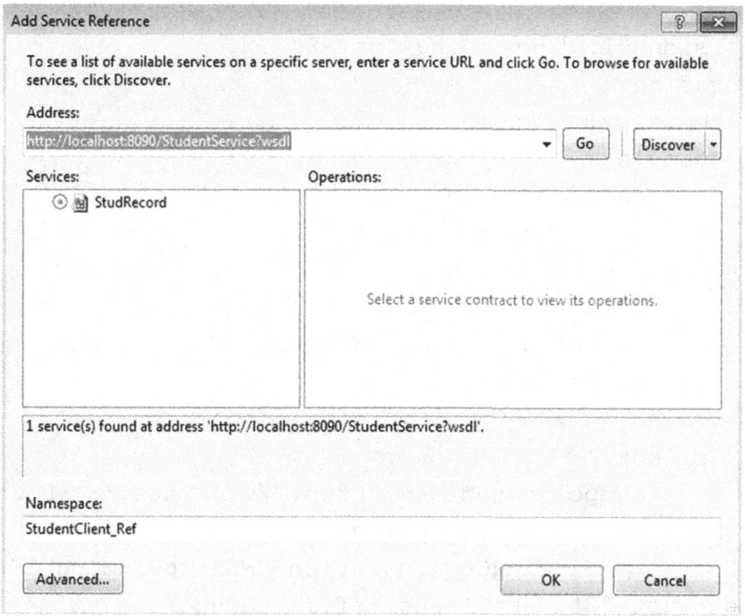

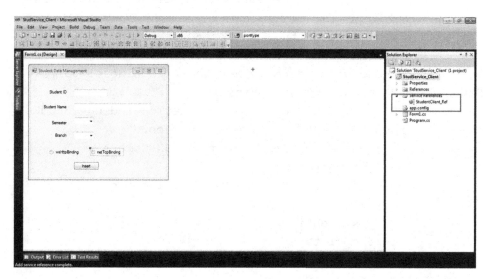

Figure 7. Added service reference in client project

Example 5. Content of App.Config file of client project:

```xml
<?xml version="1.0" encoding="utf-8" ?>
<configuration>
    <system.serviceModel>
        <bindings>
            <netTcpBinding>
                <binding name="NetTcpBinding_IStudRecord" />
            </netTcpBinding>
            <wsHttpBinding>
                <binding name="WSHttpBinding_IStudRecord" />
            </wsHttpBinding>
        </bindings>
        <client>
            <endpoint address="http://localhost:8090/Stu-
dentService" binding="wsHttpBinding"
                bindingConfiguration="WSHttpBinding_IStudRe-
cord" contract="StudentClient_Ref.IStudRecord"
                name="WSHttpBinding_IStudRecord">
                <identity>
                    <userPrincipalName value="india1\india"
/>
                </identity>
            </endpoint>
            <endpoint address="net.tcp://localhost:9091/
StudService2" binding="netTcpBinding"
                bindingConfiguration="NetTcpBinding_IStudRe-
cord" contract="StudentClient_Ref.IStudRecord"
                name="NetTcpBinding_IStudRecord">
                <identity>
                    <userPrincipalName value="india1\india"
/>
                </identity>
            </endpoint>
        </client>
    </system.serviceModel>
</configuration>
```

The service reference i.e. StudetClient_Ref contains the proxy class. So svcutil is responsible for all these and we are not directly using it, but we

Figure 8. Showing all the items of solution explorer

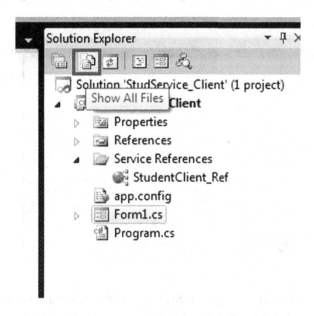

Figure 9. Contents of ServiceClient_Ref

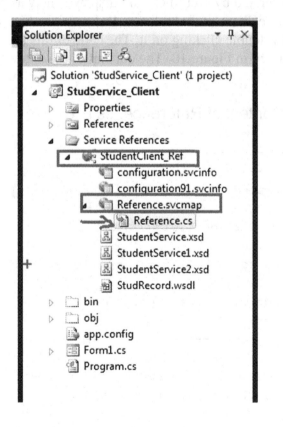

Figure 10. Content of Reference.cs file in visual studio

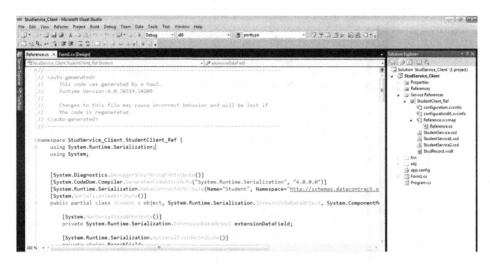

are using it through visual studio. So to view the generate proxy class click on the Show all button on solution explore as shown in Figure 8. All the components generated by svcutil.exe are displayed now as shown in Figure 9. Expand ServiceClient_Ref and locate Reference.cs file. Then open Reference.cs file by double clicking on it. The code of this file is shown visual studio as illustrated in Figure 10. The content of the entire file is presented in Example 6.

Example 6. Content of Reference. cs File

```
//----------------------------------------------------------
----------------------
// <auto-generated>
//      This code was generated by a tool.
//      Runtime Version:4.0.30319.34209
//
//      Changes to this file may cause incorrect behavior and
will be lost if
//      the code is regenerated.
// </auto-generated>
//----------------------------------------------------------
----------------------
namespace StudService_Client.StudentClient_Ref {
    using System.Runtime.Serialization;
```

```csharp
    using System;

    [System.Diagnostics.DebuggerStepThroughAttribute()]
    [System.CodeDom.Compiler.GeneratedCodeAttribute("System.
Runtime.Serialization", "4.0.0.0")]
    [System.Runtime.Serialization.DataContractAttribute(
Name="Student", Namespace="http://schemas.datacontract.
org/2004/07/DataContractDemo")]
    [System.SerializableAttribute()]
    public partial class Student: object, System.Runtime.
Serialization.IExtensibleDataObject, System.ComponentModel.
INotifyPropertyChanged {

        [System.NonSerializedAttribute()]
        private System.Runtime.Serialization.ExtensionDataO-
bject extensionDataField;

        [System.Runtime.Serialization.OptionalFieldAttrib-
ute()]
        private string BranchField;

        [System.Runtime.Serialization.OptionalFieldAttrib-
ute()]
        private int semesterField;

        [System.Runtime.Serialization.OptionalFieldAttrib-
ute()]
        private string stud_idField;

        [System.Runtime.Serialization.OptionalFieldAttrib-
ute()]
        private string stud_nameField;

        [global::System.ComponentModel.
BrowsableAttribute(false)]
        public System.Runtime.Serialization.ExtensionDataO-
bject ExtensionData {
            get {
                return this.extensionDataField;
            }
```

```
        set {
            this.extensionDataField = value;
        }
    }


    [System.Runtime.Serialization.DataMemberAttribute()]
    public string Branch {
        get {
            return this.BranchField;
        }
        set {
            if ((object.ReferenceEquals(this.Branch-
Field, value) != true)) {
                this.BranchField = value;
                this.RaisePropertyChanged("Branch");
            }
        }
    }


    [System.Runtime.Serialization.DataMemberAttribute()]
    public int semester {
        get {
            return this.semesterField;
        }
        set {
            if ((this.semesterField.Equals(value) !=
true)) {
                this.semesterField = value;
                this.RaisePropertyChanged("semester");
            }
        }
    }


    [System.Runtime.Serialization.DataMemberAttribute()]
    public string stud_id {
        get {
            return this.stud_idField;
        }
        set {
            if ((object.ReferenceEquals(this.stud_id-
```

```
Field, value) != true)) {
                this.stud_idField = value;
                this.RaisePropertyChanged("stud_id");
            }
        }
    }

    [System.Runtime.Serialization.DataMemberAttribute()]
    public string stud_name {
        get {
            return this.stud_nameField;
        }
        set {
            if ((object.ReferenceEquals(this.stud_name-
Field, value) != true)) {
                this.stud_nameField = value;
                this.RaisePropertyChanged("stud_name");
            }
        }
    }

    public event System.ComponentModel.PropertyChangedE-
ventHandler PropertyChanged;
        protected void RaisePropertyChanged(string prop-
ertyName) {
            System.ComponentModel.PropertyChangedEventHan-
dler propertyChanged = this.PropertyChanged;
            if ((propertyChanged != null)) {
                propertyChanged(this, new System.Component-
Model.PropertyChangedEventArgs(propertyName));
            }
        }
    }

    [System.CodeDom.Compiler.GeneratedCodeAttribute("System.
ServiceModel", "4.0.0.0")]
    [System.ServiceModel.ServiceContractAttribute(Configurat
ionName="StudentClient_Ref.IStudRecord")]
    public interface IStudRecord {
```

```
        [System.ServiceModel.OperationContractAttribut
e(Action="http://tempuri.org/IStudRecord/insert_stud",
ReplyAction="http://tempuri.org/IStudRecord/insert_studRe-
sponse")]
        bool insert_stud(StudService_Client.StudentClient_
Ref.Student stud);
    }


    [System.CodeDom.Compiler.GeneratedCodeAttribute("System.
ServiceModel", "4.0.0.0")]
    public interface IStudRecordChannel: StudService_Cli-
ent.StudentClient_Ref.IStudRecord, System.ServiceModel.ICli-
entChannel {
    }


    [System.Diagnostics.DebuggerStepThroughAttribute()]
    [System.CodeDom.Compiler.GeneratedCodeAttribute("System.
ServiceModel", "4.0.0.0")]
    public partial class StudRecordClient: System.Servic-
eModel.ClientBase<StudService_Client.StudentClient_Ref.IStu-
dRecord>, StudService_Client.StudentClient_Ref.IStudRecord {

        public StudRecordClient() {
        }

        public StudRecordClient(string endpointConfigura-
tionName):
                base(endpointConfigurationName) {
        }

        public StudRecordClient(string endpointConfigura-
tionName, string remoteAddress):
                base(endpointConfigurationName, remoteAd-
dress) {
        }

        public StudRecordClient(string endpointConfigura-
tionName, System.ServiceModel.EndpointAddress remoteAd-
dress):
                base(endpointConfigurationName, remoteAd-
```

```
dress) {
        }


        public StudRecordClient(System.ServiceModel.Chan-
nels.Binding binding, System.ServiceModel.EndpointAddress
remoteAddress):
                base(binding, remoteAddress) {
        }


        public bool insert_stud(StudService_Client.Stu-
dentClient_Ref.Student stud) {return base.Channel.insert_
stud(stud);
        }
    }
}
```

As shown in the above example, the proxy class StudRecordClient is generated and it contains several constructors and the operation which client project will consume. As discussed earlier, this code is generated by svcutil. exe. If you want to work directly on svcutil.exe you can find this utility under C:\Program Files (x86)\Microsoft SDKs\Windows\vx.0x\Bin or C:\Program Files (x86)\Microsoft SDKs\Windows\vx.0x\Bin folder. To execute this command, open visual studio command prompt as shown in Figure 11. It is important to note that the visual command prompt should be opened with Administrator privilege. The command prompt is opened the svcutil command can be applied as shown in Figure 12. It takes a WSDL file of service as argument. There are many switches available in this command. The /out or /o is used to generate the code file which is same as Reference.cs file shown earlier in Example 6. The /config or /c is used to generate configuration file which is same as App.Config file shown in Example 5. The other options can be tried by taking the help of this command by using svcutil/? command from the command prompt. The use of other options and switches is left to the reader as self-learning exercise. Now the last step is to write the code in Form1.cs file of client project.

Step 8: Write the code in Form1.cs file of client project as depicted in Example 7. The output is shown in Figure 13 and Figure 14 after executing the code shown in Example 7.

Figure 11. Opening visual studio command prompt

Figure 12. Working with svcutil.exe

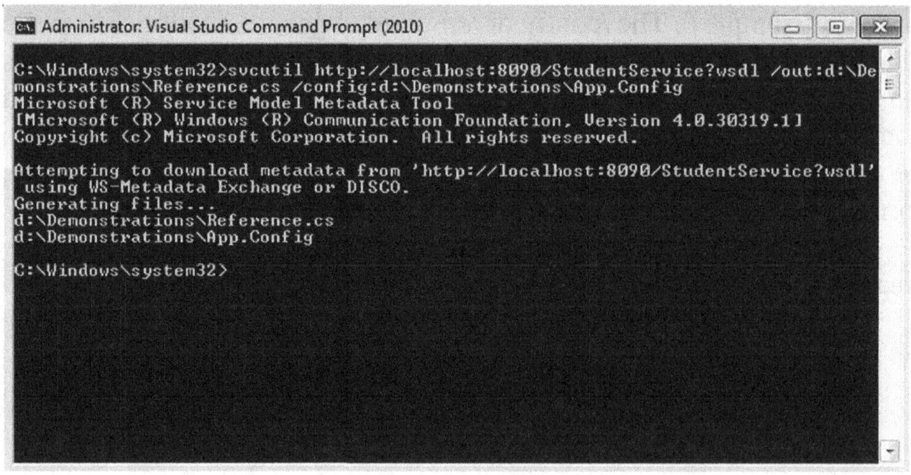

Figure 13. Taking the input from the user

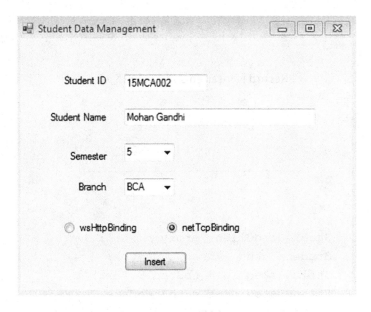

Example 7. Code of Form1.cs File

```
using System;
using System.Collections.Generic;
using System.ComponentModel;
using System.Data;
using System.Drawing;
using System.Linq;
using System.Text;
using System.Windows.Forms;
using StudService_Client.StudentClient_Ref;
namespace StudService_Client
{
    public partial class frmStudManagement: Form
    {
        public frmStudManagement()
        {
            InitializeComponent();
        }
        private void btnInsert_Click(object sender, Even-
tArgs e)
```

Figure 14. Message after successfully inserting record

```
       {
              StudRecordClient proxy = null;
              Student stud = new Student();
              String stud_id = tbStudID.Text;
              String stud_name = tbStudName.Text;
              int sem = Convert.ToInt16(cbSemester.Select-
       edItem.ToString());
              String branch = cbBranch.SelectedItem.To-
       String();

              Boolean isRecord_Inserted=false;
              String endpoint_name =null;
              if(rbwsHttpBinding.Checked==true)
                  endpoint_name="WSHttpBinding_IStudRecord";
       //setting endpoint name
                                                //having
       wsHttpBinding from App.Config file
              else
                  endpoint_name="NetTcpBinding_IStudRecord";//
       setting endpoint name

       //having netTcpBinding from App.Config file
              proxy = new StudRecordClient(endpoint_name);
              stud.stud_id = stud_id;
              stud.stud_name = stud_name;
              stud.semester = sem;
              stud.Branch = branch;
              isRecord_Inserted=proxy.insert_stud(stud);
```

```
             if(isRecord_Inserted==true)
                  MessageBox.Show("Record is inserted success-
fully");
             else
                  MessageBox.Show("Error:There is a problem.
Record is not inserted");
          }
     }
}
```

In section, you have learned a lot about how the proxy class is generated using svcutil.exe and WSDL. The WSDL file is also important for interoperability with other languages such as JAVA or PHP. You must have gained understanding that Add Service Reference option of visual studio is nothing but indirect use of svcutil.exe command. In summary, whether you deal with svcutil.exe command directly or using visual studio svcutil.exe is responsible for all the auto generated code. Now, instead of using proxy class ChannelFactory class can be used to have the same functionality as discussed above. Consuming a service using ChannelFactory class is the next topic.

Generating proxy using ChannelFactory<TChannel> class

The ChannelFactory class is available in the System.ServiceModel. We will use generic version this class i.e. ChannelFactory<TChannel>. It is a factory that is used to create different types of channels that are used by the client to communicate with the service. The communication is done using various configured service endpoints. There are many overloaded constructors available in this class and we will discuss about following constructor:

public ChannelFactory<TChannel>(string endpointConfigurationName)

Here TChannel is a user defined type which is generally an interface. This constructor takes an endpoint name which is specified in the <endpoint name> tag of configuration file. So by using this constructor object of ChannelFactory class is created. It has overloaded method CreateChannel() for establishing the channel. We will discuss following version of this method:

public TChannel CreateChannel()

This method returns TChannel which is user defined and generally an interface. The detail about other overloaded versions of this method can be found in object browse of visual studio. The last step is to call the operation of the service using the TChannel object. The code of Form1.cs file of client program using this method is illustrated in Example 8.

Example 8. Code of Client Project using ChannelFactory Class

```
using System;
using System.Collections.Generic;
using System.ComponentModel;
using System.Data;
using System.Drawing;
using System.Linq;
using System.Text;
using System.Windows.Forms;
using StudService_Client.StudentClient_Ref;
using System.ServiceModel;
namespace StudService_Client
{
    public partial class frmStudManagement: Form
    {
        public frmStudManagement()
        {
            InitializeComponent();
        }
        private void btnInsert_Click(object sender, Even-
tArgs e)
        {

            Student stud = new Student();
            String stud_id = tbStudID.Text;
            String stud_name = tbStudName.Text;
            int sem = Convert.ToInt16(cbSemester.Select-
edItem.ToString());
            String branch = cbBranch.SelectedItem.To-
String();

            Boolean isRecord_Inserted=false;
            String endpoint_name =null;
```

```
        if(rbwsHttpBinding.Checked==true)
            endpoint_name="WSHttpBinding_IStudRecord";
//setting endpoint name

//having wsHttpBinding from App.Config file
        else
            endpoint_name = "NetTcpBinding_IStudRe-
cord";//setting endpoint name

//having netTcpBinding from App.Config file
        ChannelFactory<IStudRecord> factory = new Chann
elFactory<IStudRecord>(endpoint_name);IStudRecord channel =
factory.CreateChannel();
        stud.stud_id = stud_id;
        stud.stud_name = stud_name;
        stud.semester = sem;
        stud.Branch = branch;
        isRecord_Inserted=channel.insert_stud(stud);
        if(isRecord_Inserted==true)
            MessageBox.Show("Record is inserted success-
fully");
        else
            MessageBox.Show("Error:There is a problem.
Record is not inserted");
        factory.close();
    }
  }
}
```

Here in above example, the code related to channel factory is highlighted to find the difference between this method and previous method.

Now you are familiar with both methods of consuming a WCF service. During the code client code creation, there are certain objects created which required for communication. A programmer is not involved directly in dealing with these objects as these objects are auto generated like the code of Reference.cs file of Example 6. In the following section we will learn about these objects.

OBJECTS OF CLIENT

While generating the client code certain auto generated classes and interfaces are created which are required for communication. In the following section important communication objects are discussed.

ICommunicationObject Interface

This interface is a contract for all the communication objects such as channels, service hosts, channel factories, listeners and dispatchers. Each communication object has certain state at a time and an object can be in one state a time. A communication object can move from one state to another state which is also known as state transition. Formally, a state transition is the transition from one state to another. For example, in the self-hosting program when the service is hosted successfully the object of ServiceHost class is in opened state and when the host program is stopped the object of ServiceHost class moves in closed state. This is the state transition from opened state to closed state. The ICommuncationObject interface has a single property called State which gets current state of the communication object. The value of this property comes from System.ServiceModel.CommunicationState enum. All these values are explained below:

- **Created:** A communication object comes into this state by creating its object. When an object of any communication object is instantiated its state is Created by default.
- **Opening:** It intermediate state when the communication object is being transitioned from created to opened state.
- **Opened:** It is the state which indicates the communicate object is in opened state and it is ready to be used.
- **Faulted:** It indicates that the communication is in the error state and it cannot be used any more.
- **Closing:** It is the opposite state of opening state which indicates a communication object is being transitioned from opened to the closed state.
- **Closed:** It is the opposite state of the opened state which indicates a communication object is in the closed state and it cannot be used further.

It is important to note that a communication object can communicate in opened state only. A communication object can enter in any of these states by using calling following methods available in the ICommunicationObject interface:

- **Open ():** This method causes a communication object from created to opened state. To call this method a communication object must be in created state.
- **Close ():** This method causes a communication object from any state to closed state.
- **Abort ():** This method causes a communication object from any state to close state. The difference between Abort and Close method is that the Close () method allows to complete the unfinished work to be completed before closing the object while Abort () method immediately closes the object without completing unfinished work.

Some events are fired during the state transitions which are mentioned below:

- **Opening:** This event occurs when a communication object enters into the opening state.
- **Opened:** This event occurs when a communication object enters into the opened state.
- **Faulted:** This event occurs when a communication object enters into the faulted state.
- **Closing:** This event occurs when a communication object enters into the closing state.
- **Closed:** This event occurs when a communication object enters into the closed state.

CLIENT COMMUNICATION PATTERNS

A client can communicate with service in three ways: one way or simplex, request reply and duplex. All these communication patterns are explained in below section.

Oneway

It is known as single directional communication. It is also known as simplex communication. The popular example is a radio broadcasting system in which communication is done only in a single direction. After sending the

Figure 15. One way

request a client does not wait for the reply as service does not send reply in this communication as illustrated in Figure 15. A service receives message processes it and does return anything to the client. If the service operation is one way it must have a void return type in the operation signature. In WCF all the operations are request-reply by default, so additional configuration is required to make the operation as one way even the operation is having return type as void. Only void return type is allowed in this communication otherwise following error is generated while hosting the service:

Operations marked with IsOneway=true must not declare output parameters, by-reference parameters or return values

To understand the difference between one way and void let us understand the code shown in Example 8 and Example 9.

Example 8. Code of Service Contract

```
using System;
using System.Collections.Generic;
using System.Linq;
using System.Runtime.Serialization;
using System.ServiceModel;
using System.Text;
namespace OnewayDemo
{
    [ServiceContract]
    public interface IOneway
    {
        [OperationContract(IsOneWay = true)]
        void DoNothing1();
        [OperationContract]
        void DoNothing2();
```

```
    }
}
```

As shown in Example 8 the first operation is void and IsOneWay paramter of first [OperationContract] is true which indicate that the operation is one way and it will not wait for the reply from server. The another operation is void and IsOneWay parameter of [OperationContract] is not specified which is false by default so this operation is request-reply and it will wait for the reply from the service even return type of the operation is void.

Now these operations are implemented in service code as shown in Example 9.

Example 9. Service Code

```
using System;
using System.Collections.Generic;
using System.Linq;
using System.Runtime.Serialization;
using System.ServiceModel;
using System.Text;
namespace OnewayDemo
{
    public class OneWayService: IOneway
    {
        public void DoNothing1()
        {
            System.Threading.Thread.Sleep(5000);
        }
        public void DoNothing2()
        {
            System.Threading.Thread.Sleep(5000);
        }
    }
}
```

In above example of service code the thread sleeps for 5 seconds in both operations. As first operation is one way the client will not wait for 5 seconds The client will wait for 5 seconds in after calling second operation as it is request-reply.

Figure 16. Request-Reply

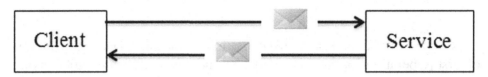

Request-Reply

It is a two way communication but not at the same time. That is either entity can send the message at time. The popular example is walky-talky in which at a time any one person can talk. In this communication a client send the request to service and waits for the reply. After receiving the request from client, a service executes the code and return reply back to the client. The process is well presented in Figure 16. As discussed earlier in service chain, a service may communicate with other service to provide the data to the client. As this is the default message pattern of communication in WCF, no additional configuration is required for this message pattern. An operation must have a return value for this communication otherwise it will result in error. Any return type is allowed in this communication. In most of the situations we use request-reply communication. Many examples of request-reply are explained in the preceding chapters so demonstration of request-reply is not illustrated here.

Duplex

It is a two way communication at the same time. Both client and service can send and receive the message at the same time in this message pattern. The popular example is the telephone communication where both sender and receiver can talk with each other at the same time. In WCF duplex communication, a service can call the function of client so there must be another contract which must be implemented by a client to make this communication possible. The entire process is presented in Figure 17. As shown in Figure 17, the communication is done in both directions. When a communication is done in both directions at the same time there must be different channels for communication from client to service and service to client. A client sends the request to the service using proxy and endpoint. The message is received by the service using endpoint available at service side. The service sends a reply to the client using endpoint. In duplex communication service sends the request to the client using callback contract and the client sends the reply

Figure 17. Duplex

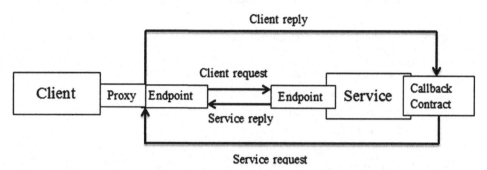

to the service using the same contract. In this communication two channels are used. One channel is for client the service communication and another channel is used for service to client communication. Following points should be considered while developing the duplex communication in WCF:

- Create two interfaces. One interface is [ServiceContract]. Another interface is CallbackContract.
- Add one way operation to the [ServiceContract]
- Relate CallbackContract with [ServiceContract] by using a parameter of [ServiceContract]
- In the host program use binding that supports duplex communication.
- Implement the CallbackContract at client side.

In the following section the implementation of duplex program is illustrated in details.

Step 1: Create the WCF service library project and write the code of service contract as shown in in Example 10.

```
Example 10. Code of Service Contract
using System;
using System.Collections.Generic;
using System.Linq;
using System.Runtime.Serialization;
using System.ServiceModel;
using System.Text;
namespace UpdateService_Duplex_Demo
{
```

```
    [ServiceContract (CallbackContract=typeof(IUpdateCallBa
ck))]
    public interface IUpdateUser
    {
        [OperationContract (IsOneWay=true)]
       void Authenticate(String software_key);
        [OperationContract (IsOneWay=true)]
        void Nofify();
    }
    public interface IUpdateCallBack
    {
        [OperationContract(IsOneWay = true)]
        void notifyUpdateCallback(String Message);
    }
}
```

Step 2: Implement the contract and write the code of service class as illustrated in Example 11. The compile the service and general the Dll of
the service.

```
Example 11. Code of Service Class
using System;
using System.Collections.Generic;
using System.Linq;
using System.Runtime.Serialization;
using System.ServiceModel;
using System.Text;
namespace UpdateService_Duplex_Demo
{
    public class UpdateUser: IUpdateUser
    {
        public void Authenticate(string software_key)
        {

            System.IO.File.WriteAllText(@"D:\Demonstra-
tions\Chapter 7\UpdateService_Duplex_Demo\key.txt", " Key= "
+ software_key);
        }
        public void Nofify()
        {
```

```
            IUpdateCallBack client_callback = OperationCon-
text.Current.GetCallbackChannel<IUpdateCallBack>();
            System.Threading.Thread.Sleep(2000);

            client_callback.notifyUpdateCallback("Key is
valid. Please update the software");

    }


        }

    }
```

Step 3: Now host the service using self-hosting. In this program, we will use windows forms to host the service. So right click on the solution and click on the add new project as illustrated in Figure 18. Select windows forms application project as shown in Figure 19. Now design the controls on the form as illustrated in Figure 20.

As shown in Figure 20 two buttons are designed to start and stop the service. In the form, one label control is placed to display current status of the service.

Next step is to write the code of the service as illustrated in Example 12.

Figure 18. Adding new project to the solution

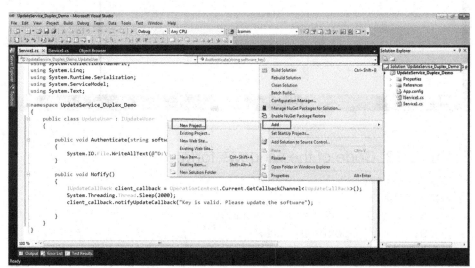

Figure 19. Windows Application Project

Figure 20. Designing controls on windows form

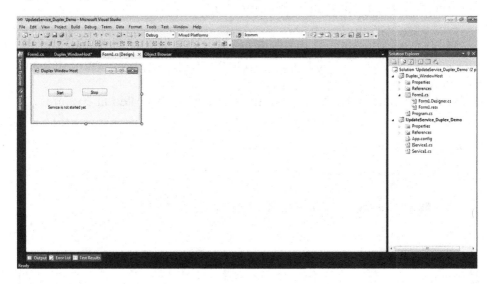

Example 12. Code of the windows form:

```
using System;
using System.Collections.Generic;
using System.ComponentModel;
using System.Data;
```

```
using System.Drawing;
using System.Linq;
using System.Text;
using System.Windows.Forms;
using System.ServiceModel;
using UpdateService_Duplex_Demo;
namespace Duplex_WindowHost
{
    public partial class Form1: Form
    {
        ServiceHost host = new ServiceHost(typeof(UpdateUs
er));
        public Form1()
        {
            InitializeComponent();
            btnStop.Enabled = false;
        }
        private void btnStart_Click(object sender, EventArgs
e)
        {
            if (host.State != CommunicationState.Created)
            {
                host = new ServiceHost(typeof(UpdateUser));

            }
            host.Open();
            btnStart.Enabled = false;
            btnStop.Enabled = true;
            lblStatus.Text = "Service is started";
        }
        private void btnStop_Click(object sender, EventArgs
e)
        {
            host.Close();
            btnStop.Enabled = false;
            btnStart.Enabled = true;
            lblStatus.Text = "Service is stopped";
        }
    }
}
```

Figure 21. Adding a new Item to the project

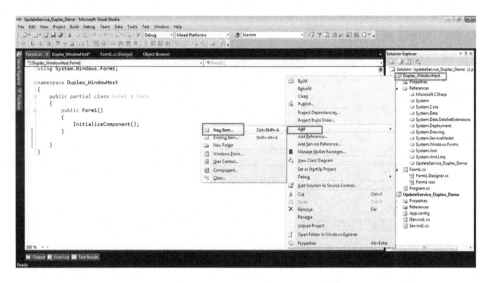

Figure 22. Adding App.Config file

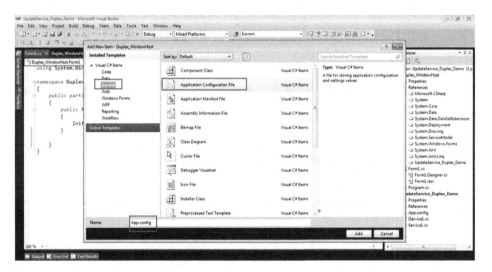

Step 4: Create endpoint using configuration file. To add the configuration file Right click on the project and click on Add->New Item option from the context menu as shown in Figure 21. Then add the App.Config file as per the steps mentioned in Figure 22. Now edit the configuration file by right clicking on it as shown in Figure 23. The service configuration

Figure 23. Opening WCF service configuration editor

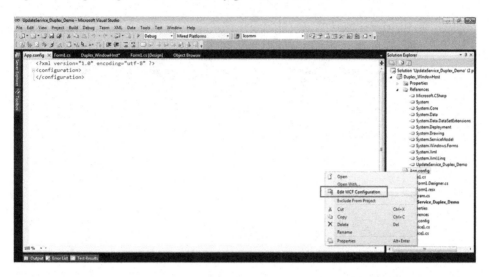

Figure 24. Service configuration editor

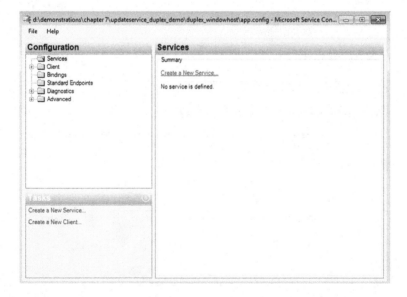

editor is opened as shown in Figure 24. Now click on the Create a new service link and follow the steps mentioned through Figure 25 to Figure 27 to add service and contract details.

Figure 25. Selecting service element

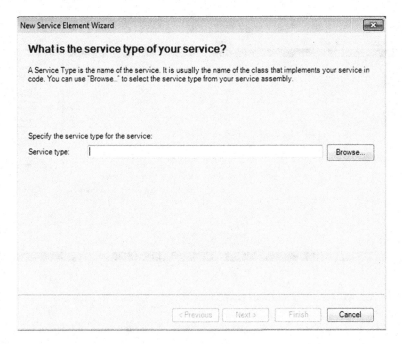

Figure 26. Selected service

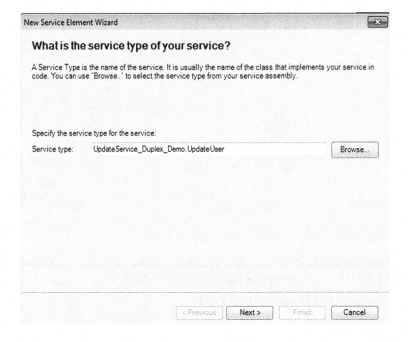

Figure 27. Selected contract

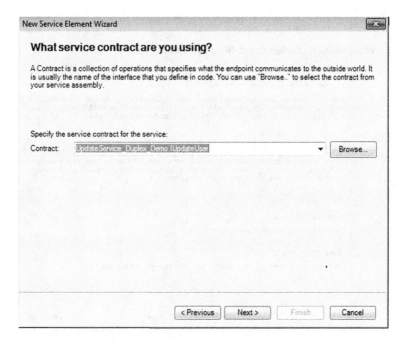

Figure 28. Selected contract

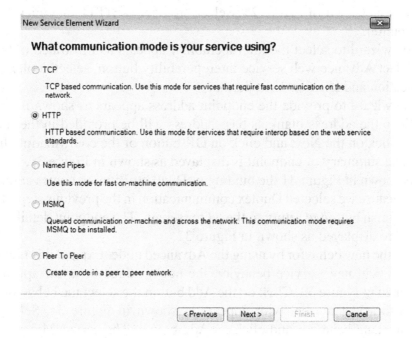

Figure 29. Interoperability selection

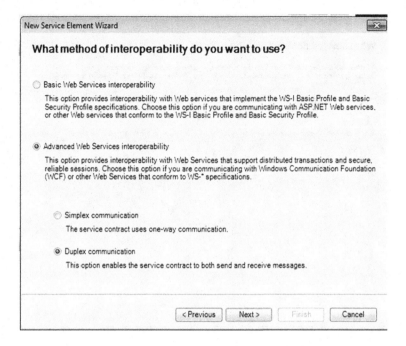

Now click on the Next button in Figure 27 the wizard appears to select the protocol as shown in Figure 28. Select protocol as HTTP and click on the Next button.

The wizard to select the interoperability appears as illustrated in Figure 29. Select Advance web service interoperability button, select duplex communication and click on Next button.

The wizard to provide the endpoint address appears as shown in Figure 30. Keep the address blank as base address will be provided in the further steps. Click on the Next and click on OK button of the confirmation dialog box. The summary of endpoint is displayed as shown in Figure 31.

As shown in Figure 31 the binding wsDualHttpBinding comes automatically because we selected Duplex communication in the previous steps. Click on the finish button to return to the editor screen. The endpoint details in the editor are displayed as shown in Figure 32.

Add the new behavior by using the Advanced node. Expand this node and click on Add new service behavior, the newly added behavior appears as illustrated in Figure 33. Click on the Add button the select the behavior. The screen to select the behavior appears as shown in Figure 34. Select serviceMetadata behavior and click on Add button. The serviceMetadata be-

Client and Service

Figure 30. Providing endpoint address

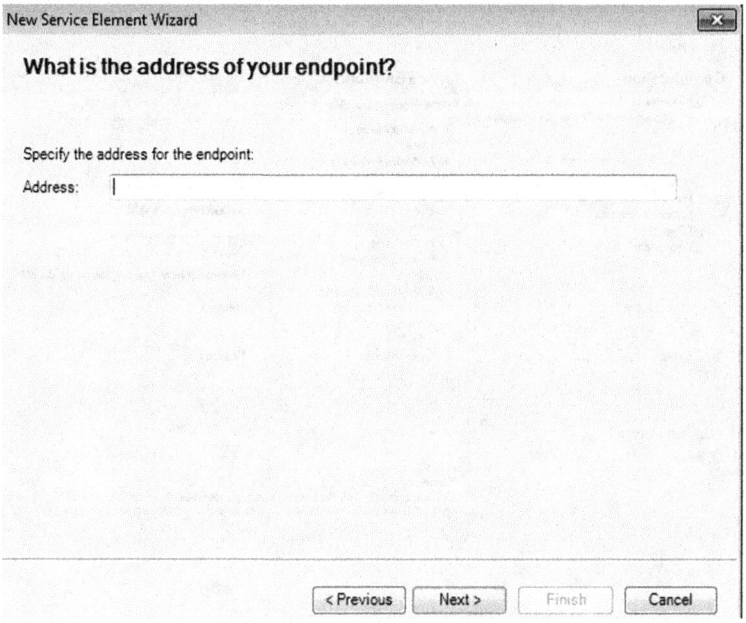

Figure 31. Endpoint summary

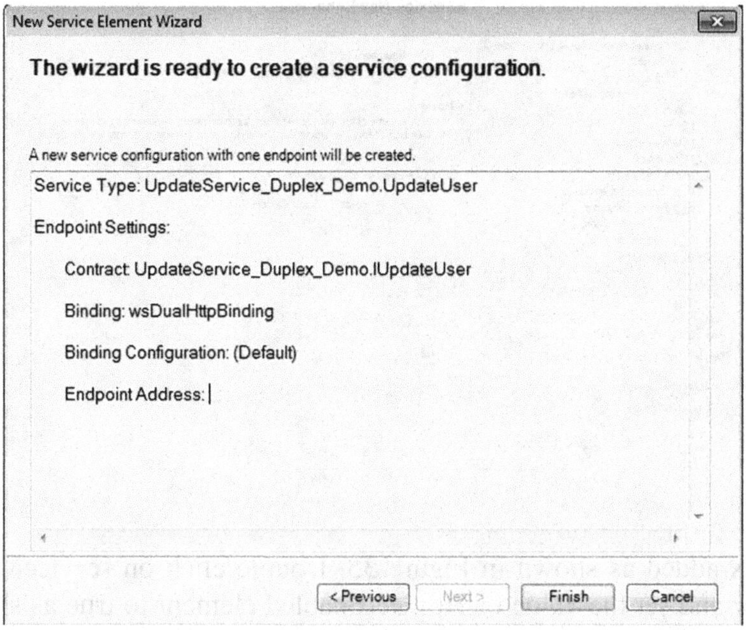

Figure 32. Endpoint summary in editor

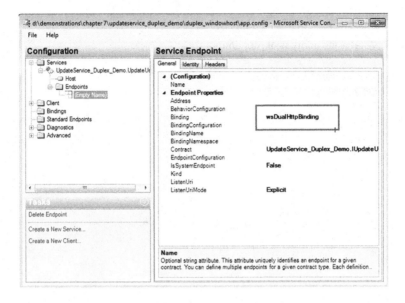

Figure 33. Adding new behavior

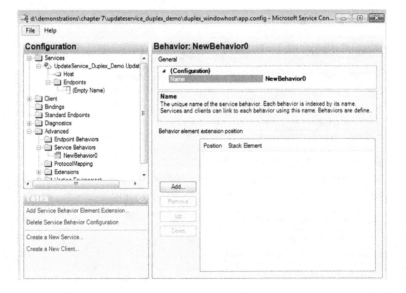

havior is added as shown in Figure 35. Double click on serviceMetadata behavior and set the value of HttpGetEnabled element to true as shown in Figure 36. Now relate the behavior with service as shown in Figure 37.

Figure 34. Selecting behavior

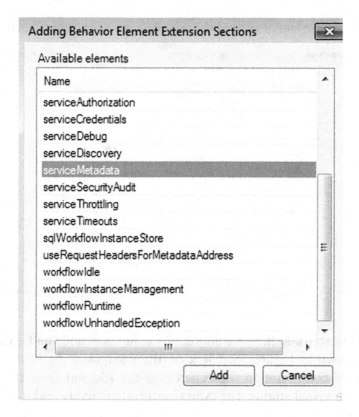

Figure 35. ServiceMetadata behavior in editor

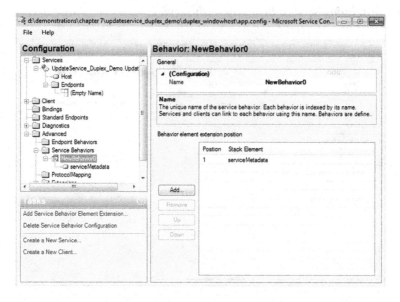

Figure 36. ServiceMetadata behavior in editor

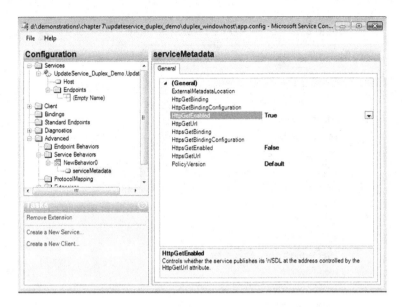

In the last step add the base address by using host node under the service node as shown in Figure 38. Click on the Ok button the base address is added to the configuration file. Then save the file and close the editor to return to the visual studio. The App.Config file is ready and it is shown in Example 13.

Figure 37. Relating service behavior with service

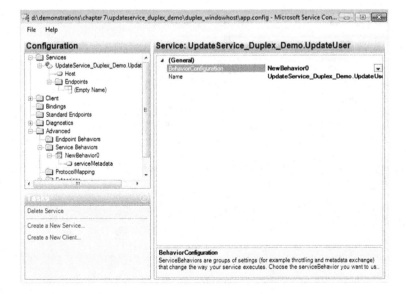

Figure 38. Adding base address

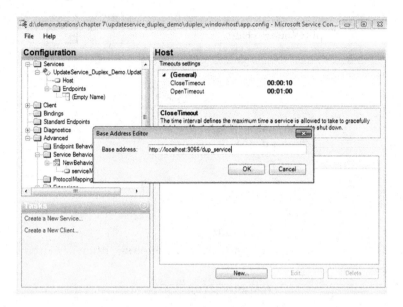

Example 13. Contents of App.Config File

```xml
<?xml version="1.0" encoding="utf-8" ?>
<configuration>
    <system.serviceModel>
        <behaviors>
            <serviceBehaviors>
                <behavior name="NewBehavior0">
                    <serviceMetadata httpGetEnabled="true"
/>
                </behavior>
            </serviceBehaviors>
        </behaviors>
        <services>
            <service behaviorConfiguration="NewBehavior0"
name="UpdateService_Duplex_Demo.UpdateUser">
                <endpoint address=""
binding="wsDualHttpBinding" bindingConfiguration=""
                    contract="UpdateService_Duplex_Demo.IUp-
dateUser" />
                <host>
```

Figure 39. Host program with start and stop buttons

```
                <baseAddresses>
                     <add baseAddress="http://local-
host:9066/dup_service" />
                </baseAddresses>
            </host>
         </service>
      </services>
   </system.serviceModel>
</configuration>
```

Step 5: Compile the windows forms application project which is the host program of WCF service. Locate the EXE of the project and run it with administration credentials the output of running the EXE of the project is shown in Figure 39. Click on the start button to start the service and see the message shown in Figure 39. Now you can start and stop the service by using these buttons and there is no need to run the host program every time.

Step 6: To consume this service create window forms application project and design the controls on form as shown in Figure 40. Now add the service reference of service by using WSDL file of the service. The client configuration file is generated which is shown in Example 14.

Example 14. App.Config file of Client Project

```
<?xml version="1.0" encoding="utf-8" ?>
<configuration>
    <system.serviceModel>
```

Figure 40. Layout of the form of the client project

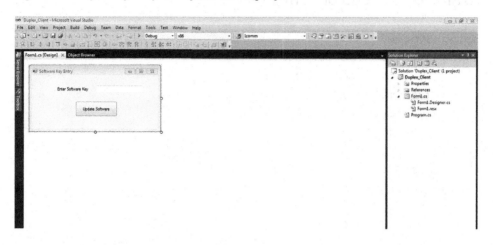

```
        <bindings>
            <wsDualHttpBinding>
                <binding name="WSDualHttpBinding_IUpdateUs-
er" />
            </wsDualHttpBinding>
        </bindings>
        <client>
            <endpoint address="http://localhost:9066/dup_
service" binding="wsDualHttpBinding"
                bindingConfiguration="WSDualHttpBinding_IUp-
dateUser" contract="DuplexClient_Ref.IUpdateUser"
                name="WSDualHttpBinding_IUpdateUser">
                <identity>
                    <userPrincipalName value="india1\india"
/>
                </identity>
            </endpoint>
        </client>
    </system.serviceModel>
</configuration>
```

Now write the code for Form.cs file as demnosrated in Example 15.

Example 15. Code of Form1.cs

```
using System;
using System.Collections.Generic;
using System.ComponentModel;
using System.Data;
using System.Drawing;
using System.Linq;
using System.Text;
using System.Windows.Forms;
using Duplex_Client.DuplexClient_Ref;
using System.ServiceModel;
namespace Duplex_Client
{
    public partial class Form1: Form
    {
        public Form1()
        {
            InitializeComponent();
        }
        private void btnUpdate_Click(object sender, Even-
tArgs e)
        {
            UpdateCallBack ucb=new UpdateCallBack();Instance
Context instance_context = new InstanceContext(ucb);UpdateUs
erClient proxy = new UpdateUserClient(instance_context);
            String software_key = tbswKey.Text;
            proxy.Authenticate(software_key);
            proxy.Nofify();
        }
    }
    public class UpdateCallBack: IUpdateUserCallback
    {
        public void notifyUpdateCallback(string Message)
        {
            MessageBox.Show(Message);
        }
    }
}
```

As shown in Example 14, one class i.e. UpdateCallBack is created which implements the CallBackContract i.e. IUpdateUserCallback. Please note that this CallBackContract was declared in service program is implemented in the client program.

The process to create proxy object is a little bit different. The first three lines of button click event are highlighted. In the first line the object of UpdateCallBack is instantiated which is passed as parameter to the constructor of InstanceContext. The object of InstanceContext class is provided in the constructor of the proxy class. The rest of the procedure of consuming the service using proxy object is same of the preceding sections.

Step 7: Compile the client project and execute it as shown in Figure 41 and Figure 42 to test the duplex communication.

Figure 41. Client program-proving the software key

Figure 42. Client Program-output message

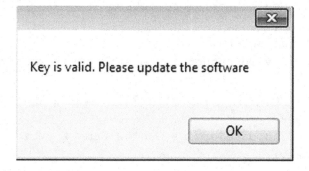

SERVICE

As service is a prograsm which provides functionality to the client by through the endpoint. It must be hosted by the host program. The host program can be the component of the system such as IIS, Windows Service or self-hosting program developed by a programmer. This is the major advantage of WCF over the other web services as there is no specific host required to host the service. The examples self-hosting using console application and windows form application project are already demonstrated and you are not aware about these methods.

Like the [ServiceContract] a service class as several behaviors to customize the service. This topic is discussed in the next section.

SERVICE BEHAVIOR

A service behavior is used to control the service runtime. One of the service behaviors is service metadata behavior which is demonstrated extensively in previous chapters and this chapter. This behavior determines whether to expose service metadata or not while the service is running. Likewise, there are many issues which is must be handled by the service when it is running. Therefore, service behavior plays vital role in controlling and handling this issues runtime. The service behavior is applied on service by using [Service-Behavior] attribute. Likewise operation behavior is applied to the operations defined in the service class by using [OperationBehavior]. The code snippet of applying [ServiceBehavior] and [OperationBehavior] is illustrated in Example 16.

Example 16. Applying Service Behavior

```
[ServiceBehavior]
public class UpdateUser: IUpdateUser
{
        [OperationBehavior]
        public void Authenticate(string software_key)
        {
            System.IO.File.WriteAllText(@"D:\Demonstrations\
Chapter
            7\UpdateService_Duplex_Demo\key.txt", " Key= "
+ software_key);
```

```
        }
}
```

In the following sections the parameters of both attributes are discussed.

Parameters of Service Behavior

The [ServiceBehavior] attribute comes from System.ServiceModel.Service-BehaviorAttribute. There are following major service behaviors listed below:

- AutomaticSessionShutdown
- ConcurrencyMode
- ConfigurationName
- IncludeExceptionDetailInFaults
- InstanceContextMode
- ReleaseServiceInstanceOnTransactionComplete
- TransactionAutoCompleteOnSessionClose
- TransactionIsolationLevel
- TransactionTimeout

AutomaticSessionShutdown

This parameter is used to specify whether to close the session or not when a client terminates the session. The data type of this parameter is a Boolean. Default value of this parameter is true which indicates that the service automatically closes the sessions when a client terminates the session. The service processes all the messages before terminating the session. Set the value false if want to control the session. The code snippet of setting this parameter is depicted in Example 17.

Example 17. Specifying AutomaticSessionShutdown Parameter

```
[ServiceBehavior (AutomaticSessionShutdown=false)]
public class DivisionService: IDivisionService
{
        public int divide_no(int no1, int no2)
        {
            return no1 / no2;
```

```
      }
}
```

ConcurrencyMode

This parameter is related to threading in a WCF service. It is used to specify the kind of thread support available with the service. The value of this parameter comes from System.ServiceModel.ConcurrencyMode enum which contains following values:

- **Single:** It indicates that the service is single threaded. It can accept one call at a time. The new call must wait until the previous call is processed. It does not process reentrant calls.
- **Reentrant:** Reentrant calls are single threaded. The reentrant call is the call which must be safely called before its previous invocation is completed. The example of reentrant call is in the operating system when one process is interrupted by an interrupt because of higher priority, its current execution is pauses and its paused execution resumed after getting back from the interrupt routine.
- **Multiple:** It indicates that service is multithreaded. It is very useful in handling concurrent calls.

Default value is Single. All these options can be helpful in different situations. A developer should take care about thread safety while using multiple and reentrant options. Single threading option is the safest option as at a time only one thread is executed but it might not be helpful to have concurrent access. The code snippet to set the concurrency mode as Multiple is illustrated in Example 18.

Example 18. Setting ConcurrencyMode

```
[ServiceBehavior (ConcurrencyMode=ConcurrencyMode.Multiple)]
public class DivisionService: IDivisionService
{
        public int divide_no(int no1, int no2)
        {
            return no1 / no2;
        }
}
```

ConfigurationName

This parameter is used to get or set the name of service in the configuration file. The data type of this parameter is a string. Default value is the fully qualified name of the service class. The snippet to apply this parameter is depicted in Example 19.

Example 19. Applying ConfigurationName

```
[ServiceBehavior (ConfigurationName="DivService")]
public class DivisionService: IDivisionService
{
        public int divide_no(int no1, int no2)
        {
            return no1 / no2;
        }
}
```

As demonstrated in the above example, the name of the service is referred as DivService without fully qualified name. So in the configuration file it must be changed written in the configuration file as illustrated in Example 20.

Example 20. Service Name in Configuration File

```
<services>
      <service name="DivService">
        <endpoint address="" binding="wsHttpBinding"
                                contract="ServiceBehavior_
Demo.IDivisionService">
        </endpoint>
      </service>
</services>
```

IncludeExceptionDetailInFaults

This parameter is used to show the exception details to the client. In WCF service the exception details are not shown to the client when an exception occurs in the service. The data type of this parameter is a Boolean. The default value of this parameter is false. For example, in the division operation

Figure 43. Error message (IncludeExceptionDetailInFaults=false)

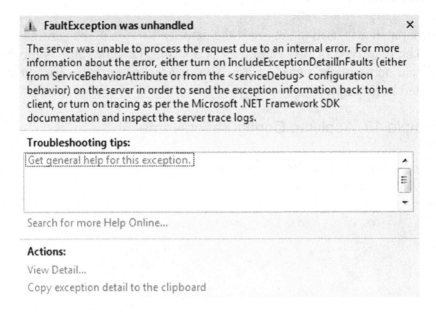

if we provide the second number as 0 (zero) from the client program and the value of this parameter is false then the error message appears as shown in Figure 43.

As shown in Figure 43 actual error is shown to the client. To view the actual error details value of this parameter must be set to true as demonstrated in Example 21.

Example 21. Applying INcldueExceptionDeaillnFaults

```
[ServiceBehavior(IncludeExceptionDetailInFaults=true)]
public class DivisionService: IDivisionService
{
        public int divide_no(int no1, int no2)
        {
            return no1 / no2;
        }
}
```

Now the value is set to true. So the client will get the actual error message as shown in Figure 44.

Figure 44. Error message (IncludeExceptionDetailInFaults=true)

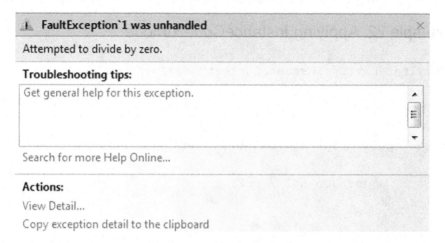

Please note that this parameter is to show the actual exception only. It cannot be used to handle the exception. For debugging purpose, set it as true and handle the exception after knowing about the actual exception. It must be set to false in actual developement. The exception handling mechanism in WCF is explained later in this chapter.

InstanceContextMode

It is used to determine how many objects of service should be created when the client calls the service. It decides when to create new service object and when to destroy it. The value of this parameter comes from System.ServiceModel.InstanceContextMode enum. It has following three values:

- **Single:** A single service object is created when the service is called first time. This object is shared to all the clients and all the calls. No matter how many clients calls operations of service, a single service object is shared among all the clients.
- **PerCall:** A new service object is created each time a client calls operation of the service. For example if there are two clients and each client calls three operations of a service, then total six service objects will be created.
- **PerSession:** A new service object is created when a client starts the session with the service. For each session single object of the service is created. For example, if there are ten sessions then ten service object will be created.

The code snippet of applying the parameter is shown in Example 22.

Example 22. Applying InstanceContextMode

```
[ServiceBehavior(InstanceContextMode=InstanceContextMode.
PerSession)]
public class DivisionService: IDivisionService
{
        public int divide_no(int no1, int no2)
        {
            return no1 / no2;
        }
}
```

Default value of this parameter is PerCall. It is not advisable to provide values as Single.

ReleaseServiceInstanceOnTransactionComplete

It determines the recycle point of the service object when the transaction is finished. The data type of this parameter is a Boolean. The default value is true. The code snippet to set this parameter is illustrated in Example 23.

Example 23. Applying ReleaseServiceInstanceOnTransactionComplete Parameter

```
[ServiceBehavior(ReleaseServiceInstanceOnTransactionComplet
e=false)]
public class DivisionService: IDivisionService
{
        public int divide_no(int no1, int no2)
        {
            return no1 / no2;
        }
}
```

TransactionAutoCompleteOnSessionClose

It determines whether to complete the pending transactions when the session is closed. The data type of this parameter is a Boolean. Setting the value true completes the transaction when the session is closed. The default value of this parameter is false. The code snippet of applying this parameter is shown in Example 23.

Example 23. Applying TransactionAutoCompleteOnSessionClose

```
[ServiceBehavior(ReleaseServiceInstanceOnTransactionComplet
e=false)]
    public class DivisionService: IDivisionService
    {
        public int divide_no(int no1, int no2)
        {
            return no1 / no2;
        }
    }
```

TransactionIsolationLevel

This parameter determines the isolation level of the transaction. An isolation level is used to specify determine what to do when multiple transactions are accessing the data concurrently. It comes from System.Transactions.IsolationLevel enum. To use this enum, reference of System.Transactions must be added in the service project. Following are the possible isolation level:

- **Chaos:** It used to deny overwriting the highly visible transactions.
- **ReadCommitted:** The committed data can be read and the volatile data cannot be read but can be modified. This means delete or update query can be applied to volatile data.
- **ReadUnCommitted:** The uncommitted data can be read. This means that the volatile data can be read but cannot be modified and only select query can be applied to volatile data.
- **RepeatableRead:** It specifies that the volatile data can be read but cannot be modified and new data can be added. This means that select and insert query can be applied to volatile data.

- **Snapshot:** It indicates that volatile data can be read. Before applying any update on the data the transaction checks whether any other transaction has applied the changes to this data. If the data has been changed by another transaction an error is raised. This allows the current transaction to access previously committed data.
- **Serializable:** It allows volatile data to be read only and no other operations are allowed. This means that only select query can be applied to volatile data.
- **Unspecified:** It is undetermined state. If this level is set from service, the isolation level can be specified by the client program.

The code snippet to apply this parameter is illustrated in Example 24.

Example 24. Applying TransactionIsolationLevel

```
[ServiceBehavior(TransactionIsolationLevel=System.Transac-
tions.IsolationLevel.Snapshot)]
public class DivisionService: IDivisionService
{
        public int divide_no(int no1, int no2)
        {
            return no1 / no2;
        }
}
```

A volatile data is the data affected by a transaction. While developing the transaction program, it is required to specify the isolation level of transaction. Highest level of isolation level is Serializable and default value is Unspecified.

There can be a question about which isolation is better. It depends on the development requirement. The isolation level Serializable ensures consistency of data and there is no chance of corruption of data using this level, but it allows only one transaction at a time. So there is no concurrent access which affects the performance of the system. Likewise the isolation level ReadCommitted allows multiple transactions to work on volatile data, but there is a risk of inconsistency and data corruption using this level.

So it is left to the developer to choose the right isolation level based on requirements of the system.

TransactionTimeout

It determines the amount of time in which a transaction must be completed. The data type of this parameter is a string, but it takes values in the form of time span. Care should be taken while providing time out value as higher time out value may put a system in not responding state while low time out value may generate frequent exceptions. So it is left to the programmer to choose a right TransactionTimeout value. The code snippet to apply this parameter is illustrated in Example 25.

Example 25. Applying TransactionTimeou

```
[ServiceBehavior(TransactionTimeout="00:02:00")]
 public class DivisionService: IDivisionService
{
        public int divide_no(int no1, int no2)
        {
            return no1 / no2;
        }
}
```

As shown in the above example, the format is hh:mm ss. So above transaction should be completed in 2 minutes. The default value of this parameter is 0 seconds, which indicates that there is not transaction time out.

Parameters of Operation Behavior

[OperationBehavior] attribute comes from System.ServiceModel.OperationBehaviorAttribute class. It contains several parameters The important parameters are listed below:

- AutoDisposeParameters
- ReleaseInstanceMode
- TransactionAutoComplete
- TransactionScoreRequired

In the following section above parameters are explained.

AutoDisposeParameters

It specifies whether the parameters of an operation should be disposed or not. The data type of this parameter is Boolean. Default value of this parameter is true. Setting the value false, stores the parameter values in the cache memory which is shown in Example 26.

Example 26. Applying AutoDisposeParameters

```
public class DivisionService: IDivisionService
{
        [OperationBehavior (AutoDisposeParameters=false)]
        public int divide_no(int no1, int no2)
        {
            return no1 / no2;
        }
}
```

ReleaseInstanceMode

This parameter is used to specify the recycle point of the service object. It comes from System.ServiceModel.ReleaseInstanceMode enum. It decides when to dispose the service object. It has following values:

- **AfterCall:** It recycles the service object after the operation is called.
- **BeforeCall:** It recycles the service object before the operation is called.
- **BeforeAndAfterCal:** It recycles the service object before and after calling the operation.
- **None:** It recycles service object based on the value set by the InstanceContextMode parameter of service behavior attribute.

The code snippet is shown in Example 27.

Example 27. Applying ReleaseInstanceMode

```
public class DivisionService: IDivisionService
{
        [OperationBehavior (ReleaseInstanceMode=ReleaseInst
anceMode.AfterCall)]
```

```
        public int divide_no(int no1, int no2)
        {
            return no1 / no2;
        }
}
```

The value other than None overrides the value of InstanceContextMode parameter of [ServiceBehavior] attribute. For example if InstanceContextMode is set as PerSession and value of ReleaseInstanceMode is set as AfterCall then the service object is recycled after each call and object is created at each operation call not at each session. So it overrides value of PerSession to PerCall. So care should be taken while using this parameter. Default value of this parameter is None.

TransactionAutoComplete

It specifies whether to complete the transaction or not if there is no unhandled exceptions. The data type of this parameter is a Boolean. The default value of this parameter is true. Setting the value false means that transaction should be committed or rolled back manually by the developer and developer has to deal with the exception handling mechanism. The code snippet to apply this parameter is shown in Example 28.

Example 28. Applying TransactionAutoComplete

```
public class DivisionService: IDivisionService
{
        [OperationBehavior (TransactionAutoComplete=false)]
        public int divide_no(int no1, int no2)
        {
            return no1 / no2;
        }
}
```

It is advisable to set this value as true which is by default.

TransactionScoreRequired

It is used to specify whether the operation requires a transaction scope. The data type of this parameter is Boolean. Default value is false. Setting the true value of this parameter executes the operation under the flowed transaction if flowed transaction is available. If flowed transaction is not available then new transaction is created and the operation is executed under new transaction. The code snippet of applying this parameter is illustrated in Example 29.

Example 29. Applying TransactionScoreRequired

```
public class DivisionService: IDivisionService
{
        [OperationBehavior (TransactionScopeRequired=true)]
        public int divide_no(int no1, int no2)
        {
            return no1 / no2;
        }
}
```

Specifying the Service Behaviors Using the Configuration File

So far we have discussed on how to specify the behavior using the declarative method. The behaviors can be specified via configuration file also. The App.Config of host program is shown in Example 30 to demonstrate writing behaviors using the configuration file.

Example 30. Specifying Behaviors using Config File

```
<?xml version="1.0" encoding="utf-8" ?>
<configuration>
  <system.serviceModel>
    <behaviors>
      <serviceBehaviors><behavior name="NewBehavior0"><serviceMetadata httpGetEnabled="true" /><serviceDebug includeExceptionDetailInFaults="false"/><serviceTimeouts transaction-Timeout="00:01:00"/></behavior></serviceBehaviors>
    </behaviors>
    <services>
      <service behaviorConfiguration="NewBehavior0" name="ServiceBehavior_Demo.DivisionService">
        <endpoint address="" binding="basicHttpBinding" bindingConfiguration=""
```

```
                contract="ServiceBehavior_Demo.IDivisionService"
/>
        <host>
          <baseAddresses>
            <add baseAddress="http://localhost:9912/service"
/>
          </baseAddresses>
        </host>
      </service>
    </services>
  </system.serviceModel>
</configuration>
```

It left to the developer to choose the appropriate method to apply the service behaviors.

SERVICE THROTTLING

It is necessary to control the amount of work a service accepts in the situation when there are concurrent users of the service. This can be done by using the addition behavior called throttling which limits the amount of work a service can accept. It can be specified by <serviceThrottling> element within <behavior> of the configuration file. The code snippet of this element is illustrated in Example 31.

Example 31. Throttling Behavior in App.Config File

```
<?xml version="1.0" encoding="utf-8" ?>
<configuration>
  <system.serviceModel>
    <behaviors>
      <serviceBehaviors>
        <behavior name="NewBehavior0">
          <serviceMetadata httpGetEnabled="true" />
          <serviceDebug includeExceptionDetailInFaults="fal
se"/>
          <serviceTimeouts transactionTimeout="00:01:00"/>
          <serviceThrottling maxConcurrentCalls="20" maxConc
urrentSessions="5"maxConcurrentInstances="5"/>
```

```
      </behavior>
    </serviceBehaviors>
  </behaviors>
  <services>
    <service behaviorConfiguration="NewBehavior0"
name="ServiceBehavior_Demo.DivisionService">
 ......
...... .
</service>
    </services>
  </system.serviceModel>
</configuration>
```

As shown in the above example, this behavior has three values which are explained below:

- **MaxConcurrentCalls:** Attribute specifies the maximum number of concurrent calls a service can accept. If maximum number of calls are met and a new call comes is placed in queue. The call inside the queue will be processed when concurrent calls are below maxConcurrent-Calls. Default value of this attribute is 16. Setting the value 0 is equal toInt32.MaxValue.

- **MaxConcurrentInstances:** Attribute specifies the maximum number of concurrent service instances of a service should be created. If maximum numbers of instances are created and new request for creating an instance comes then it is placed in the queue. The request in the queue is processed when number of instances in the queue are below maxConcurrentInstances. Default value is of this attribute is Int32. MaxValue.

- **MaxConcurrentSessions:** Attribute allows you to specify maximum number of concurrent sessions a service can have. If the maximum number of sessions are created and a request to create new session, it is placed inside a queue. The request in the queue is processed when number of sessions in queue are below maxConcurrentSessions. The default value of this attribute is 10. Setting it to 0 is equal to Int32. MaxValue.

HANDLING EXCEPTIONS

We have discussed earlier on how to view the exception details at client program using IncludeExceptionDetailInFaults behavior. Please note this behavior is not used for handling the exception it is just to show actual error. So to handle the exception in WCF service it must be converted to the SOAP faults before sending it to the client over the wire. There are two types of SOAP faults mentioned below:

- **Declared:** This kind of fault is declared using [FaultContract] attribute on operation contract.
- **Undeclared:** [FaultContract] attribute is not used on operation contract.

It is advisable to use declared soap faults for interoperability with any system. Undeclared SOAP fault can be useful for debugging purpose only. The exception can be thrown and handled by FaultException class which is discussed in below section.

FaultException<T>

FaultException class is used to throw the custom error to the client program. It is the generic version of FaultException class which can be useful to catch undeclared SOAP faults. The FaultException<T> class is used to catch declared SOAP faults in the client program. Because of this generic version of exception can be easy sent to any type of client and client can handle it easily. The practical demonstration of fault exception is illustrated in following section.

Handling Exceptions Programmatically

In this section step by step explanation of the program is mentioned.

Step 1: Create WCF service library and write the code of service contract class as depicted in Example 32.

Example 32. Service Contract Code

```
using System;
using System.Runtime.Serialization;
using System.ServiceModel;
```

275

```
using System.Text;
namespace ServiceBehavior_Demo
{
    [ServiceContract]
     public interface IDivisionService
     {
         [FaultContract (typeof(DivisionFault))]
         [OperationContract]
         int divide_no(int no1, int no2);
     }
     [DataContract]
     public class DivisionFault
     {
         [DataMember]
       public int error_code;
         [DataMember]
         public String msg;
     }
}
```

As shown in the above example, a custom class DivisionFault is created which is considered as [FaultContract] of the [OperationContract] divide_no. This defines the boundary of this operation as either integer or exception and it satisfies one of the tenets of SOA-i.e. Explicit boundary.

Step 2: Write the code of service class as illustrated in Example 33.

Example 33. Code of Service Class

```
using System;
using System.Collections.Generic;
using System.Linq;
using System.Runtime.Serialization;
using System.ServiceModel;
using System.Text;
namespace ServiceBehavior_Demo
{
    public class DivisionService: IDivisionService
    {
        public int divide_no(int no1, int no2)
```

```
        {
            if (no2 == 0)
            {
                DivisionFault df = new DivisionFault();df.
error_code = -999;df.msg = "Can't divide. It will lead to in
finity";FaultException<DivisionFault> fe = newFaultException
<DivisionFault>(df);throw fe;
            }
            else
            {
                return no1 / no2;
            }
        }
    }
}
```

The code of sending custom exception to the client is highlighted in the above example. First the object of [FaultContract] is created and its data members are assigned user defined values. Then the object of generic FaultException class is created in which the object of [FaultContract] class is passed. Finally the exception is thrown using throw keyword.

Step 3: Compile WCF service and generate the Dll. Create the console host program to host this service and write the code of Program.cs file as illustrated in Example 34.

Example 34. Code of Console Host Program

```
using System;
using System.Collections.Generic;
using System.Linq;
using System.Text;
using System.ServiceModel;
using ServiceBehavior_Demo;
namespace Division_Host
{
    class Program
    {
        static void Main(string[] args)
        {
```

277

```
        ServiceHost host = new ServiceHost(typeof(Divis
ionService));
        host.Open();
        Console.WriteLine("Service is running. Press any
key to stop");
        Console.ReadKey();
        host.Close();
    }
  }
}
```

Step 4: Create App.Config file host program as shown in Example 35.The compile the host program and run it with administrator privilege.

Example 35. App.Config File of Host Program

```xml
<?xml version="1.0" encoding="utf-8" ?>
<configuration>
  <system.serviceModel>
    <behaviors>
      <serviceBehaviors>
        <behavior name="NewBehavior0">
          <serviceMetadata httpGetEnabled="true" />
          <serviceDebug includeExceptionDetailInFaults="fal
se"/>
        </behavior>
      </serviceBehaviors>
    </behaviors>
    <services>
      <service behaviorConfiguration="NewBehavior0"
name="ServiceBehavior_Demo.DivisionService">
        <endpoint address="" binding="basicHttpBinding"
bindingConfiguration=""
          contract="ServiceBehavior_Demo.IDivisionService"
/>
        <host>
          <baseAddresses>
            <add baseAddress="http://localhost:9912/service"
/>
          </baseAddresses>
```

```
        </host>
      </service>
    </services>
  </system.serviceModel>
</configuration>
```

Step 5: Create window forms application project as client to consume the service. Design the layout of the form as shown in Figure 45.

Step 6: Write the code of Form1.cs file as depicted in Example 36.

Example 36. Code of Form1.cs File

```
using System;
using System.Collections.Generic;
using System.ComponentModel;
using System.Data;
using System.Drawing;
using System.Linq;
using System.Text;
using System.Windows.Forms;
using Div_test.DivisionClient_Ref;
using System.ServiceModel;
namespace Div_test
{
    public partial class frmDivision: Form
    {
```

Figure 45. Design of the client form

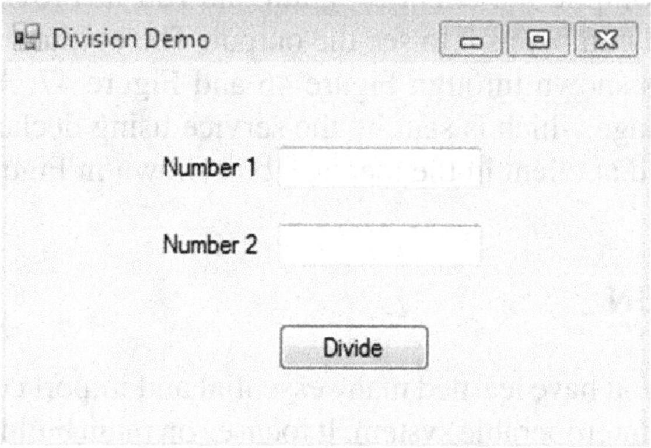

```
        public frmDivision()
        {
            InitializeComponent();
        }
        private void btnDivide_Click(object sender, Even-
tArgs e)
        {
            int no1, no2;
            no1 = Int16.Parse(tbNumber1.Text);
            no2 = Int16.Parse(tbNumber2.Text);
            DivisionServiceClient proxy=new DivisionService-
Client();
            int ans = 0;
            try
            {
                ans = proxy.divide_no(no1, no2);}catch
(FaultException<DivisionFault> fe){MessageBox.Show("Error
code=" + fe.Detail.error_code + " " +
                fe.Detail.msg);}
        }
    }
}
```

As shown in the above example the error handling code is highlighted. As discussed earlier the generic version FaultException class is used to catch the exception. To use this class in client program System.ServiceModel reference must be imported into the program by *using* keyword. In this code, it is imported on the top which is also highlighted.

Step 7: Now compile the client program and run it. Provide the value of the second number as 0 to see the output. The output of running client program is shown through Figure 46 and Figure 47. As expected the error message which is sent by the service using declared SOAP fault is displayed at client in the message box shown in Figure 47.

CONCLUSION

In this chapter you have learned many essential and import concepts to build distributed and interoperable system. It focuses on main building blocks such

Figure 46. Client program – providing inputs

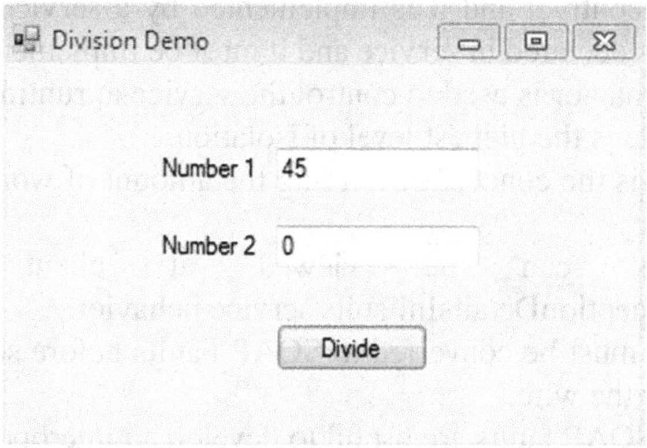

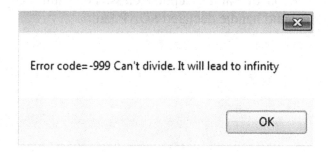

Figure 47. Client program – output message

as client and service. The client code to consume WCF is explained in depth. The service behavior is explored in depth to understand its impact on service. Following are the key points to learn from this chapter:

- The client is a piece of program which consumes the service.
- Generally a client initiates communication.
- Client code can be generated by two ways: By using svcutil and by ChannelFactory class.
- The Svcutil is a powerful command line tool to generate the client code using WSDL file of the service.
- There are three client communication patterns: one way or simplex, request reply and duplex.
- All the operations are request-reply by default.

- In duplex communication two interfaces are required. One interface is service contract and it is implemented by a service while another interface is declared in service and it must be implemented by a client.
- Service behavior is used to control the service at runtime.
- Serializable is the highest level of isolation.
- Throttling is the concept of limiting the amount of work a service can accept.
- Exceptions can be viewed at client by using IncludeExceptionDetailsInFaults service behavior.
- Exception must be converted to SOAP Faults before sending it to the client over the wire.
- Declared SOAP faults are useful to develop an interoperable system.
- Declared SOAP faults are defined using [FaultContract] attribute on operation contract.
- Generic version of FaultException class, i.e. FaultException<T> is used to send and handle declared SOAP faults.

Chapter 8
Managing Transactions in WCF

After completing this chapter, you will be able to:

- Learn about transaction.
- Gain the knowledge about properties of transaction.
- Understand the protocols used in transaction.
- Implement transaction practically.

INTRODUCTION TO TRANSACTION

This chapter covers very important concept of transaction. Transaction management is vital in the real time applications. In daily life we deal with transaction processing directly or indirectly.

A transaction is a logical unit of work. In other words it is group of one or more operations and all operations work as unit. If one operation fails entire transaction fails. For example when you purchase the item online by placing the order a transaction occurs. Let us understand how this transaction works. You place order of number of items and then you pay the money online banking system through the payment gateway. The bill amount is credited to the

DOI: 10.4018/978-1-5225-1997-3.ch008

vendor's bank account and same amount is debited from your account. So this transaction involves two operations, credit and debit.

Now imagine that from these two operations only debit operation is executed, but credit is not executed. This means that the bill amount is debited from your bank account and not credited in the vendor's account. You will not be happy! Likewise, if credit operation is executed and debit operation is not executed, you will be happy. These two situations are annoying from any of the related entities. There must be a solution to overcome this problem.

The solution to this problem is the use of the transaction mechanism in such situations. Put both debit and credit operations in the transaction. Commit the transaction if all the operations are executed successfully. Undo all the operations if any one operation fails to execute. The process of undoing the operations is known as rolling back the transaction. Now the both entities in the online purchase example are happy as there is no inconsistency because of the transaction management.

A transaction contains following ACID properties:

- **Atomic:** The operations of a transaction should work like an atom. This means you cannot separate the operations either all the operations should be executed or none of the operations should be executed. In other words, either transaction should be completed 100% or 0% there is no intermediate status such as 50%. Here 100% transaction should be committed and 0% means transaction should be rolled back.

- **Consistent:** The operations of a transaction should put a data base in consistent. For example, if Account 1 has a balance of amount 12000 and Account2 has a balance of amount 8000. Now if we perform a balance transfer of amount 1000 from account 1 to account 2, at the end of transaction Account 1 should have a balance of 11000 and Account 2 should have a balance of 9000. This involves two operations: One is the debit operation which deducts amount of 1000 from the balance of Account 1 and another is credit operation which adds amount of 1000 to the balance of Account 2. If either of the operations fails, then all the operations should be rolled back and the Account 1 and Account 2 should have an amount which was there prior to initiating the transaction. That is Account 1 should have an amount of 12000 and Account 2 should have an amount of 8000. In summary, if the transaction is committed, then Account 1 should have a balance of 11000 and Account 2 should have a balance of 9000 and if the transaction is rolled back, then Account 1 should have a balance of 12000 and Account 2 should have a balance of 8000.

- **Isolated:** When more than transactions are accessing the same data, each transaction should work in isolated manner, i.e. transaction might not be aware about each other. For example, I am purchasing items online using net banking and at the same time my friend is withdrawing money from ATM using my debit card. Here both transactions should be executed in isolated manner and both not aware about it. The transaction should be done in such manner that it should not put the database in the inconsistent state.
- **Durable:** Durable means long lasting. It means that transaction should survive in case of any failure. Once the transaction is committed or rolled back then it should persist in the database even in case of power failure.

Transactions in WCF Service

In WCF, transaction support can be integrated by using the System.Transactions name space. The support for transactions is available in.NET since version 2.0. In WCF transaction can be easily integrated by using service behaviors and the binding which supports transaction. There are main two components to manage the transactions. One is the transaction manager which is responsible to manage the state of a particular resource utilized in a transaction. A resource manager deals with durable or volatile data. It communicates with the transaction manager to commit or rollback particular transaction. To dig more into the practical implementation of transaction understanding of following concept is required.

Two Phase Commit Protocol

Two phase commit protocol (2PC) works in two phases to maintain the atomicity among the participating resource managers (Bustamante). In this protocol the coordinator plays important role to coordinate all the participating resource manages. It works in 2 phases as shown below:

Phase 1: The coordinator asks all the resource managers to respond with their votes to commit or roll back the transaction. Each resource manager responds with commit or rollback. The coordinator collects all the votes and gets ready to decide on to commit or rollback the entire transaction.

Phase 2: The coordinator informs all the resource managers to commit or rollback based on its decision. If the resource manager informed to commit, it commits and sends an acknowledgement to the coordinator otherwise it rolls back. The coordinator waits for the acknowledgement from all the resource managers regarding the transaction commit.

This protocol provides flexibility to the WCF developers to provide greater reliability and consistency while developing transaction oriented service.

In this section and previous section I discussed about resource managers. A resource manager can be durable or volatile. Following section covers detail about these resource managers.

Durable and Volatile Resource Managers

A durable resource manager saves data during the first phase of 2PC. So in case of any system failure it, can reenlist the details to the transaction coordinator to commit or roll back the transaction. Major RDBMS providers have durable resource managers to coordinate with the coordinator. Microsoft SQL server 2008 has support of the durable resource manager.

A volatile resource manager works in the second phase of 2PC. It works on data available in the primary memory. The volatile resource manager is not able to survive in the case of system failure. This is the key difference between durable resource manager and volatile resource manager. System. Transactions namespace supports volatile resource manage and Lightweight Transaction Manager.

Web Service Atomic Transaction (WS-AT)

WS-Atomic Transaction (WS-AT) is an interoperable transaction protocol (https://msdn.microsoft.com/en-us/library/dd936243.aspx).It uses the 2PC protocol which is discussed in the previous section. A WCF service using WS-AT protocol controlled under Microsoft Distribute Transaction Coordinator (MSDTC) transaction manager. The benefit of using this protocol is to flow the WCF transaction with other technologies too. In WCF some bindings such as wsHttpBinding uses WS-AT by default while netTcpBinding uses oleTransaction(oleTx).

Microsoft Distributed Transaction Coordinator(MSDTC)

This component is available in windows operation system. To access it locate component services from the control panel and under control panel find local DTC as shown in Figure 1.

Now right click on Local DTC and click on the properties menu to see the properties of this component as shown in Figure 2. The properties window

Figure 1. Local DTC under component services

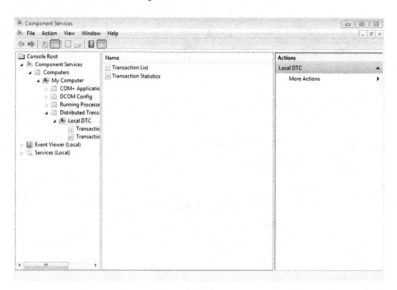

has three tabs. The first tab contains tracing information regarding the transaction. Select the appropriate option to trace by clicking on the related check box. The second tab is to log the transaction data. The third tab is related to security of transaction which is shown in Figure 3. You can allow access to different entities by clicking on related options.

The local DTC works as coordinator which takes the final decision on to commit or roll back (abort) particular transaction. To view the decision click on the Transaction Statistics option as shown in Figure 4. As shown in Figure 4, the list of active, committed and aborted transactions are shown. As of now there is no active, no committed and no aborted transaction so it shows 0 for all type of transactions.

Transaction Attributes in WCF

In previous chapter I have already discussed following parameters of service behavior and operation behavior:

Parameters of [ServiceBehavior]:

- TransactionAutoCompleteOnSessionClose
- TransactionIsolationLevel
- TransactionTimeOut

Figure 2. Property of local DTC- tracing tab

Parameters of [ServiceBehavior]:

- TransactionAutoComplete
- TransactionScopeRequired

Apart from these parameters we need to enable transaction in binding as shown in Example 1.

Example 1. Enabling Transactions in Binding

```
<wsHttpBinding>
      <binding name="NewBinding0" transactionFlow="true"
useDefaultWebProxy="false">
        <reliableSession enabled="false" />
      </binding>
</wsHttpBinding>
```

Figure 3. Security tab

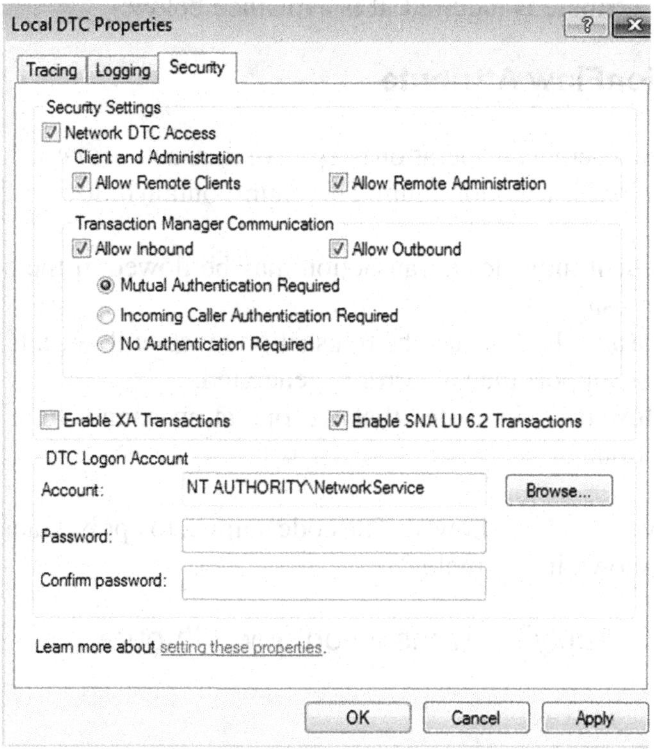

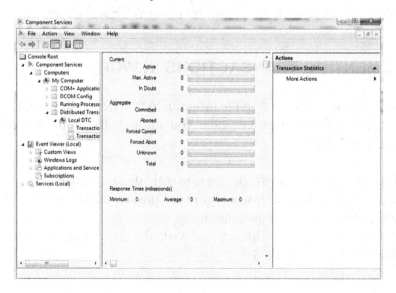

Figure 4. Transaction statistics of local DTC

To consider the particular operation as a part of a transaction or not, TransactionFlow attribute is required. It is explained below:

TransactionFlow Attribute

It determines whether an operation is a part of transaction or not. It takes value from TransationFlowOption enum. This enum contain following three values:

- **Allowed:** It indicates a transaction may be flowed, if the binding supports transaction.
- **Mandatory:** It indicates the transaction must be flowed. If the binding does not support then an error is generated.
- **NotAllowed:** It indicates that the operation cannot be a part of the transaction.

Default value is NotAllowed. The code snippet to apply TransactionFlow attribute is shown in Example 2.

Example 2. Applying TransactionFlow Attribute

```
[OperationContract]
[TransactionFlow(TransactionFlowOption.Mandatory)]
int Debit(int AccountNo, int Amt);
```

The following section explains the practical implementation of transaction program of account balance transfer using WCF service and NET client.

IMPLEMENTING TRANSACTIONS IN WCF

In this section we will develop the program to transfer money from account 1 to account2. Following steps take you through the implementation of transaction in WCF.

Step 1: Create one table in the database to store the.account details and insert data in that table as shown in Figure 5. Consider data type of AccountNo and Balance columns as numeric.

Step 2: Crete WCF service library and write the code of service contract as illustrated in Example 3.

Figure 5. Account Master Table

Account_Master:...KACCOUNTDB.MDF)

	AccountNo	Balance
	11000101	60000
▶	11200001	40000

Example 3. Service Contract Code

```
using System;
using System.Collections.Generic;
using System.Linq;
using System.Runtime.Serialization;
using System.ServiceModel;
using System.Text;
namespace BalanceTransferDemo
{
    [ServiceContract]
    public interface IBalanceTransfer
    {
        [OperationContract]
        [FaultContract (typeof(TransactionError))]
        [TransactionFlow(TransactionFlowOption.Allowed)]
        int Debit(int AccountNo, int Amt);
        [OperationContract]
        [FaultContract (typeof(TransactionError))]
        [TransactionFlow(TransactionFlowOption.Allowed)]
        int Credit(int AccountNo, int Amt);
    }
    [DataContract]
    public class TransactionError
    {
        [DataMember]
        public int error_code;
        [DataMember]
        public String error_msg;
```

```
    }
}
```

Step 3: Write the code of service class as depicted in Example 4. You need to add the reference of System.Transactions and it must be imported in the code as shown in Example 4.

Example 4. Code of Service Class

```
using System;
using System.Collections.Generic;
using System.Linq;
using System.Runtime.Serialization;
using System.ServiceModel;
using System.Text;
using System.Data.SqlClient;
using System.Transactions;
namespace BalanceTransferDemo
{
    [ServiceBehavior(TransactionIsolationLevel = Isolation-
Level.Serializable)]
    public class BalanceTransfer: IBalanceTransfer
    {
        [OperationBehavior(TransactionScopeRequired = true)]
        public int Debit(int AccountNo, int Amt)
        {
            SqlConnection conn = new SqlConnection(@"Data
Source=.\SQLEXPRESS;AttachDbFilename=D:\Demonstrations\
Chapter8\BankAccountdb.mdf;Integrated Security=True;Connect
Timeout=30;User Instance=True");
            SqlCommand cmd = new SqlCommand();
            String sql = "update Account_master set
Balance=Balance-" + Amt + " where Accountno=" + AccountNo;
            cmd.Connection = conn;
            cmd.CommandText = sql;
            conn.Open();

            int records_affected = cmd.ExecuteNonQuery();
            conn.Close();
```

```
            if (records_affected == 0)
            {
                TransactionError te = new TransactionEr-
ror();
                te.error_code = -88;
                te.error_msg = "Unable to debit due to wrong
account number";
                FaultException<TransactionError> fe = new Fa
ultException<TransactionError>(te);
                throw fe;
            }
            return Amt;
        }
        [OperationBehavior(TransactionScopeRequired = true)]
        public int Credit(int AccountNo, int Amt)
        {
            SqlConnection conn = new SqlConnection(@"Data
Source=.\SQLEXPRESS;AttachDbFilename=D:\Demonstrations\
Chapter8\BankAccountdb.mdf;Integrated Security=True;Connect
Timeout=30;User Instance=True");
            SqlCommand cmd = new SqlCommand();
            String sql = "update Account_master set
Balance=Balance+" + Amt + " where Accountno=" + AccountNo;
            cmd.Connection = conn;
            cmd.CommandText = sql;
            conn.Open();

            int records_affected = cmd.ExecuteNonQuery();
            conn.Close();
            if (records_affected == 0)
            {
                TransactionError te = new TransactionEr-
ror();
                te.error_code = -88;
                te.error_msg = "Unable to credit due to
wrong account number";
                FaultException<TransactionError> fe = new Fa
ultException<TransactionError>(te);
                throw fe;
```

```
            }
            return Amt;
        }
    }
}
```

Step 4: Compile WCF service library and host the service using console application project. Write the code in the Program.cs file of console application project as illustrated in Example 5.

Example 5. Code of Program.cs of Console Application Project

```
using System;
using System.Collections.Generic;
using System.Linq;
using System.Text;
using System.ServiceModel;
using BalanceTransferDemo;
namespace Transaction_Console_Host
{
    class Program
    {
        static void Main(string[] args)
        {
            ServiceHost host = new ServiceHost(typeof(Balan
ceTransfer));
            host.Open();
            Console.WriteLine("Service is running. Press any
key to stop");
            Console.ReadKey();
            host.Close();
        }
    }
}
```

Step 5: Prepare the App.Config file and write the code of this file as illustrated in Example 6.

Example 6. App.Config file of Console Application Project

```xml
<?xml version="1.0"?>
<configuration>
    <system.serviceModel>
        <behaviors>
            <serviceBehaviors>
                <behavior name="NewBehavior0">
                    <serviceMetadata httpGetEnabled="true"/>
                </behavior>
            </serviceBehaviors>
        </behaviors>
        <bindings>
            <wsHttpBinding>
                <binding name="NewBinding0"
transactionFlow="true"/>
            </wsHttpBinding>
        </bindings>
        <services>
            <service behaviorConfiguration="NewBehavior0"
name="BalanceTransferDemo.BalanceTransfer">
                <endpoint address=""
binding="wsHttpBinding" bindingConfiguration="NewBinding0"
contract="BalanceTransferDemo.IBalanceTransfer"/>
                <host>
                    <baseAddresses>
                        <add baseAddress="http://local-
host:9067/TransactionService"/>
                    </baseAddresses>
                </host>
            </service>
        </services>
    </system.serviceModel>
</configuration>
```

Step 6: Compile the application project and generate EXE of console application project. Run locate the EXE and run it with the administrator
credentials. Keep the host program in running mode and create the client
to consume the service.

Figure 6. Layout of form

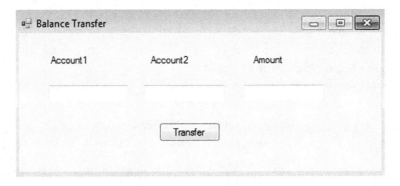

Step 7: Create a windows forms application project and design the layout of form as shown in Figure 6.

Step 8: Add the reference of service by using add service option and generate the proxy class. Also add the reference of System.ServiceModel and System.Transactions in windows forms project. The App.Config file is auto generated which is shown in Example 7.

Example 7. App.Config File of Client Project

```xml
<?xml version="1.0" encoding="utf-8" ?>
<configuration>
    <system.serviceModel>
        <bindings>
            <wsHttpBinding>
                <binding name="WSHttpBinding_IBalanceTrans-
fer" transactionFlow="true" />
            </wsHttpBinding>
        </bindings>
        <client>
            <endpoint address="http://localhost:9067/Trans-
actionService"
                binding="wsHttpBinding" bindingConfiguration
="WSHttpBinding_IBalanceTransfer"
                contract="Transaction_ClientRef.IBalance-
Transfer" name="WSHttpBinding_IBalanceTransfer">
                <identity>
                    <userPrincipalName value="india1\india"
```

```
/>
                </identity>
            </endpoint>
        </client>
    </system.serviceModel>
</configuration>
```

Write the code of Form1.cs file of client program as shown in Example 8.

Example 8. Code of Form1.cs of Client Project

```
using System;
using System.Collections.Generic;
using System.ComponentModel;
using System.Data;
using System.Drawing;
using System.Linq;
using System.Text;
using System.Windows.Forms;
using Transaction_ClientProj.Transaction_ClientRef;using
System.Transactions;using System.ServiceModel;
namespace Transaction_ClientProj
{
    public partial class frmBalanceTransfer: Form
    {
        public frmBalanceTransfer()
        {
            InitializeComponent();
        }
        private void btnTransfer_Click(object sender, Even-
tArgs e)
        {
            int account1 = Int32.Parse(tbAccount1.Text);
            int account2 = Int32.Parse(tbAccount2.Text);
            int amt = Int16.Parse(tbAmount.Text);
            BalanceTransferClient proxy = new BalanceTrans-
ferClient();
            using (TransactionScope ts = new Transaction-
Scope())
            {
```

```
                    try
                    {
                        proxy.Debit(account1,amt);
                        proxy.Credit(account2,amt);
                        ts.Complete();
                        MessageBox.Show("Amount is Transferred
successfully");
                    }
                    catch (FaultException<TransactionError> fe)
                    {
                        MessageBox.Show("Unable to transfer the
amount due to error. "+
                        fe.Detail.error_msg);
                        ts.Dispose();
                    }
                }
            }
        }
}
```

In the above code, the TransactionScope class is used to commit or rollback a transaction. It contains two methods. The Complete() method sends signal to Distributed Transaction Coordinator (DTC) to commit the transaction while the Dispose() method sends signal to Distributed Transaction Coordinator (DTC) abort (rollback) the transaction. The Complete() method is written in try block after writing both operations. This means that all the operations are completed successfully, there is not error and transaction should be completed which accomplished by Complete() method. The Dispose() method is written in catch block which means that there is some error either in the first operation, second operation or both operations. So transaction must be aborted, which is done by using Dispose() method.

Step 9: Compile the client project and execute it. The output of successful transaction is shown in Figure 7 and Figure 8, and the screen of DTC confirming the committed transaction is shown in Figure 9.

Likewise the output of unsuccessful transaction is shown in Figure 10 and Figure 11, which is rolled back (aborted) by DTC as shown in Figure 12.

Figure 7. Client program output of commit operation of transaction – user input

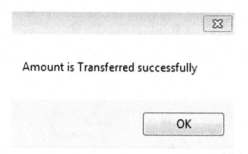

Amount is Transferred successfully

OK

Figure 8. Client program output of commit operation of transaction – output message

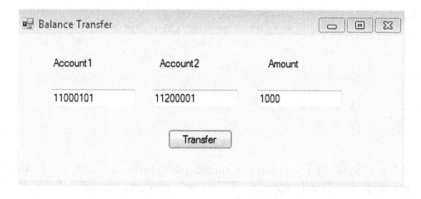

CONCLUSION

This chapter covers important concepts of transaction. It provided in depth knowledge of different protocols available for transaction management. The practical implementation of transaction using WCF service and .NET client is explained in depth. Following points should be remembered from this chapter.

- A transaction is a logical unit of work. It is a group of operations which are executed as a whole unit.
- A transaction can be in 0% state or 100% state.
- For 2 phase commit protocol (2PC) there should be a coordinator and more than one resource managers.
- In windows operating system Local Distributed Transaction Coordinator is available to deal with the transactions.

Figure 9. DTC after committing transaction

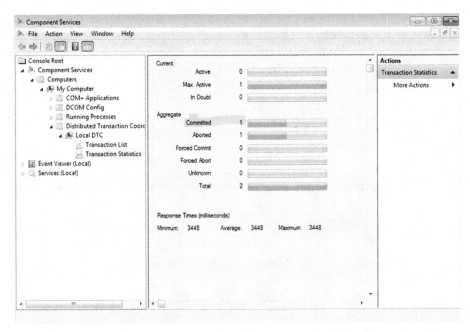

- In.NET System.Transactions namespace provides support to develop transaction related program. This namespace is available from.NET2.0 version onwards.
- There are two transaction protocols: Web Service Atomic Transaction (WS-AT) and oleTransaction (oleTx).
- The wsHttpBinding uses WS-AT by default.

Figure 10. Client program output of abort (rollback) operation of transaction – user input

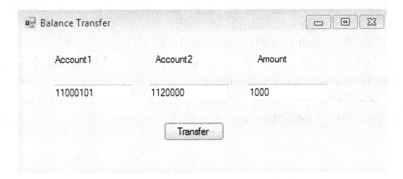

Figure 11. Client program output of abort (rollback) operation of transaction – output message

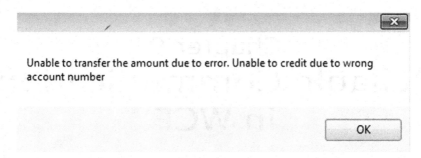

Figure 12. DTC after rolling back (aborting) transaction

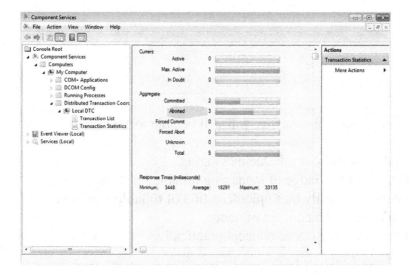

- In.Net, transaction support is provided by System.Transactions name space. The reference of this namespace must be added in WCF service and client in order to have transaction support.
- In.Net client TransactionScope class is used to commit or abort (rollback) the transaction.

Chapter 9
Reliable Communication in WCF

After completing this chapter, you will be able to:

- Understand about reliable messaging.
- Gain the knowledge of managing reliable sessions.
- Learn practically on implementation of reliable sessions.
- Understand the concept of queue.
- Implement the queue concept practically.

INTRODUCTION

Reliable messaging is the mechanism to successfully deliver the message in case of failure of dependent components in service oriented applications. The failure can be due to network, transport failure or any other failure. In WCF reliable messing is provided by reliable sessions using WS-reliable messaging protocol. When you send any message you make sure that it is reached to the destination. If it is not reached you may send it again to guarantee the delivery of the message. This mechanism is adopted by TCP and name pipes, but HTTP does have this mechanism. For TCP and named pipe

DOI: 10.4018/978-1-5225-1997-3.ch009

communication guarantee of message delivery is only from point-point. If other components such as a proxy server or router exist, then it is difficult to get the message delivery assurance. Now reliable sessions in WCF provide following advantages:

- End-to-end message delivery is guaranteed.
- The entire message is delivered not just packet of messages are delivered.
- There is no chance of duplication of message i.e. a message is sent exactly once.
- The reliable messaging protocol works on all types of binding so reliable delivery of message possible in HTTP protocol also.
- The reliable messaging protocol is interoperable so guarantee of message delivery is possible between diverse machines and diverse platforms. For example, because of this protocol a message is surely delivered between WCF service and JAVA program running on Linux.

In the following section, reliable sessions are explained in depth. For durable transfer message queuing is used which is discussed after the section of reliable sessions.

WORKING WITH RELIABLE SESSIONS

To enable reliable messaging in WCF, you must use binding which supports reliable messaging. The bindings such as wsHttpBinding, netTcpBinding, wsDualHttpBinding etc support the reliable messaging. The reliable messaging can be enabled by adding new binding configuration and relating that binding configuration to the endpoint as illustrated in the code snippet of configuration file in Example 1.

Example 1. Adding Support for Reliable Session in Binding

```
<bindings>
<wsHttpBinding>
<binding name="NewBinding0">
<reliableSession enabled="true" />
</binding>
</wsHttpBinding>
</bindings>
```

```
<services>
<service behaviorConfiguration="NewBehavior0"
name="ReliableSessionDemo.MathOperations">
<endpoint address="" binding="wsHttpBinding" bindingConfigu
ration="NewBinding0"
contract="ReliableSessionDemo.IMathOperations"
/>
<host>
<baseAddresses>
<add baseAddress="http://localhost:9090/ReliableService" />
</baseAddresses>
</host>
</service>
</services>
```

The bindings which support reliable session have following properties which can be configured in the configuration file:

- **InactivityTimeout:** It is a time span which controls the inactivity time during the session. If no communication is done during the elapsed inactivityTimeout, the session is faulted and an error is generated. The format of this property is "hh:mm:ss". The default time out value is 00:02:00 i.e. 2 minutes. Following is the syntax to generate in activity timeout of session to 2 minutes:

```
<wsHttpBinding>
<binding name="NewBinding0">
<reliableSession inactivityTimeout="00:02:00"/>
</binding>
</wsHttpBinding>
```

So as per above code if there is no communication between service and client after two minutes the session is faulted and trying to send the message results in following error:

The underlying secure session has faulted before the reliable session fully completed. The reliable session was faulted.

- **Enabled:** It is used to determine whether a reliable session is allowed or not. It takes Boolean value. So, specifying a true value allows having a reliable session while a false value does allow having reliable session. In some binding it is enabled by default while in the binding such as wsHttpBinding it is not enabled so we need to enable it by specifying the true value as shown below:

```
<wsHttpBinding>
<binding name="NewBinding0">
<reliableSession inactivityTimeout="00:01:00"
enabled="true"/>
</binding>
</wsHttpBinding>
```

- **Ordered:** This property takes care about the order. It takes Boolean value. It is enabled by default in all the bindings. If a reliable session is enabled, setting the true value of this property the messages are delivered in order. Following is the syntax of specifying this property:

```
<wsHttpBinding>
<binding name="NewBinding0">
<reliableSession inactivityTimeout="00:01:00" enabled="true"
ordered="true" />
</binding>
</wsHttpBinding>
```

In most of the situations the default values are sufficient and appropriate, but you can chbange the inactivity time out for long sessions by increasing its value. Many of the available bindings support reliable session except a few such as basicHttpBinding. It is also possible to enable reliable session in the custom binding. Following example shows how to configure reliable session in custom binding:

```
<customBinding>
<binding name="NewBinding1">
<reliableSession inactivityTimeout="00:05:00"
ordered="true"/>
<textMessageEncoding />
<httpTransport />
</binding>
```

Following are the steps to write the WCF service with reliable messaging support:

Step 1: Create new WCF service library project and write the code of service contract class as shown in Example 2.

Example 2. Code of Service Contract Class

```
using System;
using System.Collections.Generic;
using System.Linq;
using System.Runtime.Serialization;
using System.ServiceModel;
using System.Text;
namespace ReliableSessionDemo
{
[ServiceContract]
    public interface IMathOperations
    {
[OperationContract]
int add_nos(int no1, int no2);
[OperationContract]
int subtract_nos(int no1, int no2);
    }
}
```

Step 2: Write the code of service class as depicted in Example 3.

Example 3. Code of Service Class

```
using System;
using System.Collections.Generic;
using System.Linq;
using System.Runtime.Serialization;
using System.ServiceModel;
using System.Text;
namespace ReliableSessionDemo
{
public class MathOperations: IMathOperations
{
```

```
public int add_nos(int no1, int no2)
{
return no1 + no2;
}
public int subtract_nos(int no1, int no2)
{
return no1 - no2;
}
}
}
```

Step 3: Compile the service project and create a console application project to host the service. Write the code in Program.cs file to host the service. The code of Program.cs file is shown in Example 4.

Example 4. Code of Program.cs File

```
using System;
using System.Collections.Generic;
using System.Linq;
using System.Text;
using ReliableSessionDemo;
using System.ServiceModel;
namespace Session_Host
{
class Program
{
static void Main(string[] args)
{
ServiceHost host = new ServiceHost(typeof(MathOperations));
host.Open();
Console.WriteLine("Service is running. Press any key to
stop");
Console.ReadKey();
host.Close();
}
}
}
```

Step 4: Create App.Config file with the binding having reliable session support as shown in the Example 5.

Example 5. App.Config File with Reliable Session Support

```
<?xml version="1.0" encoding="utf-8" ?>
<configuration>
<system.serviceModel>
<behaviors>
<serviceBehaviors>
<behavior name="NewBehavior0">
<serviceMetadata httpGetEnabled="true" />
</behavior>
</serviceBehaviors>
</behaviors>
<bindings><wsHttpBinding><binding name="NewBinding0"><reliab
leSession ordered="true" inactivityTimeout="00:01:00"enabled
="true" /></binding></wsHttpBinding></bindings>
<services>
<service behaviorConfiguration="NewBehavior0"
name="ReliableSessionDemo.MathOperations">
<endpoint address="" binding="wsHttpBinding" bindingConfigu
ration="NewBinding0"
contract="ReliableSessionDemo.IMathOperations" />
<host>
<baseAddresses>
<add baseAddress="http://localhost:9090/ReliableService" />
</baseAddresses>
</host>
</service>
</services>
</system.serviceModel>
</configuration>
```

As shown in above configuration a binding element is added under <bindings> tag. This binding is related to endpoint under binding Configuration property as highlighted in Example 5. If you forget to relate it with the endpoint, the reliable session will not be applied to the endpoint.

Step 5: Now compile the console application project (host) and execute it with administrator privileges. After it is executed successfully the WSDL file of the service is generated as shown in Example 6.

Example 6. WSDL File of Service

```
<?xml version="1.0" encoding="utf-8" ?>
- <wsdl:definitions name="MathOperations"
targetNamespace="http://tempuri.org/" xmlns:wsdl="http://
schemas.xmlsoap.org/wsdl/" xmlns:xsd="http://www.w3.
org/2001/XMLSchema" xmlns:soapenc="http://schemas.xmlsoap.
org/soap/encoding/" xmlns:wsu="http://docs.oasis-open.org/
wss/2004/01/oasis-200401-wss-wssecurity-utility-1.0.xsd"
xmlns:soap="http://schemas.xmlsoap.org/wsdl/soap/"
xmlns:soap12="http://schemas.xmlsoap.org/wsdl/soap12/"
xmlns:tns="http://tempuri.org/" xmlns:wsa="http://schemas.
xmlsoap.org/ws/2004/08/addressing" xmlns:wsx="http://sche-
mas.xmlsoap.org/ws/2004/09/mex" xmlns:wsap="http://schemas.
xmlsoap.org/ws/2004/08/addressing/policy"
xmlns:wsaw="http://www.w3.org/2006/05/addressing/wsdl"
xmlns:msc="http://schemas.microsoft.com/ws/2005/12/wsdl/con-
tract" xmlns:wsp="http://schemas.xmlsoap.org/ws/2004/09/
policy" xmlns:wsa10="http://www.w3.org/2005/08/addressing"
xmlns:wsam="http://www.w3.org/2007/05/addressing/metadata">
- <wsp:Policy wsu:Id="WSHttpBinding_IMathOperations_policy">
- <wsp:ExactlyOne>
- <wsp:All>
- <wsrm:RMAssertion xmlns:wsrm="http://schemas.xmlsoap.org/
ws/2005/02/rm/policy">
<wsrm:InactivityTimeout Milliseconds="60000" />
<wsrm:AcknowledgementInterval Milliseconds="200" />
</wsrm:RMAssertion>
- <sp:SymmetricBinding xmlns:sp="http://schemas.xmlsoap.org/
ws/2005/07/securitypolicy">
- <wsp:Policy>
- <sp:ProtectionToken>
- <wsp:Policy>
- <sp:SecureConversationToken sp:IncludeToken="http://
schemas.xmlsoap.org/ws/2005/07/securitypolicy/IncludeToken/
AlwaysToRecipient">
```

```
- <wsp:Policy>
<sp:RequireDerivedKeys />
- <sp:BootstrapPolicy>
- <wsp:Policy>
- <sp:SignedParts>
<sp:Body />
<sp:Header Name="To" Namespace="http://www.w3.org/2005/08/
addressing" />
<sp:Header Name="From" Namespace="http://www.w3.org/2005/08/
addressing" />
<sp:Header Name="FaultTo" Namespace="http://www.w3.
org/2005/08/addressing" />
<sp:Header Name="ReplyTo" Namespace="http://www.w3.
org/2005/08/addressing" />
<sp:Header Name="MessageID" Namespace="http://www.w3.
org/2005/08/addressing" />
<sp:Header Name="RelatesTo" Namespace="http://www.w3.
org/2005/08/addressing" />
<sp:Header Name="Action" Namespace="http://www.w3.
org/2005/08/addressing" />
</sp:SignedParts>
- <sp:EncryptedParts>
<sp:Body />
</sp:EncryptedParts>
- <sp:SymmetricBinding>
- <wsp:Policy>
- <sp:ProtectionToken>
- <wsp:Policy>
- <sp:SpnegoContextToken sp:IncludeToken="http://schemas.
xmlsoap.org/ws/2005/07/securitypolicy/IncludeToken/AlwaysTo-
Recipient">
- <wsp:Policy>
<sp:RequireDerivedKeys />
</wsp:Policy>
</sp:SpnegoContextToken>
</wsp:Policy>
</sp:ProtectionToken>
- <sp:AlgorithmSuite>
- <wsp:Policy>
<sp:Basic256 />
```

```
</wsp:Policy>
</sp:AlgorithmSuite>
- <sp:Layout>
- <wsp:Policy>
<sp:Strict />
</wsp:Policy>
</sp:Layout>
<sp:IncludeTimestamp />
<sp:EncryptSignature />
<sp:OnlySignEntireHeadersAndBody />
</wsp:Policy>
</sp:SymmetricBinding>
- <sp:Wss11>
<wsp:Policy />
</sp:Wss11>
- <sp:Trust10>
- <wsp:Policy>
<sp:MustSupportIssuedTokens />
<sp:RequireClientEntropy />
<sp:RequireServerEntropy />
</wsp:Policy>
</sp:Trust10>
</wsp:Policy>
</sp:BootstrapPolicy>
</wsp:Policy>
</sp:SecureConversationToken>
</wsp:Policy>
</sp:ProtectionToken>
- <sp:AlgorithmSuite>
- <wsp:Policy>
<sp:Basic256 />
</wsp:Policy>
</sp:AlgorithmSuite>
- <sp:Layout>
- <wsp:Policy>
<sp:Strict />
</wsp:Policy>
</sp:Layout>
<sp:IncludeTimestamp />
<sp:EncryptSignature />
```

```
<sp:OnlySignEntireHeadersAndBody />
</wsp:Policy>
</sp:SymmetricBinding>
- <sp:Wss11 xmlns:sp="http://schemas.xmlsoap.org/ws/2005/07/
securitypolicy">
<wsp:Policy />
</sp:Wss11>
- <sp:Trust10 xmlns:sp="http://schemas.xmlsoap.org/
ws/2005/07/securitypolicy">
- <wsp:Policy>
<sp:MustSupportIssuedTokens />
<sp:RequireClientEntropy />
<sp:RequireServerEntropy />
</wsp:Policy>
</sp:Trust10>
<wsaw:UsingAddressing />
</wsp:All>
</wsp:ExactlyOne>
</wsp:Policy>
- <wsp:Policy wsu:Id="WSHttpBinding_IMathOperations_add_nos_
Input_policy">
- <wsp:ExactlyOne>
- <wsp:All>
- <sp:SignedParts xmlns:sp="http://schemas.xmlsoap.org/
ws/2005/07/securitypolicy">
<sp:Body />
<sp:Header Name="Sequence" Namespace="http://schemas.xml-
soap.org/ws/2005/02/rm" />
<sp:Header Name="SequenceAcknowledgement" Namespace="http://
schemas.xmlsoap.org/ws/2005/02/rm" />
<sp:Header Name="AckRequested" Namespace="http://schemas.
xmlsoap.org/ws/2005/02/rm" />
<sp:Header Name="To" Namespace="http://www.w3.org/2005/08/
addressing" />
<sp:Header Name="From" Namespace="http://www.w3.org/2005/08/
addressing" />
<sp:Header Name="FaultTo" Namespace="http://www.w3.
org/2005/08/addressing" />
<sp:Header Name="ReplyTo" Namespace="http://www.w3.
org/2005/08/addressing" />
```

```
<sp:Header Name="MessageID" Namespace="http://www.w3.
org/2005/08/addressing" />
<sp:Header Name="RelatesTo" Namespace="http://www.w3.
org/2005/08/addressing" />
<sp:Header Name="Action" Namespace="http://www.w3.
org/2005/08/addressing" />
</sp:SignedParts>
- <sp:EncryptedParts xmlns:sp="http://schemas.xmlsoap.org/
ws/2005/07/securitypolicy">
<sp:Body />
</sp:EncryptedParts>
</wsp:All>
</wsp:ExactlyOne>
</wsp:Policy>
- <wsp:Policy wsu:Id="WSHttpBinding_IMathOperations_add_nos_
output_policy">
- <wsp:ExactlyOne>
- <wsp:All>
- <sp:SignedParts xmlns:sp="http://schemas.xmlsoap.org/
ws/2005/07/securitypolicy">
<sp:Body />
<sp:Header Name="Sequence" Namespace="http://schemas.xml-
soap.org/ws/2005/02/rm" />
<sp:Header Name="SequenceAcknowledgement" Namespace="http://
schemas.xmlsoap.org/ws/2005/02/rm" />
<sp:Header Name="AckRequested" Namespace="http://schemas.
xmlsoap.org/ws/2005/02/rm" />
<sp:Header Name="To" Namespace="http://www.w3.org/2005/08/
addressing" />
<sp:Header Name="From" Namespace="http://www.w3.org/2005/08/
addressing" />
<sp:Header Name="FaultTo" Namespace="http://www.w3.
org/2005/08/addressing" />
<sp:Header Name="ReplyTo" Namespace="http://www.w3.
org/2005/08/addressing" />
<sp:Header Name="MessageID" Namespace="http://www.w3.
org/2005/08/addressing" />
<sp:Header Name="RelatesTo" Namespace="http://www.w3.
org/2005/08/addressing" />
<sp:Header Name="Action" Namespace="http://www.w3.
```

```
org/2005/08/addressing" />
</sp:SignedParts>
- <sp:EncryptedParts xmlns:sp="http://schemas.xmlsoap.org/
ws/2005/07/securitypolicy">
<sp:Body />
</sp:EncryptedParts>
</wsp:All>
</wsp:ExactlyOne>
</wsp:Policy>
- <wsp:Policy wsu:Id="WSHttpBinding_IMathOperations_sub-
tract_nos_Input_policy">
- <wsp:ExactlyOne>
- <wsp:All>
- <sp:SignedParts xmlns:sp="http://schemas.xmlsoap.org/
ws/2005/07/securitypolicy">
<sp:Body />
<sp:Header Name="Sequence" Namespace="http://schemas.xml-
soap.org/ws/2005/02/rm" />
<sp:Header Name="SequenceAcknowledgement" Namespace="http://
schemas.xmlsoap.org/ws/2005/02/rm" />
<sp:Header Name="AckRequested" Namespace="http://schemas.
xmlsoap.org/ws/2005/02/rm" />
<sp:Header Name="To" Namespace="http://www.w3.org/2005/08/
addressing" />
<sp:Header Name="From" Namespace="http://www.w3.org/2005/08/
addressing" />
<sp:Header Name="FaultTo" Namespace="http://www.w3.
org/2005/08/addressing" />
<sp:Header Name="ReplyTo" Namespace="http://www.w3.
org/2005/08/addressing" />
<sp:Header Name="MessageID" Namespace="http://www.w3.
org/2005/08/addressing" />
<sp:Header Name="RelatesTo" Namespace="http://www.w3.
org/2005/08/addressing" />
<sp:Header Name="Action" Namespace="http://www.w3.
org/2005/08/addressing" />
</sp:SignedParts>
- <sp:EncryptedParts xmlns:sp="http://schemas.xmlsoap.org/
ws/2005/07/securitypolicy">
<sp:Body />
```

```
</sp:EncryptedParts>
</wsp:All>
</wsp:ExactlyOne>
</wsp:Policy>
- <wsp:Policy wsu:Id="WSHttpBinding_IMathOperations_sub-
tract_nos_output_policy">
- <wsp:ExactlyOne>
- <wsp:All>
- <sp:SignedParts xmlns:sp="http://schemas.xmlsoap.org/
ws/2005/07/securitypolicy">
<sp:Body />
<sp:Header Name="Sequence" Namespace="http://schemas.xml-
soap.org/ws/2005/02/rm" />
<sp:Header Name="SequenceAcknowledgement" Namespace="http://
schemas.xmlsoap.org/ws/2005/02/rm" />
<sp:Header Name="AckRequested" Namespace="http://schemas.
xmlsoap.org/ws/2005/02/rm" />
<sp:Header Name="To" Namespace="http://www.w3.org/2005/08/
addressing" />
<sp:Header Name="From" Namespace="http://www.w3.org/2005/08/
addressing" />
<sp:Header Name="FaultTo" Namespace="http://www.w3.
org/2005/08/addressing" />
<sp:Header Name="ReplyTo" Namespace="http://www.w3.
org/2005/08/addressing" />
<sp:Header Name="MessageID" Namespace="http://www.w3.
org/2005/08/addressing" />
<sp:Header Name="RelatesTo" Namespace="http://www.w3.
org/2005/08/addressing" />
<sp:Header Name="Action" Namespace="http://www.w3.
org/2005/08/addressing" />
</sp:SignedParts>
- <sp:EncryptedParts xmlns:sp="http://schemas.xmlsoap.org/
ws/2005/07/securitypolicy">
<sp:Body />
</sp:EncryptedParts>
</wsp:All>
</wsp:ExactlyOne>
</wsp:Policy>
- <wsdl:types>
```

315

```
- <xsd:schema targetNamespace="http://tempuri.org/Imports">
<xsd:import schemaLocation="http://localhost:9090/
ReliableService?xsd=xsd0" namespace="http://tempuri.org/" />
<xsd:import schemaLocation="http://localhost:9090/
ReliableService?xsd=xsd1" namespace="http://schemas.micro-
soft.com/2003/10/Serialization/" />
</xsd:schema>
</wsdl:types>
- <wsdl:message name="IMathOperations_add_nos_InputMessage">
<wsdl:part name="parameters" element="tns:add_nos" />
</wsdl:message>
- <wsdl:message name="IMathOperations_add_nos_OutputMes-
sage">
<wsdl:part name="parameters" element="tns:add_nosResponse"
/>
</wsdl:message>
- <wsdl:message name="IMathOperations_subtract_nos_InputMes-
sage">
<wsdl:part name="parameters" element="tns:subtract_nos" />
</wsdl:message>
- <wsdl:message name="IMathOperations_subtract_nos_Output-
Message">
<wsdl:part name="parameters" element="tns:subtract_nosRe-
sponse" />
</wsdl:message>
- <wsdl:portType name="IMathOperations">
- <wsdl:operation name="add_nos">
<wsdl:input wsaw:Action="http://tempuri.org/IMathOperations/
add_nos" message="tns:IMathOperations_add_nos_InputMessage"
/>
<wsdl:output wsaw:Action="http://tempuri.org/IMathOpera-
tions/add_nosResponse" message="tns:IMathOperations_add_nos_
OutputMessage" />
</wsdl:operation>
- <wsdl:operation name="subtract_nos">
<wsdl:input wsaw:Action="http://tempuri.org/IMathOperations/
subtract_nos" message="tns:IMathOperations_subtract_nos_In-
putMessage" />
<wsdl:output wsaw:Action="http://tempuri.org/IMathOpera-
tions/subtract_nosResponse" message="tns:IMathOperations_
```

```
subtract_nos_OutputMessage" />
</wsdl:operation>
</wsdl:portType>
- <wsdl:binding name="WSHttpBinding_IMathOperations"
type="tns:IMathOperations">
<wsp:PolicyReference URI="#WSHttpBinding_IMathOperations_
policy" />
<soap12:binding transport="http://schemas.xmlsoap.org/soap/
http" />
- <wsdl:operation name="add_nos">
<soap12:operation soapAction="http://tempuri.org/IMathOpera-
tions/add_nos" style="document" />
- <wsdl:input>
<wsp:PolicyReference URI="#WSHttpBinding_IMathOperations_
add_nos_Input_policy" />
<soap12:body use="literal" />
</wsdl:input>
- <wsdl:output>
<wsp:PolicyReference URI="#WSHttpBinding_IMathOperations_
add_nos_output_policy" />
<soap12:body use="literal" />
</wsdl:output>
</wsdl:operation>
- <wsdl:operation name="subtract_nos">
<soap12:operation soapAction="http://tempuri.org/IMathOpera-
tions/subtract_nos" style="document" />
- <wsdl:input>
<wsp:PolicyReference URI="#WSHttpBinding_IMathOperations_
subtract_nos_Input_policy" />
<soap12:body use="literal" />
</wsdl:input>
- <wsdl:output>
<wsp:PolicyReference URI="#WSHttpBinding_IMathOperations_
subtract_nos_output_policy" />
<soap12:body use="literal" />
</wsdl:output>
</wsdl:operation>
</wsdl:binding>
- <wsdl:service name="MathOperations">
- <wsdl:port name="WSHttpBinding_IMathOperations"
```

Figure 1. Screen design of form of client project

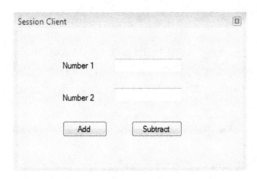

```
binding="tns:WSHttpBinding_IMathOperations">
<soap12:address location="http://localhost:9090/ReliableSer-
vice" />
- <wsa10:EndpointReference>
<wsa10:Address>http://localhost:9090/ReliableService</
wsa10:Address>
- <Identity xmlns="http://schemas.xmlsoap.org/ws/2006/02/ad-
dressingidentity">
<Upn>INDIA1\india</Upn>
</Identity>
</wsa10:EndpointReference>
</wsdl:port>
</wsdl:service>
</wsdl:definitions>
```

In above WSDL file the header part contains policy information about service. This part indicates that the service need to provide reliable session in the communication.

Step 5: Create windows forms application project to consume the service. Design the layout of the form as shown in Figure 1.

Step 6: Generate the proxy class by adding the reference of the service and write the code of client program as illustrated in Example 7.

Example 7. Code of Client Program

```
using System;
using System.Collections.Generic;
```

```
using System.ComponentModel;
using System.Data;
using System.Drawing;
using System.Linq;
using System.Text;
using System.Windows.Forms;
using Session_Client.MathServiceRef;
namespace Session_Client
{
public partial class Form1: Form
{
MathOperationsClient proxy = new MathOperationsClient();
public Form1()
{
InitializeComponent();
}
private void btnAdd_Click(object sender, EventArgs e)
{
int no1 = Int16.Parse(tbNumber1.Text);
int no2 = Int16.Parse(tbNumber2.Text);
int ans = proxy.add_nos(no1, no2);
MessageBox.Show("Answer of additions is " + ans);
}
private void btnSubtract_Click(object sender, EventArgs e)
{
int no1 = Int16.Parse(tbNumber1.Text);
int no2 = Int16.Parse(tbNumber2.Text);
int ans = proxy.subtract_nos(no1, no2);
MessageBox.Show("Answer of additions is " + ans);
}
}
}
```

The App.Config file of client program is shown in Example 8.

Example 8. Content of App.Config File

```
<?xml version="1.0" encoding="utf-8" ?>
<configuration>
<system.serviceModel>
```

```
<bindings>
<wsHttpBinding>
<binding name="WSHttpBinding_IMathOperations">
<reliableSession enabled="true" />
</binding>
</wsHttpBinding>
</bindings>
<client><endpoint address="http://localhost:9090/Reliable-
Service" binding="wsHttpBinding"
bindingConfiguration="WSHttpBinding_IMathOperations"
contract="MathServiceRef.IMathOperations"
name="WSHttpBinding_IMathOperations">
<identity>
<userPrincipalName value="INDIA1\india" />
</identity>
</endpoint>
</client>
</system.serviceModel>
</configuration>
```

Step 7: Now execute the client program and click on the Add button after providing the input as shown in Figure 2. As the communication is done within 1 minute the client gets correct output as shown in Figure 3.

Figure 2. Client output-providing inputs

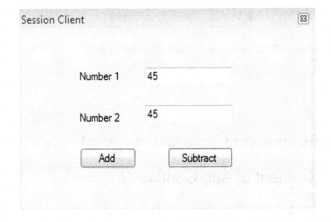

Figure 3. Client output-Successful message

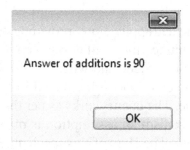

Now click on the Subtract button after one minute. As inactivity time out is 1 minute, the session is faulted and error message is displayed as shown in Figure 4. This mechanism of having lower inactivity timeout can be very useful in the sensitive system such as net banking in which system should terminate the session after few minutes of inactivity.

In the above section you learned about marinating the session and sending the message using reliable sessions. Now if you want to transfer the message if either of service or client is not available then queue is the solution. This is one of the features of WCF to integrate with the message queue of windows operating system. In the following section, queue support in WCF is explained in depth.

Figure 4. Error message of session inactivity time out

⚠ **CommunicationException was unhandled**	✕
The underlying secure session has faulted before the reliable session fully completed. The reliable session was faulted.	

Troubleshooting tips:

Get general help for this exception.

Search for more Help Online...

Actions:

View Detail...

Copy exception detail to the clipboard

WORKING WITH QUEUES

In distributed service oriented applications, providing the durability of message is must. In durable communication if either sender or receiver is not available, the message is stored in the queue and when the sender or receiver is available, the message is delivered to it and removed from the queue. This is the basic behavior the queue. The queue works as per the mechanism illustrated in Figure 5. In the mechanism an assumption is made that queue available at both service and client. The flow of this mechanism is explained below:

1. A client sends message to the service. Now if service is unavailable the message is stored in the queue of the service. Before sending the message to the incoming queue of service a client puts the message in its outgoing queue.
2. Similarly, same thing happens when the service sends a message to the client.
3. If the receiver is not available, then message remains in the queue and it is delivered to the receiver when it is available. The message in the queue will be deleted after successfully delivering the message to the receiver.
4. The order of message delivery is as per First Come First Serve (FCFS) basis.
5. The messages which are never delivered to the receiver from the queue are moved in the dead letter queue. Sometimes it is also known as poison queue.

The queue can be useful in following scenarios:

1. Indirect transfer in which either party is not available.
2. The error can be easily detected as the error can be checked by running either service or client at a time. There for error can be easily isolated.

Figure 5. Basic queue mechanism

Figure 6. Message queuing component in Windows OS

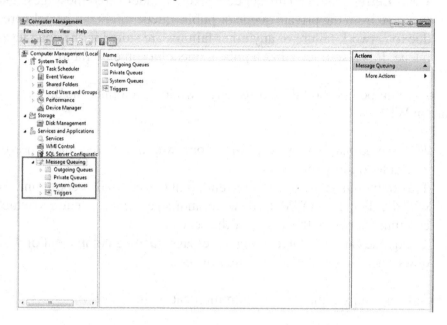

3. The use of queue is ideal for loosely coupled systems as client can communicate with the service even when service is not running.

4. Flow control becomes easily if either service or client is sending the message too fast. Because of the queue the message is first sent to the queue and then it is processed, which help to control the flow of data between client and service.

Implementing Queue in WCF

In WCF the queue can be implemented by using the MSMQ protocol as discussed earlier. In Windows operating system the message queuing component is responsible for handing the queues. It is available under the computer management, which is shown in Figure 6. The Message Queuing must be installed by using *Programs and Features* option if it is not available. There are following types of queues available:

- **Private Queue:** A private queue resides in the local machine. It is used to store the message within the local machine.
- **Public Queue:** A public queue resides in the network. It is used to store the message in the distributed environment.

- **Dead Letter Queue:** This queue stored all undelivered messages. The message from the private queue or public queue might not be delivered due to network failure or any other failures are stored in the dead letter queue. It is also referred as a poison queue in some literature.

Following points should be considered while developing the queue program in WCF:

1. The operations of service must be one way as service might not be available to reply immediately.
2. Two endpoints are required. One endpoint can be used to communicate with the client using WSDL file while another endpoint is required which communicate with the queue of the service.
3. The queue can be created using a message queuing component of windows operating system or through the code.

Following steps explain queue communication in WCF:

Step 1: Create WCF service library project and write the code of service contract class as illustrated in Example 9.

Example 9. Code of Service Contract

```
[ServiceContract]
public interface IMessageSender
{
[OperationContract(IsOneWay =true)]
void SendMessage(String msg);
}
```

Step 2: Write the code of service class as shown in Example 10.

Example 10. Code of service class:

```
public class MessageSender: IMessageSender
{
public void SendMessage (string msg)
{
Console.WriteLine("This is message number " + msg);
}
}
```

324

Step 3: Compile the service project and create new console application project to host the service.

Step 4: The code of the host program is shown in Example 11.

Example 11. Code of Console Host Program

```
using System;
using System.Collections.Generic;
using System.Linq;
using System.Text;
using QueueService;
using System.ServiceModel;
using System.Messaging;
namespace Console_Host
{
class Program
{
static void Main(string[] args)
{
String queue_name = ".\\private$\\WCF";
ServiceHost sh = null;
if (!MessageQueue.Exists(queue_name))MessageQueue.
Create(queue_name,false);
sh = new ServiceHost(typeof(MessageSender));
sh.Open();
Console.WriteLine("Service is running. Press Any Key to
Stop");
Console.ReadKey();
sh.Close();
}
}
}
```

In above code, to integrate MSMQ a reference of System.Messaging is required. So first add the reference of System.Messaging name space in the console application project and then import it in the top of code as highlighted in Example 11. In the code of the host program, first the existence of queue is checked using Exists method and if does not exists, it is created by using the Create () method. These two methods are explained below:

- **MessageQueue.Exists(String queuepath):** This method checks whether the queue exists at the specified path. It returns true if queue exists and false value is returned if the queue does not exists.
- **MessageQueue.Create(String queuepath, Boolean Transactional):** This method creates the queue in the message queuing at specified queue path. It takes two parameters. The first parameter is queue path. The second parameter determines whether the queue is transactional or not. Specifying the true value creates a transactional queue. The false value indicates the queue is not transactional. In this example false is provided as this program does have any transaction.

In Example 11, the queue is created using code. Now a queue can also be created using the messaging queuing component as shown in Figure 7 and Figure 8. As shown in Figure 7, right click on the private queue and select New->Private Queue. The dialog box to create private queue appears as shown in Figure 8. As shown in Figure 8, a text box is provided to enter the queue name. So it behaves same as the first parameter of Create() method. There is one checkbox which asks whether the queue is transactional or not. It is same as the second parameter of Create() method. After providing all the values, click on the OK button. The private queue is created. If you are using this option there is no need to create a queue using code and Create() method is not required in code.

Figure 7. Selecting type of queue as private queue

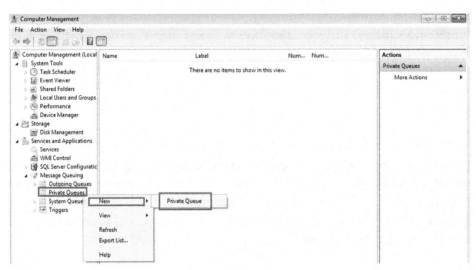

Figure 8. Proving queue details

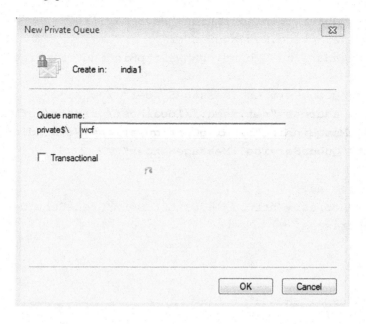

Step 5: Create the endpoint using the configuration file. The content of configuration file is shown in Example 12

Example 12. Content of App.Config File

```
<?xml version="1.0" encoding="utf-8" ?>
<configuration>
<system.serviceModel>
<bindings>
<netMsmqBinding>
<binding name="NewBinding0" exactlyOnce="false"><security
mode="None" /></binding>
</netMsmqBinding>
</bindings>
<behaviors>
<serviceBehaviors>
<behavior name="NewBehavior0">
<serviceMetadata httpGetEnabled="true" />
</behavior>
</serviceBehaviors>
</behaviors>
```

```
<services>
<service behaviorConfiguration="NewBehavior0"
name="QueueService.MessageSender">
<endpoint address="" binding="wsHttpBinding" bindingConfigu-
ration=""
contract="QueueService.IMessageSender" />
<endpoint address="net.msmq://localhost/private/wcf" bin
ding="netMsmqBinding"bindingConfiguration="NewBinding0"
contract="QueueService.IMessageSender" />
<host>
<baseAddresses>
<add baseAddress="http://localhost:9099/QueueService" />
</baseAddresses>
</host>
</service>
</services>
</system.serviceModel>
</configuration>
```

In above App.Config file, there are two endpoints. The first endpoint is a regular http endpoint to communicate with the client using WSDL file. The second endpoint is used to communicate with the private queue when service is not available. Apart from this additional binding configuration is required, which contains following property:

- **ExactlyOnce:** The default value of this element is true. A true value is required for transactional queue. In this program transactional queue is not implemented so set this value as false.

The default security mode is message and system tries to authenticate with active directory users on windows service operating system. As this program is written on a computer without server operating system, set the security mode to None as highlighted in Example 12. Now compile the host program and execute it with administrator privileges. Upon successful hosting the service, create the client project to consume the service.

Step 6: Open visual studio and create windows forms project. Design the form layout as shown in Figure 9.

Step 7: Add the service reference of hosted service. The generated App. Config file of client is shown in Example 13.

Figure 9. Layout of client program

Example 13. App.Config File of Client Program

```
<?xml version="1.0" encoding="utf-8" ?>
<configuration>
<system.serviceModel>
<bindings>
<netMsmqBinding>
<binding name="NetMsmqBinding_IMessageSender"
exactlyOnce="false">
<security mode="None" />
</binding>
</netMsmqBinding>
<wsHttpBinding>
<binding name="WSHttpBinding_IMessageSender" />
</wsHttpBinding>
</bindings>
<client>
<endpoint address="http://localhost:9099/QueueService"
binding="wsHttpBinding"
bindingConfiguration="WSHttpBinding_IMessageSender"
contract="QueueServiceRef.IMessageSender"
name="WSHttpBinding_IMessageSender">
<identity>
<userPrincipalName value="INDIA1\india" />
</identity>
</endpoint>
<endpoint address="net.msmq://localhost/private/wcf" binding
="netMsmqBinding"bindingConfiguration="NetMsmqBinding_IMes-
```

```
sageSender" contract="QueueServiceRef.IMessageSender"name="N
etMsmqBinding_IMessageSender" />
</client>
</system.serviceModel>
</configuration>
```

In above code there are two endpoints generated. The first endpoint is http endpoint and second endpoint is msmq endpoint to communicate with the queue of service. So while creating proxy object in the client program name of this endpoint should be provided. The code of Form1.cs file of the client program is shown in Example 14.

Example 14. Code of Client Program

```
using System;
using System.Collections.Generic;
using System.ComponentModel;
using System.Data;
using System.Drawing;
using System.Linq;
using System.Text;
using System.Windows.Forms;
using Queue_Client.QueueServiceRef;
namespace Queue_Client
{
public partial class Form1: Form
{
public Form1()
{
InitializeComponent();
}
private void button1_Click(object sender, EventArgs e)
{
MessageSenderClient proxy = new MessageSenderClient("NetMsmq
Binding_IMessageSender");
proxy.SendMessage(txtMsg.Text) ;
}
}
}
```

In the above code, the object of the proxy class is created by using the name of MSMQ endpoint. So the client will communicate with this endpoint when service is available or not available.

Step 8: Compile the client project and run it. The output window of the client program is shown in Figure 10. Provide the value in the text box and click on the Send button. Right now the service is running so it will receive this message which is displayed in console as shown in Figure 11. Now stop the service by stopping the console host program and send two more messages to the service to see what happens to the messages which are sent to the service. In the normal direct transfer the messages are lost and client can get an error message regarding non-availability of service. But in this queue program the messages are not lost and stored in the queue as shown in Figure 11. To view the messages in the queue open the computer management screen and locate your private queue i.e.wcf in this example as shown in Figure 11.

Figure 10. Output of client program

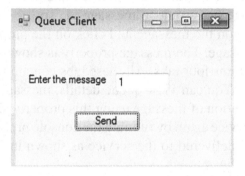

Figure 11. Console host-received the message from client

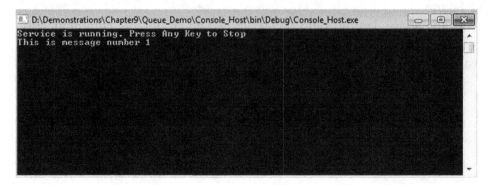

Figure 12. Console host-received the message from the client

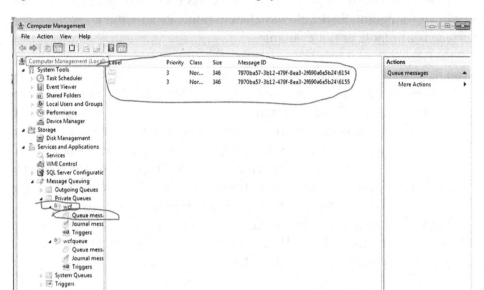

In this queue the two messages stored in the queue are shown in right side panel. Each message has a unique message id. To see the property of the message right click on the message and click on the properties to view the property of the message. The message property is shown in Figure 12. The property sheet contains four tabs. All these tabs contain useful information regarding message. You can view queue details, message body details and other useful information of message using this property sheet.

Now start the service again by running the console program. The message from the queue are delivered to the service as shown in Figure 13 and wcf queue gets empty.

As depicted in Figure 14, the messages arrive in order only. This is the characteristics of the queue which provides reliable communication in case of failure.

In the above demonstration, you learned about durable communication between client and service using queue. The queue is integrated in WCF using MSMQ transport, which provides reliable message transfer.

Figure 13. Property of message

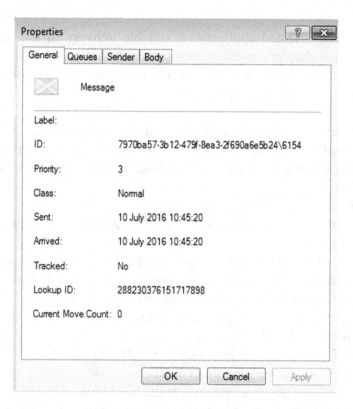

Figure 14. Host program – receiving message from queue

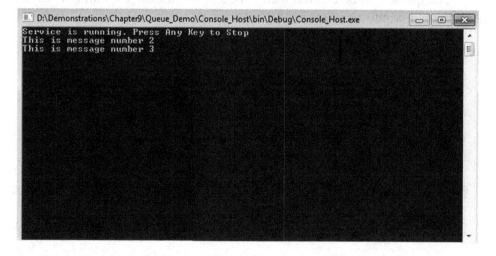

SUMMARY

In any service oriented applications, reliable delivery of the message is expected. This chapter covers various concepts such as reliable messaging and message queuing to accomplish this functionality. The following are important points to ponder in this chapter:

- Reliable session can be enabled by adding a new binding configuration element in the configuration file of the host program of service.
- To enable reliable session, use the binding which supports the reliable session.
- For indirect transfer queue is useful.
- There are three types of queue: private queue, public queue and dead letter queue.
- The private queue is used to communicate the message in local machine.
- The public queue is used to communicate the message in the network. The public queue resides in the active directory services.
- The undelivered messages are also known as poison message which are stored in dead letter queue.
- In WCF queue support is provided by MSMQ protocol.
- To integrate queue support in WCF, window operating system must have message queuing component installed in it.
- The queue can be used in transaction program, i.e. the queue can be transactional also.
- The queue can be created using code or the message queuing component of windows system.

Chapter 10
Securing Message

After completing this chapter, you will be able to:

- Gain knowledge of type of security mechanisms available in WCF.
- Understand security infrastructure available in WCF.
- Secure the message using various security options.
- Learn about the service trace viewer tool to trace the message.

INTRODUCTION

In a distributed environment a message can travel across several nodes to reach to the destination. It is necessary to secure the message to avoid the security breaches and to have the integrity of the message. WCF provides robust and powerful security infrastructure to provide the security in distributed communication. The following security concepts must be implemented in any service oriented applications:

DOI: 10.4018/978-1-5225-1997-3.ch010

- Integrity
- Confidentiality
- Authentication
- Authorization

Integrity

Integrity means the message sent to the receiver is not altered. It is received in the same as sent by the sender. For instance, if a sender sends message as "Hello" and if the receiver receives as "Hello" then it is because of integrity. Digital signature option can be useful to provide integrity in the distributed environment.

Confidentiality

Confidentiality means the message is secret and only the intended recipients can receive it. Other entities cannot access the message while it is travelling over the wire. Any unintended receive should not be aware about the message being transmitted.

Authentication

Authentication is a technique to request the identity of sender or receiver. In real life, requesting someone to show his/her identity proof is an example of authentication. The distributed environment authentication should happen at both sides to avoid penetrations to enter in the system. In operating system entering login credentials is the popular example of authentication we observe in our daily life. There are various ways to provide authentication in WCF which will be discussed later in this chapter.

Authentication

By using authentication the identity of the user is fetched but what about restricting the users to access resources at certain level? The answer to this question is authorization which allows only authorized users to access particular operations of service in distributed environment. There are numerous options to provide authorization in WCF. Each of these options is discussed later in this chapter.

Security in WCF

In WCF security is provided through the binding. Each binding has its own default security settings which can be overridden if required. For Internet based communication, HTTP protocol is useful and bindings such as basicHttpBinding or wsHttpBinding can be useful for communication. For reliable and secured transfer wsHttpBinding is better as compared to basicHttpBinding. Similarly, for federated security wsFederationBinding is the preferred choice. For intranet communication netTCPBinding can be useful which also offers secured and reliable communication. All the bindings support following type of security modes:

- **Transport Level Security:** A transport level security is a point-to-point security.
- **Message Level Security:** Message level security provides end-to-end security which means that the entire message is secured during the transfer.
- **Both:** It is security mode which combines transport level as well as message security and only netMsmqBinding supports this option.
- **None:** It is means the binding does not provide any security to the message. It is not recommended to use this option.
- **TransportCredentialOnly:** Using this option client credentials can be passed over the transport protocol, message is not protected during the transfer.
- **TransportWithMessageCredential:** Using this option the message credentials are passed and message is protected during the transfer. The server provides transport level authentication using this option.

A developer can choose to turn on or off the security setting based on the need of the organization. The transport level security is point to point security which entire message is not secured while the message level security provides end to end security so entire message remains secured during the transfer.

The Figure 1 illustrates communication between client and service using transport level security. As shown in Figure 1, the message is not secured after it is passed from intermediary 1 and it remains unsecured in further communication towards service. This is the major problem with transport level security as it provides only point to point security.

The message level security is illustrated in Figure 2. In this communication the entire message remains secured no matter how many intermediaries are there in between client and service. Therefore this level of security is

Figure 1. Message transfer in transport security

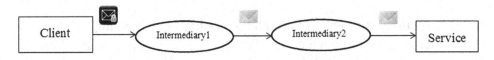

Figure 2. Message transfer in message level security

very useful when you want to hide your message from any third party. Recently WhatsApp provided end to end security to ensure the privacy of the users' data.

The difference between transport level security and message level security is mentioned below in Table 1:

Transport Credentials

In transport level security following client credentials can be provided:

- **None:** In this mode any client can communicate with the service without any authentication. That means the anonymous client can consume the service without any restriction.
- **Basic:** In this mode the authentication is done based on the user name and password stored in the active directory server. The password is stored in unencrypted form.

Table 1. Transport level security vs. message level security

Transport Level Security	Message Level Security
It is Faster	It is Slower
It provides point to point communication. So if service forwards the message it is not secured.	It provides end to end encryption. So if message is forwarded by service from one hope to another hope it remains secured during entire transfer.
Less number of options are available to provide the credentials	More options are available to provide credentials.

- **Digest:** This option works with active directory user authentication. It sends hash value over the network for authentication.
- **NTLM:** The Security Support provider Interface (SSPI) is used for client authentication.
- **Windows:** In this mode the client is authenticated using windows credentials.
- **Certificate:** The X.509 certificate is used to authenticate the client in this mode.

Message Credentials

In message level security following client credentials can be provided:

- **None:** Any client can communicate with service. That means anonymous client can communicate with the service.
- **Windows:** Credentials of windows operating system can be supplied i.e. windows login id and password are allowed.
- **UserName:** The client can be authenticated using the UserName of windows operating system or ASP.NET membership provider account.
- **Certificate:** In this mode the authentication is done by X.509 certificate.
- **Windows Cardspace:** The windows card space is used to authenticate the client.

Following program depicts different between the secured message and unsecured message by using default settings of basicHttpBinding and wsHttpBinding.

Default Security Settings

Default security settings for commonly used binding are shown in the following Table 2.

In netNamedPipe binding client credential as only Windows is supported and other client credentials are not supported.

Default Security Settings Programming Example

Let us understand the default security settings by using the programming example in this section. In this example we will create WCF service using two bindings: basicHttpBinding and wsHttpBinding to observe the default security setting in both bindings.

Table 2. Default security settings for various bindings

Binding	Default Security	Default Client Credentials
basicHttpBinding	None	Basic
wsHttpBinding	Message Level	Windows
netTcpBinding	Transport Level	Windows
netMSMQBinding	Transport Level	Windows
netNamedPipeBinding	Transport Level	Windows

Step 1: Create the WCF service library and write the code of the service contract and service class as shown in Examples 1 and 2 respectively.

Example 1. Code of Service Contract Class

```
using System;
using System.Collections.Generic;
using System.Linq;
using System.Runtime.Serialization;
using System.ServiceModel;
using System.Text;
namespace Basic_Security_Demo
{
    [ServiceContract]
    public interface IMessageSender
    {
        [OperationContract]
        string SendMessage(String message);
    }
}
```

Example 2. Code of Service Class

```
using System;
using System.Collections.Generic;
using System.Linq;
using System.Runtime.Serialization;
using System.ServiceModel;
using System.Text;
namespace Basic_Security_Demo
```

```
{
    public class MessageSender: IMessageSender
    {
        public string SendMessage(string message)
        {
            return "Your message is:" + message;
        }
    }
}
```

Step 2: Create console application project to host the service, add the reference of service library, System.ServiceModel and write the hosting code as illustrated in Example 3.

Example 3. Code of Host Program

```
using System;
using System.Collections.Generic;
using System.Linq;
using System.Text;
using System.ServiceModel;
using System.ServiceModel.Description;
using Basic_Security_Demo;
namespace Console_Host
{
    class Program
    {
        static void Main(string[] args)
        {
            ServiceHost host = new ServiceHost(typeof(Messa
geSender));
            host.Open();
            foreach (ServiceEndpoint endpoint in host.De-
scription.Endpoints)
            {
                Console.WriteLine("Service is running at: "
+ endpoint.Address);
                Console.WriteLine("Binding=" + endpoint.
Binding);
                Console.WriteLine("");
```

```
        }
        Console.WriteLine("Press any key to stop");
        Console.ReadKey();
        host.Close();
    }
  }
}
```

Step 3: Create the App.Config file of host program as show in Example 4.

Example 4. App.Config of Host Program

```xml
<?xml version="1.0" encoding="utf-8" ?>
<configuration>
    <system.serviceModel>
        <services>
        <service name="Basic_Security_Demo.MessageSend-
er">
            <endpoint address="basic"
binding="basicHttpBinding" bindingConfiguration=""
                contract="Basic_Security_Demo.IMessag-
eSender" />
            <endpoint address="ws"
binding="wsHttpBinding" bindingConfiguration=""
                contract="Basic_Security_Demo.IMessag-
eSender" />
            <host>
                <baseAddresses>
                    <add baseAddress="http://local-
host:9056/securityDemo" />
                </baseAddresses>
            </host>
        </service>
        </services>
    </system.serviceModel>
</configuration>
```

Now see trace the message for viewing default settings, you need to add diagnostics tab in the configuration file. It can be added in configuration file using service configuration editor too. We will use service configuration

Figure 3. Diagnostics node in service configuration editor

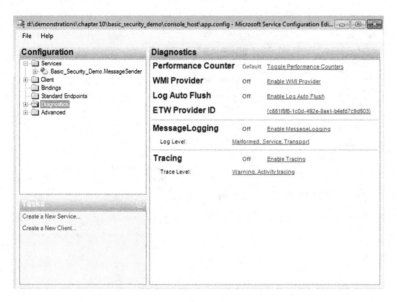

editor to add this tag. Right click on App.Config file and click on Edit WCF Configuration, the editor is displayed and click on the diagnostics node as shown in Figure 3. Expand this node to explore other options available. The elements under this node are displayed as shown in Figure 4. Now enable the MessageLogging option which is off by default. This is toggle link and you can enable or disable it by click on it. You need to provide the path of message logging listener where the trace file is save. It can be specified by clicking ServiceModelMessageLogginListener link. The dialog box to change the path of listener appears as shown in Figure 5. To change the default path click on browse button and provide new path and click on OK button. If you don't want to change the path then click on Cancel button. The extension of trace file is.svclog, which can be opened in special tool called service trace viewer which is discussed in the next section.

Finally click on the Message Logging node and set the value to true for all the three types of messages: service, transport and malformed as shown in Figure 6.

Now save the file and get back to the visual studio. The App.Config is updated and it looks like as shown in Example 5.

Figure 4. Elements under diagnostics node

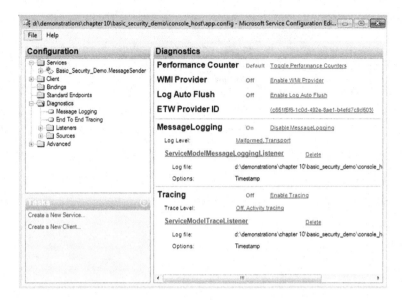

Figure 5. Dialog box to change the path of listener

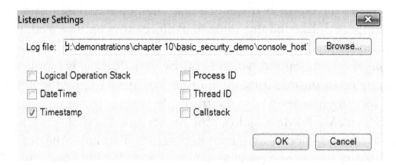

Example 5. Updated App.Config of Host Program

```xml
<?xml version="1.0" encoding="utf-8" ?>
<configuration>
    <system.diagnostics><sources><source
propagateActivity="true" name="System.ServiceMod-
el" switchValue="Off, ActivityTracing"><listeners><
add type="System.Diagnostics.DefaultTraceListener"
name="Default"><filter type="" /></add><add name="Serv
iceModelTraceListener"><filter type="" /></add></lis-
```

Figure 6. Setting message logging levels

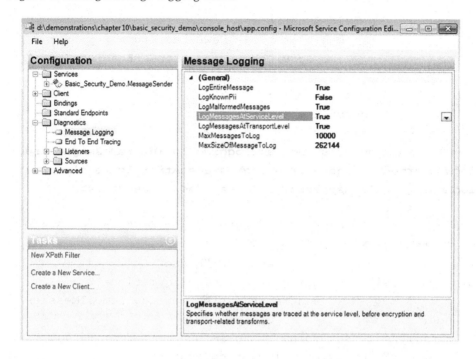

```
teners></source><source name="System.ServiceModel.Mes-
sageLogging" switchValue="Warning, ActivityTracing"><li
steners><add type="System.Diagnostics.DefaultTraceLis-
tener" name="Default"><filter type="" /></add><add name="
ServiceModelMessageLoggingListener"><filter type="" /></
add></listeners></source></sources><sharedListeners><add
initializeData="d:\demonstrations\chapter 10\basic_secu-
rity_demo\console_host\app_tracelog.svclog"type="System.
Diagnostics.XmlWriterTraceListener, System, Version=4.0.0.0,
Culture=neutral, PublicKeyToken=b77a5c561934e089"name="Serv
iceModelTraceListener" traceOutputOptions="Timestamp"><filt
er type="" /></add><add initializeData="d:\demonstrations\
chapter 10\basic_security_demo\console_host\app_messages.
svclog"type="System.Diagnostics.XmlWriterTraceListener, Sys-
tem, Version=4.0.0.0, Culture=neutral, PublicKeyToken=b77a5c
561934e089"name="ServiceModelMessageLoggingListener" traceOu
tputOptions="Timestamp"><filter type="" /></add></sharedLis-
teners></system.diagnostics>
     <system.serviceModel>
```

```
        <behaviors>
            <serviceBehaviors>
                <behavior name="NewBehavior0">
                    <serviceMetadata httpGetEnabled="true"
/>
                </behavior>
            </serviceBehaviors>
        </behaviors>
        <diagnostics><messageLogging logEntireMessage="true"
logMalformedMessages="true"logMessagesAtServiceLevel="true"
logMessagesAtTransportLevel="true" /></diagnostics>
        <services>
<service behaviorConfiguration="NewBehavior0"  name="Basic_
Security_Demo.MessageSender">
                <endpoint address="basic"
binding="basicHttpBinding" bindingConfiguration=""
                contract="Basic_Security_Demo.IMessag-
eSender" />
                <endpoint address="ws"
binding="wsHttpBinding" bindingConfiguration=""
                contract="Basic_Security_Demo.IMessag-
eSender" />
                <host>
                <baseAddresses>
                    <add baseAddress="http://local-
host:9056/securityDemo" />
                </baseAddresses>
                </host>
            </service>
        </services>
    </system.serviceModel>
</configuration>
```

Step 4: Compile the host program and execute it with administrator privileges. The output of host program is shown in Figure 7.

Step 5: Create windows forms application project as client application to consume the service. Design the controls of form as shown in Figure 8. Add the reference of service project. The automatically generated App. Config of client program is shown in Example 6.

Figure 7. Output of host program

```
D:\Demonstrations\Chapter10\Basic_Security_Demo\Console_Host\bin\Debug\Console_Host.exe
Service is running at: http://localhost:9056/securityDemo/basic
Binding=System.ServiceModel.BasicHttpBinding

Service is running at: http://localhost:9056/securityDemo/ws
Binding=System.ServiceModel.WSHttpBinding

Press any key to stop
```

Figure 8. Design of form of client project

```
Security Client (Message Sender)

Enter Your Message:  [          ]

Please Select the Binding

  ○ BasicHttpBinding   ○ WSHttpBinding

        [  Send  ]
```

Example 6. App.Config File of Client Program

```xml
<?xml version="1.0" encoding="utf-8" ?>
<configuration>
    <system.serviceModel>
        <bindings>
            <basicHttpBinding>
                <binding name="BasicHttpBinding_IMessag-
eSender" />
            </basicHttpBinding>
            <wsHttpBinding>
```

```
                <binding name="WSHttpBinding_IMessageSender"
/>
            </wsHttpBinding>
        </bindings>
        <client>
            <endpoint address="http://localhost:9056/securi-
tyDemo/basic"
                binding="basicHttpBinding" bindingConfigurat
ion="BasicHttpBinding_IMessageSender"
                contract="SecurityClient_Ref.IMessageSender"
name="BasicHttpBinding_IMessageSender" />
            <endpoint address="http://localhost:9056/securi-
tyDemo/ws" binding="wsHttpBinding"
                bindingConfiguration="WSHttpBinding_IMessag-
eSender" contract="SecurityClient_Ref.IMessageSender"
                name="WSHttpBinding_IMessageSender">
            <identity>
                <userPrincipalName value="INDIA1\india"
/>
            </identity>
            </endpoint>
        </client>
    </system.serviceModel>
</configuration>
```

Now write the code of client program as illustrated in Example 7.

Example 7. Code of client program:

```
using System;
using System.Collections.Generic;
using System.ComponentModel;
using System.Data;
using System.Drawing;
using System.Linq;
using System.Text;
using System.Windows.Forms;
using Security_Client.SecurityClient_Ref;
namespace Security_Client
{
```

```
public partial class Form1: Form
{
    public Form1()
    {
        InitializeComponent();
    }
    private void btnSend_Click(object sender, EventArgs
e)
    {
        MessageSenderClient proxy = null;
        String binding_name = null;
        if (rbBasicHttpBinding.Checked == true)
            binding_name = "BasicHttpBinding_IMessag-
eSender";
        else
            binding_name = "WSHttpBinding_IMessageSend-
er";
        proxy = new MessageSenderClient(binding_name);
        String message = tbMessage.Text;
        String ans = proxy.SendMessage(message);
        MessageBox.Show("Reply from service is "+ ans);
    }
}
}
```

Step 6: Execute the client program. Provide the value of input in text box, select BasicHttpBinding radio button first time and click on Send button. Repeat this step by selecting the WSHttpBinding radio button. The output of client program is shown in Figure 9.

Figure 9. Output of client program with BasicHttpBinding

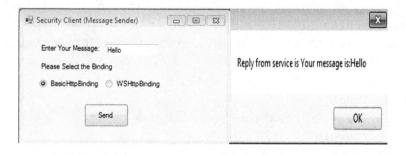

Figure 10. Service trace viewer

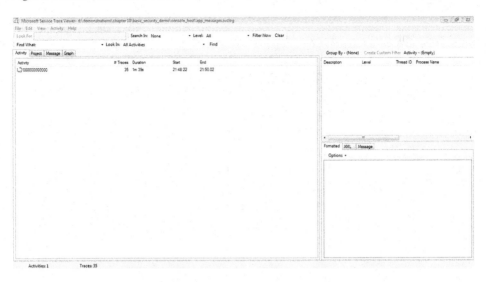

Then close the host and client program. The svclog file is generated which contains the tracing of the messages sent via BasicHttpBinding and WSHttp-Binding. So locate the svclog file and double click on it to open it in the Service Trace Viewer which is shown in Figure 10.

Click on the Messages tab to view the message details. As it is shown in Figure 11, for each binding there are two copies of request and reply as highlighted in Figure 11. One copy is unencrypted message which is prepared before sending it over the wire and second copy is actual message which is sent over the wire. In the first run we consumed the service using BasicH-ttpBinding so both copies of request are shown in Example 8 and Example 11.

Example 8. BasicHttpBinding Request First Copy Prepared by Client

```
<E2ETraceEvent xmlns="http://schemas.microsoft.com/2004/06/
E2ETraceEvent">
<System xmlns="http://schemas.microsoft.com/2004/06/windows/
eventlog/system">
<EventID>0</EventID>
<Type>3</Type>
<SubType Name="Information">0</SubType>
<Level>8</Level>
```

Figure 11. Message details in service trace viewer

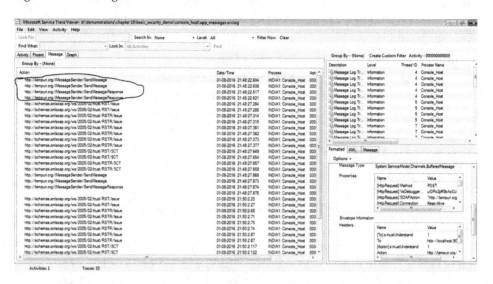

```
<TimeCreated SystemTime="2016-08-01T16:18:22.6041676Z" />
<Source Name="System.ServiceModel.MessageLogging" />
<Correlation Activity-
ID="{00000000-0000-0000-0000-000000000000}" />
<Execution ProcessName="Console_Host" ProcessID="1204"
ThreadID="4" />
<Channel />
<Computer>INDIA1</Computer>
</System>
<ApplicationData>
<TraceData>
<DataItem>
<MessageLogTraceRecord Time="2016-08-
01T21:48:22.5991673+05:30" Source="TransportReceive"
Type="System.ServiceModel.Channels.BufferedMessage"
xmlns="http://schemas.microsoft.com/2004/06/ServiceModel/
Management/MessageTrace">
<HttpRequest>
<Method>POST</Method>
<QueryString></QueryString>
<WebHeaders>
<VsDebuggerCausalityData>uIDPo2pff0bAoOJEkhMd+sgwrswAAAAANB
3GJZY3MUS+zPd1TqrxPMd4QARBrH9Mojy5qucgqPAACQAA</VsDebugger-
```

```
CausalityData>
<SOAPAction>"http://tempuri.org/IMessageSender/SendMes-
sage"</SOAPAction>
<Connection>Keep-Alive</Connection>
<Content-Length>173</Content-Length>
<Content-Type>text/xml; charset=utf-8</Content-Type>
<Accept-Encoding>gzip, deflate</Accept-Encoding>
<Expect>100-continue</Expect>
<Host>localhost:9056</Host>
</WebHeaders>
</HttpRequest>
<s:Envelope xmlns:s="http://schemas.xmlsoap.org/soap/enve-
lope/">
<s:Header>
<To s:mustUnderstand="1" xmlns="http://schemas.microsoft.
com/ws/2005/05/addressing/none">http://localhost:9056/secu-
rityDemo/basic</To>
<Action s:mustUnderstand="1" xmlns="http://schemas.micro-
soft.com/ws/2005/05/addressing/none">http://tempuri.org/
IMessageSender/SendMessage</Action>
</s:Header><s:Body><SendMessage xmlns="http://tempuri.
org/"><message>Hello</message></SendMessage></s:Body>
</s:Envelope>
</MessageLogTraceRecord>
</DataItem>
</TraceData>
</ApplicationData>
</E2ETraceEvent>
```

As shown in the above example, the body part of request shows the actual message which is unencrypted as expected. Now the copy of message which is sent over the wire is shown in Example 9.

Example 9. BasicHttpBinding copy of message sent over the wire:

```
<E2ETraceEvent xmlns="http://schemas.microsoft.com/2004/06/
E2ETraceEvent">
<System xmlns="http://schemas.microsoft.com/2004/06/windows/
eventlog/system">
```

Securing Message

```
<EventID>0</EventID>
<Type>3</Type>
<SubType Name="Information">0</SubType>
<Level>8</Level>
<TimeCreated SystemTime="2016-08-01T16:18:22.6061677Z" />
<Source Name="System.ServiceModel.MessageLogging" />
<Correlation Activity-
ID="{00000000-0000-0000-0000-000000000000}" />
<Execution ProcessName="Console_Host" ProcessID="1204"
ThreadID="4" />
<Channel />
<Computer>INDIA1</Computer>
</System>
<ApplicationData>
<TraceData>
<DataItem>
<MessageLogTraceRecord Time="2016-08-
01T21:48:22.6061677+05:30" Source="ServiceLevelReceiveReq
uest" Type="System.ServiceModel.Channels.BufferedMessage"
xmlns="http://schemas.microsoft.com/2004/06/ServiceModel/
Management/MessageTrace">
<HttpRequest>
<Method>POST</Method>
<QueryString></QueryString>
<WebHeaders>
<VsDebuggerCausalityData>uIDPo2pff0bAoOJEkhMd+sgwrswAAAAANB
3GJZY3MUS+zPd1TqrxPMd4QARBrH9Mojy5qucgqPAACQAA</VsDebugger-
CausalityData>
<SOAPAction>"http://tempuri.org/IMessageSender/SendMes-
sage"</SOAPAction>
<Connection>Keep-Alive</Connection>
<Content-Length>173</Content-Length>
<Content-Type>text/xml; charset=utf-8</Content-Type>
<Accept-Encoding>gzip, deflate</Accept-Encoding>
<Expect>100-continue</Expect>
<Host>localhost:9056</Host>
</WebHeaders>
</HttpRequest>
<s:Envelope xmlns:s="http://schemas.xmlsoap.org/soap/enve-
lope/">
```

```
<s:Header>
<To s:mustUnderstand="1" xmlns="http://schemas.microsoft.
com/ws/2005/05/addressing/none">http://localhost:9056/secu-
rityDemo/basic</To>
<Action s:mustUnderstand="1" xmlns="http://schemas.micro-
soft.com/ws/2005/05/addressing/none">http://tempuri.org/
IMessageSender/SendMessage</Action>
</s:Header>
<s:Body><SendMessage xmlns="http://tempuri.
org/"><message>Hello</message></SendMessage></s:Body>
</s:Envelope>
</MessageLogTraceRecord>
</DataItem>
</TraceData>
</ApplicationData>
</E2ETraceEvent>
```

Now both copies of request message are exactly same as BasicHttpBinding is not secured by default. For WSHttpBinding similar copies are created by the service trace viewer.

The unencrypted copy which is prepared before sending is not shown as it is same as the Example 9. The copy of message which is sent over the wire using WSHttpBinding is shown in Example 10.

Example 10. WSHttpBinding Copy of Message Sent Over the Wire

```
<E2ETraceEvent xmlns="http://schemas.microsoft.com/2004/06/
E2ETraceEvent">
<System xmlns="http://schemas.microsoft.com/2004/06/windows/
eventlog/system">
<EventID>0</EventID>
<Type>3</Type>
<SubType Name="Information">0</SubType>
<Level>8</Level>
<TimeCreated SystemTime="2016-08-01T16:18:27.8694688Z" />
<Source Name="System.ServiceModel.MessageLogging" />
<Correlation Activity-
ID="{00000000-0000-0000-0000-000000000000}" />
<Execution ProcessName="Console_Host" ProcessID="1204"
```

Securing Message

```
ThreadID="5" />
<Channel />
<Computer>INDIA1</Computer>
</System>
<ApplicationData>
<TraceData>
<DataItem>
<MessageLogTraceRecord Time="2016-08-
01T21:48:27.8694688+05:30" Source="TransportReceive"
Type="System.ServiceModel.Channels.BufferedMessage"
xmlns="http://schemas.microsoft.com/2004/06/ServiceModel/
Management/MessageTrace">
<s:Envelope xmlns:s="http://www.w3.org/2003/05/soap-en-
velope" xmlns:a="http://www.w3.org/2005/08/addressing"
xmlns:u="http://docs.oasis-open.org/wss/2004/01/oasis-
200401-wss-wssecurity-utility-1.0.xsd">
<s:Header>
<a:Action s:mustUnderstand="1" u:Id="_2">http://tempuri.org/
IMessageSender/SendMessage</a:Action>
<a:MessageID u:Id="_3">urn:uuid:b4b15001-821b-4eb8-8c9d-
7abfcedd9d5f</a:MessageID>
<a:ReplyTo u:Id="_4">
<a:Address>http://www.w3.org/2005/08/addressing/anonymous</
a:Address>
</a:ReplyTo>
<a:To s:mustUnderstand="1" u:Id="_5">http://localhost:9056/
securityDemo/ws</a:To>
<o:Security s:mustUnderstand="1" xmlns:o="http://docs.oasis-
open.org/wss/2004/01/oasis-200401-wss-wssecurity-secext-
1.0.xsd">
<u:Timestamp u:Id="uuid-b2afc061-11a6-4598-b9b4-
bedf65d14e6">
<u:Created>2016-08-01T16:18:27.851Z</u:Created>
<u:Expires>2016-08-01T16:23:27.851Z</u:Expires>
</u:Timestamp>
<c:SecurityContextToken u:Id="uuid-0cce91ca-4114-4e18-
a92d-8613be1fc308-2" xmlns:c="http://schemas.xmlsoap.org/
ws/2005/02/sc">
<c:Identifier>urn:uuid:56990a04-f843-423e-b86b-
3a963b11d74c</c:Identifier>
```

```
</c:SecurityContextToken>
<c:DerivedKeyToken u:Id="uuid-b2afc061-11a6-4598-b9b4-
bedf65d14e4" xmlns:c="http://schemas.xmlsoap.org/ws/2005/02/
sc">
<o:SecurityTokenReference>
<o:Reference ValueType="http://schemas.xmlsoap.org/
ws/2005/02/sc/sct" URI="#uuid-0cce91ca-4114-4e18-a92d-
8613be1fc308-2"></o:Reference>
</o:SecurityTokenReference>
<c:Offset>0</c:Offset>
<c:Length>24</c:Length>
<c:Nonce>
<!-- Removed-->
</c:Nonce>
</c:DerivedKeyToken>
<c:DerivedKeyToken u:Id="uuid-b2afc061-11a6-4598-b9b4-
bedf65d14e5" xmlns:c="http://schemas.xmlsoap.org/ws/2005/02/
sc">
<o:SecurityTokenReference>
<o:Reference ValueType="http://schemas.xmlsoap.org/
ws/2005/02/sc/sct" URI="#uuid-0cce91ca-4114-4e18-a92d-
8613be1fc308-2"></o:Reference>
</o:SecurityTokenReference>
<c:Nonce>
<!-- Removed-->
</c:Nonce>
</c:DerivedKeyToken>
<e:ReferenceList xmlns:e="http://www.w3.org/2001/04/xm-
lenc#">
<e:DataReference URI="#_1"></e:DataReference>
<e:DataReference URI="#_6"></e:DataReference>
</e:ReferenceList>
<e:EncryptedData Id="_6" Type="http://www.w3.org/2001/04/
xmlenc#Element" xmlns:e="http://www.w3.org/2001/04/xmlenc#">
<e:EncryptionMethod Algorithm="http://www.w3.org/2001/04/
xmlenc#aes256-cbc"></e:EncryptionMethod>
<KeyInfo xmlns="http://www.w3.org/2000/09/xmldsig#">
<o:SecurityTokenReference>
<o:Reference ValueType="http://schemas.xmlsoap.org/
ws/2005/02/sc/dk" URI="#uuid-b2afc061-11a6-4598-b9b4-
```

Securing Message

bedf65d14e5"></o:Reference>
</o:SecurityTokenReference>
</KeyInfo>
<e:CipherData>
<e:CipherValue>rVhk9h+22HRXsXA/+Dj4bG7dF56CSpIMPjdFinE6Q1YW
XmRpZlQJmPS7g1nEFe2mRXQ/SIKU0Y+U8Gl68vD+ZXxl9osP/Xs7UVAww/
O1CUpo6lNZcbjMcjyQGkIqUzqgXis3//onAmth6g9lIb7mewqdRqPAf-
prXRzcJ36T475S3U2atIoIb/a2RdOu9M+EjLREZhh3aksqA4P18TF0hrg8b
u4qGO+o5KUm7hJQCV/+PfVAg7nW5l0+XoyXpTtHysfuF313Q+PInJCXbqg
xXG2WMgUttcr2FBpgOKxB33TwSejzBKz1KH9XglYHEA4f2mCOLYkOjcXGJ
NN0myrcH+jjmYkR+kgmdlFNqSxiIjLxI81Gmft2+N5G/52uj2ZxPSk6ew0
GrNFTP04i2p+EiEc0EDv0ez9q7M2gjvdwly1YYEkR4mOigtspD3Mf4kw6x
vhqqyqqCDWpZz5U5BwxQdY+l8ML4jrCnk/ZZdeIb2EYdpBk/nU2mih2uD/
Hlay4AW2KRqreaj7GyuDHQ1zAokR1tKaHpn5VGK7kb0ONOmlxC/YIfv-
HEW584Qos0zbGfW7nslpLNbwc+BjlHYaKLn3vMz2k+syVt+g3jEgOI6CGYd
rKvJxZwX4eVVmkV+KAAlD7k1poMt09lXaafzmw1GaDV52y9AoMwRy5cDfK8
FFp07QJn2g7kiN8b/utS+jRINuRlne+U8OiywuQM6mo2gx0X+cXEOU1ecjb
zDS8d2Q9SeqpK5kaQP7ax3i6M6K6iQXeVhlu6Kw+xXyf01KSWMewCgjIC37
dsT8hRweGhN+RtzGJnbJ+aIB+2NgkCDfGFQQq7+zAGHZSyYtm+zbasthl8
3b4U+xwi19o9Jvkawr+j2o/otzA6lBfpeg/P/9ApCX68Wn9rXwdRug3O9-
2iChyq8ape95k8RVvY0fOzqQdsBxp8xYASxD3exwSaWQ2YXSiaGZwal47H
4oqgvfiLfscdrHC7uxuetuFah1BJl0epRh+MsFgrQQrzTi0Rx7a9raDf-
MeCftlUCsc3lq6vFqjTGU3clQ4vkgypUGIuVOj5D4zvk15mMgdbOihZtCYE
AUqI27iUy+ZFd8Jo0R8hxs6P4p9ylEBltTyRMSL6Xljsfz6Tq8svH4SaSq
TeOxFsOm+c0G8rd5uERuqlT5yvkUKk60aOtPnk4wmhIeKKS5QlYjZB7xx-
85ByPa7fu60Q4JEsXcrb/R1NXOLyRlfdkGJ7Z0bU1YI7v1qXPs6o/2vHz7eJ
1sKpGOcjdD6YE0PyY2BsZvp/h96gc0admagNfRzcmzMTCKXdzXjDbWfpIZ-
R4QLkeiUGFtD/INAyNtwIG+BwZuhvhc1h86ITB1P/tKdqniMAZ0MhBS1G/
EL8gohEOF+arTbvefCQp8sht1WC1/MFnbfjTD8aek79m6BvZ4JxzEqYkzK3F
aIORV9OmiT3AmoW2oFmi9HMrmc2+p6ecTD8TzgtLFa8YZc/jYlLIpNxdT9Ye
8RtsNgAn2Yrf4pgaJldS+IKc77zoqCQCXzDwxbEuXxaYWyxP5zZc0b4v5jDQ
QhBc1sQIFI2xeLwP0ujplp0I1Yg8VrG6cxllgcyaz+q5F8/s6XAuSDMSYb-
UtVAh5YaZG0zvVoClvz69Baqub5yXoL1j11cPP6YXre4ZItXsZXAsKibN-
nJGOBz0hNc6i80qxck13roiAfMN/Am/I0sIBB87L2T1vQfLnTcr9pcWM-
2vIfTZ7D4dRVtmphB8iZfPRdf6roTZ8TWw1uTL4+tKXFmvFFTkijFfqQdqkg
aW+4ElIHDNRHYIDzoDSZZ1Vb87mLQ7E+iLn1joS1aMZoK1G4rlmauF43Ka-
osPYN4QWe9qar0yAYXPiAQ3DANe+zZ7/GXhiahIhr+Y67F3Thu8Cw5cQYio
FPlZB0cWfoeiUVOrWVDd0BKW6vASct/SQzwbdpp2CUTCs49Pf8BiZXFq4/
I9zgFRIRwcVwGPMl0W4ehaxehcHJitpp1qRewqmBXmrpFb4eVEjuM-
li6oAo2NR3G8UmaQ9kEjPY0JYqFhlg3aoZUFrZIiEWcXte6xck2rauuCEG-

zxoHLiZusEPJdI6JCz4ZMCjSmHyCuvcIZhPtYfk9pqbwR1lGCy+QOX6xaU-
CCLwg0IJR8yhXXSmLGMPaaje4FO9792fOgYsTWWn81X2cCF07z84jZp+xbn3
taD8VpGyulwPwidSTRa5nei8WnURCsA6oRGgka7QG4AW4btQ5QhUVHy6bz9y
EyHXUof5XUMbz2vIVki426JjuHH4hH6Gyf+KzVvpN/dxb44QMyhsfEId4pK-
Mp5USfCBUEVs7BEMWE6tU5ZrEZ3KsZz6lAU8kthTjtNQ6V/EEFKEcHBfw8K
1N/7s9ABWKFRJ6VKzPDF91jiOJG7pPWKm6g6dWvTxuW6ZPLWzKeEZpON2aS
rhYsOuWCsqYkKTVYm5YWJ02TA1gE+Or8R9ETBTaoAKT+RTu3SrAn1+Idk28
RTVOjR+0BZ4o3qq0mq9vBb/NDQgNL/vdrjsQPQB5LjS9lBLK2rFQqoK8ob-
cJrB0A43Vd3lZg3KTMRQxeAsNKhr4lnBxB7mBMTk1U2ag3Xc3ORnK2MkaR-
cxJIN7sSW26ueVGrvQiyY8HBM4bV7tyK1P19PvP5QPHXfuCm+nq2Q3on7Rk-
gKmvvsJM9uD4DO8u1apQUn537KDpB6BeTIh+34F9aJTNLPIqYsxOwTnLp1HL
WvdkGyiFgrdluzATzdypMjdmWV6ZCUDfQi0rKKaebqTjXxhBu6JMSEoFw2tU
3BugCh4zwqkB7hNO9DjJYETYs1YsRByzGf</e:CipherValue>
</e:CipherData>
</e:EncryptedData>
</o:Security>
</s:Header>
<s:Body u:Id="_0"><e:EncryptedData Id="_1" Type="http://
www.w3.org/2001/04/xmlenc#Content" xmlns:e="http://
www.w3.org/2001/04/xmlenc#"><e:EncryptionMethod
Algorithm="http://www.w3.org/2001/04/xmlenc#aes256-
cbc"></e:EncryptionMethod><KeyInfo xmlns="http://
www.w3.org/2000/09/xmldsig#"><o:SecurityTokenReferen
ce xmlns:o="http://docs.oasis-open.org/wss/2004/01/oa-
sis-200401-wss-wssecurity-secext-1.0.xsd"><o:Reference
ValueType="http://schemas.xmlsoap.org/ws/2005/02/sc/
dk" URI="#uuid-b2afc061-11a6-4598-b9b4-bedf65d14e5"></
o:Reference></o:SecurityTokenReference></KeycInfo><e:Ciph-
erData><e:CipherValue>GN68MsPeqInvR5aVZKAnjESR8OApO0Ccmp
LJTLfdIX731y+24HxwHsznkgcbgytgy+q5CbmoiU9VXM06Ab6Rr3m08q
PMgHrqjjMkiubCB3U64m31UaSz1Q2fkC9cI6cR</e:CipherValue></
e:CipherData></e:EncryptedData></s:Body>
</s:Envelope>
</MessageLogTraceRecord>
</DataItem>
</TraceData>
</ApplicationData>
</E2ETraceEvent>

As show in above example the message body is encrypted and the actual message is not visible to us. It is shown in the encrypted form as WSHttp-Binding is secured by default having message level security. Likewise you can inspect copies of reply message of both bindings.

We are able to inspect the messages using message logging feature of WCF. To open the message a tool called service trace view is used. In the following section the service trace viewer is explained in depth.

SERVICE TRACE VIEWER

Service Trace Viewer is a tool available at C:\Program Files\Microsoft SDKs\ Windows\vX.0A\Bin\SvcTraceViewer.exe. This tool is used to trace the message to and from the service. The display screen of this tool is shown in Figure 10. The traces can be viewed in four ways by using four different tabs available as shown in Figure 10.

- Activity
- Project
- Message
- Graph

Each of the above options is discussed below.

Activity

The activity tab contains the details about all the traces in the one group as activity. The activities are color coded. Exceptions are shown in the red color and warnings are shown in yellow color. To view the activity details click on the activity. The detail of activity is shown in the right pane as shown in Figure 12.

Project

Group of activities can be saved as project. The project tab contains one or more activities inside it. Click on this tab to view all the activities available under the project as shown in Figure 13. The project extension is stvproj. The project can be saved using File-> Save As menu. Multiple activities can be clubbed together in single project.

Figure 12. Viewing activity

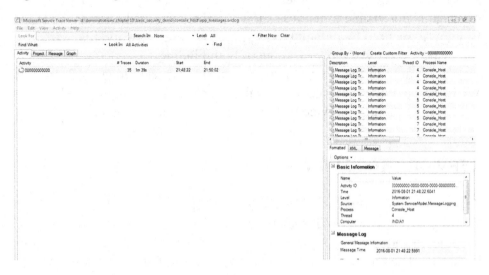

Figure 13. Viewing project

Message

The message tab contains details about request and reply message. It contains two copies of request and two copies of reply message as discussed in the previous section. As shown in Figure 14 after clicking on the message tab the message details are displayed. The first two copies are prepared for the request and the other two copies are prepared for reply. The details about these copies are already discussed in previous section.

Figure 14. Viewing message

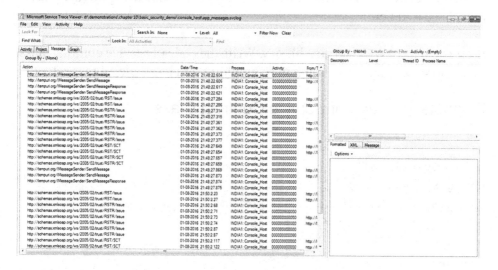

Figure 15. Viewing graph

Graph

The graph tab helps you to view activity in graphical manner. It allows you to see the events in the step by step manner as shown in Figure 15.

Authentication Example

The authentication is the process to check the identity of client. By default basicHttpBinding is not secured so it does not check the identity by default. Other bindings such as wsHttpBinding and netTcpBinding are secured by default. As discussed before wsHttpBinding has message level security by default. Setting the Transport level security in wsHttpBinding an https address is required for which secured certificate is required. The netTcpBinding has transport level security by default.

In this section the authentication process is explained using all three bindings discussed here.

Step 1: Create a WCF service library. Write the code of service contract class and service class as shown in Example 11 and Example 14 respectively.

Example 11. Code of Service Contract Class

```
using System;
using System.Collections.Generic;
using System.Linq;
using System.Runtime.Serialization;
using System.ServiceModel;
using System.Text;
namespace AuthenticationDemo
{
    [ServiceContract]
    public interface IStudRecord
    {
        [OperationContract]
        Boolean insert_stud(Student stud);
    }
    [DataContract]
    public class Student
    {
        [DataMember]
        public String stud_id;
        [DataMember]
        public String stud_name;
        [DataMember]
        public int semester;
        [DataMember]
        public String Branch;
    }
}
```

Example 12. Code of service contract class:

```
using System;
using System.Collections.Generic;
```

```
using System.Linq;
using System.Runtime.Serialization;
using System.ServiceModel;
using System.Text;
namespace AuthenticationDemo
{
    public class StudRecord: IStudRecord
    {
        public bool insert_stud(Student stud)
        {
            Console.WriteLine(System.Threading.Thread.Cur-
rentPrincipal.Identity.Name +" Has Called the service");
            List<Student> all_students = new
List<Student>();
            if (stud != null)
            {
                all_students.Add(stud);
                return true;
            }
            else
                return false;
        }
    }
}
```

As shown in the above example, the identity of the client consuming the operation is printed in the first line of the code which is highlighted. This code will print the identity on the console host when a service is consumed by the client using different bindings.

Step 2: Compile the WCF service library project and create console application project to host the service. Add the reference of WCF service library and System.ServiceModel. Write the code of Program.cs file as depicted in Example 13.

Example 13. Code of Program.cs File

```
using System;
using System.Collections.Generic;
using System.Linq;
```

```
using System.Text;
using System.ServiceModel;
using System.ServiceModel.Description;
using AuthenticationDemo;
namespace Console_Host
{
    class Program
    {
        static void Main(string[] args)
        {
            ServiceHost host = new ServiceHost(typeof(StudR
ecord));
            host.Open();
            foreach (ServiceEndpoint endpoint in host.De-
scription.Endpoints)
            {
                Console.WriteLine("Service is running at: "
+ endpoint.Address);
                Console.WriteLine("Binding=" + endpoint.
Binding);
                Console.WriteLine("");
            }
            Console.WriteLine("Press any key to stop");
            Console.ReadKey();
            host.Close();
        }
    }
}
```

Step 3: Create multiple endpoints in the configuration file which is shown in Example 14. It is advisable to use service configuration editor to create multiple endpoints.

Example 14. App.Config of Console Application Project

```
<?xml version="1.0" encoding="utf-8" ?>
<configuration>
  <system.serviceModel>
    <behaviors>
      <serviceBehaviors>
```

Figure 16. Output of console application project

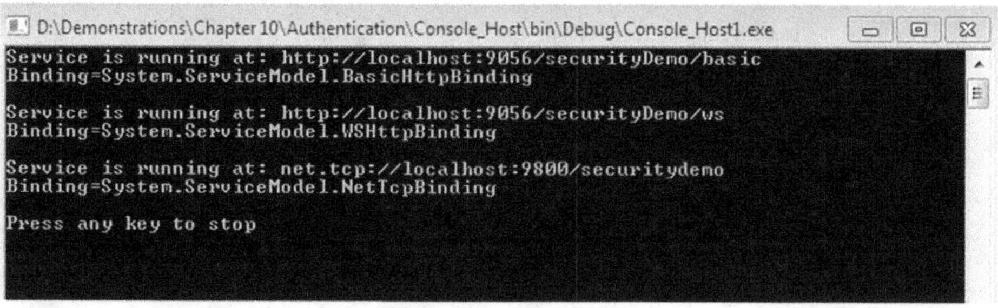

```xml
        <behavior name="NewBehavior0">
          <serviceMetadata httpGetEnabled="true" />
        </behavior>
      </serviceBehaviors>
    </behaviors>
    <services>
      <service behaviorConfiguration="NewBehavior0"
name="AuthenticationDemo.StudRecord">
        <endpoint address="basic" binding="basicHttpBinding"
bindingConfiguration=""
                contract="AuthenticationDemo.IStudRecord" />
        <endpoint address="ws" binding="wsHttpBinding" bind-
ingConfiguration=""
                contract="AuthenticationDemo.IStudRecord" />
        <endpoint address="net.tcp://localhost:9800/securi-
tydemo" binding="netTcpBinding"
                bindingConfiguration=""
contract="AuthenticationDemo.IStudRecord" />
        <host>
          <baseAddresses>
            <add baseAddress="http://localhost:9056/securi-
tyDemo" />
          </baseAddresses>
        </host>
      </service>
    </services>
  </system.serviceModel>
</configuration>
```

Figure 17. Design of form of client project

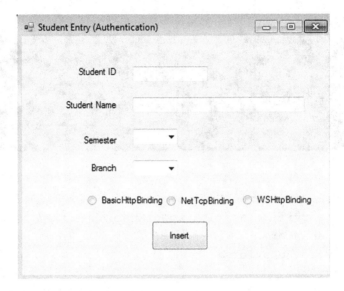

Step 4: Compile the console application project and execute it. The output of running this host program is shown in Figure 16.

Step 5: Create a windows forms application project as client project to consume the service. Design the layout of form this project as shown in Figure 17.

Step 6: Add the service reference of service in client project. The App.Config is auto generated which is shown in Example 15.

Example 15. App.Config File of Client Program

```xml
<?xml version="1.0" encoding="utf-8" ?>
<configuration>
    <system.serviceModel>
        <bindings>
            <basicHttpBinding>
                <binding name="BasicHttpBinding_IStudRecord"
/>
            </basicHttpBinding>
            <netTcpBinding>
                <binding name="NetTcpBinding_IStudRecord" />
            </netTcpBinding>
            <wsHttpBinding>
```

```
                        <binding name="WSHttpBinding_IStudRecord" />
                    </wsHttpBinding>
                </bindings>
                <client>
                    <endpoint address="http://localhost:9056/securi-
tyDemo/basic"
                        binding="basicHttpBinding" bindingConfigurat
ion="BasicHttpBinding_IStudRecord"
                        contract="SecurityClient_Ref.IStudRecord"
name="BasicHttpBinding_IStudRecord" />
                    <endpoint address="http://localhost:9056/securi-
tyDemo/ws" binding="wsHttpBinding"
                        bindingConfiguration="WSHttpBinding_IStudRe-
cord" contract="SecurityClient_Ref.IStudRecord"
                        name="WSHttpBinding_IStudRecord">
                        <identity>
                            <userPrincipalName value="INDIA1\india"
/>
                        </identity>
                    </endpoint>
                    <endpoint address="net.tcp://localhost:9800/se-
curitydemo" binding="netTcpBinding"
                        bindingConfiguration="NetTcpBinding_IStudRe-
cord" contract="SecurityClient_Ref.IStudRecord"
                        name="NetTcpBinding_IStudRecord">
                        <identity>
                            <userPrincipalName value="INDIA1\india"
/>
                        </identity>
                    </endpoint>
                </client>
        </system.serviceModel>
</configuration>
```

Then write the code of Form1.cs file as shown in Example 16

Example 16. Code of Form1.cs File of Client Program

```
using System;
using System.Collections.Generic;
```

```
using System.ComponentModel;
using System.Data;
using System.Drawing;
using System.Linq;
using System.Text;
using System.Windows.Forms;
using Security_Client.SecurityClient_Ref;
namespace Security_Client
{
    public partial class Form1: Form
    {
        public Form1()
        {
            InitializeComponent();
        }
        private void btnSend_Click(object sender, EventArgs
e)
        {
            StudRecordClient proxy = null;
            String studid, studname;
            int sem;
            String Branch;
            studid = tbStudID.Text;
            studname = tbStudName.Text;
            sem = Int32.Parse(cbSemester.SelectedItem.To-
String());
            Branch = cbBranch.SelectedItem.ToString();
            String binding_name = null;
            if (rbBasicHttpBinding.Checked == true)
                binding_name = "BasicHttpBinding_IStudRe-
cord";
            else if (rbwsHttpBinding.Checked == true)
                binding_name = "WSHttpBinding_IStudRecord";
            else
                binding_name = "NetTcpBinding_IStudRecord";
            proxy = new StudRecordClient(binding_name);

            Student stud = new Student();
            stud.stud_id = studid;
            stud.stud_name = studname;
```

Figure 18. Output of client program

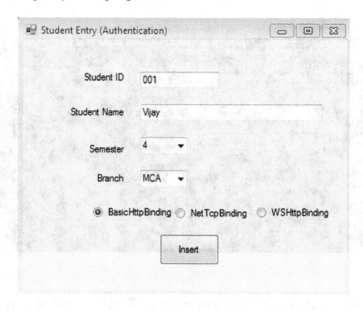

```
        stud.semester = sem;
        stud.Branch = Branch;
        Boolean is_record_inserted = proxy.insert_
stud(stud);
        if(is_record_inserted==true)
                MessageBox.Show("Record is inserted
successfully");
        else
                        MessageBox.Show("Error: There
is some problem in inserting record");
        }
    }
}
```

Step 7: Compile the client program and execute it to see the identity details in console host by consuming service using different binding. The output of client program is shown in Figure 18.

Execute the code for basicHttpBinding, netTcpBinding and wsHttpBinding and the output of the console host is shown in Figure 19. As shown in Figure 19, first we consumed the service basicHttpBinding so the identity of the user is not checked and not shown.

Figure 19. Displaying client identity on console host

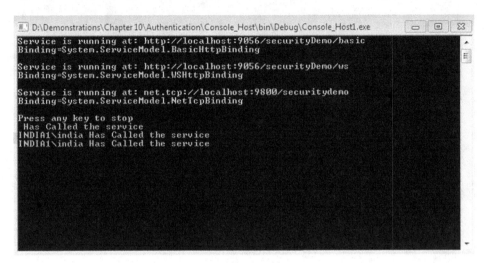

The service is consumed again by using netTcpBinding and wsHttpBinding respectively. As it is shown in Figure 19, the identity of the user is displayed when the service is consumed by using both bindings.

All the client credentials are not supported in all the bindings. The following Table 3 summarizes supported client credentials type and protection level in major bindings.

Table 3. Client credentials supported in various bindings

Binding	Protection Level	Client Credentials Supported
basicHttpBinding	None, Sign, EncryptAndSign	Transport Level: None, Basic, Digest, Windows, Certificate, Ntlm Message Level: UserName, Certificate
wsHttpBinding	None, Sign, EncryptAndSign	Transport Level: None, Basic, Digest, Windows, Certificate, Ntlm Message Level: None, IssuedToken, Certificate, Windows, UserName
netTcpBinding	None, Sign, EncryptAndSign	Transport Level: None, Windows, Certificate Message Level: None, IssuedToken, Certificate, Windows, UserName
netMSMQBinding	None, Sign, EncryptAndSign	Transport Level: None, Windows, Certificate Message Level: None, Issued Token, Certificate, Windows, UserName
netNamedPipeBinding	None, Sign, EncryptAndSign	Transport Level: None, Windows

As depicted in Table 3, the netNamedPipeBinding supports only Transport level security and it supports only two client credential types: None and Windows. The other bindings support both transport level and message level security and having various client credentials at each level of security.

Authorization Example

Authorization is the process of allowing access to particular resource based on the rights assigned to the user. The authorization can be done by using by using various options such as PrincipalPermission attribute, ASP.NET membership provider, ASP.NET role provider etc.

Following section demonstrates authorization using PrincipalPermission attribute which comes from System.Security.Permissions.

Step 1: Create WCF service library. Write the code of service contract and service class as shown in Example 17 and Example 20 respectively.

Example 17. Code of Service Contract

```
using System;
using System.Collections.Generic;
using System.Linq;
using System.Runtime.Serialization;
using System.ServiceModel;
using System.Text;
namespace AuthorizationDemo
{
    [ServiceContract]
    public interface IStudRecord
    {
        [OperationContract]
        Boolean Insert_Stud(Student stud);
        [OperationContract]
        Boolean Update_Student(String studid,String
studname,int studsem,String studbranch);
        [OperationContract]
        List<Student> Display_All();

    }
```

```
[DataContract]
public class Student
{
    [DataMember (Order=1)]
    public String stud_id;
    [DataMember(Order = 2)]
    public String stud_name;
    [DataMember(Order = 3)]
    public int semester;
    [DataMember(Order = 4)]
    public String Branch;
}
}
```

In above example, three operations are defined. The first two operations are created to test the authorization based on the user rights. The third operation is used to verify whether the data is inserted or updated properly or not.

Example 18. Code of Service Class

```
using System;
using System.Collections.Generic;
using System.Linq;
using System.Runtime.Serialization;
using System.ServiceModel;
using System.Text;using System.Security.Permissions;
namespace AuthorizationDemo
{
    public class StudRecord: IStudRecord
    {
        List<Student> all_students = new List<Student>();
        [PrincipalPermission (SecurityAction.
Demand,Role="India1\\India")]
        public bool Insert_Stud(Student stud)
        {
            if (stud != null)
            {
                all_students.Add(stud);
                return true;
            }
```

```
            else
                return false;
        }
        [PrincipalPermission(SecurityAction.Demand, Role =
"India1\\testuser")]
        public bool Update_Student(string studid, string
studname, int studsem, string studbranch)
        {
            foreach (Student stud in all_students)
            {
                if (stud.stud_id == studid)
                {
                    Student updated_stud = new Student();
                    updated_stud.stud_id = studid;
                    updated_stud.stud_name = studname;
                    updated_stud.semester = studsem;
                    updated_stud.Branch = studbranch;
                    all_students.Remove(stud);
                    all_students.Add(updated_stud);
                    return true;   //record is found. It is
updated so return true
                }
            }
            return false; //if record is found it is not
updated
        }
        public List<Student> Display_All()
        {
            return all_students;
        }
    }
}
```

As shown in Example 18 above, the Insert_Student operation can be consumed by user India1\India only. If other user tries to consume this operation then access denied error will be displayed. Likewise, the Update_Student operation can be consume by the user India1\TestUser only. If other user tries consume this operation then access denied error is generated. The Display_All operation can be consumed by any user as no PrincipalPermission is applied on it.

Step 2: Compile the WCF service library and create console application project to host the WCF service. Write the code in Program.cs file as shown in Example 19.

Example 19. Code of Program.cs File

```
using System;
using System.Collections.Generic;
using System.Linq;
using System.Text;
using System.ServiceModel;
using System.ServiceModel.Description;
using AuthorizationDemo;
namespace Console_Host
{
    class Program
    {
        static void Main(string[] args)
        {
            ServiceHost host = new ServiceHost(typeof(StudR
ecord));
            host.Open();
            foreach (ServiceEndpoint endpoint in host.De-
scription.Endpoints)
            {
                Console.WriteLine("Service is running at: "
+ endpoint.Address);
                Console.WriteLine("Binding=" + endpoint.
Binding);
                Console.WriteLine("");
            }
            Console.WriteLine("Press any key to stop");
            Console.ReadKey();
            host.Close();
        }
    }
}
```

Then prepare the App.Config file of host project as shown in Example 20.

Example 20. App.Config File Console Application Project

```xml
<?xml version="1.0" encoding="utf-8" ?>
<configuration>
  <system.serviceModel>
    <behaviors>
      <serviceBehaviors>
        <behavior name="NewBehavior0">
          <serviceMetadata httpGetEnabled="true" />
        </behavior>
      </serviceBehaviors>
    </behaviors>
    <services>
      <service behaviorConfiguration="NewBehavior0"
name="AuthorizationDemo.StudRecord">
        <endpoint address="ws" binding="wsHttpBinding" bind-
ingConfiguration=""
          contract="AuthorizationDemo.IStudRecord" />
        <host>
          <baseAddresses>
            <add baseAddress="http://localhost:9056/securi-
tyDemo" />
          </baseAddresses>
        </host>
      </service>
    </services>
  </system.serviceModel>
</configuration>
```

Execute the host program. The output of host program is shown in Figure 20.

Step 3: Create a Windows forms application project to consume the service. Add the service reference of service and design the layout as shown in Figure 21.

Step 4: Write the code of Form1.cs file as show in Example 21.

Example 21. Code of Form1.cs File

```csharp
using System;
using System.Collections.Generic;
```

Figure 20. Output of console application project

Figure 21. Form design of client project

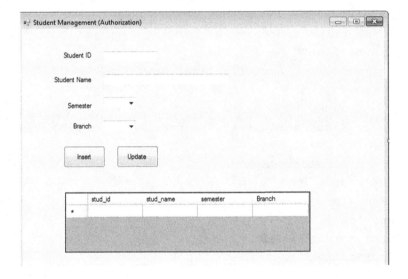

```
using System.ComponentModel;
using System.Data;
using System.Drawing;
using System.Linq;
using System.Text;
using System.Windows.Forms;
using Security_Client.SecurityClient_Ref;
using System.ServiceModel.Security;
namespace Security_Client
{
```

```
    public partial class Form1: Form
    {
        StudRecordClient proxy   = new StudRecordClient();
        public Form1()
        {
            InitializeComponent();
        }
        private void btnInsert_Click(object sender, Even-
tArgs e)
        {

            String studid, studname;
            int sem;
            String Branch;
            studid = tbStudID.Text;
            studname = tbStudName.Text;
            sem = Int32.Parse(cbSemester.SelectedItem.To-
String());
            Branch = cbBranch.SelectedItem.ToString();


            Student stud = new Student();
            stud.stud_id = studid;
            stud.stud_name = studname;
            stud.semester = sem;
            stud.Branch = Branch;
            Boolean is_record_inserted = false;
            try{is_record_inserted = proxy.Insert_
Stud(stud);}catch (SecurityAccessDeniedException sae){Mes-
sageBox.Show("Access denided. You are not authorized user to
consume this operation");}
            if(is_record_inserted==true)
            MessageBox.Show("Record is inserted successful-
ly");
            else
            MessageBox.Show("Error: There is some problem in
inserting record");
            studentBindingSource.DataSource = proxy.Display_
All();
```

```
            }
        private void btnUpdate_Click(object sender, Even-
tArgs e)
        {
            if (btnUpdate.Text == "Update")
            {
                tbStudID.Clear();
                tbStudName.Clear();
                btnUpdate.Text = "Save";
            }
            else
            {
                String studid, studname;
                int sem;
                String Branch;
                studid = tbStudID.Text;
                studname = tbStudName.Text;
                sem = Int32.Parse(cbSemester.SelectedItem.
ToString());
                Branch = cbBranch.SelectedItem.ToString();
                Boolean is_record_updated = false;
                try{is_record_updated = proxy.Update_
Student(studid, studname, sem, Branch);}catch (SecurityAc-
cessDeniedException sae){MessageBox.Show("Access denided.
You are not authorized user to consume this operation");
                }
                if (is_record_updated == true)
                {
                    MessageBox.Show("Record is updated suc-
cessfully");
                }
                else
                {
                    MessageBox.Show("Error: Unable to up-
dated record");
                }
                btnUpdate.Text = "Update";
            }
            studentBindingSource.DataSource = proxy.Display_
All();
```

378

```
              }
        }
  }
```

As shown in above code accessing the operation by using unauthorized user results in SecurityAccessDeniedException which comes from System. ServiceModel.Security as shown in Figure 22. So to catch this exception, reference of System.ServiceModel.Security must be imported in the client program which is highlighted at the top of the program

We tried to access the method Update_Student () by using user account other than testuser. As only testuser can access the method the error is generated as shown in Figure 22.

SUMMARY

This chapter provides very important concepts of security for any distributed applications. It also focuses on implementing these concepts using robust security infrastructure available in WCF.

Following are the important points to summarize from this chapter:

Figure 22. Error message on unauthorized access

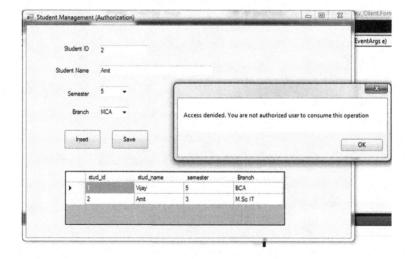

- In any service oriented applications following security concepts must be implemented: Integrity, Confidentiality, Authentication and Authorization.
- BasicHttpBinding is not secured by default.
- Transport level security is point to point and faster.
- Message level security is end to end but it is slow as compared to transport level security.
- In Transport level security message may not remain secured during the transfer while message level security provides end-to-end encryption of message so entire message remains secured and no third party can access it.
- Most of the bindings support Transport level and message level security but netNamedPipeBinding supports on Transport level security.
- Authentication is the concept to check the identity of the client program.
- Authorization is the concept of providing access based on the privileges given to the client program.
- To have transport level security using basicHttpBinding or wsHttpBinding the address must be https and valid certificate must be obtained from certification authority in order to provide this level of security.
- The attribute [PrincipalPermission] is used to provide role based authorization based on the windows user account. It comes from System.Security.Permissions.

Chapter 11
Hosting WCF Service

After completing this chapter, you will be able to:

- Learn about various hosting options available in WCF
- Understand various hosting and self-hosting options available in WCF
- Host the WCF service practically using all the hosting options available.
- Understand difference between hosting and self-hosting

INTRODUCTION

A WCF service can be hosted using various hosting options available. This is the important aspect of WCF as there are multiple hosting options available to host any WCF service. A developer is not bound to choose any particular hosting option or component. Following hosting options are available in WCF:

- Internet Information Services (IIS)
- Windows Service Hosting
- Windows Activation Service (WAS)
- Self-hosting using console application

DOI: 10.4018/978-1-5225-1997-3.ch011

- Self-hosting using windows form application

In the absence of IIS, a developer can use any of the self-hosting options also to host the service. This is the major advantage of WCF which distinguishes it from other technology. In following section, each of these options is explored with great details.

Internet Information Services (IIS)

When you host the service on IIS, you don't need to manage hosting process of the service. IIS itself takes care of heath, recycling and other issues related to the service. To host the service on IIS svc (service) file is required which must be added manually when WCF service library option is used. From. NET 3.5, you can create WCF service application which adds svc file automatically. The demonstration of hosting the service using IIS is illustrated in following steps.

Step 1: Select File->New Project as shown in Figure 1. The wizard is displayed to select the project type and other details.

In the wizard, select WCF from the installed templates and click on the WCF Service Application as highlighted in Figure 2. Then click on the OK button, the project is created, which is shown in the Visual studio as shown

Figure 1. Creating new project

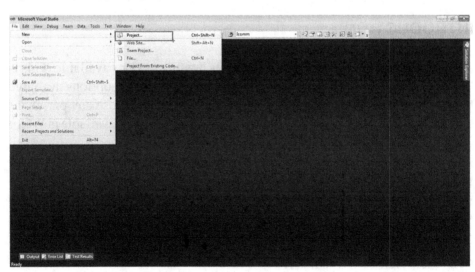

Figure 2. Selecting WCF service application project

in Figure 3. As shown in this figure, there are three files. One is IService1. cs in which the service contract is written. The Service1.svc file contains the information to host the service which is discussed later on in this section. The Service.svc.cs file contains the service class which implements the service contract. The Web.config is also available which should be modified with service and endpoint details. So the benefit of this kind project is that we don't need to create a new configuration file for preparing the endpoint, just modify the web.config file with updated service and endpoint details.

Step 2: Open IService1.cs file and rename the service contract name using the refactor option as illustrated in Figure 4. Click on the Rename option from the context menu and provide the new name of the contract in the dialog box as shown in Figure 5. Click on the button after providing new name of the service contract. The changes are shown in preview dialog box as illustrated in Figure 6. Click on the apply button to confirm the rename operation. The service contract is renamed in IService.cs file. Write the code of service contract as illustrated in Example 1.

Example 1. Code of Service Contract

```
using System;
using System.Collections.Generic;
using System.Linq;
using System.Runtime.Serialization;
```

Figure 3. WCF Service Application project in Visual Studio

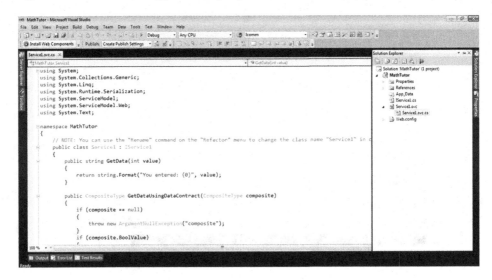

Figure 4. Renaming service contract

Figure 5. Changing the name of service contract

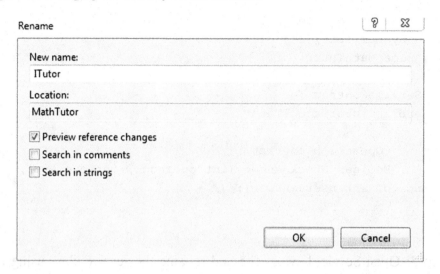

Figure 6. Previewing the changes of rename operation

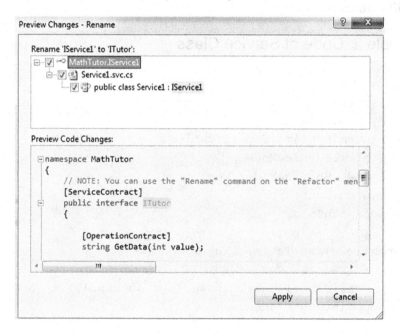

```csharp
using System.ServiceModel;
using System.ServiceModel.Web;
using System.Text;
namespace MathTutor
{
    [ServiceContract]
     public interface ITutor
     {
         [OperationContract]
         Boolean Check_Answer(int operand1, int operand2,
String op, int user_answer);
     }
}
```

Step 3: Open Service1.svc.cs file and rename the service class using the refactor option as discussed in previous step. This is the service class which implements the service contract. Write the code of this class as illustrated in Example 2.

Example 2. Code of Service Class

```csharp
using System;
using System.Collections.Generic;
using System.Linq;
using System.Runtime.Serialization;
using System.ServiceModel;
using System.ServiceModel.Web;
using System.Text;
namespace MathTutor
{
     public class Tutor: ITutor
     {
         public bool Check_Answer(int operand1, int operand2,
string op, int user_answer)
         {
             int correct_ans = 0;
             if (op == "+")
                 correct_ans = operand1 + operand2;
             else if (op == "-")
                 correct_ans = operand1 - operand2;
```

```
            else if (op == "*")
                correct_ans = operand1 * operand2;
            else //operation is division
                correct_ans = operand1 / operand2;
            //mathching the actual answer i.e.correct_ans
            //and answer entered by user i.e. user_answer
            if (correct_ans == user_answer)
                return true;
            else
                return false;
        }
    }
}
```

Step 4: Right click on the Service1.svc file and click on the view markup option to open the content of this file as double clicking on Service1.svc file opens the code file i.e. Service1.svc.cs file. So to view the content of this file view markup option is used as shown in Figure 7.

This file includes following code:

```
<%@ ServiceHost Language="C#" Debug="true"
Service="MathTutor.Tutor" CodeBehind="Service1.svc.cs" %>
```

Figure 7. Opening Service1.svc file

The above code is very important to host the WCF service on IIS or development server provided by visual studio. It contains ServiceHost directly which is similar as ServiceHost class we discussed earlier to host the service. Now update the Web.Config with by adding the service and endpoint details as illustrated in Example 3.

Example 3. Web.Config File

```
<?xml version="1.0"?>
<configuration>
  <system.web>
    <compilation debug="true" targetFramework="4.0" />
  </system.web>
  <system.serviceModel>
    <services>
      <service name="MathTutor.Tutor">
        <endpoint address="" binding="wsHttpBinding" bind-
ingConfiguration=""
          contract="MathTutor.ITutor" />
      </service>
    </services>

    <behaviors>
      <serviceBehaviors>
        <behavior>
          <!-- To avoid disclosing metadata information, set
the value below to false and remove the metadata endpoint
above before deployment -->
          <serviceMetadata httpGetEnabled="true"/>
          <!-- To receive exception details in faults for
debugging purposes, set the value below to true.  Set to
false before deployment to avoid disclosing exception infor-
mation -->
          <serviceDebug includeExceptionDetailInFaults="fal
se"/>
        </behavior>
      </serviceBehaviors>
    </behaviors>
    <serviceHostingEnvironment multipleSiteBindingsEnabled=
"true" />
```

```
  </system.serviceModel>
<system.webServer>
    <modules runAllManagedModulesForAllRequests="true"/>
  </system.webServer>
  </configuration>
```

It is important to note that there is not base address defined and serviceMetadata behavior is added but there will not be any error as the base address is provided by ASP.NET development server or IIS.

The Service1.svc file is required when hosting WCF service on IIS. In the absence of IIS, ASP.NET development server is used to host the service. To host the service on ASP.NET development server right click on Service1.svc file and click on view in browser option as shown in Figure 8. The browser is opened and the browser displays metadata about service as shown in Figure 9. It is important to note here that we have not created any endpoint or configuration but still service is hosted. This is possible because while we create this project the web.config is available in this project with default endpoint having wsHttpBinding. When you open the svc file in browser, visual studio hosts WCF service on ASP.NET development service and runs this server. The development server can be found at the taskbar as shown in Figure 10. To open it right click on it and click on show details as shown in Figure 11. The development server appears as illustrated in Figure 12. Using this service is good for developing and debugging purpose but it cannot be used for real development as service hosted on this server is accessible to local machine only it cannot be accessing by other machine which does not serve the purpose of developing service oriented and distributed applications.

Hosting WCF service on IIS is discussed in the next step onwards.

Step 5: After updating the Web.Config file compile the project and correct the syntax error if any. Then close the visual studio and open it again with administrator privileges. Open the wcf service application in visual studio. The administrator privileges are required while hosting the service on IIS so it is compulsory to open visual studio with administrator privileges.

To publish the service on IIS, right click on the project and click on the publish option as shown in Figure 13. The wizard is displayed to provide the service publishing options. In this wizard, specify the publish method as File System, specify the Target Location by providing path of the service as illustrated in Figure 14. This is the virtual directory path and the service

Figure 8. Selecting option to view svc file in browser

will be accessible using this address only. Before clicking on publish button click on browse button besides the path to view whether the service is hosted on IIS. The Target Location is displayed as shown in Figure 15. Select Local IIS option if it is not selected and click on Open button to get back to the screen shown in Figure 14.

Now click on the publish button shown in Figure 14. The WCF service is hosted on IIS and the confirmation is displayed in the output window as shown in Figure 16.

Figure 9. Service metadata in browser

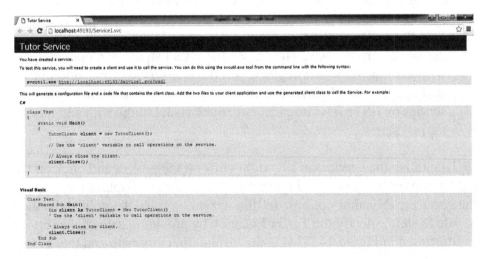

Figure 10. Locating ASP.NET development server

Figure 11. Selecting option to open ASP.NET development server

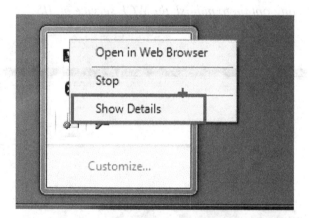

Open IIS to view the published WCF service on IIS. The WCF service is displayed under the Default Website as shown in Figure 17. It shows the virtual directly which is accessible in browser but the files are located physically in the c:\inetpub\wwwroot folder as shown in Figure 18.

Now get back to the IIS and click on the Browse button as shown in Figure 17 to open the service in browser. It shows the error as shown in Figure 19. The main cause of this error is that I have not configured the default document for this service. In this service the default document is Service1. svc which must be configured to open the service using the above path. So

Figure 12. ASP.NET development server

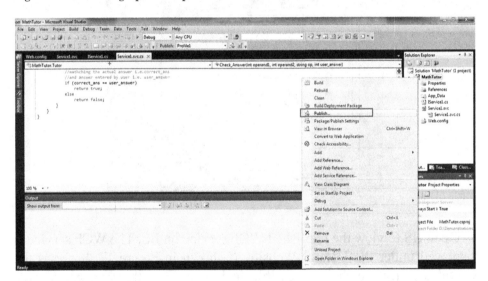

Figure 13. Selecting option to publish the WCF service on IIS

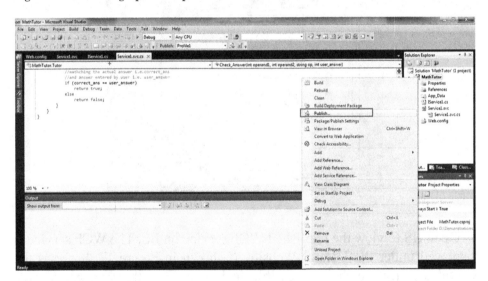

Hosting WCF Service

Figure 14. Specifying publishing options

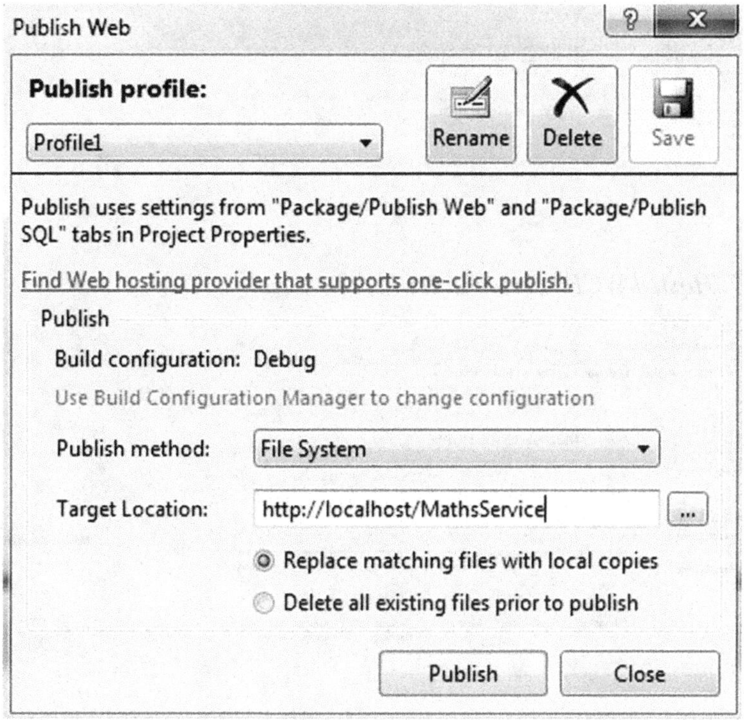

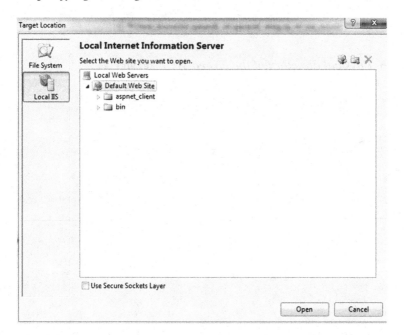

Figure 15. Specifying the Target Location

Figure 16. Output of publishing WCF service on IIS

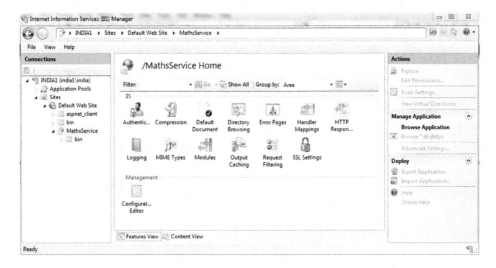

Figure 17. Hosted WCF Service in IIS

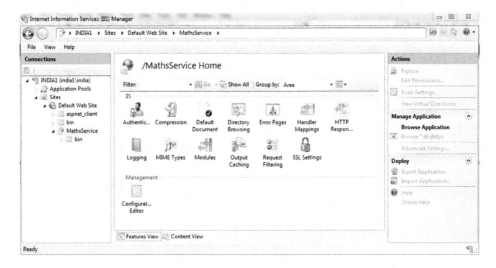

Figure 18. Physical directory of the hosted WCF service

get back to IIS screen as shown in Figure 17 and click on the Default Document option. The screen appears as shown in Figure 20 to manage the default document for this website. Click on the Add option under the Actions menu to add a new default document. In this service the default document name is Service1.svc so specify it as shown in Figure 21. Click on the OK button and get back to the IIS screen. Now try to browse the MathsService website again to explore it in browse. This time correct output is displayed as shown in Figure 22. Now by using WSDL file the service can be consumed in most of the client applications.

Sometime it is quite possible that after doing this stuff the service is not displayed in browser. In such situation, you need to register the WCF service with IIS using the servicemodelreg command. To apply this command you need to open visual studio command prompt using administer privileges. Write the command mentioned in the Figure 23 to register WCF with IIS. This command has several switches such as i, u, c,a etc. The switch i is used to register WCF with IIS while the switch u is used to unregister WCF with IIS.

In this section we took enough pain to host the WCF service on IIS. The process of consuming the service is same as the methods discussed in previous chapters so the client program is not discussed here.

Figure 19. Error on browsing WCF service

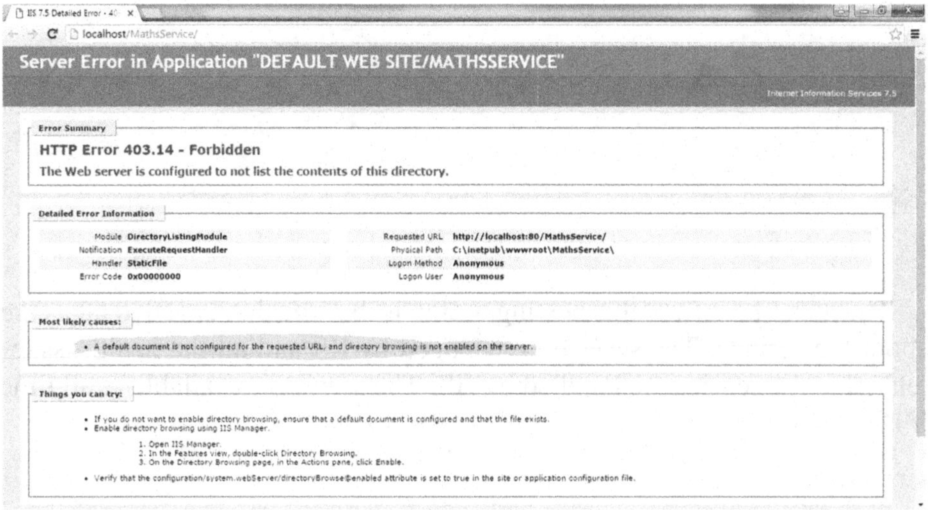

Figure 20. Managing default document

Figure 21. Specifying default document name

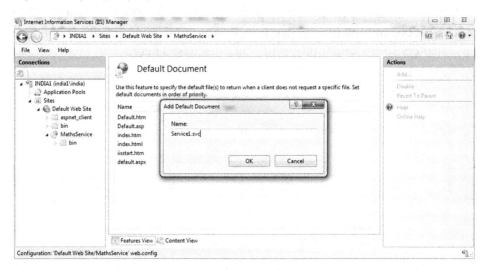

The major benefit of this hosting option is that you don't need to take care about the service. The service is managed by IIS and all the health issues related to the service are handled by IIS. The service is available at all time if IIS is not stopped.

Figure 22. Viewing Hosted WCF service in the browser

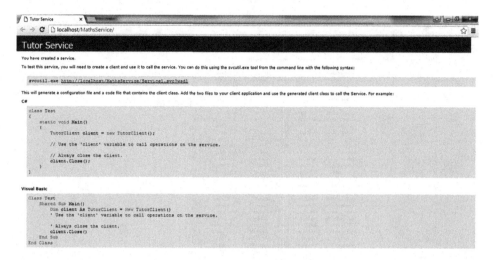

Figure 23. Registering WCF service with IIS

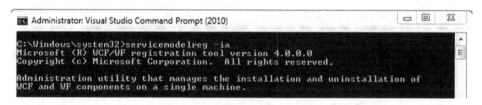

Windows Service Hosting

In windows operating system, all the services run at services.msc. To open it type services.msc in run menu. The list of services is displayed as shown in Figure 24. Using this option you can host your WCF service at this place. Like IIS you don't need to manage the service through the program as it takes care about the service. A program hosted under windows service can different start up option such as Automatic, Manual and Disabled. For example let us observe the properties of SQLExpress program hosted as windows service in Figure 25. As it shown in Figure 25, it contains three types Automatic, Manual and Disabled. This options are explained below:

- **Automatic:** This option automatically starts the service when computer is restarted. You don't need to start it by using start button. This option is very useful when human intervention is not needed to start service every time.

Figure 24. Services of windows operating system

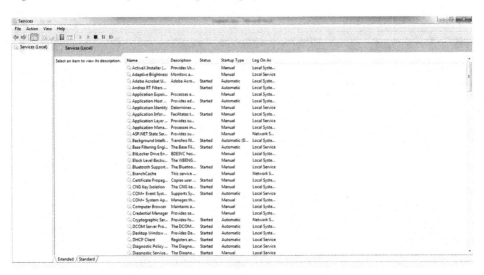

Figure 25. Properties of SQLExpress

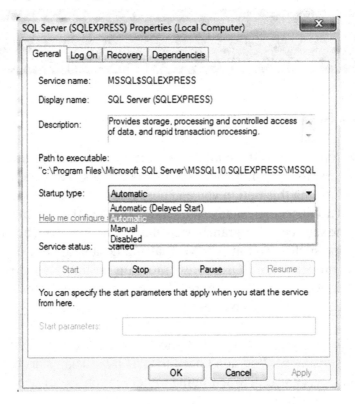

- **Manual:** This option provides control to the user to start and stop the service manually. You need to start the service by clicking on the start button. When computer is restarted the service is stopped and you need to start it again by clicking on start button as it will not start automatically.
- **Disabled:** This option is used to disable service and you cannot start the service.

Hosting WCF service using this option is explained in the following steps:

Step 1: Create WCF Service library project and write the code of service contract and service class shown in Example 4 and Example 5 respectively.

Example 4. Code of Service Contract

```
using System;
using System.Collections.Generic;
using System.Linq;
using System.Runtime.Serialization;
using System.ServiceModel;
using System.Text;
namespace FirstWCFService_Calc
{
    [ServiceContract]
    public interface ICalculator
    {
        [OperationContract ]
        int add(int no1, int no2);
        [OperationContract]
        int sub(int no1, int no2);
        [OperationContract]
        int mul(int no1, int no2);
        [OperationContract]
        int div(int no1, int no2);
    }
}
```

Example 5. Code of Service Class:

```
using System;
using System.Collections.Generic;
using System.Linq;
using System.Runtime.Serialization;
using System.ServiceModel;
using System.Text;
namespace FirstWCFService_Calc
{
    public class Calculator: ICalculator
    {
        public int add(int no1, int no2)
        {
            return no1 + no2;
        }
        public int sub(int no1, int no2)
        {
            return no1 - no2;
        }
        public int mul(int no1, int no2)
        {
            return no1 * no2;
        }
        public int div(int no1, int no2)
        {
            return no1 / no2;
        }
    }
}
```

Step 2: Compile WCF service library. Right click on the solution and add new project. The wizard to select the project appears as shown in Figure 26. Select windows from the installed template, select Windows Service project, provide name of the project and click on the OK button. The Windows Service project appears in visual studio as shown in Figure 27. As this is windows service project there not design view available for this kind of project. To view the code click on Service1.cs file or

Figure 26. Adding new project

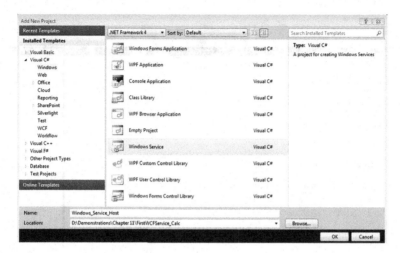

click on the link switch to code view. The code file is opened as shown in Figure 28. In this code there are two methods available OnStart() and OnStop().The OnStart method is attached with Start button of windows service so in this method the logic for starting the service must be written while the OnStop method is attached with Stop button of windows service so in this method logic for stopping the service must be written.

Figure 27. Widows service project in visual studio

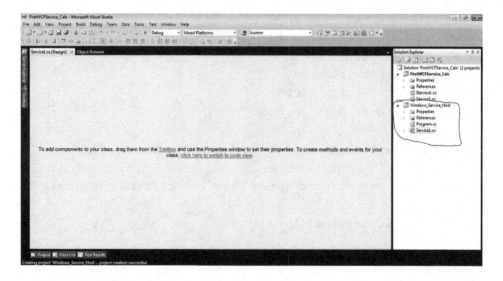

Figure 28. Widows service project in visual studio

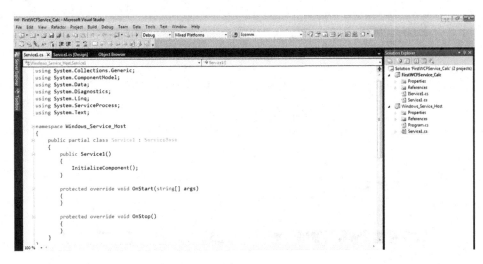

Step 3: Add the reference of theWCF service, System.ServiceModel and write the code of Service1.cs file as illustrated in Example 6.

Example 6. Code of Service1.cs File

```
using System;
using System.Collections.Generic;
using System.ComponentModel;
using System.Data;
using System.Diagnostics;
using System.Linq;
using System.ServiceProcess;
using System.Text;
using System.ServiceModel;
using FirstWCFService_Calc;
namespace Windows_Service_Host
{
    public partial class Service1: ServiceBase
    {
        ServiceHost host = new ServiceHost(typeof(Calculat
or));
        public Service1()
        {
            InitializeComponent();
```

```
    }
    protected override void OnStart(string[] args)
    {
        host.Open();
    }
    protected override void OnStop()
    {
        host.Close();
    }
  }
}
```

Here in above code we don't need to check the state of the ServiceHost object as it will be handled by the windows service.

Step 4: Add App.Cofig file to create the endpoint. To add the configuration file right click on the project and select Add->new item option. The template appears to add the item as shown in Figure 29. Select Application configuration file and click on the Add button. The App.config file is added in visual studio. To edit the App.Config file right click on it and click on Edit WCF Configuration option as shown in Figure 30. To add the new service click on Create a New Service Link and follow the steps through Figure 31 to Figure 35 to add service and contract details in App.Config file.

Select the protocol as TCP as shown in Figure 36 and click on Next button. In the next step, provide the address in net.tcp format as shown in Figure 37 and click on Next button. The endpoint is created and summary is displayed as shown in Figure38. Click on the Finish button to return to the Editor again.

Now add mex endpoint to expose the existing endpoint to the client program. To add another endpoint right click on the Endpoints node and select New Service Endpoint option as shown in Figure 39. In the wizard provide relative address of the endpoint. As it is mex address I have provided address as mex. Select binding and mexTcpBinding from the list of available bindings as shown in Figure 40. Write the name of contract as IMetadataExchange as shown in Figure 41.

It is required to have service metadata behavior when mex endpoint is added in the service. To add the service metadata behavior click on the Advanced->Service Behavior node as illustrated in Figure 42. Click on the New Service Behavior Configuration link to add new behavior which is

Figure 29. Template to add new item

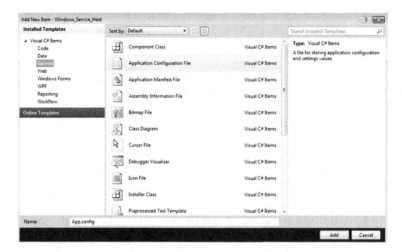

Figure 30. Selecting option of Edit App.Config file

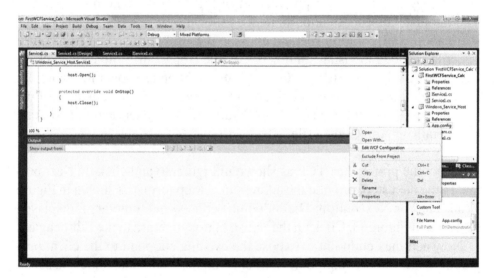

added as shown in Figure 43. To add new behavior, click on the Add button. Select serviceMetata behavior and click on the Add button as shown in Figure 44. In this program the binding is netTcpBinding so httpGetEnabled property must be set to false as shown in Figure 45.

Relate the service behavior with service using behaviorConfiguration property of service as shown in Figure 46. When a service behavior is added it is required to have the base address on the service. To add the base address

Figure 31. Create a New Service Link in editor

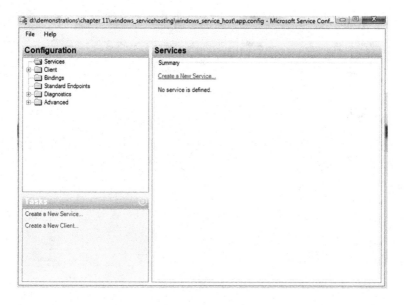

Figure 32. Browsing for service DLL

Figure 33. Locating service DLL

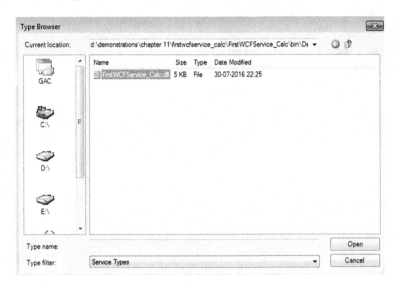

Figure 34. Selecting service

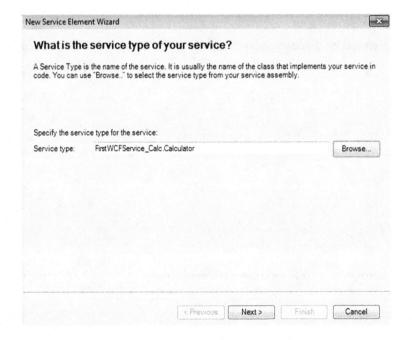

Figure 35. Selecting contract

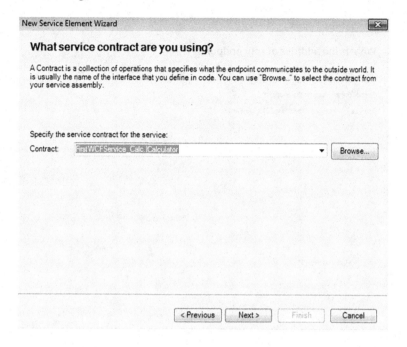

Figure 36. Selecting protocol

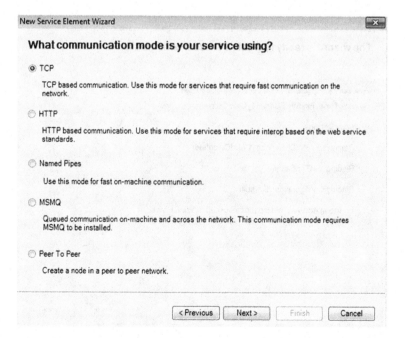

Figure 37. Specifying address

Figure 38. Endpoint in editor

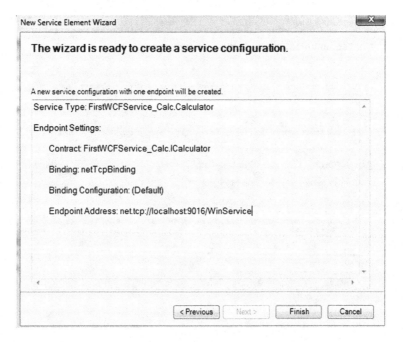

Figure 39. Adding new endpoint

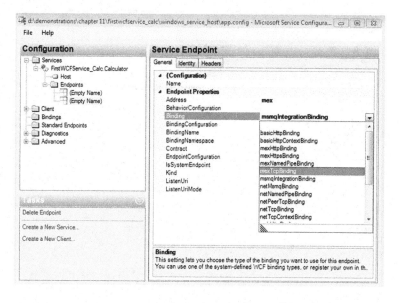

Figure 40. Selecting binding

Figure 41. Specifying the contract

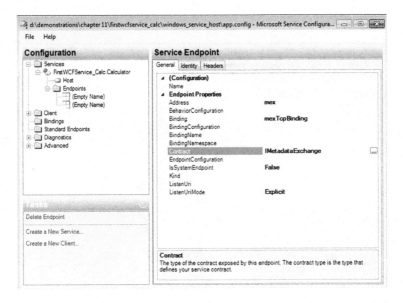

Figure 42. Adding Service Behavior

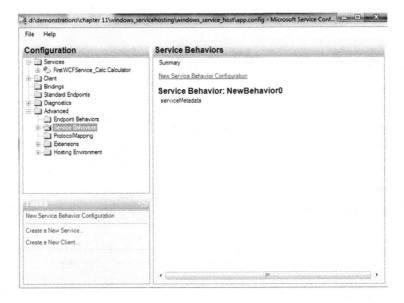

Figure 43. Newly added behavior

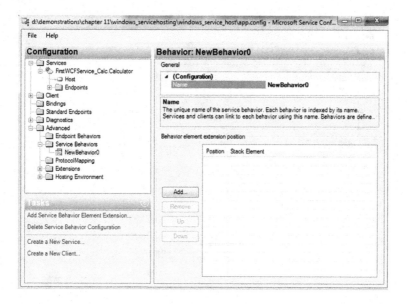

Figure 44. Adding serviceMetadata behavior

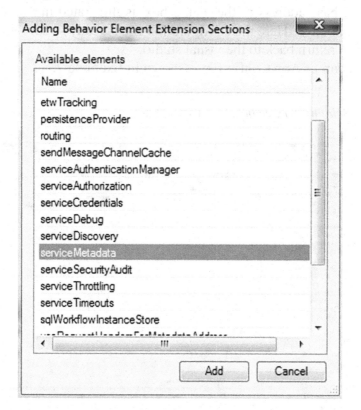

Figure 45. setting property of serviceMetadata behavior

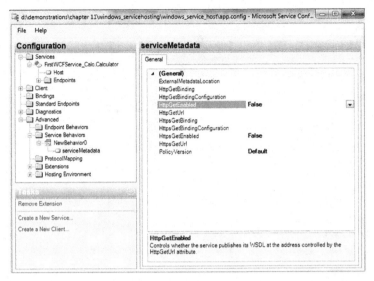

click on the host node under the service node and click on New button. Then provide the base address in the dialog box as illustrated in Figure 47 and click on OK button. Here the configuration file is ready so save it and close the editor to return back to the visual studio.

The content of App.Config file is shown in Example 7.

Figure 46. Relating service behavior with service

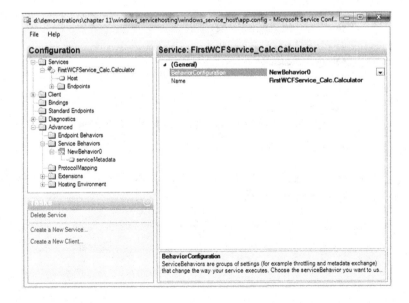

Figure 47. Adding base address

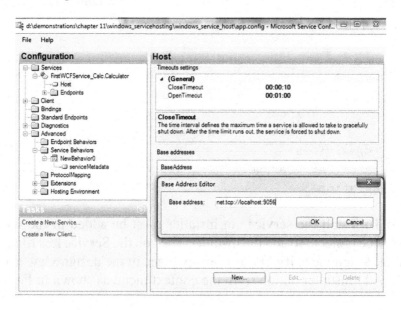

Example 7. Content of App.Config File

```xml
<?xml version="1.0"?>
<configuration>
    <system.serviceModel>
        <behaviors>
            <serviceBehaviors>
                <behavior name="NewBehavior0">
                    <serviceMetadata/>
                </behavior>
            </serviceBehaviors>
        </behaviors>
        <services>
            <service behaviorConfiguration="NewBehavior0"
name="FirstWCFService_Calc.Calculator">
                <endpoint address="net.tcp://localhost:9016/
WinService" binding="netTcpBinding"
                    bindingConfiguration=""
contract="FirstWCFService_Calc.ICalculator" />
                <endpoint address="mex"
binding="mexTcpBinding" bindingConfiguration=""
```

```
                contract="IMetadataExchange" />
        <host>
            <baseAddresses>
                <add baseAddress="net.tcp://local-
host:9056" />
            </baseAddresses>
        </host>
      </service>
    </services>
  </system.serviceModel>
</configuration>
```

Step 5: To install the service, an installer must be added to the windows service project. To add the installer, click on the Service1.cs file to open it in design view. Right click on any place in the design view and click on Add Installer option from the context menu as shown in Figure 48.

It adds ProjectInstaller.cs file which contains two installers: serviceProcessInstaller1 and serviceInstaller1 as shown in Figure 49. Open the property page of serviceProcessInstaller1 and set the Account as NetworkService which will run the service under network service account of windows system so it will not ask credentials to execute the service. Then after open the property page of serviceInstaller1 and set the different properties of it as

Figure 48. Adding installer

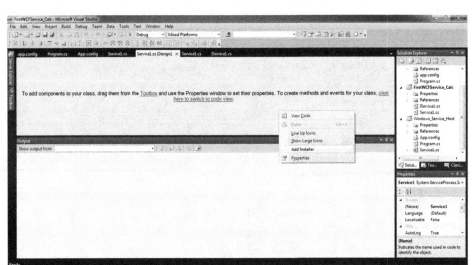

Figure 49. Content of project installer

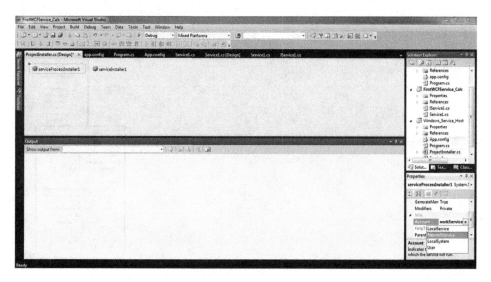

shown in Figure 50. Following are the important properties of servicpIn-staller1:

- **ServiceName:** It is actual name by which the service can be referred.
- **Service Type:** This property sets the type of service which can be Automatic, Manual or Disabled. These types are discussed earlier in this section.
- **DisplayName:** This property sets the display name of service which is displayed in the list of service. The default name is ServiceName.
- **Description:** This property displays the description of service when it is displayed under the list of services.

After setting all these values service must be installed in the windows services list which is explained in the next step.

Step 6: Open visual studio command prompt with administrator privileges as shown in Figure 51. The command prompt is opened. Locate the EXE of the windows service project in command prompt by reaching up to bin/debug folder as shown in Figure 52. Then, write installutil command with switch i as shown in Figure 52 to install the service. In case of no error the service is installed successfully and the message is shown at the command prompt as illustrated in Figure 53.

415

Figure 50. Setting property of serviceInstaller1

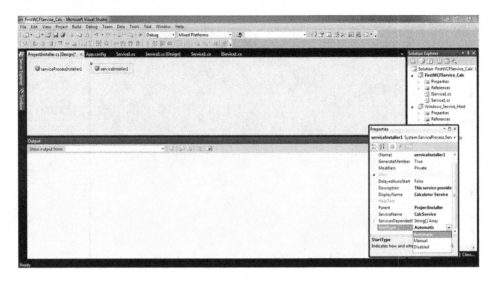

Figure 51. Opening visual studio command prompt

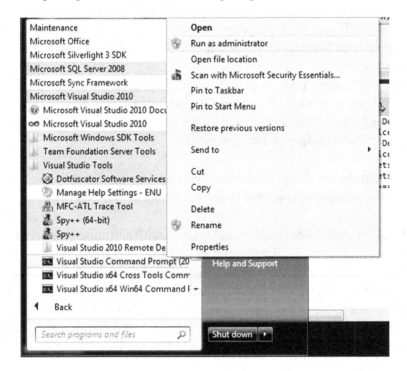

Figure 52. Opening visual studio command prompt

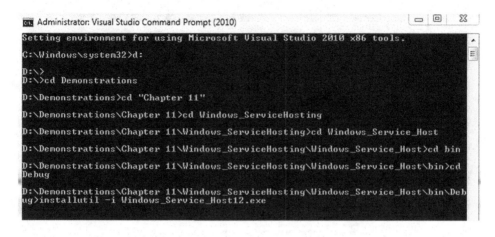

Figure 53. Successfully installation of service

Figure 54. Locating the installed service

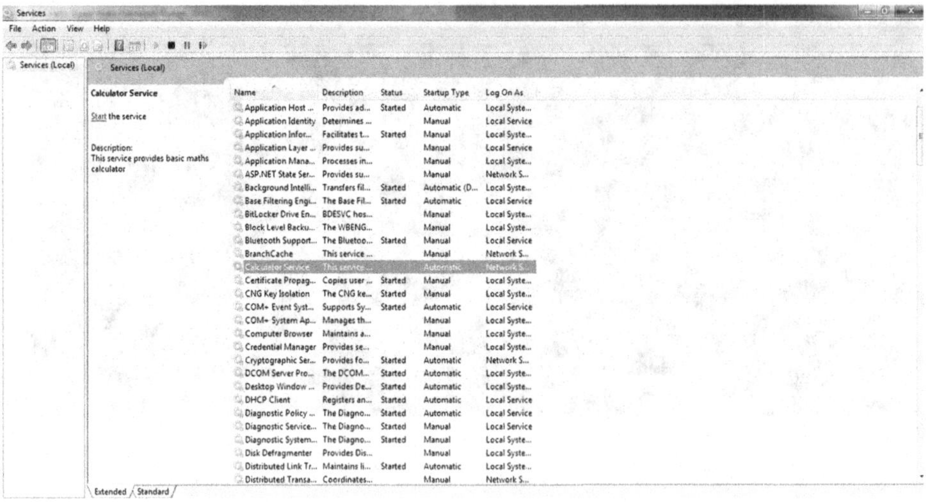

Likewise the service can be uninstalled by using -u switch with instal-lutil command. The installutil.exe file is located at.Net framework folder i.e.C:\Windows\Microsoft.NET\Frameworkxx\vxxx.

The switch i is default value so it is not required to write if you want to install a service i.e. following two commands are exactly same:

installutil –i or installutil

Here service is successfully installed. The next step is to start the service.

Step 7: To start the service open the list of services (services.msc from run menu) and find the installed service from the list as illustrated in Figure 54. The service can be started by using the Start button locate at left most side or right clicking on it as shown in Figure 55. If there is no error then service get started and it status is changed to Started as shown in Figure 56. There are the occasions in which service is not able to start due to some errors. In such situation the errors can be found under windows event logs. Find the error from it, uninstall the service, correct the errors, recompile the service, install the service again try to run it again. To view the property of service right click on the service and select property to view the property dialog box of service as shown in Figure 57.

Figure 55. Starting the service

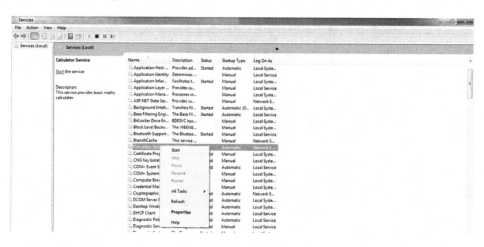

Figure 56. Started service

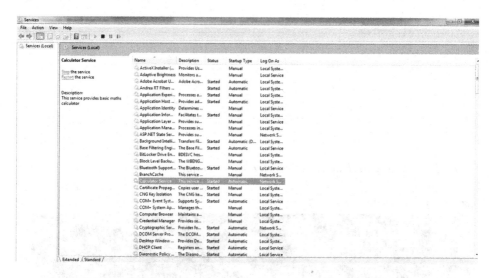

As you can see in Figure 57, the property dialog of service contains all the properties which are set using the program in the earlier step. You can change it from here also.

Now a service can be started and stop using Start and Stop buttons. It is also possible to start and stop the service using command prompt by using the commands net start and net stop as shown in Figure 58.

So, now service is hosted and running successfully. So let us consume it by creating client project in the next step.

Figure 57. Service properties

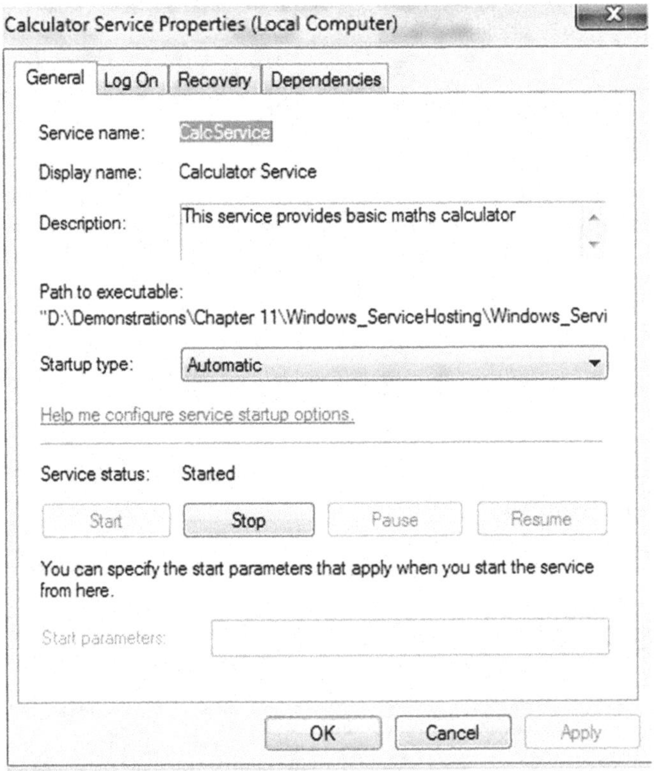

Figure 58. Starting and stopping service using commands

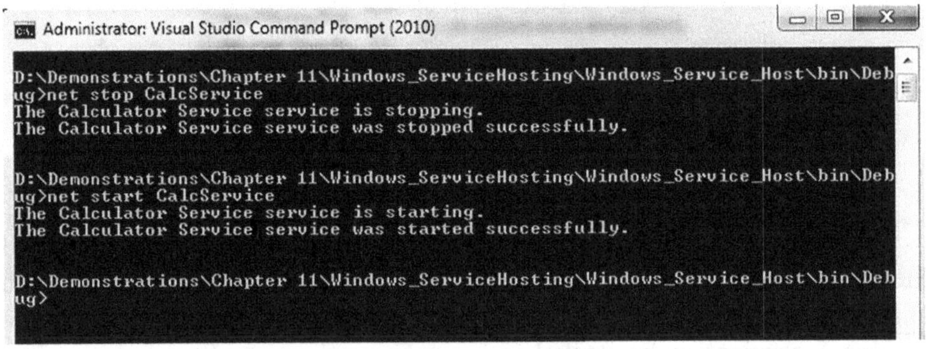

Figure 59. Design of the form

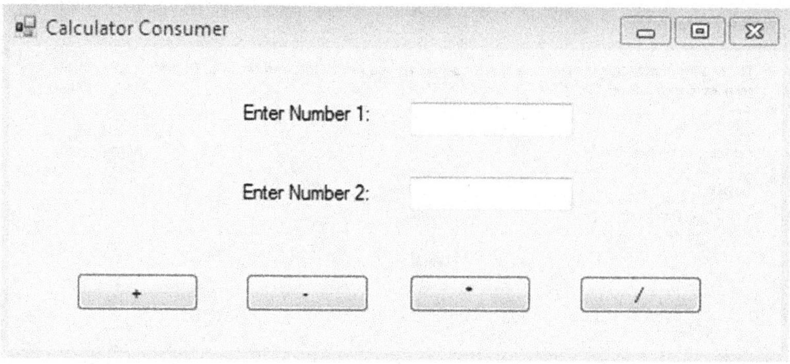

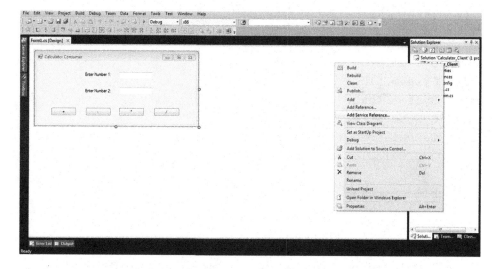

Step 8: Create windows forms application project and design the layout of form as depicted in Figure 59. Right click on the project and add the service reference of service as shown in Figure 60.The dialog appears to write the address of service. Write the base address of service and click on the Go button. Once the service details are loaded provide the name of the namespace as shown in Figure 61 and click on the OK button. Then write the code of Form1.cs file as shown in Example 8.

Figure 60. Adding service reference

Figure 61. Adding service reference

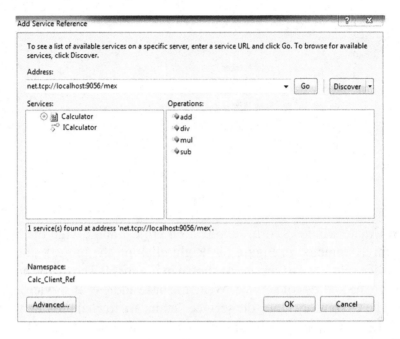

Example 8. Code of Form1.cs File

```csharp
using System;
using System.Collections.Generic;
using System.ComponentModel;
using System.Data;
using System.Drawing;
using System.Linq;
using System.Text;
using System.Windows.Forms;
using Calculator_Client.Calc_Client_Ref;
namespace Calculator_Client
{
    public partial class Form1: Form
    {
        int no1, no2;
        int ans;
        CalculatorClient proxy = new CalculatorClient();

        public Form1()
```

```
        {
            InitializeComponent();
        }
        private void btnPlus_Click(object sender, EventArgs
e)
        {

            no1 = Int16.Parse(tbNumber1.Text);
            no2 = Int16.Parse(tbNumber2.Text);
            ans = proxy.add(no1, no2);
            MessageBox.Show("Answer is "+ans);


        }
        private void btnMinus_Click(object sender, EventArgs
e)
        {

            no1 = Int16.Parse(tbNumber1.Text);
            no2 = Int16.Parse(tbNumber2.Text);
            ans = proxy.sub(no1, no2);
            MessageBox.Show("Answer is " + ans);
        }
        private void btnMult_Click(object sender, EventArgs
e)
        {
            no1 = Int16.Parse(tbNumber1.Text);
            no2 = Int16.Parse(tbNumber2.Text);
            ans = proxy.mul(no1, no2);
            MessageBox.Show("Answer is " + ans);
        }
        private void btnDiv_Click(object sender, EventArgs
e)
        {
            no1 = Int16.Parse(tbNumber1.Text);
            no2 = Int16.Parse(tbNumber2.Text);
            ans = proxy.div(no1, no2);
            MessageBox.Show("Answer is " + ans);
        }
    }
}
```

Figure 62. Enabling WAS

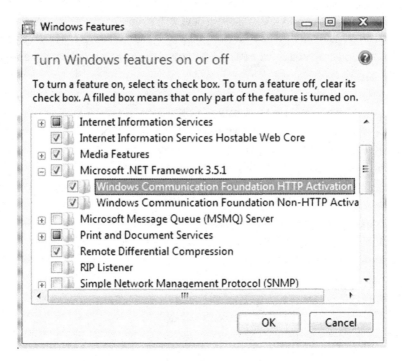

Finally, execute the code to validate the program. The execution of the program is not shown as it is similar as the other client programs discussed in earlier chapters.

Hosting WCF Service Using Windows Activation Service (WAS)

The Windows Activation Service (WAS) supports non-HTTP protocols in IIS 7.0. To have the support of these protocols you must enable the support for WAS by turning on the feature to support non-HTTP protocol in windows operating system as shown in Figure 62. After selecting this feature click on OK button to enable this feature.

To enable the support for various protocols such and net tcp and named pipe, a command to register the protocol must be written in command prompt as illustrated in Figure 63.

The configuration settings for these protocols are saved in C:\Windows\ System32\inetsrv\config\ applicationHost.config file which contains configuration details of all the allowed protocols in the bindings. The bindings

Figure 63. Enabling support for non-Http bindings

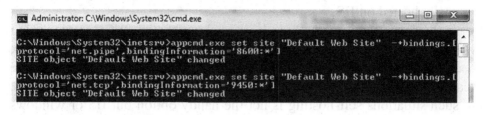

which are added using above command are also added in this file. The part of applicationHost.config is shown in Example 9.

Example 9. AapplicationHost.Config File Content:

```
...
                <bindings>
                        <binding protocol="http" bindingInforma-
tion="*:80:" />
                        <binding protocol="net.tcp" bindingIn-
formation="808:*" />
                        <binding protocol="net.pipe" bindingIn-
formation="*" />
                        <binding protocol="net.msmq" bindingInf
ormation="localhost"/>
                        <binding protocol="msmq.formatname"
bindingInformation="localhost" />
                        <binding protocol="net.tcp" bindingIn-
formation="9200:*" />
                        <binding protocol="net.tcp" bindingIn-
formation="9300:*" />
                        <binding protocol="net.tcp" bindingIn-
formation="9400:*" />
                        <binding protocol="net.pipe" bindingIn-
formation="9000:*" />
                        <binding protocol="net.pipe" bindingIn-
formation="8600:*" />
                        <binding protocol="net.tcp" bindingIn-
formation="9450:*" />
                </bindings>
...
```

After enabling these protocols, a WCF service with those protocols can be easily hosted on IIS.

In the above section, you have learned about hosting WCF service using windows operating system i.e. windows takes care about service startup, health and other related issues. These options are very powerful for the large scale system in which service handles huge numbers of concurrent requests. In such situations self-hosting is not the handy option but IIS or windows service or WAS might be really useful for better performance. Self-hosting is useful when a programmer needs to control the service startup, health and other issues related to the service. In the following section, self-hosting concepts are explained in depth.

Hosting Under the Managed Code: Self Hosting

A managed code is a.NET application which contains.NET framework components and runs under the control of Common Language Runtime (CLR). Hosting WCF under managed code is known as self-hosting. This option requires least infrastructure to host WCF service. The ServiceHost class is used to host service using this option. There are two self-hosting options available: console application and windows forms application. These options are explained in below section.

Self-Hosting Using Console Application Revisited

In the preceding chapters we have already discussed about hosting the WCF service using console application project. In this section I will recall the steps once again to revisit this option.

Step 1: Create WCF service library project and write code of service contract and service class as illustrated in Example 10 and Example 11 respectively.

Example 10. Code of Service Contract Class

```
using System;
using System.Collections.Generic;
using System.Linq;
using System.Runtime.Serialization;
using System.ServiceModel;
using System.Text;
namespace FirstWCFService_Calc
```

```
{
    [ServiceContract]
    public interface ICalculator
    {
        [OperationContract ]
        int add(int no1, int no2);
        [OperationContract]
        int sub(int no1, int no2);
        [OperationContract]
        int mul(int no1, int no2);
        [OperationContract]
        int div(int no1, int no2);
    }
}
```

Example 11. Code of Service Class

```
using System;
using System.Collections.Generic;
using System.Linq;
using System.Runtime.Serialization;
using System.ServiceModel;
using System.Text;
namespace FirstWCFService_Calc
{

    [ServiceBehavior]
    public class Calculator: ICalculator
    {
        public int add(int no1, int no2)
        {
            return no1 + no2;
        }
        public int sub(int no1, int no2)
        {
            return no1 - no2;
        }
        public int mul(int no1, int no2)
        {
            return no1*no2;
```

```
        }
        public int div(int no1, int no2)
        {
            return no1 / no2;
        }


    }
}
```

Step 2: Compile the WCF service library and add the console application project. Add the reference of the WCF service and System.ServiceModel. Write the code of Program.cs file as depicted in Example 12 to host the service.

Example 12. Code of Program.cs File:

```
using System;
using System.Collections.Generic;
using System.Linq;
using System.Text;
using FirstWCFService_Calc;
using System.ServiceModel;
namespace Calculator_Host_Console
{
    class Program
    {
        static void Main(string[] args)
        {

            ServiceHost host = new ServiceHost(typeof(Calcu
lator));
            host.Open();
            Console.WriteLine("Service is running press any
key to stop");
            Console.ReadKey();
            host.Close();
        }
    }
}
```

Step 3: Add App.Config in console application project to create the endpoint. The content of App.Config file is shown in Example 13.

Example 13. App.Config of Host Program

```xml
<?xml version="1.0"?>
<configuration>
    <system.serviceModel>
        <behaviors>
          <serviceBehaviors>
            <behavior name="NewBehavior">
                <serviceMetadata httpGetEnabled="true"/>
            </behavior>
          </serviceBehaviors>
        </behaviors>
        <services>
            <service behaviorConfiguration="NewBehavior"
name="FirstWCFService_Calc.Calculator">
            <endpoint address=""
binding="basicHttpBinding" bindingConfiguration=""
contract="FirstWCFService_Calc.ICalculator"/>
                <host>
                    <baseAddresses>
                        <add baseAddress="http://local-
host:9087/CalculatorDemo"/>
                    </baseAddresses>
                </host>
            </service>
        </services>
    </system.serviceModel>
</configuration>
```

Step 4: Compile the console application project. Run the EXE of console application project with administrator privileges to host the service. Write the base address in the browse to view the WSDL file. By using WSDL file consume the service in the client program which is already discussed in many chapters so it is not explained again here.

Figure 64. Form design of host program

Self-Hosting Using Windows Forms Application Revisited

This is also a self-hosting option but it has GUI to control the start and stop event of the ServiceHost class. The important steps to host the WCF service using windows forms application project are explained below:

Step 1: Create WCF service library and write the code of service contract and service class as illustrated in Example 10 and Example 11.

Step 2: Add Windows forms application project. Add the reference of the WCF service and System. ServiceModel. Design the form layout of the form as illustrated in Figure 64. As it is shown in Figure 64, there are two buttons. The Start button is used to start the service while the Stop button is used to stop the service. You can start and stop service multiple times without the closing or restarting the program. This provides the flexibility over the console application project in which you can start the service once only. If the service is stopped you need to run the program again.

Step 3: Write the code of the form as shown in Example 14.

Example 14. Code of the Form:

```
using System;
using System.Collections.Generic;
using System.ComponentModel;
using System.Data;
using System.Drawing;
using System.Linq;
using System.Text;
using System.Windows.Forms;
```

```csharp
using System.ServiceModel;
using FirstWCFService_Calc;
namespace Windows_Form_Host
{
    public partial class Form1: Form
    {
        ServiceHost host = new ServiceHost(typeof(Calculat
or));
        public Form1()
        {
            InitializeComponent();
        }
        private void btnStart_Click(object sender, EventArgs
e)
        {
            if (host.State != CommunicationState.Created)
            {
                host = new ServiceHost(typeof(Calculator));
            }
            host.Open();
            btnStart.Enabled = false;
            btnStop.Enabled = true;
            lblStatus.Text = "Service is started";
        }
        private void btnStop_Click(object sender, EventArgs
e)
        {
            host.Close();
            btnStop.Enabled = false;
            btnStart.Enabled = true;
            lblStatus.Text = "Service is stopped";
        }
    }
}
```

The code written in this example is robust enough. It takes care of all the kinds of validation for starting and stopping service. Most important thing is that a service can be started and stopped as many times as you want without restarting the program.

Now windows service hosting has an advantage over this option as in windows service hosting option we don't need to write any validation in OnStart() and OnStop() methods while the validation code is required in a windows forms application hosting option.

Step 4: Add App.Config file in the windows forms application project and create an endpoint in it as illustrated in Example 15.

Example 15. App.Config File of Windows Forms Application Project

```xml
<?xml version="1.0" encoding="utf-8" ?>
<configuration>
  <system.serviceModel>
    <behaviors>
      <serviceBehaviors>
        <behavior name="NewBehavior0">
          <serviceMetadata httpGetEnabled="true" />
        </behavior>
      </serviceBehaviors>
    </behaviors>
    <services>
      <service behaviorConfiguration="NewBehavior0"
name="FirstWCFService_Calc.Calculator">
        <endpoint address="" binding="basicHttpBinding"
bindingConfiguration=""
          contract="FirstWCFService_Calc.ICalculator" />
        <host>
          <baseAddresses>
            <add baseAddress="http://localhost:9099/calc_
service" />
          </baseAddresses>
        </host>
      </service>
    </services>
  </system.serviceModel>
</configuration>
```

Compile the windows application project and execute it with the administrator privileges. Click on the Start button to start the service. Once the service is

Table 1. Comparison between hosting and self-hosting

Hosting	Self-Hosting
Service is hosted under windows operating infrastructure	A program must be written to host the service. The object of ServiceHost class must be created to host the service.
Examples: IIS,WAS, Windows Service	Examples: Console Application, Windows Forms Application
Service activation is automatic	You need to start the service to activate it.
Health of service is managed.	The health of the service is not managed.
The OS can control the service hosted under Windows Service	The OS cannot control the self-hosted service.
IIS 6.0 supports only http protocol. But IIS 7.0 onwards support for multiple protocols such as http, net.tcp, net.pipe etc. is available.	Support for multiple protocols such as http, net.tcp, net.pipe etc. is available in this hosting.

started open the base address of service in browse and find the WSDL file. Consume the service using WSDL file in the client program. This step is not shown here as it is also well explained in most of the chapters.

Difference between Hosting and Self-Hosting

In this chapter we have explored all the hosting options available in WCF. There are mainly two categories of hosting: Hosting and Self-hosting. In the *hosting* the windows operating system infrastructure is used to host WCF service. Hosting using IIS, Windows service and WAS are example of hosting. In *self-hosting* we need to write a program to host the WCF service. Hosting using console application project and windows forms application project are examples of self-hosting.

In the Table 1, both hosting options are compared.

Advice on Programming WCF Service

In traditional programming, there is a single program or single unit while in WCF there are more than one component. This increase the chances of making logical errors while wring the program. To correct or prevent the errors the advice provided in following points can very handy:

- Always have a habit of using interface as [ServiceContract].
- Don't write the return type of the one-way operation.

- For debugging purpose set IncludeExceptionInDetails service behavior to true. After knowing the actual exception, set IncludeExceptionInDetails to false. Handle the exception using declared SOAP fault, i.e. using [FaultContract] attribute.
- For intermittent connectivity always use reliable sessions and queue.
- For disconnected operations always use a queue.
- Use BasicHttpBinding with default settings for interoperability with other platforms.
- Always use secured binding while transmitting sensitive information over the wire.

CONCLUSION

This chapter provides in depth understanding of hosting a WCF service using various hosting options available. Following are the important takeaways from this chapter:

- There are mainly two categories of hosting a WCF service: hosting and self-hosting.
- Hosting means hosting WCF service using available components of windows operating system. Examples are IIS, window service and WAS.
- Self-hosting means hosting WCF service using managed code. Examples are windows forms application project and console application project.
- A managed code uses.NET framework components and runs under the control of Common Language Runtime(CLR).
- .svc file is required to host the service on IIS.
- IIS 7.0 supports multiple protocols.
- In the absence of IIS a service can be hosted on ASP.NET development server provided that the WCF service has.svc file.
- In IIS the physical path of virtual directory is stored at c:\inetpub\ wwwroot.
- A service hosted under windows service can be Automatic, Manual or Disabled.
- A service hosted under windows service is under the control of windows operating system.

- To install / uninstall the windows service installutil.exe command is used. The switch i is used to install the service while the switch u is used to uninstall the service.
- For WAS support non-HTTP support features must be installed from windows features.
- To have more protocol support in WAS appcmd.exe command is used.
- In console application project a program must be restarted to restart the service.
- In windows forms application project it is not required to restart the program to restart the service.
- IIS hosting is the most powerful hosting option among all the hosting options available.

Chapter 12

Interoperability with Other Platforms

After completing this chapter, you will be able to:

- Know about the history of interoperability.
- Learn how to consume WCF service in various platforms such as JAVA, PHP and Android.
- Practically implement the client program in other platform to consume WCF service.

INTRODUCTION

The WCF was born to provide distributed system which can interoperate with other platforms seamlessly. Today, interoperability between different programming languages has become easier. In earlier days different vendors had their own standards to consume the web service. So a web service developed in one programming language cannot be consumed in another programming language. To overcome this problem, different vendors such as

DOI: 10.4018/978-1-5225-1997-3.ch012

Sun, Microsoft, Apache etc. jointly decided open standard to have interoperability among diverse platforms. Due to their rigorous efforts there were able to invent Web Service - Interoperability (WS-I) basic profile.

The WS-I 1.0 version was released in 2004. These forced other organization to adhere to follow the common standards of WS-I rather than sticking to their proprietary standards. So nowadays major organizations follow WS-I basic profile. Because of this reason if you compare the WSDL file of a JAVA web service and.NET web service both are identical as Oracle (Formerly known as Sun) and Microsoft follow WS-I basic profile. The later version of WS-I basic profile is 2.0. Following are the core components of the WS-I basic profile:

- SOAP
- WSDL
- UDDI
- XML
- XML Schema Part1: Structures
- XML Schema Part 2: Data types
- SSL

The current version 2.0 was release in 2010. It contains UDDI 3.0, SOAP 1.2 and WS-Addressing. The details about all the profiles can be found at http://www.ws-i.org/Profiles. Following is the list of the frameworks which are compliant with WS-I basic profile:

- ASP.NET 2.0
- Apache Axis2
- GlassFish Metro
- Microsoft BizTalk Server
- Oracle Weblogic Server

In the following sections, I will demonstrate how to consume WCF service in following platforms:

- JAVA
- PHP
- Android

Consuming WCF Service in Java

A Java program can be developed using various IDEs such as eclipse, Net Beans and event in notepad. In this demonstration I will use Net Beans IDE to develop the Java program. Following are the steps to interoperate Java program with WCF service.

Step 1: Create a WCF service with binding as basicHttpBinding as shown in the web.config file of the service program in Example 1.

Example 1.Web.Config File of the Service

```xml
<?xml version="1.0"?>
<configuration>
  <system.web>
    <compilation debug="true" targetFramework="4.0" />
  </system.web>
  <system.serviceModel>
    <services>
      <service name="MathTutor.Tutor">
        <endpoint address="" binding="basicHttpBinding" bind
ingConfiguration=""contract="MathTutor.ITutor" />
      </service>
    </services>
    <behaviors>
      <serviceBehaviors>
        <behavior>
          <serviceMetadata httpGetEnabled="true"/>
          <serviceDebug includeExceptionDetailInFaults="fal
se"/>
        </behavior>
      </serviceBehaviors>
    </behaviors>
    <serviceHostingEnvironment multipleSiteBindingsEnabled=
"true" />
  </system.serviceModel>
  <system.webServer>
    <modules runAllManagedModulesForAllRequests="true"/>
  </system.webServer>
</configuration>
```

Figure 1. Viewing WSDL file

Host the service using any of the hosting options available and view the WSDL file of the hosted service as shown in Figure 1. In this example the service is hosted on IIS. The content of a WSDL file is shown in Example 2.

Example 2. WSDL File of Hosted Service

```
<wsdl:definitions xmlns:wsdl="http://schemas.xmlsoap.org/
wsdl/" xmlns:wsx="http://schemas.xmlsoap.org/ws/2004/09/
mex" xmlns:wsa10="http://www.w3.org/2005/08/addressing"
xmlns:tns="http://tempuri.org/" xmlns:soap12="http://sche-
mas.xmlsoap.org/wsdl/soap12/" xmlns:wsu="http://docs.oasis-
open.org/wss/2004/01/oasis-200401-wss-wssecurity-utility-
1.0.xsd" xmlns:wsp="http://schemas.xmlsoap.org/ws/2004/09/
policy" xmlns:wsap="http://schemas.xmlsoap.org/ws/2004/08/
addressing/policy" xmlns:msc="http://schemas.microsoft.
com/ws/2005/12/wsdl/contract" xmlns:wsa="http://schemas.
xmlsoap.org/ws/2004/08/addressing" xmlns:wsam="http://www.
w3.org/2007/05/addressing/metadata" xmlns:wsaw="http://www.
w3.org/2006/05/addressing/wsdl" xmlns:soap="http://schemas.
xmlsoap.org/wsdl/soap/" xmlns:xsd="http://www.w3.org/2001/
XMLSchema" xmlns:soapenc="http://schemas.xmlsoap.org/soap/
encoding/" name="Tutor" targetNamespace="http://tempuri.
org/">
```

```
<wsdl:types>
<xsd:schema targetNamespace="http://tempuri.org/Imports">
<xsd:import schemaLocation="http://localhost/MathsService/
Service1.svc?xsd=xsd0" namespace="http://tempuri.org/"/>
<xsd:import schemaLocation="http://localhost/MathsService/
Service1.svc?xsd=xsd1" namespace="http://schemas.microsoft.
com/2003/10/Serialization/"/>
</xsd:schema>
</wsdl:types>
<wsdl:message name="ITutor_Check_Answer_InputMessage">
<wsdl:part name="parameters" element="tns:Check_Answer"/>
</wsdl:message>
<wsdl:message name="ITutor_Check_Answer_OutputMessage">
<wsdl:part name="parameters" element="tns:Check_AnswerRe-
sponse"/>
</wsdl:message>
<wsdl:portType name="ITutor">
<wsdl:operation name="Check_Answer">
<wsdl:input wsaw:Action="http://tempuri.org/ITutor/Check_An-
swer" message="tns:ITutor_Check_Answer_InputMessage"/>
<wsdl:output wsaw:Action="http://tempuri.org/ITutor/Check_
AnswerResponse" message="tns:ITutor_Check_Answer_OutputMes-
sage"/>
</wsdl:operation>
</wsdl:portType>
<wsdl:binding name="BasicHttpBinding_ITutor"
type="tns:ITutor">
<soap:binding transport="http://schemas.xmlsoap.org/soap/
http"/>
<wsdl:operation name="Check_Answer">
<soap:operation soapAction="http://tempuri.org/ITutor/Check_
Answer" style="document"/>
<wsdl:input>
<soap:body use="literal"/>
</wsdl:input>
<wsdl:output>
<soap:body use="literal"/>
</wsdl:output>
</wsdl:operation>
</wsdl:binding>
```

Figure 2. Creating new project

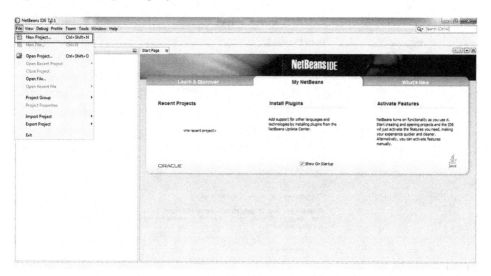

```
<wsdl:service name="Tutor">
<wsdl:port name="BasicHttpBinding_ITutor"
binding="tns:BasicHttpBinding_ITutor">
<soap:address location="http://localhost/MathsService/Ser-
vice1.svc"/>
</wsdl:port>
</wsdl:service>
</wsdl:definitions>
```

Step 2: Open NetBeans IDE and select New Project from the File menu as illustrated in the Figure 2. A wizard is displayed to select the type of project you want to create.

Step 3: From the type of project, select Java and Java application project as shown in Figure 3. You can also select any other project available in this template. Click on the Next button.

Step 4: Select the folder to save the project and write name of project as show in Figure 4.Click on Finish button to return to the NetBeans IDE. The project contains a Java file which is under the package as shown in Figure 5. All the components are placed under the project which is similar as the solution in.NET.

Step 5: To add the reference of service, right click on the project and select New->Web Service Client option as shown in Figure 6.

Figure 3. Creating new project

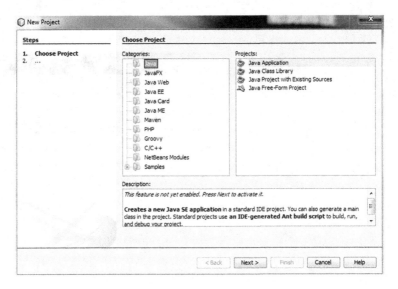

The wizard displays to provide the location of the WSDL file as shown in Figure 7. Select the WSDL URL radio button and type or copy the URL WSDL file of hosted WCF service. Then click on Finish button to generate code of consume the WCF service in java. The code is generated automatically and it is shown in the output window as shown in Figure 8. Now in

Figure 4. Providing project details

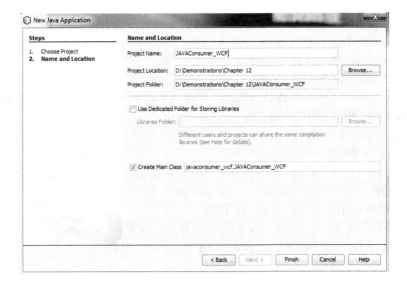

Figure 5. Java program in NetBeans IDE

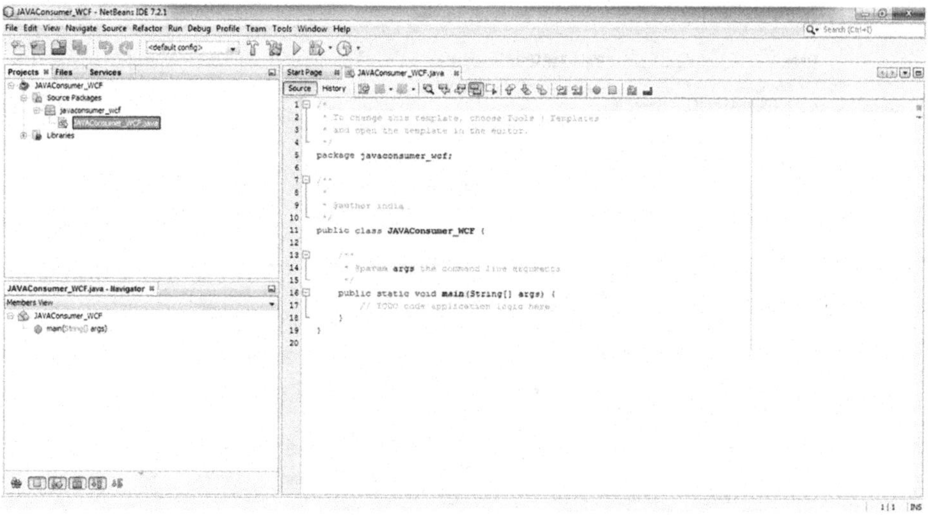

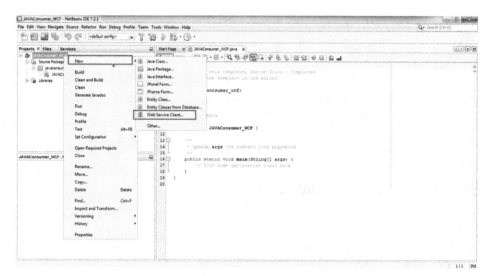

Figure 6. Adding web service client

project explores the auto generated classes are placed under org.tempuri package as shown in Figure 9. It contains several classes which also includes two classes Tutor.Java and ITutor.Java. In WCF the service name is Tutor and contract name is ITutor which is an interface too. The content of Tutor. Java file is shown in Example 3.

Figure 7. Providing WSDL file

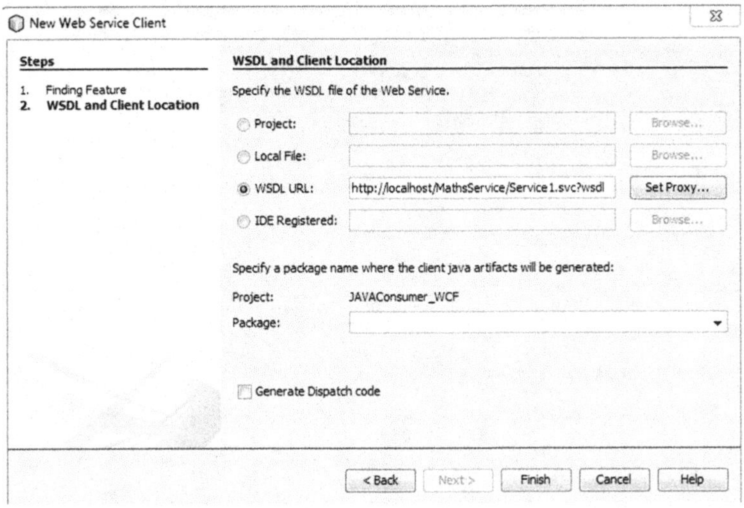

Figure 8. Output window of NetBeans

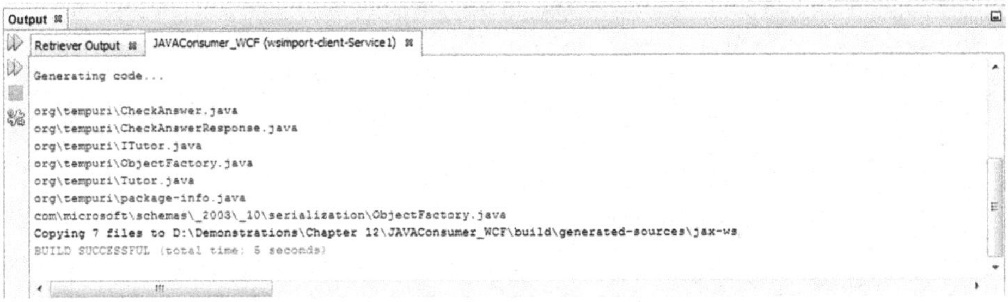

Example 3. Code of Tutor. Java

```
package org.tempuri;
import java.net.MalformedURLException;
import java.net.URL;
import javax.xml.namespace.QName;
import javax.xml.ws.Service;
import javax.xml.ws.WebEndpoint;
import javax.xml.ws.WebServiceClient;
import javax.xml.ws.WebServiceException;
import javax.xml.ws.WebServiceFeature;
/**
```

Figure 9. Generated classes in NetBeans IDE

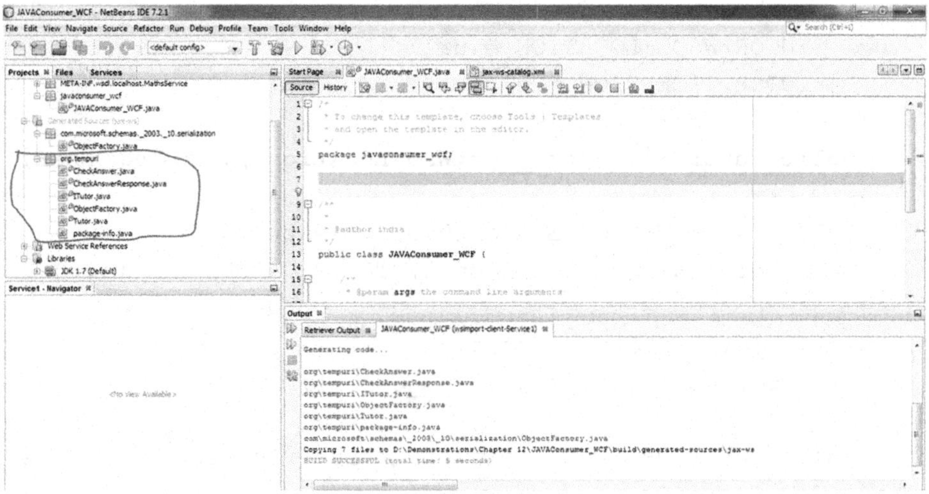

```
* This class was generated by the JAX-WS RI.
* JAX-WS RI 2.2.6-1b01
* Generated source version: 2.2
*
*/
@WebServiceClient(name = "Tutor", targetNamespace = "http://
tempuri.org/", wsdlLocation = "http://localhost/MathsSer-
vice/Service1.svc?wsdl")
public class Tutor
    extends Service
{
    private final static URL TUTOR_WSDL_LOCATION;
    private final static WebServiceException TUTOR_EXCEP-
TION;
    private final static QName TUTOR_QNAME = new
QName("http://tempuri.org/", "Tutor");
    static {
        URL url = null;
        WebServiceException e = null;
        try {
            url = new URL("http://localhost/MathsService/
Service1.svc?wsdl");
        } catch (MalformedURLException ex) {
```

```
            e = new WebServiceException(ex);
        }
        TUTOR_WSDL_LOCATION = url;
        TUTOR_EXCEPTION = e;
    }
    public Tutor() {super(__getWsdlLocation(), TUTOR_QNAME);
    }
    public Tutor(WebServiceFeature... features) {
        super(__getWsdlLocation(), TUTOR_QNAME, features);
    }
    public Tutor(URL wsdlLocation) {
        super(wsdlLocation, TUTOR_QNAME);
    }
    public Tutor(URL wsdlLocation, WebServiceFeature... features) {
        super(wsdlLocation, TUTOR_QNAME, features);
    }
    public Tutor(URL wsdlLocation, QName serviceName) {
        super(wsdlLocation, serviceName);
    }
    public Tutor(URL wsdlLocation, QName serviceName, WebServiceFeature... features) {
        super(wsdlLocation, serviceName, features);
    }
    /**
     *
     * @return
     *      returns ITutor
     */
    @WebEndpoint(name = "BasicHttpBinding_ITutor")public ITutor getBasicHttpBindingITutor() {return super.getPort(new QName("http://tempuri.org/", "BasicHttpBinding_ITutor"), ITutor.class);
    }
    /**
     *
     * @param features
     *      A list of {@link javax.xml.ws.WebServiceFeature}
to configure on the proxy. Supported features not in the
<code>features</code> parameter will have their default val-
```

```
ues.
   * @return
   *      returns ITutor
   */
   @WebEndpoint(name = "BasicHttpBinding_ITutor")
   public ITutor getBasicHttpBindingITutor(WebServiceFeatu
re... features) {
       return super.getPort(new QName("http://tempuri.
org/", "BasicHttpBinding_ITutor"), ITutor.class, features);
   }
   private static URL __getWsdlLocation() {
       if (TUTOR_EXCEPTION!= null) {
          throw TUTOR_EXCEPTION;
       }
       return TUTOR_WSDL_LOCATION;
   }
```

Now in the above example, the WCF operation Check_Answer is not available. In Java program, we need to consume it but it is not available in Tutor.java file. Let us view the content of ITutor.Java file as illustrated in Example 4.

Example 4. Content of ITutor.java

```
package org.tempuri;
import javax.jws.WebMethod;
import javax.jws.WebParam;
import javax.jws.WebResult;
import javax.jws.WebService;
import javax.xml.bind.annotation.XmlSeeAlso;
import javax.xml.ws.RequestWrapper;
import javax.xml.ws.ResponseWrapper;
/**
 * This class was generated by the JAX-WS RI.
 * JAX-WS RI 2.2.6-1b01
 * Generated source version: 2.2
 *
 */
@WebService(name = "ITutor", targetNamespace = "http://tem-
puri.org/")
```

```
@XmlSeeAlso({
    com.microsoft.schemas._2003._10.serialization.ObjectFac-
tory.class,
    org.tempuri.ObjectFactory.class
})
public interface ITutor {
    /**
     *
     * @param userAnswer
     * @param operand2
     * @param operand1
     * @param op
     * @return
     *     returns java.lang.Boolean
     */
    @WebMethod(operationName = "Check_Answer", action =
"http://tempuri.org/ITutor/Check_Answer")
    @WebResult(name = "Check_AnswerResult", targetNamespace
= "http://tempuri.org/")
    @RequestWrapper(localName = "Check_Answer", targetNam-
espace = "http://tempuri.org/", className = "org.tempuri.
CheckAnswer")
    @ResponseWrapper(localName = "Check_AnswerResponse",
targetNamespace = "http://tempuri.org/", className = "org.
tempuri.CheckAnswerResponse")
    public Boolean checkAnswer(
        @WebParam(name = "operand1", targetNamespace =
"http://tempuri.org/")
        Integer operand1,
        @WebParam(name = "operand2", targetNamespace =
"http://tempuri.org/")
        Integer operand2,
        @WebParam(name = "op", targetNamespace = "http://
tempuri.org/")
        String op,
        @WebParam(name = "user_answer", targetNamespace =
"http://tempuri.org/")
        Integer userAnswer);
```

As shown in above example, the operation Check_Answer is declared in the ITutor interface. So it can be consumed using the object of ITutor interface. The interface object cannot is instantiated using the new keyword. In the code of Tutor. Java file one method getBasicHttpBindingITutor() returns ITutor object. So if we create an object of Tutor class and then using that object the ITutor object can be initialized. Then by using the object of ITutor object the method Check_Answer can be easily called which is shown in the next step.

It is important to note that the autogenerated code is prepared by a tool JAX-WS which is part of GlassfishMetro discussed at the beginning of this chapter.

Step 6: Write the code in the JAVAConsumer_WCF.java file as shown in Example 5.

Example 5. Code of JAVAConsumer_WCF.java:

```
/*
 * To change this template, choose Tools | Templates
 * and open the template in the editor.
 */
package javaconsumer_wcf;
import java.util.Scanner;
import org.tempuri.ITutor;
import org.tempuri.Tutor;
/**
 *
 * @author india
 */
public class JAVAConsumer_WCF {
    /**
     * @param args the command line arguments
     */
    public static void main(String[] args) {

        // TODO code application logic here
        int no1=0, no2=0,correct_ans=0;
        String op="";
        Boolean is_correct=false;
        Scanner sc=new Scanner(System.in);
        System.out.println("Please enter value of Number
```

```
1:");
        no1=sc.nextInt();
        System.out.println("Please enter value of Number
2:");
        no2=sc.nextInt();

        System.out.println("Please enter Operator (+,-,* or
/):");
        op=sc.next();
        System.out.println("Please enter correct answer:");
        correct_ans=sc.nextInt();
        Tutor tutor=new Tutor();
        ITutor proxy=tutor.getBasicHttpBindingITutor();
        is_correct=proxy.checkAnswer(no1, no2, op, correct_
ans);
        if(is_correct==true)
            System.out.println("Your answer is correct");
        else
            System.out.println("Your answer is incorrect");
    }
}
```

Compile the project and execute the program. The output of the program is shown in Example 6.

Example 6. Output of Executing Java Program

```
ant -f "D:\\Demonstrations\\Chapter 12\\JAVAConsumer_WCF"
run
init:
Deleting: D:\Demonstrations\Chapter 12\JAVAConsumer_WCF\
build\built-jar.properties
deps-jar:
Updating property file: D:\Demonstrations\Chapter 12\JAVA-
Consumer_WCF\build\built-jar.properties
wsimport-init:
wsimport-client-Service1:
files are up to date
wsimport-client-generate:
Compiling 2 source files to D:\Demonstrations\Chapter 12\
```

```
JAVAConsumer_WCF\build\classes
compile:
run:
Please enter value of Number 1:
50
Please enter value of Number 2:
30
Please enter Operator (+,-,* or /):
*
Please enter correct answer:
1200
Your answer is incorrect
BUILD SUCCESSFUL (total time: 51 seconds)
```

Here in the example, I developed simple Java application and wrote the client code to consume WCF service inside it. You can develop any other type of Java application; the code to consume WCF service remains same.

Consuming WCF Service in PHP

PHP stands for Hypertext Pre-Processor. A PHP program can be written in any editor such as notepad, notepad++, Dreamweaver etc.. In the example I have used notepad++ to write the PHP code. The following steps will guide you on how to develop PHP client.

Step 1: Write the PHP code to design the form as shown in Example 7.

Example 7. PHP Code to Design the Form

```
<html>
<body>
<h1> Mathematics Tutor </h1>
<form action="checkAnswer.php" method="post">
Number 1:         &n
bsp;<input type="text" name="Number1"><br> <br>
Number 2:         &n
bsp;<input type="text" name="Number2" ><br><br>
Operator:         &n
bsp; <input type="text" name="op" > <br><br>
Correct Answer: <input type="text" name="user_ans" ><br><br>
```

Figure 10. Design of PHP client program

```
<input type="submit" value="Check Answer">
</form>
</body>
</html>
```

This code is written in the file WCF_Consumer.php which is placed in the c:\xampp\htdocs folder as I have used XAMPP for PHP development. Executing this code shows the output in the browser as shown in Figure 10.

Step 2: The code written in Example 7 redirects to the checkAnswer.php file on click event of Check Answer button. Write the code of checkAnswer. php file as shown in Example 8.

Example 8. Code of checkAnswer.php File

```
<?php
    try
    {
            $client = new SoapClient("http://localhost/
MathsService/Service1.svc?wsdl");

            $no1=$_POST['Number1'];
            $no2=$_POST['Number2'];
            $op=$_POST['op'];
            $user_answer=$_POST["user_ans"];

            // Set parameters
```

```
                $parms['operand1'] =$no1;
                $parms['operand2'] = $no2;
                $parms['op'] = $op;
                $parms['user_answer'] = $user_answer;

                // Call web service method
                $webService = $client->Check_
Answer($parms);

                //get the reply
                $wsResult = $webService->Check_AnswerRe-
sult;

                if ($wsResult==true)
                {
                            echo "Your answer is cor-
rect";
                }
                else
                {
                    echo "Your answer is not correct";
                }

} catch (Exception $e)
  {
      echo 'Caught exception:', $e->getMessage(), "\n";
  }
?>
```

In above the method SoapClient is used to communicate with WSDL file of a WCF service. The variable $parms is used to pass the parameters to the service method Check_Answer. To view the method details open the xsd0 file of the service in browser as shown in Figure 11.

All the information related to the method such as method name, return type and parameter detail is available in this file. This information is very vital for interoperability as other platform is not aware about your code. The PHP code is ready now, execute it and view the output in the next step.

Figure 11. xsd0 file contents

Step 3: Open the webpage WCF_Consume.php in browser, provide the values in the inputs and click on the Check Answer button as shown in Figure 12. The page is redirected to the checkAnswer.php page, which consumes WCF service and displays whether the answer is correct or not as shown in Figure 13.

CONSUMING WCF SERVICE IN ANDROID

Android is the operating system and SDK for developing mobile based applications or Apps. Nowadays App development is getting popular and focus is shifted from web site development to mobile application development. Most of the mobile applications require web service connectivity, so WCF

Figure 12. Providing inputs

Figure 13. Output of client program in PHP

Figure 14. Android Studio welcome screen

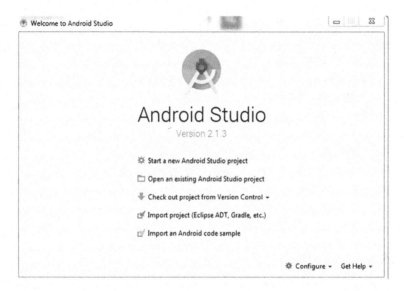

is the ultimate solution for such situation as it provides superior options of message encoding and security over the traditional web service. Following is the step by step walk-through to develop android app using Android Studio.

Step 1: Open Android studio. The welcome screen is shown in Figure 14. Click on the Start a New Android Studio Project as shown in Figure 14. The wizard appears to provide the application details as shown in Figure 15. Click on the Next button.

Step 2: Select minimum SDK for Phone as shown in Figure 16. Selecting the lower SDK version allows the app to run on more number of devices, but it might have less number of features. Therefore, Android 4.1 SDK is selected in the project. Click on the Next button then.

Step 3: A wizard is displayed to select the type of activity as illustrated in Figure 17. You can create different types of activities by using this

Figure 15. Wizard to provide project details

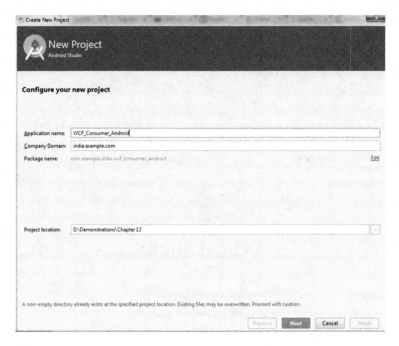

Figure 16. Selecting SDK

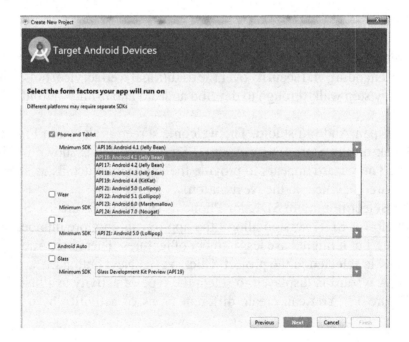

Figure 17. Selecting type of activity

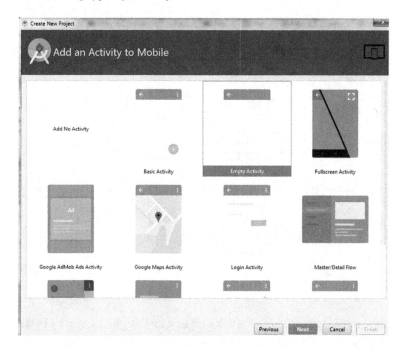

wizard. Select Blank Activity for this project and click on the Next button to customize the activity.

Step 4: The default activity name is MainActivity. Change name of the activity as shown in Figure 18 and click on Finish button to return to the Android studio which is shown in Figure 19. The layout of the app can be designed by using XML file as shown in this figure. The code is written in the JAVA file. Design the layout of application as shown in Figure 19. The code of the layout design written in XML file is shown in Example 9.

Example 9. Code of Layout Design

```
<?xml version="1.0" encoding="utf-8"?>
<RelativeLayout xmlns:android="http://schemas.android.com/
apk/res/android"
    xmlns:tools="http://schemas.android.com/tools"
    android:layout_width="match_parent"
    android:layout_height="match_parent"
    android:paddingBottom="@dimen/activity_vertical_margin"
```

Figure 18. Customizing activity

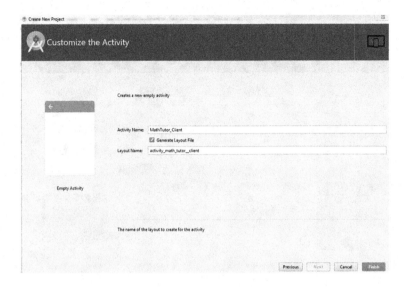

```
android:paddingLeft="@dimen/activity_horizontal_margin"
android:paddingRight="@dimen/activity_horizontal_margin"
android:paddingTop="@dimen/activity_vertical_margin"
tools:context=".MathTutor_Client"
android:id="@+id/layout_relative">
<TextView
```

Figure 19. Layout design of app

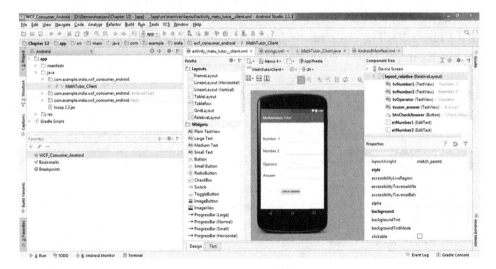

```
        android:layout_width="wrap_content"
        android:layout_height="wrap_content"
        android:textAppearance="?android:attr/textAppear-
anceLarge"
        android:text="Number  1"
        android:id="@+id/tvNumber1"
        android:layout_marginTop="67dp"
        android:layout_alignParentTop="true"
        android:layout_alignParentLeft="true"
        android:layout_alignParentStart="true" />
    <TextView
        android:layout_width="wrap_content"
        android:layout_height="wrap_content"
        android:textAppearance="?android:attr/textAppear-
anceLarge"
        android:text="Number 2"
        android:id="@+id/tvNumber2"
        android:layout_marginTop="46dp"
        android:layout_below="@+id/tvNumber1"
        android:layout_alignLeft="@+id/tvNumber1"
        android:layout_alignStart="@+id/tvNumber1" />
    <TextView
        android:layout_width="wrap_content"
        android:layout_height="wrap_content"
        android:textAppearance="?android:attr/textAppear-
anceLarge"
        android:text="Operator"
        android:id="@+id/tvOperator"
        android:layout_marginTop="52dp"
        android:layout_below="@+id/tvNumber2"
        android:layout_alignLeft="@+id/tvNumber2"
        android:layout_alignStart="@+id/tvNumber2" />
    <TextView
        android:layout_width="wrap_content"
        android:layout_height="wrap_content"
        android:textAppearance="?android:attr/textAppear-
anceLarge"
        android:text="Answer"
        android:id="@+id/tvuser_answer"
        android:layout_below="@+id/tvOperator"
```

```
        android:layout_alignLeft="@+id/tvOperator"
        android:layout_alignStart="@+id/tvOperator"
        android:layout_marginTop="40dp" />
    <Button
        android:layout_width="wrap_content"
        android:layout_height="wrap_content"
        android:text="Check Answer"
        android:id="@+id/btnCheckAnswer"
        android:layout_below="@+id/etUserAnswer"
        android:layout_toRightOf="@+id/tvNumber1"
        android:layout_toEndOf="@+id/tvNumber1"
        android:layout_marginTop="42dp" />
    <EditText
        android:layout_width="wrap_content"
        android:layout_height="wrap_content"
        android:inputType="number"
        android:ems="10"
        android:id="@+id/etNumber1"
        android:layout_alignTop="@+id/tvNumber1"
        android:layout_alignParentRight="true"
        android:layout_alignParentEnd="true" />
    <EditText
        android:layout_width="wrap_content"
        android:layout_height="wrap_content"
        android:inputType="number"
        android:ems="10"
        android:id="@+id/etNumber2"
        android:layout_alignTop="@+id/tvNumber2"
        android:layout_alignLeft="@+id/etNumber1"
        android:layout_alignStart="@+id/etNumber1" />
    <EditText
        android:layout_width="wrap_content"
        android:layout_height="wrap_content"
        android:inputType="number"
        android:ems="10"
        android:id="@+id/etOperator"
        android:layout_centerVertical="true"
        android:layout_alignLeft="@+id/etNumber2"
        android:layout_alignStart="@+id/etNumber2" />
    <EditText
```

```
        android:layout_width="wrap_content"
        android:layout_height="wrap_content"
        android:inputType="number"
        android:ems="10"
        android:id="@+id/etUserAnswer"
        android:layout_alignTop="@+id/tvuser_answer"
        android:layout_alignLeft="@+id/etOperator"
        android:layout_alignStart="@+id/etOperator" />
</RelativeLayout>
```

Step 5: In WCF, the communication is done using SOAP. Therefore, in android ksoap.jar file is used provide functionality related to the SOAP communication in android. Download jar file of ksoap. In this program ksoap 2.3.jar is used. Copy ksoap2.3.jar file in the libs folder of the project.

Step 6: Write the code in java file as shown in Example 10.

Example 10. Code of Java File

```java
package com.example.india.wcf_consumer_android;
import android.net.Uri;
import android.os.AsyncTask;
import android.support.v7.app.AppCompatActivity;
import android.os.Bundle;
import android.util.Log;
import android.view.View;
import android.widget.Button;
import android.widget.EditText;
import android.widget.TextView;
import android.widget.Toast;
import com.google.android.gms.appindexing.Action;
import com.google.android.gms.appindexing.AppIndex;
import com.google.android.gms.common.api.GoogleApiClient;
import org.ksoap2.*;
import org.ksoap2.serialization.SoapObject;
import org.ksoap2.serialization.SoapPrimitive;
import org.ksoap2.serialization.SoapSerializationEnvelope;
import org.ksoap2.transport.HttpTransportSE;
public class MathTutor_Client extends AppCompatActivity {
    /**
```

```
    * ATTENTION: This was auto-generated to implement the
App Indexing API.
    * See https://g.co/AppIndexing/AndroidStudio for more
information.
    */
    private GoogleApiClient client;
    @Override
    protected void onCreate(Bundle savedInstanceState) {
        super.onCreate(savedInstanceState);
        setContentView(R.layout.activity_matu_tutor__cli-
ent);
        Button btnCheck = (Button) findViewById(R.
id.btnCheckAnswer);
        btnCheck.setOnClickListener(new View.OnClickListen-
er() {
            @Override
            public void onClick(View arg0) {
                // TODO Auto-generated method stub
                new BackWork().execute();
            }
        });
        // ATTENTION: This was auto-generated to implement
the App Indexing API.
        // See https://g.co/AppIndexing/AndroidStudio for
more information.
        client = new GoogleApiClient.Builder(this).
addApi(AppIndex.API).build();
    }
    @Override
    public void onStart() {
        super.onStart();
        // ATTENTION: This was auto-generated to implement
the App Indexing API.
        // See https://g.co/AppIndexing/AndroidStudio for
more information.
        client.connect();
        Action viewAction = Action.newAction(
                Action.TYPE_VIEW, // TODO: choose an action
type.
                "MathTutor_Client Page", // TODO: Define a
```

```
title for the content shown.
                // TODO: If you have web page content that
matches this app activity's content,
                // make sure this auto-generated web page
URL is correct.
                // Otherwise, set the URL to null.
                Uri.parse("http://host/path"),
                // TODO: Make sure this auto-generated app
URL is correct.
                Uri.parse("android-app://com.example.india.
wcf_consumer_android/http/host/path")
        );
        AppIndex.AppIndexApi.start(client, viewAction);
    }
    @Override
    public void onStop() {
        super.onStop();
        // ATTENTION: This was auto-generated to implement
the App Indexing API.
        // See https://g.co/AppIndexing/AndroidStudio for
more information.
        Action viewAction = Action.newAction(
                Action.TYPE_VIEW, // TODO: choose an action
type.
                "MathTutor_Client Page", // TODO: Define a
title for the content shown.
                // TODO: If you have web page content that
matches this app activity's content,
                // make sure this auto-generated web page
URL is correct.
                // Otherwise, set the URL to null.
                Uri.parse("http://host/path"),
                // TODO: Make sure this auto-generated app
URL is correct.
                Uri.parse("android-app://com.example.india.
wcf_consumer_android/http/host/path")
        );
        AppIndex.AppIndexApi.end(client, viewAction);
        client.disconnect();
    }
```

```
    public class BackWork extends AsyncTask<String, Object,
Object> {
        String url = "http://10.0.2.2/MathsService/Service1.
svc?wsdl";
        public final String SOAP_ACTION = "http://tempuri.
org/ITutor/Check_Answer";
        public final String METHOD_NAME = "Check_Answer";
        public final String NAMESPACE = "http://tempuri.
org/";
        public Object response;
        @Override
        protected Object doInBackground(String... params) {
            //
            SoapObject request = new SoapObject(NAMESPACE,
METHOD_NAME);
            SoapSerializationEnvelope envelope = new SoapSe-
rializationEnvelope(
                    SoapEnvelope.VER11);
            envelope.dotNet = true;
            EditText tvno1, tvno2, tvoperator, tvuser_ans;
            int no1, no2;
            String op;
            int user_ans;
            tvno1 = (EditText) findViewById(R.id.etNumber1);
            tvno2 = (EditText) findViewById(R.id.etNumber2);
            tvoperator = (EditText) findViewById(R.
id.etOperator);
            tvuser_ans = (EditText) findViewById(R.
id.etUserAnswer);
            no1 = Integer.parseInt (tvno1.getText().to-
String());
            no2 = Integer.parseInt(tvno2.getText().to-
String());
            op = tvoperator.getText().toString();
            user_ans = Integer.parseInt(tvuser_ans.get-
Text().toString());
            //request.addProperty("no1", 25);
            // request.addProperty("no2", 30);
            request.addProperty("operand1", no1);
            request.addProperty("operand2", no2);
```

```
            request.addProperty("op", op);
            request.addProperty("user_answer", user_ans);
            envelope.setOutputSoapObject(request);
            try {
                HttpTransportSE androidHttpTransport = new
HttpTransportSE(url);
                androidHttpTransport.call(SOAP_ACTION, enve-
lope);
                response = (SoapPrimitive) envelope.getRe-
sponse();
                //here SoapPrimitive is an important part
            } catch (Exception e) {
                e.printStackTrace();
                Log.e("-9999", e.getMessage());
            }
            return response;
            // TODO Auto-generated method stub
        }
        @Override
        protected void onPostExecute(Object result) {
            String message = null;
            if ((Boolean)result == true) {
                message = "Correct";
            } else {
                message = "Incorrect";
            }
            Toast.makeText(getApplicationContext(),
                    "Your answer is  =  " + message + "",
Toast.LENGTH_LONG)
                    .show();
        }
    }
}
```

It is interesting to note that the localhost in service address does not work while executing the code in the emulator. In android, while consuming the web service the IP Address 10.0.2.2 is used to run the app on the emulator. Therefore, in Example 10, this address is used in the code in the path of WSDL file.

Step 7: Update the AndroidManifest.xml file to have the permission to execute access the permission of using Internet for consuming the web service. The content of AndroidManifest.xml file is illustrated in Example 11.

Example 11. Content of AndroidManifest.xml File

```xml
<?xml version="1.0" encoding="utf-8"?>
<manifest xmlns:android="http://schemas.android.com/apk/res/
android"
    package="com.example.india.wcf_consumer_android">
    <application
        android:allowBackup="true"
        android:icon="@mipmap/ic_launcher"
        android:label="@string/app_name"
        android:supportsRtl="true"
        android:theme="@style/AppTheme">
        <activity android:name=".MathTutor_Client">
            <uses-permission
                android:name="android.permission.INTERNET"/>
            <intent-filter>
                <action android:name="android.intent.action.
MAIN" />
                <category android:name="android.intent.cat-
egory.LAUNCHER" />
            </intent-filter>
        </activity><!-- ATTENTION: This was auto-generated
to add Google Play services to your project for
    App Indexing.  See https://g.co/AppIndexing/AndroidStu-
dio for more information. -->
        <meta-data
            android:name="com.google.android.gms.version"
            android:value="@integer/google_play_services_
version" />
    </application>
</manifest>
```

Step 8: Compile the project. Add the Android virtual device to run the app in emulator. The output in the emulator is shown in Figure 20.

Figure 20. Output of android app

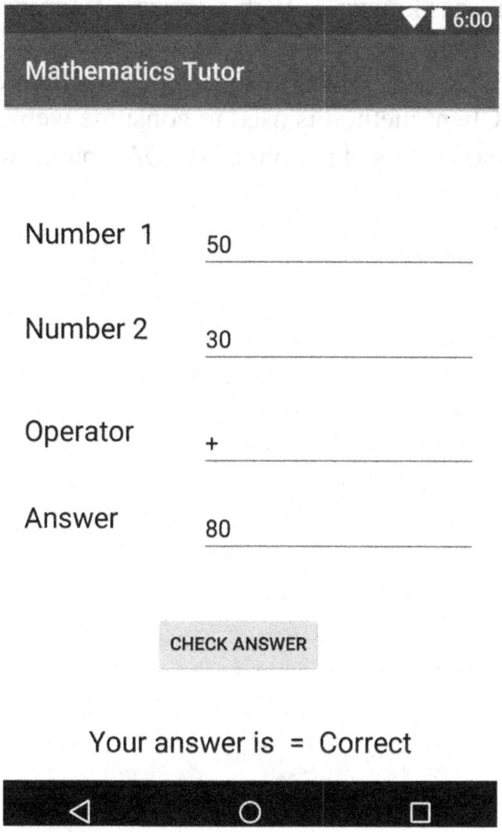

CONCLUSION

In this chapter the interoperability of WCF with three different platforms is demonstrated in depth. This is a SOAP based communication in which WSDL file plays vital role as it holds glue between WCF and other platforms.

The code to consume a WCF service in different platform is focused in this chapter. It helps developers to write the client code in their programming language. The technical details or constructs regarding these platforms are not explained as the focus of this book is to provide in depth knowledge of WCF only. Therefore, it gives directions to the programmer of other platform to consume a WCF service in their applications.

Following are the important points to remember:

- Interoperability is possible nowadays as organizations are following common standards known as Web Service – Interoperability (WS-I).
- Major organizations support WS-I basic profile.
- In NetBeans JAX-WS is used to auto generate client code in Java.
- In PHP SoapClient method is used to consume web services.
- In Android, ksoap is used to consume SOAP based web services.

Appendix

Service Chain Example

INTRODUCTION

In all the chapters I have demonstrated all the kinds of program of WCF but the service chain program is not explained in any of the chapters. In this chapter I will implement this program in depth to explain the concept practically .You are already familiar about the theoretical concept of service chain in Chapter 7 so it is not repeated. Developing such program is a bit challenging and clumsy as two or more services communicate with one another and a service may become client and service both. If the return type of an operation is primitive then there will not be any issue of data type conversion. But if the return type of an operation is user defined or complex (data contract) then it becomes difficult to type cast that return type when service to service communication is done. This issue is well handled in this chapter.

Developing Service Chain Program

In this section, we will create two WCF services and both will fetch the data from database. One service will provide data of one branch and another service will fetch the data of another branch to reduce the load. The client will communicate with first service only. The first service will communicate with second service if it is not having the data and it will provide the data to the client. The concept is explained in Following Figure 1. As shown in this figure, a client communicates with first service only. If Service1 is unable to provide the data it communicates with Service2 service. The Service2 provides data to Service1 and then the Service1 provides data to the client. In the entire communication the Service1 becomes client also for Service2. So it is both in this situation. Therefore, while developing the Service1 keep in mind that there must a code of service as well client in it. Here Service1

Figure 1. Service chain

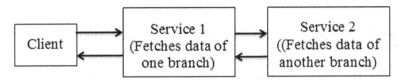

consumes Service2 so Service2 must be developed first, then Service1 should be developed. Finally client can be developed. In this demonstration IIS hosting is used to host both services so the WCF service application project must be created for both services.

Let me explain the program in brief. The services fetch data of graduate students of two branches MCAL and MSIT, who have got the job offer in the company. The first service fetches data of branch MCAL only. The second service fetches data of branch MSIT only. The client communicates with first service only. If the client requests to provide data of MSIT branchm then first service fetches it from second service and provides the data to the client. The client is unaware of this process, this is the power of service chain.

Following are the steps to develop the service chain program:

Step 1: Create two tables in SQL service or SQL Express and establish relationship between them as shown in Figure 2. Here Company_Master is the primary key table and Stud_Master is a foreign key table. The field CompanyID is primary key in Company_Master table and foreign key in Stud_Master table.

Insert appropriate data in both tables. Create one view to join both tables for easy retrieval of data through services. The definition of view is shown in Figure 3. In this example I have used SQL server, but you can create table in any other RDBMS such as MS Access, Oracle etc.

Figure 2. Database design

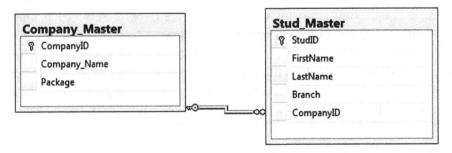

Figure 3. Design of view

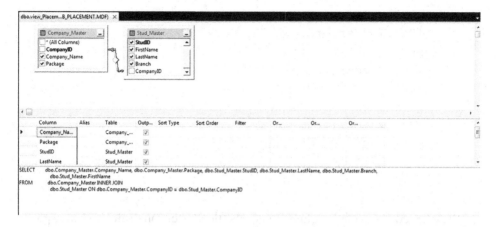

Step 2: Create Service2 by creating the WCF service application. Write the code of service contract as shown in Example 1.

Example 1. Code of service contract:

```
using System.Collections.Generic;
using System.Linq;
using System.Runtime.Serialization;
using System.ServiceModel;
using System.ServiceModel.Web;
using System.Text;
using System;
namespace WcfService1
{
    [ServiceContract]
    public interface IPlacement
    {
        [OperationContract]
        List<Student> find_placed(String bname);
    }
    [DataContract]
    public class Student
    {
        [DataMember(Order = 0)]
        public String Sid;
```

```
        [DataMember(Order = 1)]
        public String Fname;
        [DataMember(Order = 2)]
        public String Lname;
        [DataMember(Order = 4)]
        public int Package;

        [DataMember(Order = 3)]
        public String Company_name;
    }
}
```

Write the code of service class (in svc.cs file) as demonstrated in Example 2.

Example 2. Code of service class:

```
using System;
using System.Collections.Generic;
using System.Linq;
using System.Runtime.Serialization;
using System.ServiceModel;
using System.ServiceModel.Web;
using System.Text;
using System.Data.SqlClient;
namespace WcfService2
{
    public class Placement: IPlacement
    {
        public List<Student> find_placed(string bname)
        {
            List<Student> all_students = new
List<Student>();
            SqlConnection con = new SqlConnection(@"Data
Source=.\SQLEXPRESS;AttachDbFilename=D:\Demonstra-
tions\Appendix A\studdb_placement.mdf;Integrated
Security=True;Connect Timeout=30;User Instance=True");
            SqlCommand cmd = new SqlCommand();

            String query = "select * from view_Placement
where branch=@bname";
```

```
            cmd.Connection = con;
            cmd.CommandText = query;
            cmd.Parameters.AddWithValue("@bname", bname);
            con.Open();
            SqlDataReader sdr = cmd.ExecuteReader();
            while (sdr.Read())
            {
                Student stud = new Student();
                stud.Sid = sdr["studid"].ToString();
                stud.Fname = sdr["FirstName"].ToString();
                stud.Lname = sdr["LastName"].ToString();
                stud.Company_name = sdr["company_name"].
ToString();
                stud.Package = Convert.
ToInt16(sdr["Package"].ToString());
                all_students.Add(stud);
            }
            con.Close();
          return all_students;
        }
    }
}
```

The content of svc file is shown below:

<%@ ServiceHostLanguage="C#"Debug="true"Service="WcfService2.
Placement" CodeBehind="Service2.svc.cs" %>

Step 3: Create endpoint in web.config file. The content of web.config is illustrated in Example 3.

Example 3. web.config file of Service 2:

```
<?xml version="1.0"?>
<configuration>
  <system.serviceModel>
    <services>
      <service behaviorConfiguration="WcfService2.Service-
1Behavior"
        name="WcfService2.Placement">
        <endpoint address="" binding="basicHttpBinding"
```

```
contract="WcfService2.IPlacement">
            <identity>
              <dns value="localhost" />
            </identity>
          </endpoint>
        </service>
    </services>
    <behaviors>
      <serviceBehaviors>
        <behavior name="WcfService2.Service1Behavior">
          <serviceMetadata httpGetEnabled="true"/>
          <serviceDebug includeExceptionDetailInFaults="tr
ue"/>
        </behavior>
      </serviceBehaviors>
    </behaviors>
  </system.serviceModel>
</configuration>
```

Now publish this service on IIS by using the options discussed in Chapter 11. Please note that Visual Studio must be opened with Administrator privileges to do this.

Step 4: Create Service1 by creating a WCF service application. Add the reference of Service2 before writing the code of service contract or service class. The process of adding a service reference is same as adding service reference in client program discussed many times earlier. The code of service contract is shown in Example 4.

Example 4. Code of service contract:

```
using System;
using System.Collections.Generic;
using System.Linq;
using System.Runtime.Serialization;
using System.ServiceModel;
using System.ServiceModel.Web;
using System.Text;
using WcfService1.SecondService_Ref; //Reference of Service
2
```

```
namespace WcfService1
{
    [ServiceContract]
    public interface IPlacement
    {
        [OperationContract]
        List<SecondService_Ref.Student> find_placed(String
bname);
    }
}
```

It is important to observe here that in Service2 data contract was defined, but in this service it is not defined. The return type of the operation of Service1 should be same as Service 2 otherwise there will be type casting error while consuming Service2 in Service1. Therefore, a separate data contract is not required for Service1.

Now write the code of service class(svc.cs file) as shown in Example 5.

Example 5. Code of service class:

```
using System;
using System.Collections.Generic;
using System.Linq;
using System.Runtime.Serialization;
using System.ServiceModel;
using System.ServiceModel.Web;
using System.Text;
using System.Data.SqlClient;
using WcfService1.SecondService_Ref;
namespace WcfService1
{

    public class Placement: IPlacement
    {
        public List<SecondService_Ref.Student> find_
placed(string bname)
        {
            List<SecondService_Ref.Student> all_students =
new List<SecondService_Ref.Student>();
```

```
            if (bname == "MCAL") //fetching data of MCAL
branch
            {
                SqlConnection con = new SqlConnection(@"Data
Source=.\SQLEXPRESS;AttachDbFilename=D:\Demonstra-
tions\Appendix A\studdb_placement.mdf;Integrated
Security=True;Connect Timeout=30;User Instance=True");
                SqlCommand cmd = new SqlCommand();
                String query = "select * from view_Placement
where branch=@bname";
                cmd.Connection = con;
                cmd.CommandText = query;
                cmd.Parameters.AddWithValue("@bname",
bname);
                con.Open();
                SqlDataReader sdr = cmd.ExecuteReader();
                while (sdr.Read())
                {
                    SecondService_Ref.Student stud = new
SecondService_Ref.Student();
                    stud.Sid = sdr["studid"].ToString();
                    stud.Fname = sdr["FirstName"].To-
String();
                    stud.Lname = sdr["LastName"].ToString();
                    stud.Company_name = sdr["company_name"].
ToString();
                    stud.Package = Convert.
ToInt16(sdr["Package"].ToString());
                    all_students.Add(stud);
                }
                con.Close();
            }
            else //Finding student details of MSIT branch
(Requesting from Service2)
            {
                PlacementClient proxy = new PlacementCli-
ent();
                all_students = proxy.find_placed(bname).ToL-
ist();
            }
```

```
        return all_students;
        }
    }
}
```

The content of svc file is shown below:

<%@ ServiceHostLanguage="C#" Debug="true" Service="WcfService1.
Placement" CodeBehind="Service1.svc.cs" %>

Step 5: Update web.config file by adding the endpoint details as shown in
Example 6.

Example 6. web.config file of Service1:

```
<?xml version="1.0"?>
<configuration>

        <system.serviceModel>
                            <bindings>
        <basicHttpBinding>
            <binding name="BasicHttpBinding_IPlacement" clos-
eTimeout="00:01:00"
            openTimeout="00:01:00" receiveTimeout="00:10:00"
sendTimeout="00:01:00"
            allowCookies="false" bypassProxyOnLocal="false" hos
tNameComparisonMode="StrongWildcard"
            maxBufferSize="65536" maxBufferPoolSize="524288"
maxReceivedMessageSize="65536"
            messageEncoding="Text" textEncoding="utf-8"
transferMode="Buffered"
            useDefaultWebProxy="true">
            <readerQuotas maxDepth="32" maxStringContent-
Length="8192" maxArrayLength="16384"
            maxBytesPerRead="4096" maxNameTableChar-
Count="16384" />
            <security mode="None">
            <transport clientCredentialType="None"
proxyCredentialType="None"
                realm="" />
```

```
            <message clientCredentialType="UserName"
algorithmSuite="Default" />
          </security>
        </binding>
      </basicHttpBinding>
    </bindings>
    <client> <endpoint address="http://india1/Service2/Ser-
    vice2.svc" binding="basicHttpBinding" bindingConfiguration=
    "BasicHttpBinding_IPlacement" contract="SecondService_Ref.
    IPlacement" name="BasicHttpBinding_IPlacement" /> </client>
      <services>
          <service behaviorConfiguration="WcfService1.Service-
    1Behavior" name="WcfService1.Placement">
          <endpoint address="" binding="basicHttpBinding"
    contract="WcfService1.IPlacement">
          <identity>
                  <dns value="localhost"/>
          </identity>
            </endpoint>
</service>
</services>
<behaviors>
    <serviceBehaviors>
      <behavior name="WcfService1.Service1Behavior">
        <serviceMetadata httpGetEnabled="true"/>
                  <serviceDebug includeExceptionDetailInFa
ults="false"/>
      </behavior>
    </serviceBehaviors>
</behaviors>
</system.serviceModel>
</configuration>
```

In this file the <client> tag appears which is highlighted. This happens because reference of Service2 is added in Service1. So for Service2, Service1 is a client. This is the reason of having tags <service> and <client> both in Service1 as it behaves like a client and service both.

Now publish Service1 on IIS by using the options discussed in Chapter 11. Please note that Visual Studio must be opened with Administrator privileges to do this.

Figure 4. Design of from of client project

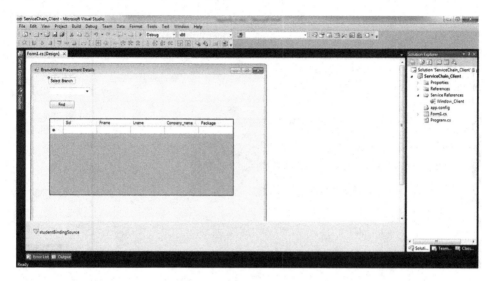

Step 6: Create Windows Forms application to consume Service1. Add the service reference of Service1. Design the layout of Form as shown in Figure 4. In this layout the grid view is in Form. Now you don't need to design from the tool box but it you can use the data source menu and select the data source as shown in Figure 5. The data source is displayed in the visual studio as shown in Figure 6.

Figure 5. Selecting data source

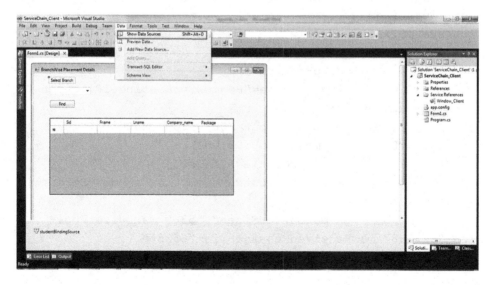

Figure 6. Data Source in visual studio

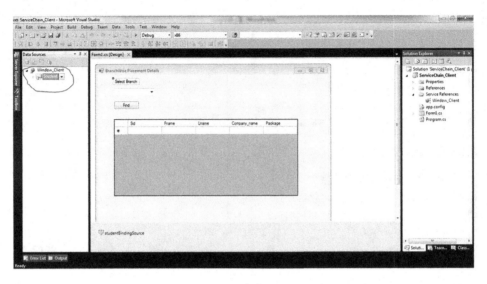

Now drag this data source on the form and the grid view will appear on the form as shown in the design of the form in Figure 4.

Step 7: The auto generated App.Config of client program is shown in Example 7.

Example 7. App.config file of client project:

```
<?xml version="1.0" encoding="utf-8" ?>
<configuration>
    <system.serviceModel>
        <bindings>
            <basicHttpBinding>
                <binding name="BasicHttpBinding_IPlacement"
closeTimeout="00:01:00"
                    openTimeout="00:01:00" receiveTime-
out="00:10:00" sendTimeout="00:01:00"
                    allowCookies="false"
bypassProxyOnLocal="false" hostNameComparisonMode="StrongWi
ldcard"
                    maxBufferSize="65536" maxBufferPool-
Size="524288" maxReceivedMessageSize="65536"
                    messageEncoding="Text"
```

```
textEncoding="utf-8" transferMode="Buffered"
                 useDefaultWebProxy="true">
                 <readerQuotas maxDepth="32" maxString-
ContentLength="8192" maxArrayLength="16384"
                     maxBytesPerRead="4096" maxNameTa-
bleCharCount="16384" />
                 <security mode="None">
                     <transport
clientCredentialType="None" proxyCredentialType="None"
                         realm="" />
              <message clientCredentialType="UserName"
algorithmSuite="Default" />
                 </security>
              </binding>
           </basicHttpBinding>
        </bindings>
        <client>
           <endpoint address="http://india1/Service1/Ser-
vice1.svc" binding="basicHttpBinding"
              bindingConfiguration="BasicHttpBinding_
IPlacement" contract="Window_Client.IPlacement"
              name="BasicHttpBinding_IPlacement" />
        </client>
     </system.serviceModel>
</configuration>
```

Write the code of Form1.cs as illustrated in Example 8.

Example 8. Code of Form1.cs:

```
using System;
using System.Collections.Generic;
using System.ComponentModel;
using System.Data;
using System.Drawing;
using System.Linq;
using System.Text;
using System.Windows.Forms;
using ServiceChain_Client.Window_Client;
namespace ServiceChain_Client
```

```
{
    public partial class Form1: Form
    {
        public Form1()
        {
            InitializeComponent();
        }
        private void btnFind_Click(object sender, EventArgs
e)
        {
            List<Student> all_student = null;
            PlacementClient proxy = new PlacementClient();
            String branch_name = cbBranch.SelectedItem.To-
String();
            all_student = proxy.find_placed(branch_name).
ToList();
            studentBindingSource.DataSource = all_student;
        }

    }
}
```

Figure 7. Output of client project

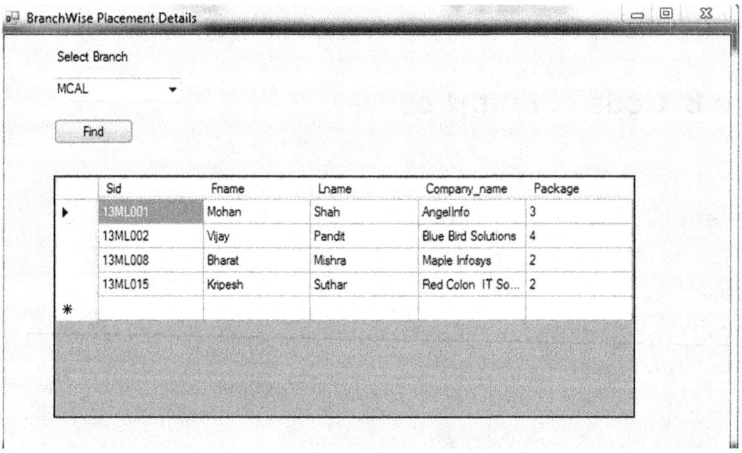

Figure 8. Data displayed in MSIT

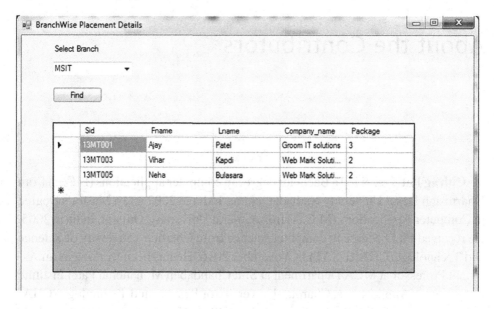

Step 8: Compile the client project and execute it. First time select branch as MCAL and the output is displayed as illustrated in Figure 7. As shown in Figure 7, the branch MCAL is selected so the Service1 will fetch the data from the database and returns data back to the client application.

Now select branch MSIT. The data of this branch are displayed as shown in Figure 8. The output is similar as branch MCAL. But the data of MSIT branch come from Service2 not from Service1 and the client is not aware about it. The client is connected with Service1 only and because of service chain concept it is able to get data from other service(s) too. This reduces the load of service 1. It also helps a lot to develop distributed services when data is distributed among difference servers.

About the Contributors

Chirag Patel received a Bachelor degree in computer applications (B.C.A) from Dharmsinh Desai University Nadiad, Gujarat, India in 2002 and a Master's Degree in Computer Applications (M.C.A) from Gujarat University, Gujarat, India in 2005. He received Ph.D degree in computer science from Charotar University of Science and Technology(CHARUSAT) in November 2016. He has been working as an Assistant Professor at MCA Department at Smt Chandaben Mohanbhai Patel Institute of Computer Applications, Charotar University of Science and Technology (CHARUSAT), Changa, Gujarat, India since June 2011. His research interests include Image Processing, Service-Oriented Architecture, and Data Mining.

Index

.NET 3, 7-8, 10, 22, 32, 54, 118

A

Apache 437
application 2-3, 12-13, 55, 65-67, 70-71, 87-88, 94, 100, 102, 141-143, 160-161, 193, 195, 199, 216, 218-219, 243-244, 256, 260, 279, 294-296, 307, 309, 318, 325, 341, 346, 363-366, 374-376, 381-384, 389, 403, 421, 426, 428-430, 432-435, 441, 449, 451, 454-455, 457, 466
ASP.NET 121, 339, 371, 389, 391-392, 434, 437
ASP.NET membership 339, 371
attribute 42, 58, 171, 177, 186, 188, 192, 202, 205, 207, 260-261, 269-271, 274-275, 282, 290, 371, 380, 434
authentication 17, 38, 175, 184, 204, 207, 211, 336-339, 361-362, 380

B

bank account 284
BasicHttpBinding 19, 22, 26, 87, 91, 93, 99-101, 104, 106, 109-116, 118, 121-123, 139, 148, 152-154, 159-160, 162, 164-165, 173, 176, 196, 199, 201, 205, 272, 278, 305, 337, 339, 342, 346-350, 352, 354, 361, 365-369, 380, 429, 432, 434, 438, 440-441, 446-447
bill amount 283-284

C

C# 2-3, 10, 23, 32, 40, 54, 57, 88, 94, 118, 219, 387
C# language 56
channel 12, 14-15, 17, 22, 24, 37-38, 54-55, 128, 229, 233, 235-236, 241, 351, 353, 355
console 12, 56, 64-67, 69-71, 87-88, 100, 110-111, 113, 141-143, 160-161, 193, 195, 216, 218, 260, 277-278, 294-295, 307, 309, 324-325, 331-332, 341-342, 345, 351, 353-354, 363-366, 369-370, 374-376, 381, 426, 428-430, 433-435
console application 12, 65-67, 70-71, 87-88, 100, 141-143, 160-161, 193, 195, 216, 218, 260, 294-295, 307, 309, 325, 341, 363-366, 374-376, 381, 426, 428-430, 433-435

D

daily life 283, 336
debit 284-285, 290-293, 298
default value 171-173, 175-177, 179-188, 190-192, 205-208, 211-212, 261-263, 266-271, 274, 290, 328, 418
directory 6, 104, 108, 328, 334, 338-339, 389, 394, 434
distributed computing 1, 5-6
distributed environment 323, 335-336
distributed system 5, 436

E

element 26-32, 41, 48, 53-55, 61, 74, 76-77, 84, 90-91, 100-101, 133-138, 142, 148, 150, 152, 156, 163, 167, 173-174, 177-178, 180-181, 188, 190, 198, 202, 205-208, 210-211, 213, 248, 252, 273, 308, 316, 328, 334, 356, 440
end-to-end 303, 337, 380
error 10, 12-14, 18, 22, 26, 36, 38, 41, 45, 47, 69-70, 72, 87, 94, 106, 116, 173, 176-178, 180, 192, 202, 205, 233, 235-236, 238, 240, 264-265, 268, 275-277, 280, 290-291, 293, 298, 304, 321-322, 331, 369, 373, 377-379, 389, 391, 395, 415, 418

F

format 4, 6-7, 14-15, 21, 25, 32, 51, 103, 105-108, 114, 119, 121, 165, 168, 269, 304, 403
functionality 2, 15, 17, 19, 233, 260, 334, 461

G

generic version 233, 275, 280, 282

H

hosting 10, 12-14, 16-17, 22, 26, 41, 53-54, 65, 67, 69, 104, 106, 108, 177-178, 180, 196, 202, 238, 328, 341, 381-382, 389, 396-397, 399, 424, 426, 432-435, 439
hosting options 12-14, 17, 54, 381, 433-435, 439

I

IIS runs 104, 119
installutil.exe 418, 435
interface 2-3, 6, 10-11, 16, 26-27, 41-43, 49-50, 55, 57-58, 62, 100, 139-140, 168-185, 193, 203, 211, 215, 227-228, 233-234, 236-238, 241-242, 276, 282, 291, 306, 324, 339-340, 362, 371, 386, 399, 427, 433, 443, 448-449
interoperability 2-6, 16, 18, 20-22, 26, 38-39, 55, 76, 78, 125, 148, 214, 233, 250, 275, 434, 436-437, 453, 467-468

J

JAVA 2-4, 6, 10, 15, 20, 54, 93, 233, 303, 436-438, 441-444, 447-451, 457, 461, 468

L

logical unit 283, 299

M

Manual 397, 399, 415, 434
message encoding 120, 165, 455
metadata 12, 49, 80, 84, 90, 101, 105, 110-111, 150, 197, 260, 309, 388-390, 403, 439
Microsoft Visual Studio 3, 19, 40
Microsoft Windows 8

N

namespace 27, 49, 55, 62-63, 69, 90, 94, 97, 111, 113, 141, 163, 171-173, 175, 180, 186-187, 193-195, 198, 200, 206, 208-209, 215-217, 219, 224-225, 231, 234, 238-239, 241-242, 245, 258, 276-277, 279, 286, 291-292, 294, 297, 300-301, 306-307, 310, 312-316, 319, 325, 330, 340-341, 348, 362-364, 368, 371-372, 374, 376, 386, 399-400, 402, 421-422, 426-428, 431, 440, 444, 464
NetTcpBinding 19, 22, 26, 104, 107, 125-127, 129, 137, 139, 154-155, 157-160, 162, 164-166, 217, 222, 232, 235, 286, 303, 337, 361, 365-370, 404, 413
node 29, 80-81, 83, 101, 134, 137, 142, 148, 152, 163, 250, 254, 343-344, 403, 412

O

object 2-4, 6, 10, 14, 43, 57, 68, 70, 88-89, 97-98, 110-112, 118-119, 122, 141, 163, 166, 182, 195, 200, 214, 219, 225-227, 231, 233-234, 236-237, 245, 258-259, 265-266, 270-271, 277, 280, 297, 319, 330-331, 349, 368, 377-378, 403, 423, 431, 449, 464-465
Oracle 437

P

path 40, 94, 96, 104, 106-107, 219, 326, 343-344, 389-391, 434, 463, 465
patterns 7, 24, 26, 35, 37, 39, 55, 165, 213, 237, 281
pen drive 25
port number 104, 106-108, 119
practical demonstration 128, 139, 275
practical implementation 120, 132, 167, 172, 213, 285, 290, 299
programmer 6-14, 16-19, 22, 26-27, 35, 38-39, 41, 53-54, 59, 104, 121, 130, 132, 166, 214, 220, 235, 260, 269, 426, 467
programming languages 3, 16, 32, 436
programming methods 57, 100, 117
protection level 175, 184, 204-205, 207, 211, 370
proxy 20, 88-89, 95, 97-98, 101, 118, 163-165, 200-201, 214, 219-220, 222, 224, 229, 232-233, 240, 258-259, 280, 296-298, 303, 318-319, 330-331, 349, 368-369, 377-378, 422-423, 446, 450
public String 187-189, 191-193, 203, 205-209, 215, 226-227, 276, 291, 341, 362, 372
purchase 283-284

Q

queuing 8, 17, 38, 107, 303, 323-324, 326, 334

R

real development 53-54, 389
Reliable messaging 17, 26, 39, 121, 124, 302-303, 306, 334
request-reply 26-27, 35-36, 39, 55, 168, 179, 238-240, 281

S

security breaches 335
security mechanisms 175, 184, 204, 207, 211, 335
self-hosting 12, 53-54, 64, 87, 236, 243, 260, 381-382, 426, 430, 433-434
serialization 3-4, 6, 15, 18, 20-21, 23, 30, 32, 53, 62-63, 90, 167-168, 185, 193-194, 198, 215-216, 224-227, 238-239, 241-242, 275-276, 291-292, 306, 316, 340, 362-363, 371-372, 383, 386, 399-400, 426-427, 440, 448, 461
service oriented 1, 5, 8, 22-23, 32, 57, 302, 322, 334-335, 380, 389
Service Oriented Applications 1, 22, 57, 302, 322, 334-335, 380
snippet 35, 115-116, 118, 122, 124, 126, 137, 172-189, 191-192, 202, 205-209, 211, 260-263, 266-273, 290, 303
SOAP faults 18, 275, 282
static void 69, 110-111, 113, 141, 195, 217, 277, 294, 307, 325, 341, 364, 374, 428, 449
student 185-189, 191-195, 199, 201, 203-211, 215-216, 225, 228-229, 232, 234, 362-363, 368, 371-373, 377-379
switch 395, 401, 415, 418, 435

T

Transaction 16, 26, 121-124, 128, 130, 132, 266-269, 271-272, 283-290, 294, 296-301, 326, 334

transaction management 283-284, 299

U

uninstall 418, 435
USB port 25

V

various hosting options 13, 54, 381, 434
vendors 436

W

web service 1-7, 17-22, 32, 76, 78, 121, 123, 148, 185, 250, 286, 300, 436-437, 441, 443, 453-455, 465-466, 468
Windows Communication Foundation 1, 8, 22-23
WSDL 3, 5-8, 14, 16, 20-21, 38, 80, 89, 91, 93-94, 96, 101, 160, 173-175, 177, 179-182, 196-197, 199-200, 219, 229, 233, 256, 281, 309, 315-318, 324, 328, 395, 429, 433, 437, 441-442, 444-447, 452-453, 464-465, 467
WSHttpBinding 19, 22, 26, 49, 60, 104, 106, 123-126, 139, 159-160, 162-164, 217, 222, 232, 235, 263, 286, 288, 295-296, 300, 303-305, 308-309, 312-315, 317-318, 320, 328-329, 337, 339, 342, 346-350, 354, 359, 361, 365-370, 375, 380, 388-389
WS-I 121, 437, 468

X

XML 3, 6-7, 15, 21, 27, 30, 32, 48, 51, 54, 60-61, 70, 86, 99, 109, 111, 114, 154, 157, 159, 162, 166, 189-192, 196-197, 201, 209-210, 216, 222, 255-256, 272-273, 278, 295-296, 308-309, 319, 327, 329, 342, 344, 347, 352-353, 364, 366, 375, 388, 413, 429, 432, 437-438, 444, 446-447, 457, 466

Printed in the United States
By Bookmasters